History after Apartheid

HISTORY AFTER APARTHEID

VISUAL CULTURE AND PUBLIC MEMORY

IN A DEMOCRATIC SOUTH AFRICA

Annie E. Coombes

Duke University Press Durham & London 2003

© 2003 Annie E. Coombes

All rights reserved

Printed in the United States of

America on acid-free paper ⊗

Designed by C. H. Westmoreland

Typeset in Scala by Tseng Information

Systems, Inc.

Library of Congress Cataloging-in-Publication Data

Coombes, Annie E.

History after apartheid : visual culture and public memory

in a democratic South Africa / Annie E. Coombes.

p. cm.

Includes bibliographical references and index.

ISBN 0-8223-3060-1 (alk. paper) —

ISBN 0-8223-3072-5 (pbk. : alk. paper)

1. Monuments—South Africa. 2. Historic Sites—Interpretive

programs—South Africa. 3. Historical museums—South

Africa. 4. Memory—Social aspects—South Africa. 5. Art, South

African—20th century. 6. Politics in art—South Africa.

7. South Africa—Cultural policy. 8. Post-apartheid—South

Africa. 9. Anti-Apartheid movements—South Africa. 10. South

Africa—Race relations. 11. South Africa—History—1961–

I. Title.

DT1725.C66 2003

968.06'5—dc21   2003007682

For Nicholas Thomas, who brings me joy.

And in memory of Fiona Coombes (1947–1997),

who had an angry young sister for most of her

life but persisted in loving me anyway.

CONTENTS

ILLUSTRATIONS

COLOR PLATES (BETWEEN PGS. 142–143)

ACKNOWLEDGMENTS

The writing and researching of this book over the past seven years has been a personal journey—by way of desultory student politics and subsequent political activity that cost me little but taught me much; the good fortune of experiencing the personal friendship of a small band of South African activists exiled in Britain and the United States; and an uncle who via Ireland and Scotland ended up as a journalist on the *Rand Daily Mail*. And of course I count myself among those who have been moved and chastened by the way the demise of apartheid was conducted, but while desperately concerned that this experiment in democracy should work, I am mindful of a friend and colleague, Benita Parry's, insightful rejoinder that "Our best hope for universal emancipation lies in remaining unreconciled to the past and discontented with the present."

I have incurred a huge number of personal and intellectual debts in the writing and research for this book. And it is certainly true that without the extraordinary generosity of many individuals, particularly in South Africa, this book would never have been possible.

Curators and directors of the many South African museums extended far more assistance than could reasonably be expected and went out of their way to facilitate my research, often drawing my attention to important references and furnishing me with obscure material, despite extremely busy schedules. In this regard my special thanks goes to Patricia Davison at the South African Museum, Sandra Prosalendis at the District Six Museum, Emma Bedford at the South African National Gallery, Rookshana Omar at KwaMuhle, André Odendaal and Barry Feinberg at the Mayibuye Centre, Hilary Bruce at MuseuMAfrica, and Robert de Jong at the National Cultural History Museum. Thanks also to Ramzay Abrahams, Rayda Becker, Gillian Berning, Kathy Brookes, Helen van Coller, Abe Dameneyt, Graham Dominy, Elda Grobler, Andrew Hall, Lindsay Hooper, Udo Küsel, Marilyn Martin, and Lalou Meltzer for facilitating all kinds of access to materials. Thanks also to Sam Nyambose, Charles Mbubana, and Marth Paya for sharing their personal histories with me and for generously traveling out to meet me. Barry Feinberg has been an invaluable guide to the resources of the Mayibuye Centre and the work of IDAF and a constant pleasure as a source of knowledge on the history and natural history of the Western Cape and, with Linda Pithers, a generous host. Thanks also to David Saks and to Alicia Monis of DACST, whose persistence finally gained me admission to the Monument to the Women of South Africa and who provided me with much supplementary material.

Other South African colleagues have provided invaluable discussion, references, documentation, and friendship: Willie Bester, Clive van den Berg, Jean Brundrit, David Bunn, Luli Callinicos, Nic Coetzee, Bronwen Findlay, Amanda Gouws, Sharmil Jeppie, David Johnson, Cynthia Kros, Maggie Makhoana, Rashidi Molapo, Zwelethu Mthethwa, Pitika Ntuli, Sarah Nuttall, Shannon Richards, Berni Searle, Jonathan Shapiro, Jayne Taylor, Jeremy and Colleen Wafer, Sue Williamson, and Nigel Worden. Michael Godby and Sandra Klopper have always been ready with hospitality when it was most needed and stimulating discussion over wonderful meals. Penny Siopis and Colin Richards, from the earliest days of my research, have generously supported this project and fed me with constant intellectual debate and invaluable source material. On numerous occasions they shared their lives, their friends, and their home with me. Isabel Hofmeyr and John Hyslop gave me the courage (or hubris) to focus the book on South Africa. Their constant and rigorous critical input has enriched its contents and alerted me to errors and absences, just as their friendship and hospitality have enriched many periods in Johannesburg and elsewhere. To my colleagues in the History Department of the University of the Western Cape I owe a special thanks for doing me the extraordinary honor of appointing me to the Chair of Public History, a position I was unable to take up, due, in large part, to various bureaucratic difficulties (a euphemistic explanation only they, and possibly Shula Marks, will fully understand). Needless to say, my own putative role has been completely redundant for their History and Heritage Program, which I trust will continue to go from strength to strength under the leadership of a terrific team of critical, inventive, and committed historians. For their support and for the many leads and references they have supplied, my thanks to Martin Legassick, Leslie Witz, Patricia Hayes, and Ciraj Rassool (who knows how to dance).

The Southern Africa History Seminar at the Institute of Commonwealth Studies in London has been a challenging and rigorous testing ground for early versions of this book. I wish to thank in particular Hilary Sapire,

Deborah Gaitskell, and Saul Dubow for their contributions to the discussion of my papers in these seminars. Shula Marks has been a constant source of support and a model of tough but also creative intellectual engagement and commitment to the dissemination of critical research on Southern Africa; many thanks indeed.

Other friends and colleagues in Britain, the United States, Canada, and Australia have supported this project in numerous ways and have always provided stimulating insights from the comparative perspective of their own work: Jeremy Beckett, Ann Curthoys, Norman Etherington, Peter Hulme, John Kraniauskas, Ruth Phillips, Adrian Rifkin, Carol Watts, and Janet Wolff. Lorna de Smidt provided me with unprecedented access to South Africa House and is a wonderful storyteller and a great cook. Paddy Donnolly generously shared his research on the building of the High Commission and his photographs of anti-apartheid activism in London. Susan Siegfried and I shared many walks during periods of writing. Her generous interest in this project, despite her own very different research concerns, helped clarify my thinking during some sticky moments. She also made me laugh. My co-editors on the collective of *Feminist Review* are, quite simply, magnificent. Without their intellectual and political fellowship and the humanity of their personal support, this book would have been even harder to write. My thanks to you all: Pam Alldred, Vicki Bertram, Lucy Bland, Avtar Brah, Helen Crowley, Dot Griffiths, Nirmal Puwar, Sadhana Sutar, Merl Storr, Lyn Thomas, and Amal Treacher.

A number of grants and fellowships have provided me with invaluable time to think and write and have given me funds for research. I am grateful to Birkbeck College for a research grant that enabled me to begin the work on this project and to the following organizations for research fellowships: the Humanities Research Centre at the Australian National University; the Leverhulme Trust, and the Arts and Humanities Research Board. I had the good fortune to be awarded visiting professorships at the University of the Witwatersrand, Brown University, and Northwestern University. My thanks to Anitra Nettleton, Dian Kriz, and Hollis Clayson respectively for these opportunities and to faculty and students who provided me with valuable intellectual exchanges at these institutions. Segments of this book have been given as lectures hosted by the Wellcome Foundation, the University of British Columbia, Oxford University, Cambridge University, the Australian National University, Columbia University, the South African Museum, and the University of Cape Town; my thanks to all those responsible in the art history, anthropology, and history departments of these universities for their invitations and for the stimulating discussions that followed:

Ken Arnold and Danielle Olsen, Rose Marie San Juan, Laura Peers, Robin Boast, Tony Bennett, Zoe Strothers, Patricia Davison, and Sandra Klopper. My own graduate students at Birkbeck College have always provided stimulating exchanges that have helped to sharpen up my thinking. Thanks in particular to Christine Boyanoski and Gabriel Koureas. Thanks also to Ken Wissoker, Christine Dahlin, and Kate Lothman at Duke University Press. It would be difficult to find a more professional team. Thanks to Christina Parragi and Jon Wilson at Birkbeck, who prepared many of the photographs. Special thanks to Jean Brundrit, who generously gave her professional expertise and who took many of the original photographs for this book.

Neville Alexander, Benita Parry, and Isabel Hofmeyr have all read chapter drafts, and their comments and criticism have been indispensable. Any oversights or errors are mine. Neil Lazarus took time out of a busy schedule and, despite considerable personal difficulties, read a draft of the manuscript and provided encouragement and criticism at a crucial moment. Many thanks. The steady support and the practical, intellectual, and human sustenance provided by Nicholas Thomas have been invaluable. I am constantly amazed and delighted that he crossed oceans and continents to share my life.

ABBREVIATIONS

AC	Amnesty Commission
ANC	African National Congress
AV	Afrikaner-Volkswag
AVF	Afrikaner Volksfront
AWB	Afrikaner Weerstandsbeweging
AZAPO	Azanian People's Organisation
BCCSA	Broadcasting Complaints Commission of South Africa
CMMH	Commission on Museums, Monuments and Heraldry
CP	Conservative Party
CPA	Cape Provincial Administration
CREATE	Commission for Reconstruction and Transformation of the Arts and Culture
DACST	Department of Arts, Culture, Science and Technology
DNE	Department of National Education
FAK	Federasie van Afrikaanse Kultuurverenigings
GEAR	Growth and Employment Policy
GNC	Griqua National Council
HODSC	Hands Off District Six Committee
HRVC	Human Rights Violation Commission
HSRC	Humanities and Social Science Research Council
ICOMOS	International Council on Monuments and Sites
IDAF	International Defence and Aid Fund
IFP	Inkatha Freedom Party
IRA	Irish Republican Army
MK	Umkhonto we Sizwe
MUSA	Museums for South Africa Intersectoral Investigation for National Policy
NEUM	Non-European Unity Movement
NGO	Nongovernmental organization

INTRODUCTION

Making History Memorable

> The strategic-political and ultimately moral-historical question is how to move towards understanding without ever forgetting, but to remember without out constantly rekindling the divisive passions of the past. Such an approach is the only one which would allow us to look down into the darkness of the well of the atrocities of the past and to speculate on their causes at the same time as we haul up the waters of hope for a future of dignity and equality.
> —Neville Alexander, *An Ordinary Country*

History after Apartheid is an analysis of how new stories of "home" and "nation" were created in the public sphere during one of the most startling periods of political and social transformation in recent history. The first democratic elections of April 1994 finally ushered in the formal demise of apartheid in South Africa. However, the difficult task of setting up a workable economic, political, and cultural infrastructure that adequately represented the transition to democracy had only just begun. This book explores how various forms of visual and material culture dramatized the tensions involved in such a momentous shift while at the same time contributing to the process of transformation itself. It argues that the visual and material manifestations of new public histories are both produced by and effectively inform changing definitions of "community" and "nation" during periods of political transition where such concepts become crucial stakes in the resolution or management of social conflict and / or renewal.

In the summer of 1999 I had an exchange with an interviewer on Australian national radio that graphically exposed both the difficulties entailed in such a project and my own reasons for persisting despite these. A paper I had just given on the complications involved in promoting Robben Island as the site of the emergence of the "new" nation (now chapter 2 in this book) had caught the eye of the Australian reporter. In the course of a telephone interview conducted while I was still in my pyjamas she asked me if it would be accurate to describe the political situation in South Africa as primarily a case of black versus white. I explained that I was neither a South African nor living in the country, but that as an "outsider" who had spent a great deal of time there since 1994 the thing I found so compelling about the situation as I encountered it was that the nature of political debate actually seemed to resist characterization in terms of a simplistic binary of black versus white. On the contrary: most black and white activists were only too well aware that while apartheid had attempted to set up the ideological and juridical structures that were intended to cement such divisions, and that indeed had produced an oppressive regime assisted by color segregation, the sophistication of political consciousness and debate in the country meant that within the broader culture of the various lefts most individuals recognized friend or foe through an identification of complex political affiliations and not on the basis of skin color alone.

Back in South Africa the shoe was on the other foot. This time I was doing the interviewing. My subject was a disconsolate Max du Preez, one of a small band of outspoken Afrikaner journalists who had been consistent critics of apartheid.[1] Harried by the draconian censorship laws of the apartheid government, many of these journalists had ended up in jail on more than one occasion.[2] My interviewee's disillusionment was due to the media row that had just broken out following an article in which he had warned against reconstructing, as he saw it, the racial categories of apartheid: "Stop using the term 'African' to mean exclusively black. As both Nelson Mandela and Thabo Mbeki did during the election campaign: they referred to 'whites, coloureds, Indians and Africans.' Because that implies absolutely that whites, coloureds and Indians can't be Africans."[3]

Du Preez's remarks also deliberately referred back to a 1996 speech by Thabo Mbeki, speaking on behalf of the African National Congress (ANC) to mark the adoption by the Constitutional Assembly of the Republic of South Africa Constitution Bill. Ironically, in 1999, at the time of du Preez's intervention, Mbeki's speech was being cited to reinforce claims of inclusivity for the "African Renaissance": "Just as there are black Jews and Europeans today, there are today European Africans and Arabic Africans."[4] The concept of the African Renaissance was early promoted as Mbeki's distinctive contribution to the presidency, as opposed to the image of South Africa as a "rainbow nation," which epitomized Mandela's government of "national unity." A sympathetic definition might describe it as a pan-Africanist philosophy attempting to identify and harness potential alliances (economic, political, and intellectual) from within the African continent as a means of shifting the axis of power away from a neocolonialist dependency on Western democracies.[5] While a potential strategy of decolonization, and one that in its "official" definitions claims to be inclusive of *all* South Africans, the African Renaissance has also lent itself to a more fundamentalist ethnic absolutism. It was partly anxiety over prioritizing this tendency that stimulated du Preez's article. Du Preez's polemic provided the ammunition for a series of attacks and counterattacks in the press concerning who had the right to call themselves "African."[6] Ironically, du Preez had found himself defending an Afrikaner's right to the title "African" and had been duly denounced as a white racist.[7] While there were certainly interesting aspects to this debate that are not reducible to racialized argument, it was nevertheless clear that much of it was being conducted on a presumption of rights on the basis of color. Once again the political goalposts had shifted. It seemed that I might be forced to revise the pronouncement I had earlier made to my Australian interlocutor.

DEFINING "COMMUNITY"

This book, however, is partly about why I believe that such a revision would be unpardonably premature. To understand the history of South Africa solely in terms of the tensions arising among ethnic groupings that were constructed under colonialism and apartheid would be to eradicate a complex political culture on the left that has proved itself to be much more resilient than either colonialism or apartheid and through which alliances and negotiations across ethnic and color divides have immeasurably complicated the complexion of the "new" nation. Of course it would be naive to imagine that the prejudices and discriminations encouraged and enacted under apartheid have not also been internalized to a certain degree, and this has had an impact on the kinds of cooperation possible among different constituencies. Both factors need to be taken into account in order to understand the stakes involved in the struggle for historical memory and public history in South Africa.

In many ways South Africa is anachronistic in the extreme. On the one hand, it is a country that to the outsider with some experience of other African states bears only a slim resemblance to many of them, having an infrastructure of roads and other support institutions (even if not always the services they should supply) that has more in common with a highly developed industrialized capitalist state. On the other hand, South Africa shares many of the problems of developing nations with histories of extremes of unevenly distributed wealth. In South Africa this resulted, during colonialism and under apartheid, with the majority population ending up with little or nothing by way of housing, education, and health care. In addition, South Africa (as a number of journalists have pointed out) remains, even now, a highly segregated society where the legacy of the 1950s Group Areas Act has ensured that the different populations of the major cities are often oddly dispersed and unintegrated. Nevertheless, despite local awareness of the ways in which colonialism and apartheid have contributed to both the artificial construction of apparently homogeneous ethnic constituencies and the destruction of other forms of viable community, the single most frequently used justification for much government expenditure in the public heritage sector is a much vaunted recourse to an ideal of "community."

For some time now, in international museum forums, there has been an expectation and an ethical injunction to establish wider consultation and active participation from members of the public not professionally engaged in museums and other publicly funded cultural institutions. In the most opportunistic scenarios the idea of "community" invoked here may simply be a bureaucratic fiction strategically deployed to legitimate an institution and its projects. On the other hand, there are many museum professionals who have a serious commitment to broadening participation at all levels, and in many instances this has resulted in genuine attempts to engage groups outside the institution. The dual legacy of colonialism and apartheid in South Africa means that such efforts are the locus of especially complicated tensions. In addition, further difficulties have arisen in South Africa, as elsewhere, since the rhetoric of "community" is the result of a genuine attempt to incorporate a more representative multicultural diversity in many aspects of public life but can also be a slipshod way of "managing" the more contradictory and potentially troublesome aspects of cultural and political diversity. The ideal of "community" on these occasions is not necessarily the same for those in whose name and interests it is invoked. Paradoxically, exclusion is therefore, to a certain extent, part of the logic of the way "community" is often mobilized in official rhetoric. Similarly, because it is a concept that is seen to provide leverage in official circles, it can precipitate problematic essentializing gestures as a means of authenticating a claim to "community."

Consequently I want to elaborate on the idea of "community" by focusing on the particularities in which such a concept is mobilized and con-

structed in instances where specific histories or sites imbued with historical significance are being contested. This is partly done in order to avoid
the reductive black versus white binary that so often applies to the way the
country's history is perceived outside South Africa. But I also believe that
such a methodological move has the additional advantage of emphasizing
the heterogeneity of the concept of "community" more generally, outside
as well as inside South Africa, and thus makes it easier to understand what
stakes might be involved in negotiating different pasts and histories at times
of social and political transition in the history of any nation when the very
notion of what constitutes a "citizen" is being radically redefined.[8] Similarly
attempting to complicate our understanding of how the concept of "community" circulated differentially at the very moment in South Africa when
in the official rhetoric of "nation-building" it is being deployed as a strategy
of unification has the effect of emphasizing the local and internal dynamic
of the debates around heritage and history, whether in response to national
or international pressures and expectations.[9] This, in turn, shifts the emphasis of the analysis away from the usual interpretative framework, which
has become fossilized as a rather monolithic representation of "global" versus "local" forces and which casts Western capitalism as the driving force
behind all exchanges and encounters to the exclusion of complex local and
regional motivations and contingencies.

"PUBLIC" HISTORY

Many commentators have written about the shortcomings of the new dispensation and the fact that so many of the promises made in the euphoric
wake of the first democratic elections have not been met. But it seems to
me that if nothing else, the South African debates on history and heritage,
on "truth" and lies, and on memory and make-believe — which are the subject of this book — demonstrate the health and vitality of a political culture
of critique and countercritique that was forged under the most difficult
of circumstances and whose main protagonists have often paid dearly for
their beliefs. Most important, this tradition is not confined to the academic
sphere alone, possibly as a result of the political education for liberation that
sometimes had the capacity to cut across class and ethnic boundaries and
that provided rigorous intellectual training and a familiarity with vociferous debate. Consequently the contested histories that form the chapters of
this book are not just internal debates among a small elite but concern a
much larger public than might normally be the case. During the period that
is the historical focus of *History after Apartheid*, the debates on what con-

stituted an appropriate public history for the "new" nation were frequently played out in the national media across different and sometimes conflicting parties. In other words, from 1989 to 2000 such questions were very much "live" issues and formative for the ways different constituencies wanted to produce themselves as part of the new nation and subsequently formative for how such an entity might then be understood by the rest of the world.

History after Apartheid is written in dialogue with and draws on important recent work on the representation of the past (or pasts) by scholars in South Africa, where history as a discipline has developed a challenging and rigorous internal dynamic. But it is also aimed at a wider audience whose frame of reference about South Africa is shaped without the benefit of the attention to internal contradictions and detailed understanding of local conditions and circumstances that informs the best work of these intellectuals.[10] However, a number of scholars (mainly anthropologists and historians) have commented on problems endemic to the area studies approach to history. In particular they cite the isolationist tendency to produce scholarship that speaks only to its own community of similarly focused academics and produces a set of internal debates that circulate among specialists in the geographical field under scrutiny and that foreground the implications of their work in a singular national arena.[11]

Recent interdisciplinary scholarship looking to the shared legacy of settler colonialism and British imperialism in New Zealand, Australia, Canada, South Africa, and the United States has sought to look comparatively at contemporary debates around belonging and identity in these countries in an attempt to better understand the particularities of how such a shared past might impinge on the ways in which new subject positions can be forged in the present. *History after Apartheid* is intended as a contribution to such comparative analysis.[12] It seeks to shed light on some of the more recent developments in debates concerning public history in South Africa by deploying some of the insights provided by an understanding of how such debates have been played out elsewhere. Most important, the book also maintains that a more detailed consideration of the South African context and the fierce debate and intelligent scholarship it has engendered provide particular insights for any emerging polity or radically transformed society. This is because South Africa encapsulates a number of dilemmas that have faced both those nation-states recovering from long periods of colonization and those that have recently emerged from a long period of totalitarian rule—the situation in both Central and Eastern Europe since the fall of the Communist regimes. In addition, some of the problems that faced South Africa on the eve of the first democratic elections were shared by developed capitalist countries with a history of settler colonialism (such as New Zealand, Australia, and Canada), where hitherto marginalized ethnic and / or autochtonous communities have, to differing degrees, emerged as constituencies with greater political clout and (as important) the organization and will to wield it in order to gain greater influence on institutions purporting to represent their histories and interests.[13] In other words, this book maintains that it is possible to see the case of South Africa during the period of transition to democracy from the late 1980s to 2000 as an example where a constellation of conditions that usually exist independently of one another come together. Here the political and social legacies left by the complex layering of histories of colonization, settler colonialism, totalitarianism, and organized resistance movements (both Boer and black) combine to produce a context where the effects of each of these historical conditions jostle against one another to produce significant tensions during periods of reconstruction.

Two events in recent years have foregrounded debates about the nature and use of historical evidence in the public sphere. These debates have carried important implications for the construction of new national histories. Both events have also served to raise questions about the nature of personal or "collective" memory as a tool for the production of historical narratives, particularly where traumatic abuses of human rights have been involved. In 1996 a small band of historians was charged with a task that would take four years to complete. In order to counter the libel suit brought against Penguin Books by David Irving, these historians would have to mount enough evidence to confirm Deborah Lipstadt's charges in her 1994 book, *Denying the Holocaust: The Growing Assault on Truth and Memory,* that Irving's denial of the Holocaust was a deliberate misrepresentation of events and a falsification of history. In April 2000 Irving's detractors successfully defended the case, and he was denounced by Justice Charles Gray as a racist anti-Semite and Holocaust denier who had manipulated historical evidence for his own ideological ends.[14] While the trial was not directly concerned with the nature of national history, it is true to say that the debates over the representation of the Holocaust, particularly in the United States and in Germany since reunification, have assumed the dimensions of a national dilemma, although for very different reasons in either case.[15]

Meanwhile, also in 1996, the South African Truth and Reconciliation Commission (TRC), chaired by Archbishop Desmond Tutu, held the first of its hearings. Set up ostensibly to investigate gross human rights violations between 1960 and 1994 and modeled in part on the Comisión National para la Verdad y la Reconciliatión (set up in 1990 in Chile to deal with abuses of human rights under the military junta between 1973 and 1990), the TRC was given the power to grant amnesty to those who made full disclosure of their crimes against humanity in cases where political motivation was proven. The declared emphasis of the commission was to enable the "truth" of events under apartheid to be spoken in order to heal the wounds of the divided society that had been so violently created. Its larger objective was to facilitate a national reconciliation between victim and perpetrator. The TRC has been heavily criticized within South Africa for the compromises made in the name of "national unity" and reconciliation that allowed so many to walk free while the conditions they had perpetrated under apartheid and that had reduced so many to poverty and powerlessness remained intact.[16] Nevertheless, the TRC has also grudgingly been acknowledged as serving a positive function.

By linking these events, I am not suggesting that they are commensurable. Both, however, were high-profile media events that raised issues about the nature of historical evidence and the role of the historian that have potentially far-reaching consequences. In particular, both have necessitated a reflection on oral witnessing and testimony. Irving's denial of the systematic killings that went on at Auschwitz was based on undermining the credibility of eyewitness accounts and oral testimony per se. It was based on the unreliability of eyewitness evidence. The TRC, on the other hand, was founded on precisely the necessity and "truth" value of such witnessing and, as a corollary, on the possibility of atonement offered by the voicing of guilt through the admission, and more particularly through the description, of deeds. In fact, one of the criticisms of the process was, as Deborah Posel has pointed out, its tendency to elide memory and truth and to equate forensic with personal evidence.[17]

History after Apartheid is premised on the understanding that all memory is unavoidably both borne out of individual subjective experience and shaped by collective consciousness and shared social processes so that any understanding of the representation of remembrances and of the past more generally must necessarily take into account both contexts.[18] In addition, research on the witnessing and testimony collected in the aftermath of genocide, war, or systematic political repression (such as in the case of South Africa) has pointed to the impact of trauma on memory and the distinction between narrative and traumatic memory.[19]

Many commentators have remarked on the somatic nature of traumatic as opposed to narrative memory, "full of fleeting images, the percussion of blows, sounds, and movements of the body—disconnected, cacophonous, the cells suffused with the active power of adrenalin, or coated with the anaesthetising numbness of noradrenalin."[20] The fragmentary nature of this somatic recall reproduces the sensation of what for many South Africans were common occurrences under apartheid—the experience of detention, displacement, or unannounced police harassment in the dead of night. Such destabilizing experiences carry with them temporal repercussions. As we now know, holding on to the possibility of a past, a present, and the prospect of a future is essential in order to stem the dissolution of self in conditions where everything conspires against the memory or imagining of any of these. Some time ago I wrote a piece about the significance of miniature objects made in secret by detainees in the infamous prison camp at Khiam on the South Lebanese border.[21] I suggested that the extraordinary miniaturized items that the detainees had manufactured were in some measure a means of countering the destructive effects of detention both by marking time (productive time) in a context designed to eradicate it and by witnessing not the terrible conditions under which they were made but their makers' ability to transcend such conditions against all odds. If the detainees expressed concern that their time in detention should not simply be "lost," then the objects they made became an embodiment of nostalgia for misplaced lives, but also and crucially they became evidence of lives spent productively—of an "other" existence. Similarly, one of the results of Primo Levi's experience in the Nazi death camps, and one that Charlotte Delbo also recalled on her return to Paris after liberation, was the terrible erasure of a capacity for feeling.[22] "The survivor must undertake to regain his memory, regain what he possessed before: his knowledge, his experience, his childhood memories, his manual dexterity and his intellectual faculties, sensitivity, the capacity to dream, imagine, laugh."[23]

In such contexts the act of making and objects themselves can become an insurance against forgetting and thus against the loss of personhood through reinstating—particularly in the case of whimsical manufactures—the capacity for fantasy. By invoking the personal, the naive, and the fantastic despite the grim context of political suppression and resistance, these objects signal the complexity and contradictions of sustaining the self while also seeking membership in an ideal of political community. These observations are also relevant in the context of a country like South Africa, scarred by the political repression and violence of apartheid but whose many activists in the struggle for liberation have all insisted on the productiveness of their years in detention and of the necessity of working toward a constructive future rather than dwelling on the destructions of the past. On the other hand, it is also true to say that such a past raises particular questions about its representation in the present and about forms of representation that can adequately act as an insurance against the amnesia of future generations but that can offer more than either a palliative or a reproduction of the pain. *History after Apartheid* is thus concerned to explore the effectivity of different kinds of expression—both pedagogic and imaginative—as appropriate means of embodying the trauma of surviving apartheid.

What interested me in the South African case was precisely the tension represented by two kinds of historical research. One of these was an important tradition of historical writing from the left that prioritized a "history from below," a history of "the people," as a strategy for redressing the absences and structural violences of the official "national" histories circulating under apartheid. This tradition also acknowledged the contribution of oral testimonies. However, for all its significant recovery work, it also had a tendency, as some critics have commented, to homogenize its subjects as primarily "representative" of a larger political ideology.[24] On the other hand, the TRC seemed to offer another significant model of historical knowledge based on an appeal to individual experience as the foundation of a new national history postapartheid. Because South Africa is a nation whose recent past has been irrevocably marked by trauma, as the testimony presented at the TRC has demonstrated, I became interested in the question of how one might embody new national histories in the public sphere that engaged larger structural narratives and material conditions *and* individual lived experiences without reducing their public expression to either some monolithic representation of "the struggle" or some unlocated and ahistorical notion of individualized experience and that might adequately signal (if not represent) the compromised, complicated texture of living under and fighting against apartheid. Contemporary South Africa provides a fertile context for such an inquiry. And indeed recent developments in the teaching of history and heritage at the University of the Western Cape, the University of Cape Town, and the University of the Witwatersrand have all worked to foster a self-reflexive awareness of, if not this particular concern, certainly the contested nature of historical memory and knowledge and of the power relations involved in the production of such knowledge.[25]

History after Apartheid makes no claim to comprehensiveness. It is neither a history of South Africa's transition to democracy nor an exhaustive account of policy decisions regarding culture and history over this period. Instead I have deliberately selected a series of case studies that seemed to me to dramatize the most significant aspects of the debates around historical representation in the public sphere during the early phase of the transition to democracy. Because the book is essentially about constructions of national history and the intersection of local and international interests in the construction of such histories, it emphasizes sites or institutions that have a national profile and have consequently been subjected to intense debate in the South African and sometimes international media. Inevitably this has meant sacrificing accounts of other important local initiatives, such as the artists' collective at the Crossroads Township outside Cape Town, the women's housing cooperative at Protea South, and the extraordinary work accomplished with abandoned and orphaned children by Maggie Makhoana at the Mokhele art therapy and education project in Soweto. Since completing the writing for this book, there have been a number of new national commemorative initiatives, many of which represent significant advances on some of the examples discussed in *History after Apartheid*. The Apartheid Museum outside Johannesburg, the Hector Pieterson Memorial Museum in Soweto, and the Women's Gaol, which forms part of the larger "Constitution Hill" project, are all immensely impressive experiments in producing appropriate models of public memorial after apartheid. They represent the beginning of a new phase in collaborative public history projects in South Africa. They are also, arguably, the result of a far greater consensus than that represented in the less resolved attempts at reinventing national history just prior to and after the first democratic elections. It is the conflict and contestation over different models of historical knowledge and narrative that are the focus of this book, and this is why I have concentrated on the formative period of Mandela's government of "national unity."

One of the objectives of *History after Apartheid* is to analyze how strategies for embodying different models of historical knowledge and experience are negotiated in public culture through a variety of material visual means—in monuments, museum narratives, the reanimation of particular sites and spaces, and through contemporary fine art.[26] I have chosen such disparate objects because they are all forms of public spectacle that together enable an analysis of the different possibilities on offer for the realization in visual and material form of narratives of belonging, of "nation" and "community," and sometimes of the impossibility of either and of the tensions between the two. The comparative frame aims to shed light on the conditions that make certain cultural strategies more appropriate in some geopolitical contexts than others and to better define the limitations and potential of these diverse forms of representation as they appeal to various constituencies.

Throughout the book instances of South African artists' engagement with their own and their nation's pasts are analyzed where their work intersects with the concerns and debates elaborated in any given chapter. This is not because I think that contemporary fine art has a more effective way of dealing with such issues or that it communicates to constituencies to whom monuments, city spaces, and museums cannot. On the contrary, the spaces in which fine art circulates are, of course, similarly delimited and are circumscribed by such factors as the art market and its institutions and by its recourse to a visual language that may rely on a vocabulary truly accessible only to a cognoscente. At the same time, artists operate within a highly privileged realm that provides a certain license (which is not to say that they do not take real risks), and this sometimes enables them to work through taboos and contradictions in a relatively "safe" space in ways that other arenas do not permit. For this reason I have found it instructive and always intellectually enlivening to draw the reader's attention to the insights and challenges provided by such work.

A number of commentators have reiterated the argument that the more monumental the scale of a public sculpture, the more likely it is to be ignored or forgotten over time.[27] My contention is that monuments are animated and reanimated only through performance and that performances or rituals focused around a monument are conjunctural. The visibility of a monument is in fact entirely contingent upon the debates concerning the reinterpretation of history that take place at moments of social and political transition. Their significance is consequently constantly being reinvented but always and necessarily in dialogue with their past. Thus the dejected political figure consigned for years to an indifferent amnesia paradoxically gets a new lease on life through the actions of later generations. When the statue of Winston Churchill in Parliament Square in London was given a Mohawk out of bright green turf, a dash of blood dribbling from the side of his mouth, and an insignia emblazoned on his lapel during May Day antiglobalization demonstrations in 2000, Prime Minister Tony Blair condemned the vandalism as "beyond contempt." However, the cause of the coalition of eco-warriors, Green Party activists, socialists, and anarchists was greatly aided by the irresistible photo opportunity provided by the "modified" Churchill, which produced an undeniably witty companion-image to the direct action that was the subject of significant coverage in the national press. The usually unremarked statue had taken center stage in the press coverage if not in the action itself (see figure 1).[28]

And so in South Africa it is also the case that even the dullest public statuary that has lain dormant and unattended for years can be and is reanimated. In 1997 *Tribute,* a glossy magazine aimed at a middle-class black entrepreneurial readership, issued a statement to accompany its action of shrouding

1. Front cover of *The Editor*. Supplement to *The Guardian*, 5 May 2000.

Below 2. Bust of J. G. Strijdom in Strijdom Square, Pretoria. Photo by the author.

in black cloth certain public statues in Johannesburg and Pretoria: "Monuments that have stood for ages, erected to men who represent all that we have struggled to change, are a little darkened this morning. *Tribute's* team has openly taken a stand against public artworks that mean nothing to the vast majority of people. With that thought weighing heavily on our conscience, we covered them up, literally. Statues in Johannesburg and Pretoria have been transformed into billboards of visual justice."[29] Among these statues thus "transformed" was the absurdly gigantesque bust of J. G. Strijdom (prime minister from 1954 to 1958) in Strijdom Square in Pretoria (figure 2). Earlier, in 1992, the ANC had held a celebratory cultural festival at the foot of Strijdom's head in the same square as a means of "liberating" Strijdom Square and reclaiming it for the black majority.[30] By the time of Thabo Mbeki's inauguration the statuary around the Union Buildings (the administrative center of the South African government) and outside the state theater in Pretoria was the focus of attention again. Plans to drape those statues connected with either colonialism or apartheid proved controversial by 1999, although the criticisms—mainly that the past should be visible as a reminder that it should not happen again or that such a gesture would undermine the importance of what the struggle had overcome—came this time from critics of the ANC, such as the New National Party, the Democratic Party, the Federal Alliance, and the Inkatha Freedom Party (IFP).[31] And the far right, who may not be seen as a particularly potent force or threat to the democratic process in South Africa now, has nonetheless also been vocal in the monument debate. In 1997 twenty-four hours after the unveiling of the statue of Steve Biko, the Black Consciousness leader murdered in 1977 in police custody (during the premiership of B. J. Vorster), the right-wing Afrikaner paramilitary organization Afrikaner Weerstandsbeweging (AWB) had spray-painted its acronym in black on the plinth of the statue.[32] Two weeks later a further attack by an unidentified group resulted in white paint over the statue.[33] It is clear that monuments in South Africa during the transition to democracy became a focus for symbolic transactions. For the time being they have become *more*, not *less*, visible. And as the following chapters will reveal, even the old stalwarts of the apartheid regime have subsequently become reanimated and reappropriated in surprising ways as the staging posts for new and competing identities.

POLICY

With the unbanning of the ANC and other liberation groups in 1990, the shaping of policy with regard to culture and heritage issues began in earnest inside the country. Earlier attempts at formulating strategy had been hosted outside the country in July 1982 in Gaborone and December 1987 in Amsterdam with the "Culture in Another South Africa" festival and conference.[34] Cape Town had attempted to host "Toward a People's Culture Arts Festival" but had been thwarted by the banning imposed through the Emergency Regulations.[35]

By 1991 the ANC had established a Commission on Museums, Monuments and Heraldry (CMMH) within the Department of Arts, Culture, Science and Technology (DACST), although by 1993 it had replaced the CMMH with the Commission for Reconstruction and Transformation of the Arts and Culture (CREATE), which was intended as a "think-tank for the ANC."[36] One of CREATE's tasks was to examine museum legislation and policy set up by the previous (National Party) government; the task led, in turn, to the scrutiny of a document produced within the museum establishment proposing strategies for transforming the museums sector. This report, entitled "The Museums for South Africa Intersectoral Investigation for National Policy" (MUSA), was the subject of considerable heated debate and derision from the ANC. In his address, " 'Give Life to Learning': The Way Ahead for Museums in a Democratic South Africa," CREATE spokesperson and Director of the Mayibuye Center for History and Culture in South Africa André Odendaal summarized the ANC view:

> The challenge to MUSA was to try to reconcile the views of a museums sector rooted in the colonial and apartheid past with a democratic vision of the liberation movement and impending democratic state structures. Almost predictably, I regret to say, the old apartheid bureaucrats and the museum establishment who dominated MUSA were unable to come up with the answer. As far as the African National Congress is concerned, MUSA does not even get out of the starting blocs. . . . The nature and timing of the report, started two months after Bloemfontein [a major ANC meeting on heritage and cultural issues] and completed one month before the onset of a democratic dispensation, can only be seen as an attempt by the old state bureaucracy and the museums establishment to unilaterally restructure the South African museums sector, preserve the status quo and pre-empt democratic processes and changes.[37]

Furthermore, according to Odendaal, "the ANC [had] serious objections to both the process by which the MUSA report was compiled and the content of the report," which it deemed unrepresentative.[38] The authors of the report were accused of blocking structural changes to their institutions on two fronts. In terms of intellectual content "the conscious and unconscious ideological functions of [their] collections" had been ignored, and "no dynamic strategy or major innovations are suggested to counter-balance the weighty baggage of the past."[39]

Odendaal drew attention to instances in the museum world where strategies reminiscent of the Federasie van Afrikaanse Kultuurverenigings (the Federation for Afrikaner Cultural Organizations—FAK) purchase of the Voortrekker Monument (discussed in chapter 1) were being deployed by museum administrators who had a vested interest in the status quo.[40] It may be tempting to see this as a conspiracy theory, but Odendaal's examples present convincing evidence. New members were obviously being hurriedly appointed to the clearly unrepresentative boards of trustees of national institutions, ensuring that these key appointments remained in the hands of the old guard.[41] A mere three months before the handover to the new government, no brakes had been put on what Odendaal describes as "the unilateral development" of Robben Island, and no assurances had been given that a more representative joint forum would be set up to decide this crucially symbolic island's future.[42] In addition, the outgoing government had in 1993 passed the Castle Management Act apparently "without consultation with the ANC or community and other interested organisations," the implication being that the castle, the oldest building in Cape Town, would be unavailable for certain kinds of educational and cultural uses once the democratic government was installed.[43]

CREATE's concerns were obviously that "Continued unilateral restructuring by the expiring minority government . . . could seriously impair the ANC ability to effectively reconstruct and transform heritage resources if these moves are not checked and reversed where necessary."[44] Evidently the MUSA document was seen by most ANC spokespeople as a last ditch attempt to secure the museums establishment for the old guard in much the same way that the hurried legislation referred to above had been designed to stem the tide of liberal reform in the panic (of some) preceding the elections.[45]

But the museum sector was not the only aspect of cultural heritage being barricaded by the outgoing government. Another crucial instance of an attempt to block changes was the reappointment of members of the National Monuments Council (NMC) as late as April 1994, reported in the last *Government Gazette* to appear before the elections—in other words before 22 April.[46] The ANC "voiced its strong opposition to this move to influence the policies of a new, democratically elected government by loading the Council of a national institution with members appointed in an arbitrary and bureaucratic manner" and further, "The ANC considers the reappointment of the old members of the National Monuments Council to be a provocative and counter-productive action and will take strong action to see that the appointment of this illegitimate Council is nullified."[47] The NMC seemed amenable to rethinking both the process of appointment and the timing and advised the ANC to take the issue up with the Department of National Education (DNE), to whom the NMC was accountable. While these organizations seem mostly to have reached an amicable settlement, the minutes of the meeting between the ANC and the DNE in Pretoria read as a much tetchier affair, with both parties standing their ground and defending their positions. The document is a good example of the kinds of entrenched positions that the more progressive recommendations of the new government would encounter in the early years of office.

This elaboration of the debates over the main bodies responsible for policy in national institutions dealing with history and heritage is similarly instructive of the significance placed on museums and other cultural heritage sites by the waning political powers—partly, one assumes, because of the desire to hang onto jobs once the new government was in power, but also because of the ideological leverage that such institutions potentially provided. By the same token, it is obviously important to recognize that the ANC was similarly invested in museums and other public institutions and monuments as purveyors of heritage and history and was aware of the potential of such institutions and sites for the new dispensation well before the elections, which is why it was keen to stop what it perceived as the blocking of positions and change by the National Party government.[48] In fact the ANC had been quite explicit about the significance of the NMC for the incoming government: "The ANC considers the composition of the National Monuments Council to be an issue akin to the appointment of the new South African Broadcasting Corporation board (SABC). The National Monuments Council has a vital role to play in the new South Africa in the conservation of the tangible historical, architectural, scientific and cultural heritage of the people of South Africa and in fostering a sense of South African nationhood."[49] These statements also tell us much about the tensions between the ANC and National Party incumbents of Mandela's new government of national unity, as well as the ANC's anxiety to maintain a strong foothold on all fronts from the outset. In April 1994, an ANC victory in the first democratic election may have been a foregone conclusion, but a new struggle over South Africa's past was just beginning.

1

TRANSLATING THE PAST

Apartheid Monuments in Postapartheid South Africa

> All Afrikaner monuments [should] be removed from the mainland and placed
> in the cells in the prison on Robben Island. It could then be called "Boeras-
> sic Park." — Evita Bezuidenhout, Ambassador to Bapetikosweti (otherwise
> known as the satirist Pieter Dirk Uys)

In July 1992 the South African History Workshop in Johannesburg hosted
a conference, "Myths, Monuments, Museums." The poster for the event depicted a crowd fighting over one of the national monuments most closely
identified with the apartheid regime — the Voortrekker Monument outside
Pretoria (figure 3). The effectiveness of the image derives partly from its
ambiguity. From one perspective the crowd is shoring up the monument,
but from another it is clearly intent on pulling it down. The thorny question
of the fate of monuments erected to commemorate regimes that have since
been discredited and disgraced is not solely a South African dilemma, of
course. In the recent past the future of most of the public statuary in Central and Eastern Europe, as well as the infamous Berlin Wall, has been the
subject of intense debate. In a moving documentary, *Disgraced Monuments*
(1994), which manages to evoke nostalgia without sentimentality, directors
Laura Mulvey and Mark Lewis explore the fate of public monuments under
successive regimes in the former Soviet Union, and the apparently endless
cycle of monumental sculptural programs celebrating the favored leader of
the moment, followed inevitably by their iconoclastic dismantling and removal. Just such a sequence was most famously captured by the Soviet filmmaker Sergei Eisenstein when he filmed the toppling of the statue of the
czar in *Oktobr* (1927). As the art historian Natalya Davidova comments in

Disgraced Monuments, in Russia it has always been a case of "a struggle with the past that was realized through a struggle with monuments." Indeed the film charts instances from Lenin's famous decree on public monuments in 1918 and the iconoclasm that followed to the more recent waves of iconoclastic fervor in the 1990s after the fall of communism.[1] In the opening scenes of the film the camera pans the shelves of a Russian factory where busts of former Soviet leaders sit mute, bundled up in brown paper packaging and tied with string, awaiting a delivery call that will probably never come. In a park in Moscow enclosed by low railings huge sculptures of Lenin, Feliks Dzerzhinsky (former head of the secret police), and Stalin lie toppled on their sides, one elbow supported by a broken column—an apt allegorical support for a fallen leader. This is the Temporary Museum of Totalitarian Art, Russia's solution to the now embarrassing memory of demoted Soviet heroes. In Budapest a similar park exists serving essentially as a cemetery for the defunct leaders of previous Communist regimes. A skeptical observer in *Disgraced Monuments* remarks that since the onset of perestroika in August 1991 the only real changes visible in Russia are a spate of new subjects for yet another wave of monuments. After all, he says pessimistically, "Concrete is easier to change than reality."

It is not surprising that similar scrutiny has been leveled at much of the public sculpture set up over the long apartheid years to commemorate key moments and figures in the Afrikaner nationalist canon and that these debates took place in the highly public forums of the national press and television, especially between 1993 and 1996. Indeed, comparisons with both the former Soviet Union and other East and Central European countries were a feature of some of these debates.[2] The humor of the moment was not lost on the acerbic South African cartoonist Zapiro, who preferred to corral the "displaced" statues and portraits of apartheid's political leaders into a wild game reserve and theme park for the benefit of tourists (figure 4).[3] As the monument debate raged, reputations were made and lost over the issue. The Voortrekker Monument provides a useful point of entry into the complexities of the debates around appropriate forms for commemorating the past and envisaging the future in the "new" South Africa. Some recommended keeping the monument as a reminder of the oppression of the apartheid era—to learn from the lessons of the past. Although some critics favored abandoning the monument altogether and demolishing the site, the South African solution has been notably unlike the East European counterparts. The ANC spokespeople involved in outlining cultural policy for the new democratic government were adamant that most of the Afrikaner monuments should remain, including the Voortrekker Monument.

3. Penny Siopis, poster for "Myths, Monuments, Museums" conference, University of the Witwatersrand, Johannesburg, 16–18 July 1992. Courtesy of the artist.

Below 4. Zapiro, *Boerassic Park. Mail and Guardian*, 1 February 1996. Courtesy of Jonathan Shapiro.

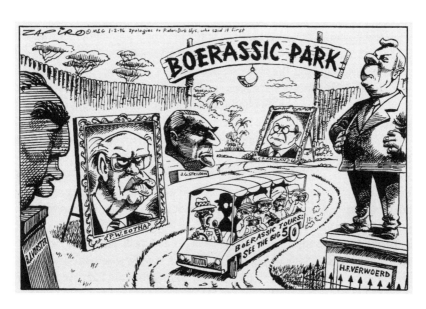

Consequently, although in practice some monuments dedicated to the memory and legacy of apartheid have been destroyed (certainly the fate of most statues of Hendrick Verwoerd, the man considered by many to be the major architect of apartheid), many of those most symbolically laden are still intact, including the Voortrekker and the Taalmonument (Afrikaans Language Monument) outside Paarl. Indeed, at various points in the debate over the future of monuments in South Africa there was criticism about the amount of government funding being apportioned to monuments dedicated to aspects of Afrikaner culture. In 1996, for example, R 1.2 million was spent on the Voortrekker Monument Museum and a further R 801,000 on the Afrikaanse Taalmuseum, as opposed to R 200,000 given to what many would regard as a key site for the commemoration of the liberation struggle—the District Six Museum.[4] According to one report, by 1999 the Voortrekker Monument was getting R 425,000 and the grant for the Afrikaanse Taalmuseum had risen from R 886,000 to R 955,000, while the grant to Robben Island had dropped from R 24.2 million to R 21.9 million.[5]

One notorious proposal was to erect a monument of Mandela's arm rising up on one of the hills opposite the Voortrekker Monument as a kind of symbolic riposte. This was one of the earliest new commissions mooted for public sculpture for the new dispensation, and the debate that ensued was to set the tone for much of the later discussions. Estimated at a cost of R 60 million in some reports, the project was highly controversial from the outset. In the first place, the chosen artist, Danie de Jager, had no reputation as a "struggle" artist. Indeed with similar hubris to Leni Riefenstahl's adamant objection to being linked in any way to the ideologies of National Socialism under the Third Reich, de Jager denied any association with the apartheid regime, despite being the artist responsible for a number of the regime's key public sculpture commissions, including the monstrous head of J. G. Strijdom in Pretoria and the statue of Hendrick Verwoerd that marks his grave. Both politicians were, in fact, responsible for the intensification of apartheid policies. De Jager saw himself as the artist best qualified for the new project precisely because, as he insisted to the *Sunday Independent,* he was "the most experienced sculptor in [the] country of heroic or larger-than-life work."[6] This is a dubious accolade at the best of times since works of such scale are historically almost always associated with totalitarian regimes of one complexion or another.[7]

To add insult to injury, the project was funded by de Jager and two businessmen, Abe and Solly Krok, whose business success was in no small measure due to their effective marketing of "skin-lightening" creams to various black constituencies. In addition, the project was apparently supported by the president's office, and the Afrikaans language daily, *Rapport,* carried photographs of Mandela in the company of Solly Krok and de Jager looking at the alarming maquette of a twenty-three-meter-high bronze forearm (apparently modeled on Mandela's) rising up out of the roof of a temple structure, looking for all the world like one of the early sets of a Hammer horror movie (figure 5). The combination of politically tainted funders and artist, together with the perceived affinity with fascist and other totalitarian monuments, was too much for many cultural commentators and elicited a spate of antagonistic criticisms in the national press on all three counts and, it would be fair to say, across a spectrum of liberal to fairly conservative opinion (see one example in figure 6).[8] Many critics were particularly dismayed at the lack of transparency in the process of assessing the project and were angered by de Jager's obvious ease of access to the president when many other causes seen as more deserving struggled for months to get a hearing. They claimed that the commission had been undemocratically handled and lacked consultative mechanisms.[9] It was also of course an opportunity for some apologists to take the side of the artist and argue (one can only say defensively) the importance of allowing individuals to be capable of change.[10] The incident also generated debate about what kind of form was appropriate for a monument to the liberation struggle, as well as obviously highlighting what one critic referred to as the "blurred borders between the state and the private sector."[11]

APARTHEID'S FOUNDATIONS

This chapter is an exploration of the possibilities and impossibilities for rehabilitating a monument with an explicit history as a foundational icon of the apartheid state. In particular, I am curious to know how far it is possible to disinvest such an icon of its Afrikaner nationalist associations and reinscribe it with new resonances that enable it to remain a highly public monument despite a new democratic government whose future is premised on the demise of everything the monument has always stood for. How is it possible for black constituencies to simply accept the coexistence of such an oppressive reminder of apartheid? Conversely, in the face of evident factionalism within the Afrikaner nationalist contingency since at least the early 1980s, how do the monument's fascist overtones square with the requirements of what some have argued is an emerging Afrikaner middle class with cosmopolitan and international pretensions.[12]

I want to argue that in the 1990s the Voortrekker Monument did not simply become a shadow of its former self (as one might anticipate) and that

5. Maquette for projected statue of President Mandela's fist, with (from right to left) Judy Sexwale, Solly Krok, Nelson Mandela, and Danie de Jager. *Rapport*, 31 August 1996.

Below 6. Zapiro, *Urban Handscape. Mail and Guardian*, 3 April 1996. Courtesy of Jonathan Shapiro.

it was not disinterest alone (even were this figured as strategic disavowal) that made it possible for the ANC and others to allow this oppressive reminder of the recent past to remain in place. Rather I want to suggest that the monument accrued significance supplemental to, and in some cases of course directly at odds with, its intended symbolic presence. I see this as not simply a symptom of the passing of time and the necessary sedimenting of meanings that accumulate as part of the process of historical change. My concern here is to reinstate the concept of agency as a way of understanding how this commemorative "shrine" has been reinvented post-apartheid. Sometimes serendipitous, sometimes strategic, and sometimes opportunistic, the monument seems to have become a staging post for self-fashioning for both white and black constituencies across the political spectrum. From Afrikaner laager to Zulu kraal—these two images span the symbolic currency of the monument today and help to resite it. The semantic distance between them foregrounds the extent to which even an apparently stable signifier of monolithic nationalist associations can be undercut by the necessarily hybridizing effects of different acts of translation.

The concept of translation is helpful here, both in the Benjaminian sense of supplemental meanings that necessarily transform the "original" through the act of translation and in the sense that Gayatri Chakravorty Spivak suggests of an active "reader as translator" capable of performing a reading against the grain and between the lines even in circumstances where the raw material reproduces a set of fairly standard colonial tropes.[13] While translation is more usually associated with the word and text, on a simple level, it is perhaps appropriate in the case of a monument such as the Voortrekker, where the iconographic register is particularly susceptible to this kind of linguistic model and the narrative of the interior frieze invites a performative reading. On a more complex level translation offers a way of articulating the operations of agency in the construction of historical memory.

My argument turns on the fact that the Voortrekker Monument has a significance for all South Africans. Any acts of translation depend on a certain familiarity with the text, a getting inside the skin of the writer. To the extent that the narrative of the Great Trek was the imposed foundational narrative of the nation-state—the only legitimate history available at any level of education—and to the extent that Afrikaans was the imposed language at all levels of public (and often private) intercourse, the Voortrekker Monument attained a certain monstrous legibility—inescapable even to those who never visited the site.[14] Most important, the monument had a historical status as the centerpiece of an orchestrated mass spectacle of Afrikaner unity and power—a legacy that has by no means receded and that provided a rallying point for various factions on the right up to and beyond the eve of the democratic elections in April 1994.

On 16 December 1938, the foundation stone of this central monument to apartheid was laid on a hill outside Pretoria. It was also the occasion of an elaborate reconstruction of the foundational event of Afrikaner nationalism—the Great Trek of 1838.[15] That year a party of Boer men, women, and children (known as the Voortrekker, or "pioneers"), dissatisfied with British rule in the Cape and its inconvenient corollary of slave emancipation, set off in a convoy of ox wagons on a grueling journey from Cape Town to form independent republics in what were to become the Orange Free State and the Transvaal. One hundred years later, twelve replica ox wagons, complete with costumed Voortrekker families, set out from various parts of the country to restage that fateful journey and finally arrived (nearly four months later) at two of the most historically significant destinations—the city of Pretoria and the site of the battle of Blood River (the Ncome River). The Voortrekker Youth Movement completed the staging of the event by forming a "river of fire," with flaming torches lit in relay fashion by hundreds of young Voortrekker scouts around the country, starting in Cape Town and culminating in a torch-lit procession up the sides of Monument Hill—"symbolic of the spread of civilization from the Cape to the far north."[16] The mass spectacle, which greeted the 1930s Trekkers and which was orchestrated around the base of what would become the Voortrekker Monument, was a calculated attempt to invent a coherent Afrikaner identity where none actually existed, borrowing the language of theater so successfully deployed by the National Socialists in Germany and epitomized by the Nazi rallies at the Nuremburg stadium.[17]

By the date of the inauguration of the monument on 16 December 1949, it was clear that the theatrical orchestration of national unity (evident in figures 7 and 8) was not the only thing the South African leaders had borrowed from the Nazis. In his inaugural address, Daniel Francis Malan, prime minister of the Union of South Africa, described the nineteenth-century Boer Trekkers: "Exclusively, and bound by their own blood ties, they had to be children of South Africa. Further, there was the realisation that as bearers and propagators of Christian civilisation, they had a national calling which had set them and their descendants the inexorable demand on the one hand to act as guardians over the non-European races, but on the other hand to see to the maintenance of their own white paramountcy and of their white race purity."[18] Furthermore, this was not simply a historical condition relegated to the past but an ongoing ideal since Afrikaners were metaphorically still on the Trek road in 1949. Malan continued: "On the Trek road! Whither?

7. Crowd in Voortrekker costume at the inauguration of the Voortrekker Monument, December 1949. Board of Control of the Voortrekker Monument, *The Voortrekker Monument*.

Below 8. Bird's-eye view of the inauguration of the Voortrekker Monument showing the extent of the reconstruction of the Great Trek, with pitched Voortrekker tents in the foreground and in the plains surrounding the monument. Board of Control of the Voortrekker Monument, *The Voortrekker Monument*.

Look ahead and judge for yourselves. . . . That which confronts you threat-eningly is nothing less than modern and outwardly civilised heathendom as well as absorption into semi-barbarism through miscegenation and the disintegration of the white race."[19] That same year the National Party passed the Prohibition of Mixed Marriages Act.

The huge monument (figure 9) still stands like some misplaced Bake-lite radio, ostentatiously positioned in the sight line of the Union Buildings, which were originally built as a symbol of South Africa's dominion status within the British Empire.[20] Inside the monument, in what is known as the "Hall of Heroes" is a carved marble frieze made up of twenty-seven panels; it is 302 feet in length and 7 feet, 6 inches high (hailed at the time as the longest frieze in existence; figure 10). Built to last, the frieze is painstak-ingly carved in Italian Quercetta (rather than Cararra) marble, known for its toughness under extreme weather conditions. The panels narrate a ver-sion of the central incidents of the Great Trek from the Cape to the Trans-vaal that became enshrined in history textbooks around the country—pre-dominantly a tale of Boer heroism and God-fearing righteousness and of Zulu and Ndebele treachery and savagery. Most significant, as an early guide stipulates, the frieze is "not only a representation of historical events. It also serves as a symbolic document showing the Afrikaner's proprietary right to South Africa. . . . A people that have sacrificed so much blood and tears, have left their mark on such a country, and therefore spiritually and physically that country belongs to them and their descendants."[21]

Historically, then, the Voortrekker Monument is of critical significance for the foundational myths of Afrikaner nationalism—in particular the idea of the Trek as the moment of emergence of the Afrikaner as the found-ing ethnic group of a new nation, "the white tribe," and the "divine right" of the Trekkers to the land. These myths are embodied through the struc-ture of the monument itself—first through the seductive resolution pro-vided by the narrative of encounter and conquest represented by the interior frieze, and second through the fact that the edifice houses what amounts to a cenotaph on its lower level, replete with "eternal flame," to the memory of Trekkers killed en route. This is strategically positioned: a shaft of sun-light was designed to strike the tomb each year on 16 December (the "day of the vow").[22] Third, of course, these foundational myths are reinforced through the prominent and confrontational positioning of the monument itself, directly opposite the Union Buildings—the site of British legislative authority.

9. Voortrekker Monument prior to the 1994 elections.

Below 10. Detail of the marbled interior and a section of the frieze inside the Voortrekker Monument. Photo by the author.

If the Voortrekker Monument had the power to symbolically muster a na-scent Afrikaner nationalism in 1938 and to consolidate this in 1949, by 1990 —just four years prior to the first democratic elections in South Africa— it still had the power to galvanize these forces. The changing fortunes of the monument's appeal as a rallying ground for Afrikaner nationalism are a good barometer of the shifting allegiances within the white right in South Africa. In particular, the mobilizations around the monument in the run-up to the elections and the way they were dealt with by both the South Afri-can Defence Force (SADF) and the National Party (NP) (who were in various stages of negotiation with the ANC by this time) serve to foreground the emergence of considerable fissures among the right in South African poli-tics over this period.

It is clear that the constant regrouping of the far right into various alli-ances over the period 1990–1993 was speeded by the NP's defections under President F. W. de Klerk from a truly segregationist apartheid and the con-solidation of liberal white supporters who were more concerned with the economic benefits of international acceptance than maintaining Afrikaner ascendancy. As Jonathan Hyslop has observed, such splits had been under way for some time: "The 1980's [then] saw a polarisation in Afrikanerdom between an elitist National Party trying to restructure classical apartheid while retaining white control, and a Conservative Party [founded in 1982] committed to reimposing the fully segregated society envisaged by Ver-woerd."[23]

One of the forms the anxiety over party allegiance has taken is a contes-tation over representations of the Great Trek by the various factions on the right. Albert Grundlingh and Hilary Sapire trace the ways the Trek narrative has been variously recuperated by different governments.[24] They argue that by 1988 acute economic and political crises and challenges to the govern-ment, both internationally and internally, "prompted Afrikaner business-men and intellectuals to express their doubts about the feasibility of a sys-tem predicated upon racial division and state intervention in the economy and to pressurize the Government into making tentative moves of 'reform.' This programme required the support of English speakers and 'moderate' black groups, precisely those groups historically portrayed as 'enemies' in traditional Great Trek representations."[25] However, rather than abandon the essentially traditionalist and archaic narrative of the Trek, this founda-tional story was "translated" to suit the agenda of the newly reformist Na-tional Party.

By the 150th anniversary celebrations of the Great Trek in 1988, the theme of "Forward South Africa" was interpreted in a particular way. Instead of a focus on the aspect of the Trek narrative that foregrounded the early Trekkers' divine right to the land and the centrality of a divinely ordained racial segregation, the emphasis in the official literature and speeches for the 1988 celebrations was on the importance of learning the spirit of self-sacrifice and compromise from these heroic predecessors in order to promote the concept of "power sharing." This concept extended, on that occasion, to acknowledging the role of various black constituencies in the historical Trek and also "in contemporary South African political, economic and social life."[26] The contest over ownership of the Trek narrative and the legitimacy of other versions and interpretations of those historic events resulted in 1988 in an alternative celebration staged in opposition to the government festivities and orchestrated by the far right Afrikaner-Volkswag (AV), who claimed that "like the Voortrekkers of 1838 who revolted against the 'social revolution' at the Cape, the right wing of the 1980s is in revolt against the 'social revolution' caused by liberalism and the 1983 constitutional arrangements."[27]

Despite the fact that lack of enthusiasm for the official celebrations suggests that a majority of prosperous, middle-class urban Afrikaners were clearly far less identified with the values and lifestyle signaled by their Voortrekker ancestry—precisely those trumpeted by the far right—it is significant that the NP evidently still felt it necessary to invoke the Voortrekkers to lend authority to its political agenda. In other words, it is clear from Grundlingh and Sapire's research that both the reforming NP and other factions on the far right were considerably invested in the representation of the Great Trek and its associated monument. If by 1988 there were clear divisions between the prosperous sector of Afrikanerdom that had benefited from the embourgeoisement of urban Afrikaner society and the sector that felt aggrieved at what were still perceived as the "corrosive influences of liberalism, communism, and materialism" manifest in the culture of the city, by 1990 these divisions had been exacerbated. One of the results was the stepping up of right-wing activism in relation to the contested terrain of the public representation of the Great Trek.

In May 1990 the Conservative Party chose the Voortrekker Monument as the meeting ground to stage a demonstration of right-wing Afrikaner solidarity against the prospect of political change presented by the forthcoming elections. About sixty-five thousand people attended the rally—a smaller turnout than had been anticipated. Ferdie Hartzenberg, who was later to become the chair of the Afrikaner People's Front (AVF) Executive Committee, addressed the crowds on behalf of the Conservative Party, stirring his listeners with incendiary language that borrowed more than a little from earlier incarnations of gatherings at the monument. He made it clear that "the Conservative Party would resort to all possible democratic, constitutional ways to fight the political changes. But if all those channels are closed for us, we would regard ourselves as an oppressed volk. Then we would have no choice but to take the path of an oppressed nation to fight for our freedom."[28] As Hyslop has pointed out, this was no empty threat. The far right in South Africa, providing it cemented certain alliances, had a leadership comprising some of the top brass from the former SADF and was fast amassing a considerable stockpile of military hardware.[29] Its success was partly due to the rise of the coalition AVF under the leadership of the influential Constand Viljoen (former chief of the SADF and an Angolan war veteran), whose message was neither the rabid racism of the AWB (under the extremist Eugene Terre'blanche) nor the backtracking return to Verwoerdian apartheid measures of the CP, but rather, as Hyslop points out, appealed on grounds of self-determination for the Afrikaner people. Such differences would eventually split the right irrevocably and cement the ANC / NP option, but at this time they presented the possibility of strengthening the right by drawing in other constituencies making similar claims who were also antagonistic to the ANC / NP negotiations, such as Mangosuthu Buthelezi's Inkhata Freedom Party.[30]

One year prior to the elections, in December 1993, the area around the Voortrekker Monument was the focus of other acts of sabotage. Hartzenberg addressed another rally at the monument, this time drawing one hundred thousand of the faithful. Another group of heavily armed right wingers—the Pretoria East Boere Kommando—took over the Schanskop Fort, situated directly opposite the monument, in what was described by their leader, Willem Ratte (a former Angolan war veteran and intelligence agent), as "a symbolic gesture by the Boere Afrikaners to show their disgust with the implementation of the Transitional Executive Council" (the transitional government formed by the ANC and NP in December).[31] The main gate providing access to both the fort and the monument was besieged by a group of supporting right wingers trying to get into the grounds but blocked by the police and a battalion of soldiers who had been mobilized after the siege on Schanskop Fort. Considerable violence was narrowly averted through the deployment of significant numbers of NP military and police forces. Among other things, this incident underlines that the military and the police force, at least in terms of their leadership, were no longer reducible to the lumpen racialist agenda of the far right but needed to be seen as bodies with vested (and opportunistic) interests in seeing the transition through to its conclusion.[32]

The fact that panic over the impending elections manifested itself as restaking a claim to certain monuments associated with key moments in the Trek narrative—the Voortrekker Monument figuring particularly prominently—had a number of interesting repercussions. Specifically, concerns about the nature of historical writing and the stakes involved in the creation of compelling versions of a shared public memory became no longer the domain of the various factions on the left—traditionally the stomping ground for such debates. Because of the very public nature of the struggle over monuments and "heritage," aided by the newfound freedom of the press, a script that had been a naturalized version of historical events and the prerogative of a more solidly identifiable right-wing Afrikaner nationalist contingent became a visibly contested domain where even the most rabid right wingers were obliged to declare their investment in certain historical narratives *as opposed* to others that they were now also forced to acknowledge (even while they may be misrepresented). For example, in 1992 one of the organs of the far right, the *Patriot,* reproduced Penny Siopis's design for the "Myths, Monuments, Museums" conference mentioned above with the caption: "The destruction of a national cultural history is symptomatic of the current revolution. Revolutions force culture back to the year dot. The ANC wants history to be rewritten. They want Verwoerdburg to be Mandelaville and they want the Voortrekker Monument to become an ANC armed struggle museum in keeping with developments in the rest of Africa where the Communists took over. Already twenty years ago the National Party started to rewrite our history and to murder it, right in keeping with ANC ideas."[33]

In further indication of election panic and its resolution through action over a monument, the main cultural organizations for the promotion and preservation of Afrikaner culture—the FAK—formed a private, nonprofit company in 1993 and bought the right to control and manage the Voortrekker Monument, effectively taking it out of the control of the presiding NP—but also, significantly, out of the control of any *subsequent* government.[34] This prompted a flurry of responses from various factions of the national press. Journalists elaborated on what was fast emerging as a hot topic. Even the Afrikaans national daily, *Die Beeld,* a fairly liberal paper with urbane pretensions, defended the monument in grandiose terms: "The Voortrekker Monument is one of the country's strongest reminders of a time when the Voortrekkers, through blood, sweat and determination, made South Africa their own." Lorette Grobler went on to claim that "In the eyes of the world the Monument is an important commemorator of South African history."[35] She gave the final word, however, to the head of the history department at the Afrikaans university of Potchefstroom, an institution with a solid reputation as one of the bastions of apartheid. The professor insisted that the monument should be kept at all costs because it was "indissolubly part of the total South African history. Maintenance of monuments is a cultural right and therefore the keeping of the [monument] should not be a controversial matter."[36]

The confident assertion of the maintenance of monuments as universally a "cultural right" by someone whose primary concern is clearly the preservation of Afrikaans culture is telling. Because of the apartheid regime's denial or destruction of most historical cultural symbols belonging to the majority black communities in South Africa, this statement poses little risk to the speaker's cultural nationalist agenda. Such a legacy has implications for the level of engagement that some constituencies may feel is possible or impossible with debates around history, heritage, and conservation. Indeed, as University of Cape Town historian Farieda Khan has pointed out, there are many reasons why black communities may be either apathetic or downright negative toward heritage or conservation issues and reluctant to engage in the debates around public culture.[37] Many of the buildings or other structures that have been proclaimed "national monuments" by the NMC have more negative than positive connotations for the majority culture. What does it mean, for example, to preserve the Cape Dutch architecture and slave quarters of Groot Constantia, built on slave labor and thriving as a profitable vineyard to this day? Other commentators have pointed out that in some ways the general emphasis on conserving the built environment may also reinforce a divide between rural and urban communities.[38] As Khan reminds us, the problem is exacerbated by the forced removals that were the direct result of the Group Areas Act in the 1950s and the subsequent demolition and destruction of areas that otherwise would have been ripe candidates for the conservation of a rich cultural heritage. Two of the most controversial casualties are District Six in Cape Town and Johannesburg's famous suburb, Sophiatown (cynically renamed Triomf by the apartheid government).

Given this legacy it is understandable that a certain degree of skepticism accompanied discussions about heritage. Nevertheless I want to suggest that the media played a significant role in engaging a broader public in the monuments debate in the lead up to the elections. Firsthand accounts of visits to the Voortrekker Monument by individuals who would have previously felt excluded were particularly effective in opening up the debate. Joe Louw, a well-known black photojournalist famous for his photographs of the aftermath of Martin Luther King's assassination, writing in the *Saturday Star*, pessimistically views the monument as "a concrete symbol of separate worlds." Louw describes his feelings on encountering the monument in 1992: "Its immense box-like granite mass imparts the feeling of a fortress—defensive, mute and immovable. For a politically aware black person to even approach the thing requires some profound self-examination."[39] He attacks the guidebook's narrative, which constantly invokes the fiction of the interior as an uninhabited land—a point contradicted by the guide writer's own narrative since "the rest of the trekker story is precisely about the bloody battles they had to fight in this supposedly 'empty' country."[40] Finally, he refers to the panel of the Zulu attack on the laager at Bloukrans as "perhaps the most provocative and nauseating scene in which Zulus treacherously attack the trekkers—beating to death mostly women and children with sticks and assegais." Louw despairs of the impression this must leave on both black and white children who visit the monument.[41] "I left the monument in a profound state of sadness," he ends. "Nowhere was there portrayed even a single gesture of kindness, mercy, magnanimity or heroism by any black. Instead they are shown either kneeling or killing. What a way to prepare the country, especially the country's youth, for the 'new' era of mutual trust and tolerance."[42]

In 1996, two years after the election of Mandela's government, a visit to the Voortrekker Monument by another prominent black public figure made national headlines. Tokyo Sexwale, at that time the charismatic premier of Gauteng Province, was photographed in a special spread in the *Sunday Times* (figure 11). Gauteng, the name given by the new government to a section of the old Boer republic of the Transvaal, is the province historically most closely associated with Afrikaner nationalism. This is an interesting article for many reasons—and significantly different in tone from Joe Louw's earlier piece. Unlike Louw, who reported on the oppressive nature of the historical narratives represented in the monument's frieze and the negative aspects of the representation of black protagonists throughout, Sexwale adopts a different strategy. While Louw pointed out the absences and distortions in the monument's representation of the past, Sexwale reads it against the grain. He effectively performs a "translation" or inversion of the prime symbols of the monument, starting with the entrance. Noticing the granite laager of sixty-four covered wagons surrounding the monument,

TOKYO'S GROOT TREK

11. Tokyo Sexwale in front of a panel from the frieze at the Voortrekker Monument depicting the battle of Kapein, fought against the Matabele. *Sunday Times,* 15 December 1996.

Right 12. Tokyo Sexwale opening the gates to the Voortrekker Monument. *Sunday Times,* 15 December 1996.

which symbolically was designed (as an early guide would have it) "to protect the tradition and sanctity of the [Afrikaner] nation against any attack," he is quoted as saying, "Now I understand the laager mentality. But I'm glad there is a gateway, or the whole Afrikaner nation would have been trapped inside."[43] The gates themselves — Sexwale insisted on being photographed opening them (figure 12) — are in the form of assegais, symbolic of the Zulu leader Dingane's power, apparently blocking the path of civilization. Sexwale inverts this symbolism: "It was precisely the assegais at its height that turned the tide. *Umkhonto we Sizwe*, the spear of the nation, opened up the path of civilisation."[44]

In a sense then, the monument becomes the focus for an active process of "translation" in the sense of Gayatri Spivak's proposition of the "reader as translator." Arguably, Sexwale's "translation" is in some ways much more effective a strategy in the case of the almost irredeemable Voortrekker Monument than it might be in another example (say Robben Island) already associated with the heroic stoicism of the liberation struggle. More than this, however, Sexwale's inversion or "Africanization" recalls a much earlier moment in the monument's history and reclaims for African consumption what was identified at its founding as the hybrid nature of the iconographic schema. By so doing, he attempts to render the structure "safe" and to disinvest the monument of the power of its oppressive legacy as a linchpin in the armory of apartheid. In terms of the politics of national unity, which was so prevalent in 1996, his strategy may well have been motivated by the diplomatic appeasement for which he became well known, but this does not diminish the broader effectivity of such a gesture.

As Elizabeth Delmont has pointed out, from its inception the Voortrekker Monument was designed to cement the historical legitimacy of an Afrikaner ascendancy.[45] To this effect the architect Gerard Moerdijk places the monument within a lineage of other internationally significant locations, including the Mausoleum of Halicarnassus. While acknowledging the disparity in scale, Moerdijk (in the official guidebook to the monument) is not reticent about marshaling the Hôtel des Invalides in Paris and India's Taj Mahal as points of comparison. He points out that detail such as the ornamental zigzag motif above the large windows is borrowed from cuneiform writing to indicate water and fertility, with a reference to the importance of procreation for the Voortrekkers. Significantly, the two examples that he sees as most appropriate to the African context and that most effectively serve to bolster the ideology of the Afrikaners' right to the African soil are taken from Egypt and what was then Southern Rhodesia:

Vastness is more than anything else a characteristic of Africa, a vastness that dwarfs the work of man. This is not so much a matter of actual size but rather one of appreciation and understanding. History teaches that one nation in particular could convey this characteristic of vastness in its works—the Egyptians. Even in their smaller edifices they succeeded in embodying a reflection of this greatness of Africa. Because of similar basic building principles it so happens that of all structures in Southern Africa this vastness of Africa is best reflected in the Zimbabwe Ruins in Southern Rhodesia.[46]

The explicit reference to the Zimbabwe Ruins or "Great Zimbabwe" (as it later came to be known) is more interesting than at first it seems. Some scholars have dismissed this as simply another instance of the degeneration-ist thesis, which made it possible to praise certain apparently ancient civilizations in Africa without conceding to them a past that spoke of cultural and political greatness.[47] This may well have been the intention. However, this argument does not take into account that the origin of the Zimbabwe Ruins was a highly contested topic at the time, and its use may well foreground the need to dispel any anxiety about the legitimacy concerning the Afrikan-ers' originary claims. Many South African intellectuals, amateur historians, archaeologists, and certainly ideologues with an interest in constructing a historical and political lineage for Afrikaner nationalism were probably only too familiar with debates concerning the origin of the ruins.

As both Saul Dubow and Henrika Kuklick have pointed out, these debates have a long history that is intimately bound up with nationalist competi-tion among South African, German, and British archaeologists.[48] More to the point in terms of how these debates might have impacted on the Voor-trekker Monument, it is important to note that Gertrude Caton-Thompson's defense of David Randall-MacIver's claim for a "Bantu" (that is, African) origin for the ruins, came to the fore in a series of highly public, volatile, and entertaining debates in South Africa, widely reported in the national press, at precisely the time when Afrikaner nationalism was beginning to be consolidated culturally.[49] By the 1950s the controversy showed no signs of abating, and the literature on the mysteries of the origins of the ruins was to continue growing exponentially well into independence.[50] The fact that the official guidebook deliberately draws attention to an iconographic forerunner for one of the founding monuments of Afrikaner nationalism— the "Zimbabwe ruins"—whose public profile has been one of contestation around its African origins, speaks of the imperative for the Afrikaner nation-alists to appropriate Africa to itself. But it was a risky gesture in the 1930s, as it was still in the 1950s. The instability of the Zimbabwe Ruins as a sign ripe for recuperation during this earlier period has effectively and unambiguously been put to work for the opposition in Sexwale's "translation," while nonetheless offering conciliatory gestures to an anxious Afrikaner contingent, very much in the way of the "concessions" made to the black majority in the opening speeches on the occasion of the consecration of the monument in 1949.[51] These are the complex underpinnings that make Sexwale's understated performance so compelling in the 1990s.

This was not the only occasion when an Afrikaner monument was used to stage a form of reconciliation in the relatively early stages of the "government of national unity." However, if Sexwale's gesture can be read as an ambivalent staging of reconciliation between Afrikaner and black constituencies under the new dispensation, Archbishop Desmond Tutu's visit to another key monument to Afrikanerdom, the Nasionale Vrouemonument, can be read as a far less ambiguous performance. The Vrouemonument, outside Bloemfontein, is the site for the commemoration of the women and children (numbering about twenty-six thousand) who died in the concentration camps set up by the British during the South African War. The monument is also the site of the graves of both Emily Hobhouse, the British woman who campaigned against the appalling conditions in the camps on behalf of the Boer women and children, and M. T. Steyn, the former president of the Orange Free State. Tutu, then chair of the recently convened TRC, was photographed in the national press praying at the foot of the monument. His reported speech is clearly conciliatory, although the focus is on the troubled relationship between two white constituencies: "If Afrikaners and English had sat down to talk about their pain and suffering, perhaps their relationship would have been different. What we are trying to do in the Truth and Reconciliation Commission is to deal with our past so that we don't have to keep coming back to it, so that it doesn't poison relationships as the relationship between Afrikaner and English was poisoned."[52] Tutu ends with the rejoinder, "We must think of all the mothers and children who have suffered in this country, like the Afrikaners in the concentration camps."[53]

SEX, CENSORSHIP, AND HERITAGE

Potentially subversive readings of the Voortrekker Monument were not the monopoly of a single sector in the "new" South Africa. Nor did they represent a simple choice between the revisionist critique offered by Louw or the "reader as translator" rendition offered by Sexwale. In June 1995 a new Afrikaans-language porn magazine, published by the owners of the South African edition of *Hustler,* hit the market. The title, *Loslyf,* roughly translates as "loose body." I want to argue here that the conjunction of image and text in the shoot featuring the Voortrekker Monument represents more than the usual disrespect for the boundaries between sacred and profane, which is the staple of much pornographic literature, and that it constitutes a more serious critique of the most oppressive version of Afrikaner ethnic absolutism. This claim rests on my understanding of the context out of which the magazine was launched: years of state censorship in South Africa and the emergence of an Afrikaner lower-middle-class constituency that the editors of the magazine saw as their readership, along with a coterie of middle-class Afrikaner dissenters and intellectuals (who provided the bulk of the editorial staff) who were in 1995 even more intent on differentiating themselves from those ideally addressed by the symbolic litany of the Voortrekker Monument.

Flagged on the cover as "Dina at the Monument," the feature is called "Dina — *Loslyf*'s Indigenous Flower of the Month" (figure 13). That the photo shoot is represented as taking place in the hallowed grounds of Monument Hill, with the Voortrekker Monument looming large in the near background, is one kind of slap in the face for the Calvinist puritanism of Afrikaner nationalists. But there are many other features that make this a more knowing trespass. Two central conceits are crucial to its effectiveness in the South African context. One of the primary conceits is that Dina is not just another porn star but is apparently related to one of the central figures in the Great Trek narrative, Gen. Andries Hendrik Potgieter (figure 14). Mobilizing the very discourses through which Afrikaner nationalism constituted itself as the guardian of the white race (civilization) — the indelible bonds of blood and family — she is quoted as saying, "My great-great-grandfather, Hendrik Potgieter, has been my hero since my childhood. He was the sort of man who inspired people to trek barefoot over the Drakensberg Mountains so that we Boere could be free and at peace living here in the Transvaal. If only we could have a leader of his caliber today."[54] To a South African reader schooled during apartheid this text is also clearly written as a pastiche of the standard children's textbook version of the Trek.[55]

The second conceit is of Dina as an "indigenous flower." Devoid of the standard boudoir accoutrements of the other models in the magazine, Dina is photographed *en plein air,* amid the long grasses at the foot of the monument. Traditionally the relationship of the Voortrekker to the concept of nature is a complex one. The idea of the Trekker as "a child of the South African wilderness" was a myth obviously calculated to enhance the Trekkers' claim to the land through demonstrating a special affinity with the rugged natural environment. Dina's description and the "natural" surroundings of the

13. "Dina—*Loslyf*'s Indigenous Flower of the Month." *Loslyf,* June 1995.

Below 14. "Dina," with the statue of Andries Hendrik Potgieter in the background. *Loslyf,* June 1995.

15. Boer mother and children, Voortrekker Monument. Board of Control of the Voortrekker Monument, *The Voortrekker Monument.*

shoot clearly rely on this association while potentially exposing the contradictions of its sexual content. Similarly, guides to the monument note that earlier Dutch or Portuguese settlers found "the interior of Africa too vast, the forces of nature too strong. . . . It was left to the Voortrekkers . . . to force, at a great price, an entry into the interior and establish a white civilisation. . . . To achieve his ideal, he had to tame nature, conquer the savages and establish his state."[56] In fact such copy could easily have found its way verbatim into the pages of a less knowing porn magazine since it conforms creditably with most of the basic requirements of pornographic writing. The conceit of Dina as an "indigenous flower" plays with the implicitly sexual content of such an ideology and the violence that underscores it.

In the symbolic schema of the Voortrekker Monument the Voortrekker ideal is achieved through the statue of the Voortrekker Mother and her two children, representing "white civilization," while "the black wildebeest [in retreat] portray the ever threatening dangers of Africa" (figure 15).[57] Far from the Calvanist puritanism of the early Voortrekker dress and *kappie* (the bonnet traditionally worn by Boer women), our "indigenous flower" is confusingly kitted out in an outfit more resonant of the threat of the African wild or of the male Voortrekkers' attempts to tame it (especially in shots of her posing in a man's bush jacket). Nor is motherhood the first thing on her mind. In fact, she disrupts the versions of both femininity and masculinity (black and white) played out in the monument, providing a kind of composite figure in which both gendered and ethnic identifications are deliberately confused. Dina's attire also makes reference to the pugilistic qualities of the Boer women, often indicated in histories of the Trek and immortalized in the monument's frieze. The effect here is to display the contradictions of the image of the demure Calvinist homemaker and procreator of the Boer nation by casting the Boer woman as Amazon—in other words, exposing the contradiction by explicitly sexualizing the Boer woman's warrior status.[58] In a timely finale, given the furor raging over heritage and monuments, the story culminates with relentless punning: "The twenty-four-year-old nurse from Pretoria doesn't beat around the bush when she speaks of her love of Afrikaans language and culture. 'All the people who are so eager to punish the Afrikaner volk by demolishing and desecrating our monuments are playing with fire. They should know: if you interfere with my symbols, you interfere with me.'"[59]

There are many levels on which such appropriations might work as potentially transgressive strategies in relation to the primary myths of Afrikaner nationalism—not the least of which is that they break down the mythic conception of the Afrikaners as a homogenous mass completely in thrall to the doctrines of apartheid and their Calvinist origins. Nevertheless, the fact that such an image is still consumed within the context of pornography might clearly mediate any critical edge by turning back on itself since the potential exposure of the sexualized violence of colonial and fascist discourse can itself become a source of titillation in its consumption as pornography. Other factors, however, support my reading of the feature as critique.[60] The editor of *Loslyf,* Ryk Hattingh, has an interesting history in relationship to campaigns against state censorship (not just vis-à-vis porn) and has long been associated with an identifiable group of Afrikaans-speaking writers against apartheid who campaigned for freedom of speech. In 1988 he wrote and staged a play, *Sing Jy Van Bomme* (Singing about bombs), which created a stir because of its caustic critique of the South African military. He was also a journalist on the now defunct social democratic independent Afrikaans weekly, *Vrye Weekblad,* and the monthly paper *Die Suid Afrikaan,* both (and especially *Vrye Weekblad*) known for their outspoken criticisms of the apartheid state. Journalists on both papers were frequently harassed and threatened, charged, and faced suspension under the terms of the emergency media regulations imposed by the state during the period of draconian censorship in the 1980s.[61] By the 1990s *Vrye Weekblad* had transformed itself into a bilingual magazine with a cultural and academic

16. Taalmonument.
Photo by the author.

emphasis; editor Max du Preez argued in an interview on the SABC English Service that "It is yesterday's cause to be an alternative newspaper" and that an alternative newspaper was no longer an effective critical platform.[62] Given this reasoning, one might ask (especially in a country where pornography of any kind was banned and where, after all, there was no television until 1975) whether a porn magazine might offer a more effective "shock" vehicle and a space for critical intervention no longer available through the alternative press.

In May 1995 du Preez himself became directly involved in the monuments and heritage debates. In this instance the monument concerned was that other canonical monument to Afrikaner nationalism—the Taalmonument (figure 16). Du Preez was responsible for an SABC *Agenda* program on the monument that resulted in a high-profile hearing by the Broadcasting Complaints Commission of South Africa (BCCSA). Complaints were brought against the SABC by the Afrikaner Kultuurbond and D. J. Malan (among others) after the broadcast on 3 April on the grounds that the language was objectionable and that descriptions of the monument as a penis were offen-sive.[63] Du Preez introduced the *Agenda* program as an inquiry into the views of Afrikaans speakers who had not been consulted when the monument had been erected on 10 October 1975, reminding the viewer that its unveiling had coincided with the commemoration of the founding of the Genootskap van Regte Afrikaners (GRA; the Society for Real Afrikaners) in Paarl one hundred twenty years ago and that there were some who considered it a monument to Afrikaner nationalism.[64]

Significantly, while the topic of the program was ostensibly a debate on the future of Afrikaner monuments like the Taalmonument, the broader and to a certain extent the more challenging agenda was a concern to re-claim Afrikaans as a language belonging to a far wider constituency than the Afrikaner nationalists who claimed it as theirs on the eve of apartheid. A number of prominent Afrikaans speakers were canvassed for their views, including the mayor of Paarl, Allan Pulse, who commented on the insig-nificant reference to the influence of Malay on the language, as did the lead-ing historian on the origins of Afrikaans, Achmat Davids, who argued in his book, *The Afrikaans of the Cape Muslims,* that Afrikaans was first writ-ten down by a Muslim imam in Arabic script. Davids suggested, "that a few words of Arabic Afrikaans be added in stone or cement, as this was the first script that was used for writing Afrikaans. Because we want to add to the language history of the monument, those important events showing friction should be illustrated, for example the uprising in Soweto against Afrikaans, when the white man claimed Afrikaans as his own and forced it upon others. And if we don't do that, we are not fairly representing the history of the language."[65] Ben Ngubane, minister of arts, culture, science, and technology in the new government, offered his views on the monument as a means of cementing Afrikaner nationalism, adding: "We are striving to devolve and evolve a national culture in South Africa, a culture of multi-lingualism, where we seek to find unity in diversity. So really, the days of celebrating group interests and culture are past."[66] Sandile Dikeni, the edi-tor of the *South African,* was less circumspect in his assessment, and his testimony was one of those that formed the basis of the prosecution in the court case:

> Aesthetically the thing is totally repulsive. . . . One feels that in its planning and symbolism, the type of thinking of a Nationalist is evident. It deters me completely. But the question is: what do you do with it? . . . If I had my way, I would've blown it up. But then, one should probably seek a different solution than dynamite. As you can see, the first guys you come across are

Westerners, and they stand out. One level down, you can see where the Coloured community with their Malay influence is placed. And here I am sitting on Africa which resembles three small turds! It tells you what was considered to be the most important when they built the monument: the Western countries are involved very significantly in the picture, and we are merely here at the bottom, us with the Malay influence. It is Afrikaner nationalism as we've known it all along. And then there is the Republic and Afrikaans that, like a penis, points upwards, and that is all that matters. We do not matter—we are merely appendages to a bigger thing.[67]

It is interesting that du Preez himself is famously passionate about the language (*Agenda* is, after all, a program transmitted in Afrikaans). Consequently he interviewed another spokesperson, W. A. de Klerk, who had also been critical of the monument at its inception but for rather different reasons and ones that offer the kinds of solutions that many were advocating in the South Africa of the new millennium. De Klerk suggested that there was no need for such an ostentatious monument and that it would have been more appropriate to simply invest a *site* with the symbolic status of a monument. His choice was the Kleinbos, the family farm of the du Toits and Malherbes in Daljosaphat, a valley near Paarl.[68] It is here that the remains exist of the school building where Afrikaans education began in 1880 and where some key Afrikaans poets were educated—D. F. Malherbe and A. G. Visser, among others.

The final nail in the coffin for the critics of the program came with comments from the head of the Daljosaphat Art Foundation, Hardie Botha. Botha compared the Taalmonument to a grave or mausoleum: "Seeing that we cannot fill it up with dynamite and blow it up, I think we should do something with it to make it look a little less like a mausoleum. It could become a playground for children of all languages. . . . It is such a lifeless monstrosity and reeks of urine. . . . Even graffiti would improve it. . . . It is a disgusting thing. Even rail tracks and bridge underpasses look better. Something has to be done to it—nothing is too precious not to be improved by a lick of paint. One can always repaint it."[69] This is exactly what Botha does on screen—a device that transforms the monument into a psychedelic version of its former self. The program ends pointedly with a satirical take on a traditional Afrikaner song by Koos Kombuis, one of the generation of Afrikaans singers known for their criticism of what they feel was the hijacking of Afrikaans for ideological and political purposes by the former apartheid regime.

Possibly anticipating the furor that would follow the program, the SABC took the precaution of airing another on 5 April to debate the issues that had come up out of the first *Agenda*. This was also introduced and chaired by du Preez, with the participation of Heinrich Willemse, professor of South African literature at the University of the Western Cape; Frits Kok, managing director of the Afrikaans Language and Culture Society; writer and actor Simon Bruijnders; and Karel Prinsloo, executive director for the GRA. Obviously the lineup was designed to dispel criticisms of bias and unrepresentativeness (although, as du Preez himself rather sheepishly acknowledged in his introduction, it was an entirely male lineup).

A feature of the program was the way the concept of "reconciliation" was used. In relation to the conciliatory gestures staged at key Afrikaner monuments by Tutu and Sexwale, the *Agenda* program offered a graphic illustration of the inherent dangers of appropriating the terms of the government of "national unity" by those who would never previously have been identified as conciliatory types! Debate focused on the nature and degree of inclusion and exclusion from the symbolic content of the Taalmonument. Both Kok and Prinsloo insisted on the inclusive nature of the monument. Willemse finally offered a corrective to this view: "We are busy with a whitewash of history. There is that history, it is very important to remember, and it happened. There was a time for keeping quiet [about the contributions of the 'coloreds']. And when the Afrikaners needed them in the 1980s, suddenly they were reincorporated as if history hadn't taken place. . . . The fact of the matter is that the monument was built as a celebration of Afrikaner nationalism. It was not inclusive. It was not intended to be inclusive. And to say afterwards that it was inclusive is an absolute distortion of those events."[70] Simon Bruijinders's case rested with the statement that "People that weren't part of this monument from the beginning will always feel [excluded]." He went on to suggest other, more appropriately inclusive, monuments to Afrikaans. "I believe that people do not really need monuments. Shakespeare, Mozart, Beethoven—they did not build monuments. They made other contributions. For me, the University of Stellenbosch (even though they produced certain guys) and the University of the Western Cape produced more important monuments for Afrikaans, because their products helped communities and contributed. That for me is a bigger monument to Afrikaans than the Taalmonument."[71] Prinsloo and Kok, once conceding that the monument may not have been intended as inclusive, were left reiterating the case for reconciliation, which, in large part, requires (as Willemse had pointed out) amnesia rather than a constructive engagement with the past. Their arguments formed a constant refrain about how "We've all moved on" now and about how things had changed. The final consensus seems to have been to leave the monument as it is, for the

Koks and Prinsloos of this world, so that it can be venerated by whomever wants to do so, and for the Willemses of this world, because the monument may act as a useful reminder of the dangers of ethnic essentialism and the exclusions to which it can lead.

By now du Preez was clearly associated in the minds of a broad public with the debate on the nature of national heritage and the symbolic manifestations of nationhood in the "new" South Africa. His mode, unlike that of Tutu and Sexwale, offered confrontation and contestation rather than reconciliation. Such a voice was an important corrective to the more temperate gestures of the politicians whose actions should be understood as motivated in part by the "nation-building" agenda of Mandela's government. But du Preez has since paid a heavy price for such outspokenness. He was eventually sacked from the SABC and further sackings and silencings have raised anxieties about new forms of censorship. In 1995, however, *Agenda* and the SABC won their legal battle against the forces of conservatism that evidently wished to quash the more controversial aspects of the debate around national heritage. There is a final twist to this story, which du Preez might have appreciated. While seeking out a pharmaceutical solution to the more prosaic problem of mosquitoes on a visit to the Taalmonument in 2000, I came across a packet of condoms marketed by an enterprising Afrikaner company making opportunistic capital out of the controversy generated over the monument's phallic status, it bore the legend "*Pollie ons gaan Pêrel toe vir die Taalvaders*" (We're going to Paarl on behalf of the fathers of our language). The packet bears an artist's impression of the Taalmonument, complete with the undeniable kitsch signature of three ducks flying in formation in the sky behind. A vindication indeed![72]

The conjuncture of particular events (including the *Agenda* controversy) at around the time of *Loslyf*'s staged sacrilege featuring the Voortrekker Monument (a sacrilege that deliberately invoked the wider monument debate) lends its appearance an even more critical dimension. For example, *Loslyf* appears at the same time that the Constitutional Court was deciding an important test case on the legality of banning pornography. The Centre for Applied Legal Studies at the University of the Witwatersrand was arguing that it was not viable to contend that although "free political discourse is an unassailable right, . . . expression on the level of pornography can justifiably be limited if this is in the common good."[73] Its opposition to such a judgment rested on the case that "with South Africa's history of censorship, all kinds of expression should be protected" and that, in answer to the Christian Lawyers' Association's position that pornography encouraged violence against women, there was little sociological evidence to support this.[74] That same year the new Film and Publications Bill, criticized in some quarters as "the latest attempt to formalise censorship in [South Africa]," was also being debated.[75]

While censorship is always a hotly debated issue among defenders of civil liberties, the moral right, and different factions of the women's movement (this latter particularly in relation to pornography), its implementation has historically carried more serious penalties in South Africa than in liberal democracies. Given the history of censorship in South Africa and its inextricable association with the apartheid state, it is understandable that those who have been most active in defending the rights of the individual against the limits set by the state are also those most anxious to ensure that such powers are never again available to the state, even under the ANC.

The critical coincidence of these events cement the view that *Loslyf*'s Voortrekker issue was a strategic intervention by a knowing body of journalists (both men and women) associated very publicly with the censorship debate. Whether or not the magazine was widely circulated, the issue received enough attention to be reported in the progressive *Weekly Mail and Guardian*, where Hattingh confirmed that the ideal readership was partly the very lower-middle-class Afrikaner entrepreneurs who had been growing steadily disaffected with the displays of "traditional" volkishness of the far right and who wished (for whatever reasons, not all of which were in any way progressive) to differentiate themselves from this group.[76]

It may not be insignificant either that *Loslyf* comes out of Larry Flynt's *Hustler* stable. Laura Kipnis's analysis of *Hustler*'s profile in terms of both gender and national politics suggests that the magazine is an unambiguously classed product intent on "rampantly transgressing bourgeois norms and sullying bourgeois property and proprieties."[77] In this sense *Loslyf* shares something with its stablemate, particularly in its scatalogical humour and its refusal to buy into the tasteful rewriting of the Trek as a romantic narrative of ecological power sharing among Boer, Ndebele, and Zulu that has been an aspect of the restaging of Afrikaner identity since 1994. As Hattingh says, "Afrikaners have always been portrayed as khaki-clad repressed people and I wanted to show them as normal, sexual, fucking human beings."[78] *Loslyf* also shares *Hustler*'s outspoken and irreverent political satire, although the South African targets in the early issues of *Loslyf* were more consistently leveled at the right than was *Hustler*'s idiosyncratic and highly problematic indiscriminate targeting. The fact that after the first issues the magazine had a complete change of editorial staff and resorted to the standard banalities of soft porn confirms my analysis of these early numbers as a strategic and knowing critique of the Afrikaner values strengthened under apartheid.

In addition, it seems that this early profanity in the form of *Loslyf* was evidently perceived as successful enough to spawn a number of other arguably less effective attempts to sully the moral and religious high ground adopted by those Afrikaners more attached to the conservative and racialized values embedded in the original conception of the Voortrekker Monument. I say "less effective" because in most cases they tended to work more as publicity vehicles for the artists than as the critical intervention I am arguing was represented by *Loslyf* in 1995. They are worth recalling here mainly because the vociferous attacks against them suggest that the values and history represented by the Voortrekker Monument clearly maintained a support base among diehard Afrikaner nationalists well into the 1990s (which is why individuals who wished to make an attack on those values often chose to do so by abusing the monument).

In January 1998 the artist Steven Cohen, dressed in drag, pitched up at the official centenary celebrations at Fort Klapperkop (a fort opened by Paul Kruger, the famous Boer commander and president of the Boer republics) on one of the hills in the vicinity of the Voortrekker Monument. Cohen was unceremoniously ejected by the right wingers and conservative Afrikaners who made up the crowd of faithful participants—an incident deemed worthy of note in two national papers.[79] Cohen's appearance was an adjunct to the highly orchestrated "intervention" in the same festivities by another artist, Kendell Geers. Geers's performance, entitled "Guilty," was initially funded by the French Cultural Institute, who withdrew its support after the German Embassy objected to the representation of Germany as a police state in Geers's publicity for his stint. Geers's objective, as he put it, was to demonstrate that "guilt remains the single most pervasive and strongest cultural force within the 'new South Africa.' One way or another we are all guilty of something whether it be the 'White guilt' of the middle-class liberal, the historical guilt associated with colonialism and Apartheid, the guilt and confessions heard at the Truth and Reconciliation Commission or personal guilt."[80] His idea had been to infiltrate the organizing of the centenary celebrations; to have a plane sporting a tail banner with the word "Guilty" in English, Afrikans, Zulu, and Xhosa fly over some of the key historical institutions venerated by Afrikaner nationalists in and around Pretoria, and to barricade himself in Fort Klapperkop "in the name of art."[81] The final component of the "action" was Geers's intention to open an account at a Johannesburg branch of Nedbank and to challenge the French Embassy to deposit the original sum it had promised him. This sum would be used to help in the restoration of Fort Klapperkop. The attempted stunt earned the ire of both the French and German embassies and the Afrikaner cultural organizations responsible for the centenary celebrations, as well as considerable publicity for Geers himself, even while it fell short of his grandiose intentions for "an exhibition that aims to explore the pervasive presence of, and silence around, the semantics of guilt in South Africa."[82]

In 1999 sex and heritage were again bedfellows at the Voortrekker Monument. Another court case ensued, this time with the Voortrekker Monument as the maligned object. On this occasion an estimated twenty-seven Afrikaner cultural and political organizations complained to the SABC over a radio program in which the presenter, Barry Ronge, in discussing a forthcoming rock concert scheduled on the grounds of the monument, explained, "I have decided the only sensible thing to do with [the monument] is to paint it pink and turn it into an enormous gay disco at which they can have drug-crazed raves."[83] Paradoxically it was the director of the Voortrekker Monument, Christie Kuun, who was besieged with death threats by angry listeners after Radio Pretoria (which also broadcast the program) made the mistake of broadcasting his home telephone number.[84] By July, in a ruling almost identical to that in relation to the 1995 *Agenda* program, the court pronounced that Ronge's remarks were just a harmless joke not calculated to inspire malice. The bold banner headline in the *Citizen* declared, " 'Pink Monument' Complaint Fails."[85]

My most recent excursion to the Voortrekker Monument (in December 2000) left a clear impression of a site that was concerned to retool itself for a multicultural audience but in a superficial rather than a structural sense. It would not be out of place to suggest that certain aspects of the site illustrate the kind of amnesia and appropriation Willemse criticized in the 1995 *Agenda* program. Perversely, in 2000 only two heritage sites associated with the liberation struggle — Robben Island and the District Six Museum — could match the Voortrekker Monument as a thriving tourist enterprise full of both local and international visitors. I was struck by the manicured lawns and the sense of prosperous expansion evident at the Voortrekker Monument. Initially, the museum at the foot of the monument was under the control of the Cultural History Museum in Pretoria. Consequently, although there were only minimal diversions from the conventional Great Trek narrative enshrined in the monument frieze, the museum presented space for a potentially disruptive counternarrative. In May 2000 this was eliminated when the FAK bought the museum from the state. (The FAK has now also bought Fort Schanskop and the accompanying amphitheater,

17. Voortrekker Monument souvenirs: ostrich eggs with a representation of the Voortrekker Monument, Ndebele doll, zebra bowl, and "big five" ceramic plate. Photo by the author.

capable of seating 365.) The Voortrekker Monument shop (which is a private enterprise but which nonetheless has the only real souvenir franchise on site), more than any other aspect of the venue, signals the ways in which some Afrikaners are seeking to accommodate the "new" South Africa. Here, cheek by jowl and for the first time on any of my many visits, embroidery from the Shangaan women's collectives was sharing shelf space with gilt wax candle replicas of the exterior of the Voortrekker Monument. Zebra print scarves sat beside ostrich eggs etched with an image of the monument, in front of which sat a beaded Ndebele doll (figure 17). At the monument itself I was able to buy a set of souvenir spoons that now sport an image of the monument facade in the spoon and the new South African flag on the handle. Conversely, the basement of the monument, which used to be empty save for the cenotaph and the eternal flame, now hangs flags of the former Boer republics around its circumference, lending an association with some clandestine Masonic gathering.

If anything, the monument has become more rather than less significant over the years for Afrikaners who, while not rabidly right wing, might still feel anxious about the new dispensation. More worrying perhaps, the confident and ostentatious spectacle of economic and cultural investment in the site suggests that the FAK believes it has a growing constituency. Since the 1994 elections, 16 December may be a day of reconciliation for other South Africans, but on Voortrekker Hill, the celebrations (certainly up until 2000) were still in honor of the Day of the Vow. If there is an argument to be made here about global tourism and cosmopolitanism, it is only on the most superficially opportunistic grounds, for nothing has changed in the narrative of the Trek and its representation in the guidebook.[86] The latter reproduces the same text, sandwiched in a slightly amended cover, which now has the new flag on the recto. Indeed, I am reminded of a visit to the monument in 1996, when I questioned the "guardian" of the monument about the extent to which he felt any changes might need to be made following the recent elections. He replied that indeed they had made some changes already and that the guidebook now had a new cover. "But," he added, he "[saw] no reason to change anything else—since history [was] history after all and nothing could alter the facts."

Clearly the Voortrekker Monument of the 1990s is not quite the monument it used to be. From a monolithic construction dedicated to a singular version of the Afrikaner nationalist narrative, it has also provided the stage upon which new identities and challenges have been launched. Each of these attempts has for different (and in some cases competing) reasons sought to disrupt the hegemony of the version of Afrikanerdom symbolized by the monument in the minds of so many South Africans. Any effectivity they might claim depends upon an acknowledgment of the residual symbolic power of the monument as a founding icon of Afrikaner nationalism. Rather than working to disinvest the monolith of its ignoble and oppressive history, the more successfully disruptive "performances" engage with that past in order to "domesticate" the apartheid state's symbolic armory as a means of offering the possibility of indifference in the future.

2

ROBBEN ISLAND

Site of Memory / Site of Nation

> John: This morning when he said: "You two! The beach!" . . . I thought,
>
> Okay, so it's my turn to empty the sea into a hole.
>
> —Athol Fugard, John Kani, and Winston Ntshona, *The Island*

In 1930 the *Cape Times* carried an advertisement asking for expressions of interest in a plot of land off the coast of Cape Town: "On April 1, 1930, Robben Island will be available to whoever makes the most attractive offer for it to the Lands Department."[1] Some of the readers might have been forgiven for treating this as an elaborate and unappealing April Fools' stunt. From its history as a British dumping ground for rebellious African chiefs in the nineteenth century to its later gruesome use as a sanatorium for victims of leprosy and mental illness by various South African governments, by 1930 the island clearly had a serious image problem. Nevertheless, the *Cape Times* attempted to reassure the potential buyer: "The leper buildings will be burnt immediately. Many of the buildings are made of wood and iron, and are old and dilapidated. But the village will be left alone. It has hundreds of trees, gardens and could house about 2000 people. There is a telephone cable from the mainland, several boreholes, and a number of windmills. There are roads, a bioscope and a landing jetty."[2] Then followed a series of imagined futures for the island that the prospective purchaser was invited to consider. These included first prize in a state lottery, a reformatory, a government farm colony for alcoholics, a home for orphans, a training ground for the defense force, and a municipal amusement park.[3] The final suggestion, with alarming hubris, was a health resort!

Since the final judgment in the Rivonia Trial in June 1964 Robben Island has been firmly fixed in international historical consciousness as the place of exile for black male political opponents of the apartheid regime—including the majority of the leadership of South Africa's first democratic government. It is no exaggeration to say that for many international observers, the island has become the foundational cornerstone of the new national image of South Africa, since it was from here that de Klerk and Mandela began the very public negotiations that were to lead eventually to the formation of the "government of national unity." Indeed such an image is not only the prerogative of the international community, but one that is also promoted internally. In January 1997 the *Argus* (a Cape Town broadsheet) was able to claim, "Robben Island, infamous for housing political prisoners, has begun its new role as the cultural showcase for the new South Africa with the first tourists allowed onto the Island last week."[4] The Robben Island Museum (RIM), as it has since been renamed, subsequently embarked on another life as the centrepiece of the "new" South Africa.

In April 1982 Mandela began another chapter in his long walk to freedom as he moved from the island prison that had been his home for eighteen years to Pollsmoor Prison, where he remained until his historic release on 11 February 1990. Some time later all political prisoners were released from the island, and finally the remaining inmates were transferred to other detention centers. With them the last of the warders and prison staff left Robben Island. Now nearly seventy years on from the attempt in 1930 to reinvent the island, it was once more on the market, as it were.

From the very beginnings of the transition to democracy the future of the island was the subject of a fraught debate—and ironically the proposals put forward bore an uncanny resemblance to those that had surfaced in 1930. The proposals ranged from a casino and leisure complex for the international moneyed classes to a Disney-style amusement park, a rehabilitation camp for street children, and a center for correctional rehabilitation running courses to reestablish the inmates' sense of moral values. The British founder of the Open University, Lord Young of Dartington, proposed reviving the reputation of the island as a "university" and formalizing Robben Island as a South African version of the Open University—but with a focus for education about the liberation struggle. Meanwhile, the nongovernmental organization (NGO) Peace Visions promoted the idea of the island as a center for international peace studies and a training ground for international brokers to learn the art of peace negotiations.[5]

In 1993 it was clear that the future of Robben Island was a preoccupation among various factions of local, regional, and national government. By May of that year reports with detailed recommendations had already been produced by the Cape Provincial Administration (CPA), the Regional Development Advisory Committee (Region A), the NMC, and the CMMH.[6] Given the complicated political terrain of the Western Cape, the recommendations were not altogether mutually compatible.

This chapter is about the possible contradictions between the concepts of "public" history, lived experience, and "national" heritage and the demands of private sponsorship and international tourism in a site of the historical magnitude of Robben Island. It is also centrally concerned with the tensions that inevitably arise internally in any project dealing with the production of a "national" history—in this instance particularly the tensions among various constituencies on the left (for example, the Pan African Congress [PAC], the Non-European Unity Movement, and the ANC), whose members all stake a claim to the public memory of the history of the liberation struggle.

PEACE VISIONS

In July 1993 Peace Visions took matters into their own hands and commissioned a feasibility study "to determine alternative options for the future utilisation of the island. The results of six months of open-ended interviews . . . conducted with non-governmental organisations, the Cape Provincial Administration, the Anglican Church, political parties, government departments, business, ex-Robben Island prisoners and youth" were published in May 1994.[7] Peace Visions described itself at the time as "committed to an inter-disciplinary approach to peace building" and saw itself primarily as a facilitator and coordinator of existing bodies and NGOs concerned with peace initiatives to "ensure a cross-fertilisation of people and ideas."[8] More significant from the point of view of this study, it evidently saw an engagement with heritage and cultural debates as central to its agenda: "Always conscious of the rich contradictions and ambiguities of South African political life we sought to actively engage the continuing debates about meanings associated with national and, in the case of Robben Island, international socio-political and cultural symbols."[9]

In the Peace Visions feasibility study respondents were asked questions such as the following: "To what extent is Robben Island a priority; how is the future of the island perceived; what are the opinions regarding commercialisation, nature conservation, militarisation, and the future of the prison; what is the opinion about a Peace Institute and who should be responsible for it? What should the curriculum consist of and which community should be served?"[10] The summary of findings suggests that by May 1994, while there was no overall consensus, there was nevertheless some agreement among certain parties that "the social, cultural and political history of the island should be protected"[11] and that the prison itself should form the basis of a museum. The report concluded, "A near consensus also exists that crass commercialisation involving hotels and casinos on the island is completely unacceptable."[12] Collective decision making was also deemed desirable by the majority of respondents, so that the responsibility of the island was understood as involving "interest groups, the new government, the state and regional government. No unilateral decision can be taken about the future of the island and any decision should involve grassroots communities as well."[13]

But if we look beyond this rather bland summary of interviews, the substance of the responses from the various organizations who agreed to participate in the feasibility study makes much more interesting reading. By elaborating some of the political stakes (nationally) in the island, they help the reader to make sense not only of the debates around its future, but also of the terms of an emerging debate concerning a new "national" history and the conflicts among conservation, preservation, and accessibility—that is, between nature and culture.

Attempts were made to interview the NP as a party rather than in its role as "government." It is clear that the NP treated the Robben Island issue as a hot potato, and the Peace Visions interviewers were referred on to the Departments of Justice or Correctional Services who in turn referred them on to the CPA. Despite serious attempts and one interview date initially agreed upon, no interviews were possible with either the IFP or the Azanian People's Organisation (AZAPO). Nor was Peace Visions able to get permission to interview any of the personnel or others living on the island itself.[14] The Conservative Party (CP) was adamant about maintaining Robben Island as a prison under the aegis of the Department of Correctional Services and also as a base for military training. It opposed the erection of casinos or hotels on the island as it opposed a peace institute or conference center since it felt that these would interfere with the "operation of the island in its present form."[15]

The PAC offered a measured response that, despite long-standing ideological differences between the PAC and ANC, had more in common with ANC proposals for the island than with any other canvassed organization: "For the PAC the significance of Robben Island lies in the triumph of the human spirit over the numerous obstacles placed by human beings upon other human beings. The history of Robben Island shows that human beings have the capacity, individually and collectively, to overcome huge obstacles. While the island is not a main priority at this time the PAC places emphasis on the history of the island and the contribution it made to the development of the PAC's understanding of non-racialism."[16] Further, the PAC wished to foreground and preserve the educational aspect of the prison, which it pointedly referred to by its Xhosa name, "Makhanda University," after the Xhosa leader who was imprisoned on the island as a result of leading a rebellion against the British in 1819.[17] The insistence on this appellation is also perhaps an indication of the bitterness that erupted over what many in the PAC regarded as the ANC leadership's willful amnesia over non-ANC initiated activism in the liberation struggle. The decision of RIM to name its two new catamarans "Makana" and "Autshumato" could be interpreted as a conciliatory gesture in this regard in acknowledgment of early Xhosa resistance to British colonialism, and also in recognition of the presence of Khoikhoi on the island since the seventeenth century, when a Khoikhoi leader, Autshumato, lived there while acting as an agent for the English.[18]

Unlike the PAC, the ANC made it clear that Robben Island was a priority for it. In no uncertain terms it similarly dismissed proposals to erect a luxury hotel or casino on the island, calling such proposals "[a] desecration of the island."[19] It also claimed that the end of any role for the Department of Correctional Services on the island was "a foregone conclusion" and criticized the department for making no effort to preserve utensils and other personal effects belonging to the political prisoners. In line with the PAC, the Anglican Church, and the ex-prisoners, the ANC claimed that "The perception exists that the island should not be a shrine to suffering and hardship but to the 'triumph of the human spirit over suffering and hardship.'"[20] In this statement the emphasis is clearly on the political history of the island, as one might expect from a party that had so many members interned there. While acknowledging the role of nature conservancy and the continuing involvement of the CPA in this capacity and in the preservation of the cultural history of the island, at this point in the debate the ANC cautioned that "This preservation should, however, not detract from the main significance of the island as a place of banishment and imprisonment."[21] As we shall see, the balance between these concerns shifts somewhat over time as part of official ANC policy vis-à-vis the island.

The CPA, in line with the ANC, endorsed the view that the island should be administered by the state. For it the island came in the top 10 percent of prioritized issues. It seems that while broadly sympathetic to the ANC, the Anglican Church, and the PAC, the CPA, as well as the Department of Nature Conservation and Museums, foregrounded the eco-tourist and nature conservancy aspects of the island, emphasizing that while "the cultural and historical aspects of the island [were] a priority," it was "especially *all* aspects of the history and not only that of the liberation struggle" that were the focus of their efforts.[22] If there was a peace institute on the island, "Both sides of the history should be reflected—that of the state's management of the island and the prison and that of the liberation struggle."[23] It added, "If a Peace Institute reflects a 'distorted' history that becomes exclusionary of certain groups, it is not worth contemplating."[24] The CPA was also adamant that the prison "should be turned into an anti-apartheid museum for the protection of its history and the artefacts of the prisoners."[25] No further role for the SADF was envisaged on the island.

The ex-prisoners were strongly opposed to commercialization of the island, "not only because of the desecration of their own personal histories, but also because it would be profit driven and not in the interest of the community."[26] All respondents in this category agreed that the prison should become a museum, conference center, or archive and certainly a place of learning, although one respondent suggested the best future for the island would be to demolish it! Most significant and similar to the PAC, the ANC, the participating NGOs, and the Anglican Church, the ex-prisoners also emphasized that they did not want the island "turned into a shrine that [would] commemorate the atrocities of the past"—and Dachau was explicitly cited as an instance of this—"but to be forward-looking while still preserving the history of the island."[27]

The Anglican Church, the only religious institution represented, was included as the other major property owner on the island besides the state. It similarly drew attention to the putative relationship *and* difference between Robben Island as a commemorative site and the Nazi death camps. As we shall see, this frequent comparison had important implications for the forging of a new national history. The Church emphasized, "The feeling exists that an apartheid museum is necessary on the island but that it should not resemble the holocaust museum," where it was felt that "people indulge in the atrocities of the past."[28] Rather it should be "a place with a positive view of the future, like the Martin Luther King Center in Atlanta in the United States."[29]

It is evident from these responses that dissent was already emerging between, on the one hand, organizations or "stakeholders" who felt that the more recent history of the liberation struggle should be a priority in the historical narratives represented on and by the island and, on the other hand, those who clearly felt that this more recent history was just one thread in a longer and more diverse historical account. Here the reader needs to be aware of what versions of the liberation narrative were prioritized for public consumption, as well as the role played by frequent comparisons with some histories of displacement, exile, and incarceration and the exclusion of others. Another potential conflict emerged between those who wished to see a political focus for the island and those whose primary concern was the development of its resources for eco-tourism. An inkling of further political rifts was evidenced by the fact that some organizations refused to take part in the Peace Visions questionnaire. Later in this story these conflicts took on a more prominent public profile, as we shall see.

"ESIQITHINI"

The impetus for the research undertaken by Peace Visions was encouraged by an unusual joint exhibition between the South African Museum (SAM; in Cape Town) and the Mayibuye Centre. This was a significant event and important for any consideration of the ways in which one might visually and materially embody the complex histories associated with Robben Island. The exhibition demonstrates in microcosm some of the difficulties facing a young democracy governed by a government of "national unity" in negotiating the investment in different and sometimes conflictual aspects of its history by diverse publics, both national and international.

On 26 May 1993 SAM and the Mayibuye Centre staged "Esiqithini" ("on the island" in Xhosa and Zulu), partly as a means of providing "members of the general public with an opportunity to learn more about the history of Robben Island and to enable them to participate in discussions about the future of the island" (the entrance to the exhibition is shown in figure 18).[30] This initiative marked one of the first collaborations between a national museum and an independent archive. The Mayibuye Centre at the University of the Western Cape was founded on the core of the International Defence and Aid Fund (IDAF) collections, accumulated by the organization in exile in London; these contain visual and written material related to the liberation struggle. SAM, on the other hand, while by no means consistently in thrall to the various apartheid governments, was nevertheless established in 1825 under British colonial rule and thrived under apartheid as one of the major national institutions devoted to natural history and anthropology (both disciplines intractably associated ideologically and practically with South Africa's colonial and apartheid pasts).

From the beginning of this liaison problems arose not only because of the sensitivity of exhibiting such politically significant material in an institution

18. Display case at the entrance to "Esiqithini: The Robben Island Exhibition," June 1993. Photo by Aubrey Byron. Courtesy of the South African Museum. Iziko Museums of Cape Town.

19. Display case from "Esiqithini: The Robben Island Exhibition" showing a photograph of ex-prisoners leaving the island with their belongings in the apple boxes shown in the display. Photo by Aubrey Byron. Courtesy of the South African Museum. Iziko Museums of Cape Town.

primarily devoted to natural history and anthropology, but also because of the ethics involved in subjecting such personally emotive material culture to the general public gaze. These issues were dealt with first by expanding the exhibit to cover the natural history of the island and the early social history of the site. (I will come back to the implications of this move below.) Also important in allaying criticism was the collaboration with former Robben Island prisoners as an active part of the organizing committee. As SAM associate director Patricia Davison explained, "One of the main aims was to interpret prison objects through the eyes of people who were there. . . . An ordinary calendar . . . takes on special significance when understood in relation to marking time in isolation. An official permit to visit a son in prison speaks volumes when a mother tells how often permits were denied by bureaucratic whim." [31]

The exhibition proceeded with an introductory timeline on the history of the island through its archaeological past to the Dutch and British colonial periods and on to its use as a leper colony and mental asylum and later a fortification during World War II, ending with its recent past as a high-security prison from 1961 to 1991. The poignant core of the exhibition consisted of displays of ex-prisoners' meager but often inventive possessions—material suggestively known now as the "apple-box archive" since this was how they carried off their belongings on their release from the island (figure 19). Running through this section were posters demanding the release of political prisoners in South Africa in order to signal visually the historical links with the international anti-apartheid movements. Among the individual stories highlighted by the exhibition, Mandela's figured prominently. As Davison herself remarked in an assessment of the exhibition written from the vantage point of hindsight, "Almost inevitably, Nelson Mandela became synonymous with Robben Island and symbolic of the liberation struggle. Mandela's image occurred frequently in the exhibition, too frequently, some viewers suggested, but he stood not only for himself but for all who were imprisoned on the island." [32]

By most accounts the exhibition was a successful venture, drawing in a large national audience and well attended by ex-prisoners and their families. The comments book in the museum is instructive, however, and worth a detour in that it reminds the reader of the kinds of volatile responses such an exhibition could provoke just prior to the first democratic elections. It also provides a corrective to skeptics who are reluctant to credit history exhibitions with the power to generate real debate or emotion, just as it demonstrates the stakes invested in the way histories were told in South Africa, then and now, even at a popular level. In addition, the comments book graphically illustrates the fierce resistance by some to the impending new order of things.

Objections to "Esiqithini" came in three categories. First was the old chestnut of scientific objectivity: "What on earth is a political history exhibition doing in a Natural History Museum? Please, rather concentrate on the intended purpose of the museum!"[33] Or: "Some will see this as a fine political gesture but I consider it out of place here, where the space could be better used for natural history and so forth. The actual display value is low and contains far too much visual trivia for absorption."[34] And again: "Blatant politics do not belong in a museum."[35] The second group of objections, relating to Mandela, was more extreme: "How can your people put up such stupid pictures of Mandela 'The son of a bitch' in our museum? Put pictures of more sensible people in our museum."[36] Or: "I wanted to see an exhibition on Robben Island. Not a *terrorist* future of the island: send Mandela back."[37]

The third kind of objection, foreshadowing what was to become a recurrent theme in the representation of the history of the island as a political prison, concerned the emphasis on the ANC: "Very biased. Are you promoting the ANC? What about other Liberation Movements? Like PAC, AZAPO, NEUM?"[38] Or: "I really enjoyed the exhibition and videos on Robben Island. All my questions have now been answered. I admire the way every aspect of the island was shown. However, only one question still remains in my mind: were ANC members the only political prisoners on Robben Island. If not, why are the other prisoners' views not expressed? Thank you!!"[39] "Very disappointed: one-sided view from an ANC perspective. It looks more like a propaganda stunt from the ANC, and to promote Nelson Mandela (President—Voting time) NB!! What about the first slaves brought to South Africa from the East? (Malaysia, Java); nothing is said about Tuan Gum, Yusuf, Nurumubeen (all slaves) and other Political Prisoners. Why were they (slaves) brought to South Africa and why were they jailed on Robben Island!! Your exhibition lacks this very important history."[40] One respondent suggested that "The exhibition gives us a picture of how those who had struggled for freedom had lived in the Island. Attempts should be made for such exhibition to be taken to the communities (black) for most of them are unable to come to town."[41]

"Esiqithini" was up from May to December 1993, and then the apple-box archive, loaned by the Mayibuye Centre and consisting of the ex-prisoners' material, was moved to a temporary exhibition site privately sponsored by the Caltex petrol company. The rationale behind the move was to establish a more permanent educational display at the point of embarkation for the island where tourists would have the opportunity to learn something of the island's role in the liberation history before their visit. The Caltex site was located in a new tourist development, primarily a trendy shopping center with expensive waterside restaurants built on Cape Town's Victoria and Alfred waterfront. Already the site of some controversy for its almost exclusive provision for international tourism, the new partnership between the Mayibuye Centre and private enterprise, called the Gateway Project, incurred considerable criticism from quarters who experienced this initiative as a commodification (as tourist attraction) of their painful personal history and one for which, to add insult to injury, an entrance fee was charged.[42] Despite its checkered past, SAM was evidently still seen by some of the protagonists whose stories formed the basis of the prison narrative as a more appropriate and authoritative venue for the exhibition, notwithstanding the Mayibuye Centre's involvement.[43]

One year after the elections, concern over the prioritizing of international over local interests in relation to Robben Island erupted when angry ex-prisoners claimed that *their* needs were not being represented by proposed developments on the island and that little attention was being given to the financial hardship that many prisoners continued to suffer since their release.[44] In other words, too much attention was being given to the *future* of Robben Island and not enough to the victims of its past and too much attention to attracting *international* interest and not enough to local needs. A number of low-level initiatives followed as attempts to redress the situation. One of them involved ex-prisoners employed by a private marketing consortium (Leading Concepts) to package pieces of rock from the island in special boxes signed by Mandela! A percentage of the sales proceeds was set aside for an ex–political prisoners' hardship fund. A more productive consequence of such antagonism was the setting up of the Association of Ex-Political Prisoners, coordinated by Ahmed Kathrada, one of the accused in the Rivonia Trial and imprisoned on the island with Mandela.[45]

Undeterred, by 1996 the courting of international celebrities at the instigation of private business interests had been taken to other extremes when a public relations company organized a corporate golf tournament on the island, an event reported in one Cape Town weekly as "marking the dawn of a new era." The staff reporter went on in an offensive parody of the literature on the prison experience: "In his autobiography *Long Walk to Freedom*, President Mandela referred to the prison on Robben Island as 'the university.' Yesterday, those who braved the tempestuous golf course were taught a lesson of their own when they failed to come to terms with the oil / sand greens and the unforgiving rough. The struggle of the golf day participants

20. The offending photograph showing participants at the golf day on Robben Island piled into Nelson Mandela's old cell. *Argus,* 16 November 1996. Courtesy of Independent Newspapers.

may not have been as tedious and energy sapping as spending days chopping rocks in the quarry, as President Mandela did, but they were well tested by the difficult course."[46] The report was accompanied by a photo of the golfing celebrities crammed into Mandela's old cell and trampling on his bed, with the caption "Chock 'n block: all the participants in the Robben Island golf day crowd inside Madiba's old cell during a visit to the jail block" (figure 20).[47] This attempt at a tasteless joke was duly picked up on by various outraged critics, including Martin Legassick, professor of History at the University of the Western Cape, who pointed out that to add insult to injury, one of the celebrities in the photo was none other than the infamous Jani Allen, formerly linked with the far right leader, Eugene Terre'blanche.

Meanwhile, once the island was actually opened for public visits on 1 January 1997, public history and private enterprise were at loggerheads again. A battle broke out when private charter companies landed parties of tourists on the island without clearance from the government authorities, who then used taxis and buses to block access to the island, forcing the chartered boats with their cargo of enthusiastic tourists to leave the small jetty immediately. One of the chartered vessels made a second attempt to dock at

Murray Harbor on the island, only to be met by navy and police boats. Others were pursued by defense force helicopters. An unseemly furor erupted, the minute details of which were gleefully covered in the national and local press.[48]

The dispute is interesting in relation to the broader issue of who has ownership of any new national history and how claims presented as being driven by moral imperatives shift significantly when the economic necessity of attracting foreign currency takes precedence. The new and current government has been insistent on the importance of Robben Island as a primary tourist venue and on the economic significance of developing the international tourist market.[49] Consequently, one of the key arguments levied against what personnel in the tourist industry viewed as the government's heavy-handed intervention over the charter "invasion" (as it was termed elsewhere) was that it would be extremely damaging to South Africa's image abroad. Insults were traded where tourist personnel described the government's intervention as "banana republic antics." André Odendaal, usually an astute and diplomatic spokesperson and at the time the interim director of RIM, was driven to retort that while it had always been the museum's intention to involve private contractors on a controlled basis, "That is what we hope to do in the long run, but it is not only a question of access for the people who are involved now. Ask the boat owners how many of their staff or co-owners are black."[50]

This time, in their defense over the government's actions, spokespeople were relatively mute on the recent historical significance of the site as a political prison. Instead their arguments capitulated to the environmentalist lobby, whose case had been seen as a potential distraction from what had earlier been deemed the primary historical significance of the island as a detention center for political prisoners. Indeed Ahmed Kathrada issued a word of warning to this effect in his opening address at the "Esiqithini" exhibition: "While we would welcome efforts of environmentalists and conservationists in the direction of the fauna and flora and historic buildings and shipwrecks, I can foresee uneasiness about activities that might adversely detract from the main focus of the island as a monument to political prisoners and the struggle for democracy in South Africa."[51] Certainly a small sample of the conflicting descriptions of the island circulated during the debates over its future illustrates some of the more serious occlusions inherent in the environmental argument that were alluded to in Kathrada's statement. Some described it (perhaps predictably in the context of discussions on its prison status) as "This barren, flat, sandy island, eight kilometers from the Cape Town mainland,"[52] and "It is itself a very harsh place

21. *Sawubona* cover with model on Robben Island. December 2000.

where only very strong grass survives . . . windswept and with a coast of rugged boulders that have brought down a number of passing ships."[53] The alternative image of the island, circulating in support of the environmental lobby, was more consistent with the following: "Robben Island is itself not only a place of natural beauty, but an ecological model for the rest of South Africa."[54] Similarly, many accounts described the island as a quaint spot full of beaten up old jalopies (since car tax was waived on the island) and cute little Victorian cottages where the community of benign jailers lived out their existence in convivial harmony with other government employees in a time warp away from the stresses and strains of big-city life in a pollutant-free eco-environment—a picture of the good and simple life![55]

The focus on the natural beauty of the island and the tendency to sideline its political history were recently graphically illustrated by the inflight magazine for South African Airways, *Sawubona* (Ndebele and Zulu for "good day"). The cover showed a fashion model strolling down one of the island's limestone roads with views of Table Mountain on the horizon (figure 21). The banner headline, "Western Cape Wonders . . . Robben Island and Beyond," flagged a journalist's twenty-eight-day journey in the Western Cape Province. The short half-page slot devoted to Robben Island, while cursorily mentioning that it was "home to political prisoners, including our beloved former President Nelson Mandela and many politicians now in government," devoted almost all the remaining space to the logistics of obtaining permission for what the magazine obviously considered a great scoop—a fashion shoot on the island.[56]

Evidently one of the more prosaic hurdles in the struggle over Robben Island was the old bugbear of conflicting interests over the public representation of history once the profit margin is prioritized by a private sector sponsor and the appeal of international revenue takes precedence over local tourism. In May 2000 these concerns were taken up in the *Sunday Independent*. Journalist Xolela Mangcu wrote an angry report entitled "Past Forgotten in Rush to Satisfy International Cultural Elites."[57] Mangcu begins: "Robben Island is a classic example of how our obsession with foreign investments and markets distorts our political culture."[58] Writing in the wake of a conference on international truth commissions held on the island, Mangcu claims regretfully that "the triumphalist chimera of 'reconciliation' has become our biggest cultural export. Cultural institutions such as Robben Island are marketed as symbols of this miracle."[59] He follows this observation up with an anecdote that demonstrates the paradoxes of this need to present a unified and harmonious face to the international community. During a Congress of South African Trade Unions (cosatu) strike for better pay and working conditions (held on 10 May), the island workers, according to Mangcu, were asked to ignore the strike action because the strike would "tarnish the good reputation of the island," and the request came, as he points out, "from an institution that is a vista of struggle."[60] Mangcu also criticized what he perceived as the narrow history told on the island tours and the marginalization of prisoners such as PAC leader Robert Sobukwe in favor of the Rivonia defendants. Tour guides drove by the house where Sobukwe was detained in solitary confinement for six years with what Mangcu describes as a cursory acknowledgment. Mangcu discovered on entering the house on his own that it was in terrible disrepair: "spider webs, cockroaches and an unbearable stench."[61] This was not the first time that such an observation had been made. Earlier reports by the PAC's Western Cape Regional Branch were supposed to be the subject of a forthcoming investigation by Lionel Mtshali, then minister of arts and culture.[62] It seems, however, that if Mangcu's report is to be believed, by May 2000 very little had changed.

Obviously these criticisms are part of a larger dissatisfaction with what some perceive as a largely ANC-driven initiative, but Mangcu's points are important in understanding the ways in which an appeal to an international tourist market can mediate the histories on offer. As Mangcu says, "[If] our cultural institutions are nothing more than saleable products for the consumption of international cultural elites, who shall provide us with the self-understandings, symbols and meanings that are the basis of modern nationhood?" He ends the report with a plea for what he terms "a new internally-driven cultural history."[63] These incidents highlight the potential conflict arising from the need, on the one hand, for national renewal and effective self-fashioning, and on the other hand, pressures arising from an international stake (largely emotional) in the island's future.

PRISONS AS REPOSITORIES FOR NATIONAL HISTORIES

The concerns regarding Robben Island are shared with similarly burdened sites worldwide. The most frequent comparisons in the national press in South Africa during the fiercest period of debate over the future of the island were with either the Nazi death camps of World War II and their association with the Holocaust or with the slave forts of Ghana and the island of Goree (Senegal) and the memory of the transatlantic slave trade. These locations are all associated at some level with state terror and attempts to systematically destroy communities on the basis of racial or ethnic discrimination and for political ends. Similarly, mass deaths or disablement were common results of incarceration in these places, although some have argued that only in one instance, the Nazi death camps, could it be claimed that systematic genocide was the state's agenda.

Such sites also represent a dilemma for contemporary local politicians and those involved in promoting and developing an international and national tourism and heritage market in Germany, Ghana, Senegal, and South Africa. At historical moments when reconciliation, renewal, and unification are the key words on most politicians' lips from within the ruling parties, these sites, tainted as they are in differing degrees with complicated histories of collusion, complicity, and betrayal, represent a potential embarrassment to their governments. This is despite the fact that they also obviously provide the potential for an experience that graphically and viscerally embodies both the horrors of political repression and the victory of surviving against the odds. In certain senses all these sites are the transitional locations that embody the ability of the new nation to rise phoenixlike from the literal ashes and debris of incarceration, death, and destruction. Consequently each has to incorporate within it the signs of both the history of total destruction and dehumanization *and* the triumph of the human spirit

Robben Island 69

over all adversity. In addition, all these sites share the further complication of providing a focus for the hopes and desires of a highly differentiated international community, and these can often run counter to the needs and interests of local constituencies.

The Ghanaian slave forts of Cape Coast Castle and Elmina Castle are a case in point. Seen as the focus of a pilgrimage of return to ancestral origins for many African Americans, the slave dungeons are the axis upon which their visit turns. The Ghanaian authorities (the Ghana Museums and Monuments Board), however, while appreciative of the revenue potential from the middle-class African American tourist market that this focus on the slave trade provides is at pains to emphasize the other histories associated with the forts. Edward M. Bruner, in an interesting analysis of the contradictions and ironies of the development of tourism in Ghana, concludes that "Most Ghanaians . . . are not particularly concerned with slavery."[64] For them Elmina Castle, to take one example, has a long and varied history, of which slavery is just a part. It is a reminder of different aspects of Ghana's colonial past—from the Portuguese, the Dutch, and the British—before being transformed (after Ghanaian independence in 1957) into a secondary school and offices of the Ghana Education Service (among other functions) until its latest incarnation as a prime tourist attraction and UNESCO World Heritage Site.

In some instances, the Ghanaian authorities have turned slave forts into exclusive tourist facilities with luxury accommodations—for example, Fort Apollonia and Fort St. Jago—and there is a plan to extend such development.[65] Clearly, as Bruner outlines, tourism is seen as an important source of revenue earmarked for economic and social development and to help provide basic infrastructural support for sanitation and roads, as well as employment opportunities for local communities.[66] Certainly tourism on Robben Island has similarly provided local jobs. However, as Bruner points out, the majority of the funds to develop the slave forts either has some direct connection with U.S. institutions (such as the Smithsonian Institution, the Central Region Development Commission, and the Midwest Universities Consortium for International Activities), or they come from USAID or the United Nations. This could place the Ghanaian authorities under considerable pressure to develop the forts in ways that are compatible with the needs of the American tourist (which for the most part means the middle-class African American tourist). According to Bruner, Enid Schildkrout, the ethnographic curator at the American Natural History Museum (and herself a West and Central African specialist), mentioned that the diaspora agenda "dominated the script of the exhibition" at a Cape Coast Castle exhibition that was largely the responsibility of a team from the Smithsonian Institution; Bruner adds that this was "at the expense of the voice of the Ghanaians."[67] Such a situation is obviously potentially volatile and compromising, and conflicts of interest in such heavily emotionally and financially invested historical sites are bound to arise. At a fund-raiser sponsored by the Minneapolis chapter of the National Association for the Advancement of Colored People (NAACP) and attended by Mandela, Minnesota businesses pledged to raise $1 million for RIM, raising the specter of similar compromises on Robben Island if foreign sponsorship is accepted.[68]

In one such conflict of interests Africans from the diaspora insisted that the names of the Ghanaian forts should be changed to represent more adequately their historical status as prisons: "dungeon" should be added after "castle" since "castle" was felt to mask the buildings' central role as holding stations in the slave trade. By 2000 no such name change had occurred. Other protests from the international community, however, have been more successful. When one of the slave dungeons at Elmina Castle was transformed into a gift shop, complaints from the African diaspora resulted in the removal of the shop to another venue and the reinstatement of the dungeon.[69] Similarly, at a conference convened by Ghana's National Commission of Culture in May 1994 to discuss the complexities of how to adequately represent histories at the slave forts and to set up policy guidelines for restoration and conservation, a restaurant that had been opened over the male dungeons at the Cape Coast Castle was closed after objections were raised that it was a desecration of a sacred site, since the dungeons were in effect burial grounds.[70] There have been other instances of protests concerning the cleaning up and repainting of the dungeons and talk of "whitewashing" black histories.[71]

It is clear that similar tensions exist on Robben Island, and similar debates have taken place around the need to leave the island untouched (one might more accurately say unretouched) or to develop it more fully as a tourist facility. In sharp contrast to the Ghanaian case, however, those in favor of leaving the island as close as possible to its original state are the ex–political prisoners and other locals who have a personal stake in the history of the island. Certainly many local observers and those associated with expolitical prisoners seem to have recognized that the symbolic resonance of District Six, kept as a derelict space in the heart of Cape Town after the forced removals of the 1960s, is far more effective than any tidied-up reconstruction might be.[72] (In the District Six case, however, the need for land restitution and adequate low-cost housing is a far more pressing consideration than debates over conservation versus reconstruction.)

The poles of the debate about the extent to which the authorities should intervene in the prison environment are graphically set out in two features in the South African press comparing Alcatraz and Robben Island.[73] Although an improbable comparison since the former prioritizes its history as a high-security prison for violent criminals and infamous mafiosi and the latter focuses on its history as a place of exile and internment for political prisoners, it is fairly frequent in both the South African and the international press.[74] The articles in question were both about visits to the respective islands in 1998. The first, by Barbara Loftus, regrets that Robben Island is unable to bring alive its extraordinary history while with Alcatraz, "smaller in size and history, . . . in terms of slick professionalism and creating a sense of place, there is no comparison."[75] Loftus describes the respective island tours. While appreciating the ex–political prisoners' guided walk through the prison on Robben Island, she thinks that it nevertheless "just missed the hard realism and vividness I had expected."[76] On the other hand, "Wandering down the corridors [of Alcatraz], listening to the authentic sound effects and personal accounts by the ex-prisoners guiding me, I truly felt the eerie spirit of the jail and its inmates. 'Sit down and imagine how it feels like to be in solitary confinement for weeks on end,' says the headphone voice when you are inside the cell."[77] The bleak surrounds of Robben Island and the "ancient, rickety buses" are not for the likes of this reporter. For her, sanitized and sensational simulacra are the desired touristic experience. It is true that the early tours on Robben Island were at breakneck speed with minimal commentary on equipment that could not stand the pace, but it is also true that "slick professionalism" and sensearound simulacra come at a cost.

The other view, represented by Hazel Friedman three months later, was clearly intended (though never directly declared) as a riposte to Loftus's article. Subtitled "South Africa's Premier Heritage Site Is a Confusing Place, for Robben Island Is No Theme-Park Alcatraz," the article is sympathetic to the island's transitional status betwixt and between different worlds: "Something has been lost in the translation of the island from site of shame to that of struggle and ultimately hope. Today, our premier heritage site struggles to free itself; it is still in the throes of a multiple-identity disorder."[78] Friedman writes about the complicated and initially ambivalent responses to the island of the RIM staff, some of whom were of course imprisoned here. One of these, Rafiq Rohan, then working on the island as head of communications and marketing, had initially felt unequivocally hostile to the continued presence of the island and was keen that it should simply be abandoned and forgotten.[79] Friedman reports that he now revels in the natural resources of the island, although he still feels keenly uncomfortable inhabiting spaces that were once the sole domain of his white jailers.[80] Her point is that there are no easy fixes: "It doesn't offer instant gratification in the form of a slick, theme-park recreation of horror. There are no pre-recorded screams of prisoners, no instant experiences offering a two-minute taste of what it would have been like to be in solitary confinement for two weeks, two years, two decades. No catharses; no easy releases."[81] And—especially in the early days of the island's reincarnation as a "museum"—the low-tech, no-frills quality of the tour seemed (at least to this visitor) one of the strengths of the visit and a feature that appeared to encourage a more intimate and reflective experience of the site.

I was lucky to be part of one of the very earliest groups allowed on the island in April 1997, before there was a full-fledged tourist operation in place. Since then I have returned on two other occasions, most recently in December 2000. On my first visit I remember going over to the island in the small tub known as the *Dias,* an antiquated vessel once used for transporting prisoners. No slick and comfortable ferry with refreshments at the ready, offering a seamless transition from the clean commodities tantalizing the tourist dollar at the waterfront shopping malls. I sat aft of the *Dias,* feeling the wash drench my hands and face as we left the harbor. What began as a bright, warm day became suddenly darker as we moved closer to the island. At one point in the journey the visibility closed down to a dense, misted gray. The *Dias* slowed to accommodate the weather, and the passengers hushed to a tense alert, chilled by the abrupt change of atmosphere. It was a fitting beginning. Finally, the island came into sight, the weather cleared, and we disembarked onto a series of recommissioned school buses with clattering gears and young guides to take us on a tour. Despite the official rhetoric of the importance of the early history of the island and its delicate ecosystem and despite the fact that in addition to the prison many other island buildings could just as easily form an integral part of a liberation narrative, in these early tours none of these other aspects was treated with anything more than the most cursory nod, hence the PAC's irritation with the scant attention paid to Robert Sobukwe's isolation unit. But for most of us on that rickety bus it was probably true to say that we were happy to collude in this truncated tour and impatient to experience what we felt to be the highlight: the moment when we stepped inside the high-security prison and exchanged our young guide for the undeniably authoritative presence of an ex-prisoner with twenty years' experience of the prison—Patrick Matanjana.

In those days, not much had been done to the interior of the prison—a few coats of paint here and there but nothing too intrusive. The infamous isolation cells in B Block were bleak reminders of the desolation of having no resources or personal objects and none of the basic amenities that allow a human being the dignity of privacy despite the obvious deprivation in every other sense. I remember being struck by the details which strung Matanjana's narrative of prison life together. They did not focus on the horror or torture. There were no tales of pain and brutality—indeed these were notably absent from his story. Instead, and somehow far more effective as a means of conveying the emotionally and physically corrosive nature of the prison, Matanjana detailed the sanitary arrangements (or rather lack of them) to which the prisoners in B Block were subjected: no doors on the toilets and no latrines or buckets in the cells. The prisoners were entirely at the mercy of the guards, who usually had other more pressing engagements (a radio commentary on the latest rugby match, for example) than attending to prisoners suffering from the painful effects of the rotting food that was often the staple prison fare. At another point in the tour, Matanjana stopped at the so-called recreation room, which after 1975 (when television was first available in South Africa) showed a restricted menu of sports and children's programs. One of the sentiments often repeated by ex–political prisoners on Robben Island is their distress at having no contact with children and youth. Matanjana's narrative was no different. Despite the patronizing and demeaning policy of only sports or children's programs, he claimed that the programs were one way of being reminded that life continued, that there was another generation coming up on the outside, and that, for the same reason, it was even a pleasure to see and hear the warders' children going off to church with their families.

On further visits I noticed changes to the prison environment. Not only were the cells in B Block painted, but there were also beds with mattresses, cupboards, and slop buckets now. Some corridors had decorative murals, and in the guides' narratives there were fewer of the details that brought to life so vividly the dehumanizing aspects of the prison experience. In addition, there was an obvious attempt to capitalize on the pulling power of one of the most (internationally) famous previous occupants. The door to Mandela's cell (number 5) was the only one with a piece of paper tacked up on it to indicate its former occupant. Given the number of other prior inhabitants and their sacrifices and significances for the fledgling democracy of 1994 it is easy to see how such a focus to the exclusion of all others might irritate a local audience. It also fuels the ignorance of many international visitors, for whom many of the other key figures in the liberation movement remain a complete mystery.[82] Indeed on my last visit a group of visitors from Soweto stayed behind to angrily question our guide, Owen Mashaba. They suggested that there was always talk of Walter Sisulu and Mandela, but they wanted to know about the others who were imprisoned on the island. After all, they said, many others spent even longer than Mandela on the island, but somehow these were never mentioned on the tour. They also made an interesting objection about the nature of the historical narrative. Why, they wanted to know, was the story always told as a tale of individuals, and why did the guides always focus on the same ones? Mashaba answered that the museum intended to produce a book that would give more information on a greater number of former prisoners. As to the emphasis on some rather than other individuals, he responded that some people's work had a greater effect on more people, and they were inevitably mentioned by name. The party from Soweto was clearly not placated by these responses, and there was an evident hum of discontent enveloping the group even after it disembarked at the waterfront.

On occasion there have been displays that have attempted to historicize the prison visit. One of these included kitting out the cells in B Block with a series of different items, depending on the year. This was a useful way of restoring a minimal historical sense of the way the prison experience changed over time—due, as readers of the many autobiographies and memoirs will be only too well aware, to the persistent and inventive protests of the prisoners themselves. What is impressive, however, is that RIM has clearly been responsive to some of the criticisms I have mapped here, and these have shaped the ways in which the young guides now narrate their tours of the island and (to a lesser extent) the ex-prisoners' narratives.

On my last visit in December 2000 the experience was clearly a far cry from my first, and there were gains and losses. The landing stage at the waterfront where one picks up one's prebooked tickets for the island now has an oddly anachronistically titled "Curio Shop." The shop sports a huge soft drinks dispenser with Ahmed Kathrada's now famous words of hope and reconciliation emblazoned rather inappropriately over its surface: "While we will not forget the brutality of apartheid we will not want Robben Island to be a monument of our hardship and suffering. . . ." (figure 22). And I am copying these very words down from one of my prized purchases from the shop, an indispensable mouse pad that sits beside my laptop.

There is no longer the seedy if sturdy little *Dias*. We are herded onto a spanking new catamaran and try to give our attention, despite the loud hum of chatter and rushing kids, to the informative video presentation on the larger colonial history of the island and the accolades about its "unspoiled" natural environment. The video also frames our visit in unambiguous terms. Hence Robben Island is not only "the birthplace of the new na-

22. Drinks dispenser at Robben Island "curio" shop reproducing a section of Ahmed Kathrada's famous speech. Photo by the author.

"WHILE WE WILL NOT FORGET THE BRUTALITY OF APARTHEID WE WILL NOT WANT ROBBEN ISLAND TO BE A MONUMENT OF OUR HARDSHIP AND SUFFERING WE WOULD WANT IT TO BE A TRIUMPH OF THE HUMAN SPIRIT AGAINST THE FORCES OF EVIL; A TRIUMPH OF WISDOM AND LARGENESS OF SPIRIT AGAINST SMALL MINDS AND PETTINESS; A TRIUMPH OF COURAGE AND DETERMINATION OVER HUMAN FRAILTY AND WEAKNESS..."

tion," but it is also the place where the new constitution was forged and "a cultural showcase" for South African democracy.[83] Certain aspects of the tour narratives reinforce this message. As we stop at the infamous lime quarry, the site of much unproductive and demoralizing labor, our guide draws our attention to the cairn of stones at the entrance and likens it to the "new South Africa"—meaning different shapes and colors. This, she says, is the only new monument on the island. For her the cairn (in figure 23) recalls the Scottish, Jewish, and Xhosa practices of placing stones in a mound as commemorative markers or as signposts on a journey. What could be a more appropriate form of monument for Robben Island? The ex-prisoner who took me around the prison on this occasion, Owen Mashaba, also had something to say regarding the symbolic status of Robben Island for different constituencies. For some people, he said, Robben Island was now a museum and for others a monument, but for South Africans it was "our national heritage," and for ex-prisoners it was a prison and "it will always remain a prison to us."[84]

After the much faster catamaran crossing we file onto luxury tour buses. Swish new signposts at the entrance (figure 24) point out what RIM considers to be the highlights of the island's tour: the Kramat, the prison, and the penguin walk. This time our young guide has been thoroughly briefed, and the narrative is much more self-reflective and thoughtful. Toward the end of the tour she tries to give the group a sense that all histories are simply versions of a truth and may be contested: "All history is usually opinion." She follows up with an invitation for us to share with the group information we may have heard that might contradict any aspect of her own account so far. My guess is that she might well be a recent graduate of the history and heritage diploma taught jointly with colleagues in the history and art history departments at the University of Cape Town and the University of the Western Cape! My companions on this tour are a mix of local and international tourists and come from Soweto, Durban, and Cape Town, as well as from Holland, the United Kingdom, and the United States. Our guide politely apologizes for speaking in English and hopes that people are comfortable with this. We are then treated to a historically informative tour of the island, and this time we are allowed off the bus for a brief refreshment stop. Across the bay, we gaze at Table Mountain, rising majestically and inevitably through the heat haze (figure 25). The poignant and cruel impression is of the tempting proximity of a mainland that remained an absolute impossibility for the prisoners. Robert Sobukwe is given special attention now—and surely this revision is in response to the angry criticisms of PAC members and their families. A coda about memory and forgetting enjoins us to remember that "there were many ordinary people involved in the struggle," both on the mainland in South Africa, but also internationally. Her final and careful thanks are directed particularly at South African visitors in recognition of the additional expense they incur by coming on the tour.

In the prison itself there are now a few displays that aim to provide more historical information about the former inmates. In the toilet block, for example, a series of display boards shaped like lookout towers and headed "Political Trials" gives details of the Rivonia defendants and others (figure 26). In Section A, which, according to our guide, was reserved primarily for young "offenders" against the state, there is now an interactive display called "Cell Stories." It is an attempt to broaden people's awareness of the range of political prisoners on Robben Island and to move beyond the reification of Mandela's story. It also opens up our knowledge of the inventive activities in which the prisoners engaged despite their restrictive environment. By implication, the installation also draws our attention to the extent of these limitations. Each cell has an intercom that, when activated by the visitor,

Top to bottom 23. Memorial cairn at the infamous lime quarry on Robben Island; 24. Gateway at the entrance to Robben Island; 25. Looking over to Table Mountain from Robben Island. Photos by the author.

can play either music or voices or discussions. Every room also has a photograph of an inmate with a statement by him, his dates on the island, and a small showcase containing an object with which he has become associated. Tokyo Sexwale's is a football trophy awarded in prison (figure 27); Marcus Solomon's is an ingenious chess set made of paper; Zakhele Mdlalose's is a buckle with a map of the African continent outlined in red, with the explanatory label, "Once they were closing a toilet pipe that was leaking. So they did not use this piece. I picked it up and made this buckle. The red colour is from a stop sign. When we make the buckle hot and press it against the sign board, then the red sticks there. Then you clean it up and you leave it like that." The necessity of moving tourists through the prison efficiently, however, has meant that there is little time for reflection, and consequently few can benefit from the knowledge that such new displays might impart. There is still the inevitable crowd with clicking cameras and home videos blocking the entrance to cell number five in B Block.

It has always struck me as inappropriate that Robben Island is likely to be compared to Alcatraz rather than any of the other prisons around the world that are associated with national liberation struggles. Perversely Alcatraz is cited for the most banal reason: its prison island status. There is never any reference to the occupation of the island in 1969 by the American Indian Movement (AIM) to draw public attention to Indian land claims—a focus that would at least have the merit of considering both islands as the home of resistance movements. Inevitably the reader wonders why some comparisons are constantly evoked in both the official literature and the press while others that may share a greater affinity are never mentioned.

Two prisons in particular seem to bear comparison with Robben Island, not because they are islands, but because of their association with nationalist liberation movements: Kilmainham Gaol in Dublin and the Maze prison near Belfast, home of the infamous H-Blocks and scene of what some would argue was the decisive turning point in Anglo-Irish relations—the hunger strikes in October 1980 and March 1981, which culminated in the tragic death of the young and freshly elected Sinn Fein MP Bobby Sands. Paradoxically the link with Robben Island and other prisons associated with nationalist liberation struggles is explicitly invoked in the literature from Kilmainham Gaol. The guidebook includes a much reproduced clandestine shot of Sisulu and Mandela deep in conversation in the prison yard, accompanied by text: "Just as men and women can be made into heroes through their imprisonment, so can their places of confinement be exalted by their presence. In this way mere places of detention for criminals are transformed into powerful symbols of political freedom."[85]

26. "Political Trials" display at Robben Island showing (top to bottom) Neville Alexander, John Pokela, and Mac Maharaj. Photo by the author.

Below 27. Tokyo Sexwale's football trophy in the "Cell Stories" exhibition at Robben Island. Photo by the author.

The core of Kilmainham Gaol today is one of those classic Benthamite prison structures designed in 1861, though the earliest sections date from 1786. The structure began life as a place of detention for the common prisoner, but its symbolic significance is due to the fact that in its time as a prison (from 1796 to 1924) most of the key players in the various Irish nationalist movements, both men and women, were incarcerated, or indeed executed, within its walls. Thus, as the guidebook points out, "The opening and closing of the Gaol more or less coincided with the making and breaking of the Union between Great Britain and Ireland."[86] Kilmainham has a small and effective museum that charts its history—and that of the Irish penal system more generally—and details the stories of the prison's more significant inmates in unsensational and historically dense accounts. The actual jail and prison yard, the cells and the outbuildings, are bleak reminders of conditions for many of the prisoners; the conservation policy has been one of minimal intervention. Most touching is the account of the salvaging and restoration of the prison. It is with this that one begins to get an inkling of the ways in which Kilmainham has been the locus of truly troubling histories that have had a continuing significance for the various governments. The result has been, on the one hand, almost criminal neglect, and on the other, a salvage operation of heroic proportions against all odds and many obstructions. By 1936 the government was intent on leaving the prison to rot into oblivion, but by 1960 a group of veterans who had participated in the events of 1916–1923 (the 1916 Rising, the War of Independence, and the Civil War) set up a board of trustees with the aim of restoring Kilmainham and gaining it recognition as a national monument. This they did with no help from state funding. The volunteer force was spurred on by dreams of celebrating the fiftieth anniversary of the 1916 Rising in the prison in 1966. Indeed a highpoint of 1966 was the visit of Kilmainham's last prisoner— and later president of Ireland—Eamon de Valera.[87] It is difficult to resist drawing the parallel with Mandela's return to his old cell on Robben Island and to the quarry after his inauguration as president of South Africa.

One of the most consistent aspects of the guided narratives of Robben Island over the years has been the emphasis on the prison as a place of learning and as a "university." This now forms the backbone of any explanation of how the prisoners maintained their morale and discipline while in prison and their fitness to take up the reins of government on their release. We probably all remember one of the extraordinary aspects of Mandela's presence on the international arena after taking power in 1994. He seemed so thoroughly and impressively familiar with the intricacies of current political affairs on the world stage, despite so many years in a maximum security prison, some of them in isolation. When the notorious Maze prison closed its gates for the final time in the summer of 2000, journalists and academics were intrigued by the discovery of a large stash of books that had been circulated in the prison among the Republican inmates. Yvonne Murphy, the librarian in charge of the political collection at the Linen Hall Library in Belfast, took on the job of cataloging the 1,700 books, convinced of the political and historical significance of recording the formative reading of leading Republicans during the same period that the peace process was ongoing. The 1,700 represent the tip of the iceberg, and estimates suggest that the total number of books in the Republican library is closer to 16,000.[88] Murphy and other academics who have had the opportunity to examine the material claim that the collection reflects an almost uniformly serious choice, with very little in the way of light entertainment and much that is taken from the staple of international left political and social theory, ranging from literature on the Palestinian Intifada to Nicaraguan, Cuban, and Kenyan revolutionary and anticolonial movements.[89] Two of the most prominently represented areas are the Middle East (especially Palestine) and South Africa. Included in the collection were a number of boxes of writings by the Republican prisoners themselves. Jackie McMullan, an ex-prisoner charged with the attempted murder of a Royal Ulster Constabulary (RUC) officer and also involved in the hunger strikes and the blanket and dirty protests of the late 1970s, claims that education was central to the Republican survival in the Maze and that it was a point of honor: "We used to say, 'You could be here for the next twenty years. You don't want to leave jail exactly as you came in. Put it to good use.' It was a driving force. It was very central to what we were about."[90]

The claim to political and intellectual self-education (the Republicans rejected the prison education service and set up their own) could be understood partly as a way for the Republican prisoners to differentiate themselves as a distinct class of prisoner. It is a self-fashioning entirely consistent with wanting recognition as political prisoners—particularly in the case of Sinn Fein, which demands that the British state recognize the "Troubles" in Ireland and the six counties of Ulster as the results of a war against British imperial forces of occupation. For different reasons, it was as crucial that certain prisoners on Robben Island receive political status, and here too differentiating themselves from the common criminal was partly achieved by the emphasis, often repeated in narratives of island life, on the "university" and the drive for self-improvement through education.

This is not to deny that educational endeavor existed or that it was simply a rehearsed narrative strategy of self-aggrandizement. There is ample evidence that it did exist—and in the most adverse conditions. But it is important to recognize how such a consistent strand in the narrative of the prisoners' existence in the case of both Robben Island and the Maze helps to cement an image that marks the political prisoners as a cut above the ordinary criminals. Similarly it softens the taint of either sabotage or political assassinations, which might otherwise mar the "heroism" of their struggle for a more liberal audience and particularly for the international tourist in need of a glorious and righteous struggle, whose outcome is not muddied by the mess and ambiguities of war, the armed struggle, and the inevitability of botched operations. Indeed while it is too soon, if it will ever be the case, for Sinn Fein to be disassociated from its armed wing, the Irish Republican Army (IRA), it is certainly the case that the armed wing of the ANC, Umkhonto we Sizwe (MK), does not feature in any way at present in the narratives of the liberation struggle on Robben Island. To many international tourists, while "MK" means nothing, "ANC" is a familiar acronym. Paradoxically, the belief in the necessity of the armed struggle is precisely what kept Mandela (for example) on the island and was the cornerstone of his heroic refusal to denounce his comrades at the Rivonia Trial.

I am not suggesting here any kind of simple equation between the Irish Republican struggle and the South African liberation movement against apartheid. Rather I am inviting the reader to consider the effects of the prominence of certain comparisons and the notable absence of others, despite pertinent analogies that could be made and despite the long and complicated historical relationship between some of the main protagonists in the political wings of both Sinn Fein and the ANC.[91] My point here is that for a South African government emphasizing unity and progress and whose honeymoon with the liberal international community rests on the extraordinary achievement of negotiating a democratic transition with a minimum of bloodshed, an identification with the Irish freedom movement would certainly do more harm than good. Similarly, the sometimes violent struggles that moved the ANC nearer to the productive resolutions of the negotiating table are evidently not perceived to enhance the mystique of that transition.

APARTHEID'S "HOLOCAUST"

During the early days of the debate regarding the future of Robben Island, another similarity frequently evoked was between apartheid and the Holocaust and between strategies for Holocaust commemoration and commemorative strategies for the liberation struggle against apartheid. In the lead-up to the declaration that bestowed World Heritage status on Robben Island, Bernd von Droste, director of the World Heritage Centre at UNESCO, reinforced these links for an international audience on the grounds that "Robben Island has international symbolic value for human rights similar to sites like Hiroshima and Auschwitz and deserved the status of a world heritage site under the auspices of the United Nations."[92]

Such links were cemented in South Africa by a series of traveling exhibitions that sought to historicize the possible relationships between apartheid and fascism. From the end of 1994 until February 1995 the Castle in Cape Town hosted "Nederland Tegen Apartheid" (the Netherlands against apartheid). An exhibition entitled "Apartheid and Resistance" was organized by the Mayibuye Centre and hosted by the South African National Gallery in Cape Town. It was coordinated with another exhibition, "Anne Frank in the World" (March–April 1994), put on in collaboration with the Anne Frank Center in Amsterdam. Designed to be seen together, the pairing sparked a number of controversial debates around the appropriateness of a comparison between fascism and apartheid and between the Holocaust and the effects of apartheid. Gordon Metz, a representative of the Mayibuye Centre, explained the thinking behind the pairing: "South Africans have lived under their own system of oppression. We can't equate the Holocaust with apartheid, but there are many parallels, and lessons to be learnt. . . . We have tried to ensure that our component of the exhibition has a wide focus. An important point that comes through is that ordinary people make history."[93] The statement was accompanied by a strong visual comparison in the form of two photographs. One was of a segregated beach in Durban sporting a plaque informing would-be bathers that "Under section 37 of the Durban beach by-laws this bathing area is reserved for the sole use of members of the white race group." The accompanying photograph, from the 1940s, shows a swimming pool in Holland with a sign at the gates barring entry to Jews (figure 28).

When "Apartheid and Resistance" and "Anne Frank in the World" were shown jointly at Museum Africa in Johannesburg, the SABC screened a program that canvassed the reactions of teenage schoolchildren. Black students from Sebokeng's Residentia High School and white students from Kempton Park's Sir Pierre van Ryneveld School (among others) were questioned. Mark Gevisser, reporting on the responses in the *Weekly Mail and Guardian,* cites a student from Residentia saying of Anne Frank's experience in occupied Holland: "I've never been to such a place, but it's as if I've seen it many times before." Another student draws parallels: "Anne Frank . . .

Painful parallel...top, a whites-only beach in Durban and, above, a swim-
ming-pool off limits to Jews in the 1940s.

28. Photographs designed to show parallels between discrimination against Jews in Holland and apartheid in
South Africa accompanying an article about the "Anne
Frank in the World" exhibition, in *On Campus: The Official Newsletter of the University of the Western Cape* 2, no. 7.

is still the same [sic] with Mr. Nelson Mandela. They did well with reconciliation."[94] Children from the more economically privileged Kempton Park
school also understood the message of the two exhibitions: "We need to
learn from history. If we had learnt from the example of Nazi Germany,
apartheid wouldn't have happened here."[95] Or again: "You don't realise the
seriousness of racism and prejudice until you see and hear the true-life story
of some of the victims of apartheid and anti-Semitism."[96] Some of the white
children, on the other hand, were clearly on the defensive and claimed that
the exhibitions were one-sided. These thought that there was some blame
to be laid at the door of the ANC for the various acts of sabotage. Gevisser's
own view of the parallel exhibitions was that the strategy was an important
one but that in "Apartheid and Resistance" the "didactic and heavy-handed
collages . . . distance the viewer by not allowing personal points of entry,"
blocking access for the children also.[97]

Gevisser's own family history (his aunt was killed in the Vilna ghetto in
Lithuania) surfaces in a special supplement to the *Weekly Mail and Guardian* that was produced in association with the Jewish Board of Deputies for

readers to take to the exhibition.[98] As always, Gevisser's writing—this time on his initially reluctant but now compulsive inquiry into his family history and the complicated denials and erasures that immigrants to South Africa inevitably mobilized as protective mechanisms—is a moving and thoughtful account that invites the reader to acknowledge the gray areas of historical investigation. Other articles in the special supplement are less reflexive and draw more didactic humanist parallels with the South African context. In one article the lives of Anne Frank and Steve Biko are said "to illustrate the monstrosities [of] mass racial repression or genocidal annihilation."[99] The article is a plea for the continuing belief against all odds in the ultimate goodness of humanity; it ends: "There is another person who was shut away for years and cut off from everyday contact with the world, yet he still dreamed of better things and never gave up his trust in humanity. His name is Nelson Mandela."[100] Another section of the supplement explicitly links the South African liberation struggle with Anne Frank's history when Govan Mbeki, one of the Rivonia defendants on Robben Island with Mandela, recalls how important Anne Frank's diary was for the prisoners. He suggests that it was seen as subversive by the prison authorities, who, together with the prisoners, recognized it as a tool in the political education of the latter: "Anne Frank's diary was very important because its circumstances were very similar to those in apartheid South Africa. It was such a moving book."[101]

The fact that the *Weekly Mail and Guardian* supplement was produced at all is an indication of the intended significance of the joint exhibitions and of the role that the Mayibuye Centre played in the early stages of reconstructing South African public history for broader consumption. In this regard it is also important to note that both exhibitions opened just prior to the first democratic elections in April 1994. In other words, a relationship between the twin atrocities of the Holocaust and apartheid was flagged early on in the contest over public history in South Africa—another reason we should take such comparisons seriously as a marker of the significant relationships that an emergent public history was attempting to instill. The *Weekly Mail and Guardian* supplement (as well as another broadsheet publication, "The Anne Frank Journal," designed to accompany the exhibition) ends with articles warning about the continuing presence of race hatred and fascism in the world.

These high-profile exhibitions also had the effect of stimulating debate about the validity of the comparison between Nazism, apartheid, and the Holocaust.[102] None of the arguments holds any real surprises, and they often surface when analogies are made between the Holocaust and any other instances of genocide on the grounds of "race" or ethnicity. Some propounded the view that nothing could compare in scale and horror to the Holocaust, which was a "unique" instance of man's inhumanity to man.[103] Others felt this argument simply reflected the embarrassment of the perpetrators of apartheid—the National Party and its supporters—who wanted to distance themselves from Nazism and its obvious ideological and historical links with apartheid. Referring to an earlier letter to the editor of the *Argus,* one correspondent retorted, "Six million (white) Jewish deaths are, in [the previous writer's] mind, obviously more significant than merely two or three million (black) African deaths caused by the apartheid government and its surrogates in neighbouring states. Nazi racism of the 1930s formed Verwoerd, Dönges and Diederichs in apartheid ideology. What is obscene in drawing parallels between nazism and apartheid is that South Africa's educated white electorate returned the Nats [National Party] to power for some 45 years. We cannot claim 'we did not know!' "[104] More to the point, such arguments were used to drive home a message to the South African electorate on the eve of the crucial first democratic election: "The only difference between the nazis and the Nats is that the Nats were less 'efficient.' A 'coloured' vote for the Nats is like a Jewish vote for Hitler."[105]

The joint exhibitions also provided the opportunity to raise other questions about national heritage and public history. One letter to the *Argus* makes the point that much of the National Party's early leadership held openly declared Nazi sympathies. The Dutch had been clearly critical of these: when Du Plessis was nominated South African ambassador to the Netherlands, they declared him a *persona non grata* in Holland because of his Nazi sympathies during World War II. However, despite the knowledge of National Party leaders' avowed admiration for Nazi ideology, there were still streets named after them and statues still stood in their honor in many of South Africa's town centers. The letter ends with sentiments that were to become a familiar refrain in the debates over public heritage: "But then I feel assured that under a non-racial administration such anomalies will be rectified. Du Plessis, Pirow and their ilk should not be honoured, but they should not be forgotten either—they should be remembered forever with the contempt they deserve."[106]

While parallels between apartheid and the Holocaust may remain controversial, there are some shared issues raised by the commemoration of both. In the case of Robben Island and District Six the commemorative terrain is a physical site marked as much by suffering and devastation as the remnants of Dachau, Auschwitz, and other camps. The primacy of location is crucial to all these examples. Similarly, neither Robben Island or District

Six nor any of the Nazi death camps have permanent collections as such, although clearly the metonymic power of personal belongings is exploited to considerable effect in all cases. In the Holocaust Memorial Museum in Washington, D.C., victims' shoes piled on either side of a narrow walkway take on the status of an intimate memorial, a parallel encouraged by the architectural restrictions: the visitor is likely to be alone in his or her encounter with these remnants of human occupation, which are in a low-lit, contained space that assumes the quality of a shrine. Less theatrically, the "apple-box archive" of political prisoners' belongings at Robben Island serves to personalize the prison experience, emphasizing the power of the individual despite the crushing uniformity of the prison regime.

The effectivity of the commemorative experience lies largely with the power of oral testimony and the notion of witnessing that both "survivors" and "place," in different ways, can offer. In all the locations noted above there is an unequivocal recognition of the need to satisfactorily evoke the horror of what took place in order to get across the message, "Never again." At the same time, there is also a desire to avoid a sensationalized account that would be more likely to encourage voyeuristic distance. Consequently reflection and intimacy are the touchstones of the more successful museums or sites that deal in such gruesome tragedy.

Various strategies have been devised to enhance these two elements. In the Holocaust Memorial Museum the visitor is offered an identification tag with data on an individual victim of the Holocaust. When the tag is inserted into interactive stations at various points in the museum, it will provide details of that individual's experience in relation to the display. On Robben Island the tour of the prison is led by ex–political prisoners, and while their narrative is oddly devoid of personal details of their own experience in the prison or even the particular circumstances of their incarceration, their very presence promotes an illusion of intimacy.

The deliberate manipulation of architectural space and the experience of the remnants of the camps or prisons themselves contribute in particular ways. One notable example of such manipulation is the Holocaust Memorial Museum, discussed above. Another is the Annex to the Jewish Museum in Berlin, designed by Daniel Libeskind. A number of commentators have noted that its architectural space conjures up a void that operates on a metonymic level to signal how the horror of the Holocaust defies description and narrative.[107] In a sense, Libeskind's design also works to defamiliarize the visitor through the physical experience of what one might call his "irrational" architecture (see figure 29)—"irrational" particularly in the context of a museum building, which by definition is usually approached with

29. Roslyn Poignant, Interior view of the Jewish Museum Extension to the Berlin Museum, 1999. Courtesy of Roslyn Poignant.

the intention of gaining some kind of edifying experience and where an explanatory rationale is often a feature of the institution. Important here is the distinction between the visual consumption and the somatic experience of Libeskind's architectural forms. These offer themselves as the consummate aesthetic object to the lens of a camera, but as an embodied experience they provoke a discomfort similar to that found in some monstrous palace of mirrors in an archaic fairground. This distinction between representation and the embodied experience of place is profound in all of the examples I discuss in this chapter and cannot be underestimated. It is the single strongest feature common to all and in all cases works partly through defamiliarization.

In the prison unit on Robben Island one of the dominant sensations is the collapsing of registers of time and space. James Young, describing a visit to Auschwitz, recalls his pleasure at the beauty of the environment and his sense of the inappropriateness of such a response.[108] The natural environment of Robben Island has a similar effect on a visitor, especially if one has been lucky enough to spend some time on it outside a guided tour. But the more noticeable disorientation comes inside the prison itself. The prevailing sensation here is also one of dissonance, with the expectation of the Gulag of popular imagination. This is a small, almost intimate, and certainly claustrophobic environment rather than the forbidding mass of a defended fortress that most of us have anticipated.

In its feasibility study, Peace Visions had drawn attention to the fact that the majority of ex-prisoners on Robben Island did not want the island turned into a shrine to commemorate the atrocities of the past (like Dachau).[109] The identification of the commemorative effort at Dachau and other Holocaust sites with an exclusive focus on victimization has been acknowledged as a problem by many of those involved in attempts to adequately honor both those who died and those who survived the Holocaust. One of the difficulties is manifest in the fragmentary nature of the necessarily limited material remnants of individuals' lives.[110] Some museums have addressed this by providing displays that emphasize the conditions and sociality of life for individuals before their tragic deportation and death.[111] By so doing, they hope to render these individuals more than just names on rosters of horror. To a certain degree this strategy is effective.

Though not in any way equivalent to the genocide represented by the Holocaust, the forced removals in District Six and other parts of South Africa have led to similar problems concerning the retrieval and recovery of memory under conditions of total destruction. Such sites engage in similar strategies for re-membering a sociality that the apartheid government attempted to permanently eradicate, through oral witnessing and through piecing together the lives of the District before dispersal. Those charged with the commemoration of those imprisoned on Robben Island, however, are faced with a rather different twist to the dilemma of how to make a remnant speak for the intricacies of the social existence of an individual. For many prisoners on the island, young adulthood and its attendant trials and tribulations and the intense relationships and experiences we might reasonably identify with this passage in a young life were all curtailed. Prisoners were sometimes on the island for a greater proportion of their life than they had been off it. Any representation of sociality has therefore to be redefined according to the parameters of the constricted universe offered by the prison and its community of political and ordinary prisoners, warders, and visitors.[112] The extent to which the prisoners become more than simply identified by the prison therefore begins to depend upon a differentiated representation of the texture of the relationships that develop within it. And this is never a feature of the narratives of a guided tour. Perhaps this is why the criticisms levelled at the absences or unilinear tale of ANC heroism as the primary prison narrative on guided tours are so persistent.

Another dilemma that the Robben Island commemorative project shares with the Holocaust is the issue of the adequacy of representation. When in 1957 the International Committee of Auschwitz convened a panel to select a fitting monument to the victims and survivors of the death camp, its chair, Henry Moore, admitted defeat in the face of such a difficult task. In a speech justifying the committee's failure to resolve the decision, he argued: "Essentially, what has been attempted has been the creation—or in the case of the jury, the choice—of a monument to crime and ugliness, to murder and to horror. The crime was of such stupendous proportions that any work of art must be on an appropriate scale. But, apart from this, is it in fact possible to create a work of art that can express the emotions engendered by Auschwitz?"[113] James Young goes on to chart the trajectory of the Auschwitz project. One of the most interesting aspects of the account is the nature of the objections raised by various constituencies to the proposals.[114] Often the designs that were most appreciated by the architects and artists on the jury were those least favored by the survivors.

Two stumbling blocks in particular are frequently encountered in this kind of commemorative project. On the one hand, the abstraction of the designs is seen as inappropriate to either the conceptual or the actual task of embodying the experience of the survivors. On the other hand, in most instances survivors are attached to the idea of some kind of monument because it provides a focal point for enactments and rituals that themselves are the symbolic and abstracted embodiment of their experiences. The other famous instance of this kind of controversy is in relation to the Vietnam Veterans' Memorial in Washington, D.C. In response to objections over abstract design, a figurative group by the sculptor Frederick Hart (representing three soldiers, one black and two white) was erected in 1984 to placate the veterans (figure 30). Paradoxically, it is Maya Ying Lin's wall that, despite the earlier protests, has become the focal point for survivors and relatives and the backdrop for commemorative services (figure 31). It is the wall, and not the figurative group, that enables ritual reappropriation and animation. Visitors make rubbings of the names of relatives and friends engraved on the wall; they place photos of their loved ones and other objects here to individuate the space of commemoration. The quality of the wall that was initially its most criticized feature—namely, its apparently "blank" abstraction—turned out to be the very quality that enables the cathartic ritual acts of commemoration through personalized inscription—the completion of the memorial through the participation of those whose memory is most at stake.

German artist Jochen Gerz's wonderful solutions to the seeming impossibility of commemorating the Holocaust are famously represented by two

30. Frederick Hart,
Vietnam memorial. Bronze.
Washington, D.C., 1984.

Below 31. Maya Ying Lin,
Vietnam Veterans'
Memorial. Polished granite.
Washington, D.C., 1983.

monuments that are more in the way of countermonuments but that also rely on processes of ritual animation to render them meaningful. In 1986 the Harburg Monument against Fascism was unveiled. Jointly designed with the Israeli artist Esther Shalev (later Shalev-Gerz), it stands as a twelve-meter-high column of hollow aluminum covered in soft lead and with an inscription at its base: "We invite the citizens of Harburg, and visitors to the town, to add their names here to ours. In doing so, we commit ourselves to remain vigilant. As more and more names cover this 12 metre tall lead column, it will gradually be lowered into the ground. One day it will have disappeared completely, and the site of the Harburg monument against fascism will be empty. In the end it is only we ourselves who can rise up against injustice" (figure 32).[115] By November 1993 the only remaining trace of the lead column was a plaque beside the site and a glass vitrine at ground level through which the sunken pillar could be seen but not the written testimonies on its leaden sides. In some sense, this is the embodiment of Pierre Nora's argument concerning the importance of the "trace" as the primary bearer of meaning in contemporary life: impermanent, mutating, and fragmentary, referring to but never entirely revealing the whole of which it is a part.[116] The countermonument is also a reflection on the nature of memory itself in the sense that it risks obliteration and repression and, conversely, that it is only in the act of remembering (paradoxically a highly subjective process) that memory exists at all.

The other Gerz countermonument is the 2,146 Stones — Monument against Racism, completed in Saarbrücken in 1997 (figure 33).[117] In the square containing the former headquarters of the Gestapo, Gerz organized a posse of students, in a logistically daring act of bravado, to lift up the cobblestones in front of the Saarbrücken Schloss, engrave them with the names of missing Jewish cemeteries in Germany, and replace them facedown and consequently invisibly.

Of course the question of finding adequate forms of commemoration for the historical atrocities of apartheid presents a rather different range of problems. In the case of Robben Island, for example, one needs to be aware of what kind of burden is represented by using the site as a means of locating and constructing "national" memory. How does the institutional location of an attempt to represent a form of collective memory mediate this process? How is it possible to produce through the exhibiting of material culture a representation of both subjective experience *and* an acceptable public narrative of the prison experience that neither undermines the complex personal responses to imprisonment nor the negotiations (both between prisoners and between prisoners and warders) necessary for sur-

32. Jochen Gerz and
Esther Shalev, The
Harburg Monument
against Fascism,
Lead, sinking into
the ground. Harburg,
1986. Photographed
in 1993. Photo
courtesy of Jochen
Gerz and Esther
Shalev-Gerz.

33. Jochen Gerz, 2,146 Stones—Monument against Racism. Saarbrücken, 1991. Photo
by M. Blancke. HBK Saar, 1997.

vival? Whose history is represented through a strategy that needs to serve simultaneously as an account of a hitherto invisible aspect of the recent national past for all South Africans *and* an account that will cement the history of the liberation struggle as a world event on the international stage? How is it possible to represent adequately the brutality of the prison regime and its significance as a symptom of the wider injustices of apartheid *and* understand Robben Island as "a monument [reflecting the] triumph of the human spirit against the forces of evil"?[118] Certainly all the debates above highlight that any threshold between public history and private experience and its intersection with the construction of nationhood is a particularly complex terrain to negotiate.

LIBERATING HISTORIES

The narrative of history foregrounded by the Robben Island story during the apartheid years is one of heroic stoicism in the face of a regime of brutalism, coupled with the deadening effects of a routine of completely unproductive labor. Many groups lay claim to this narrative in their bid to be represented as a part of the foundational struggle out of which the "new" South Africa arose phoenix-like from the ashes of apartheid. It is a narrative that is hard to challenge without sounding like some reactionary stalwart of the right. But at the same time it requires some comment since in its present form it closes off as much as it opens up for the prospect of a new national history that encompasses the experience of all South Africans.

As we have seen, part of the difficulty arises because of the international community's desire to participate in the history of South Africa's liberation. The death of apartheid represented the culmination of a huge investment of hopes and dreams for many on different lefts in Europe and America. The story of the South African revolution and the transition from racist dictatorship to democracy, negotiated via a power-sharing government of national unity, took on the status of a tremendous utopia that brooked no criticism. Central to the success of this ideal has been the status of the figure of Nelson Mandela in the international imagination. Conversely, because Mandela's story is so central to an understanding of the outcome of the liberation struggle, Robben Island figures large. Since so much of his life was spent as a prisoner there, his story was quickly transformed into best-selling biographies both in South Africa and abroad.[119] These were as speedily adapted for film for both a local and international market.[120] Rob Nixon aptly describes Mandela's appeal as a man who, despite being essentially absent from the world, incarcerated between 1964 and 1990, "lived on the cusp of time, embodying a people's hope, yet monumentalized on a scale ordinarily reserved for the dead."[121] Even the apartheid government's media ban on Mandela, his writings, and his photos seemed to have the reverse effect and guaranteed him a potent visibility and audibility: "So the South African regime helped station the idea of Nelson Mandela on the threshold between the dead and the living, between commemoration and expectation. They also unwittingly sheltered his image from the erosions of time and diversity. The ban on photographing Mandela allowed the same few images to keep circulating in a heraldic fashion perfect for the needs of an international political movement."[122]

Even after Mandela's successor, Thabo Mbeki, had taken over the reins of government, Mandela continued to figure on the international stage as a redemptive icon, capable of salvaging any number of tarnished images and regimes. Most notable in the United Kingdom was his presence during the general election and the boost his public endorsement provided for Tony Blair's Labour campaign when he addressed the party conference in Brighton on 28 September 2000, thanking the Labour Party for its historic support for the South African liberation movement and claiming a number of shared political and moral agendas (figure 34).[123] The photograph of Mandela hugging Blair was flagged on the front pages of both *The Guardian* and *The Times,* on the one hand as an endorsement of Labour and on the other as a way of foregrounding what *The Times* clearly interpreted as a cynical use of an international hero to shore up New Labour's tarnished image. The latter was cemented by Peter Brookes's cartoon of New Labour's leaders hanging onto Madiba's trademark patterned-silk shirttails (figure 35).[124]

More recently, on 29 April 2001, Mandela was the star attraction at the South Africa Freedom Day concert in Trafalgar Square (one of the only times a mass concert has been allowed in Trafalgar Square). He thrilled the crowd with references to the three decades of vigils, protests, and pickets in the square outside the South African High Commission in support of the ANC and the South African liberation movement: "I'm happy to be in Trafalgar Square where one of the most important battles for the liberation of South Africa was fought."[125] *The Guardian* sported a color picture of Mandela against the backdrop of the South African flag, with the caption, "Mandela Magic; Capital Celebrates, South Africa Style." Tony Blair was relegated, this time, to the background.[126] In addition, Mandela and Trafalgar Square are no strangers to each other since there has been an ardent and long-standing campaign to see his figure erected to fill the vacant fourth plinth directly in front of the National Gallery (see figure 36). The South African journalist and biographer of Steve Biko, Donald Woods, devoted

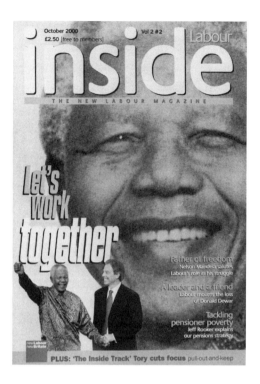

34. Cover of New Labour's magazine *Inside New Labour* foregrounding Nelson Mandela's support for the party at the time of the general election. October 2000.

Below 35. Peter Brookes, *New Labour. The Times,* 29 September 2000. Copyright Peter Brookes / Times Newspapers Limited, London.

36. Artist's impression of what a bust of Mandela might look like on the fourth plinth in Trafalgar Square. *The Voice*, 8 November 1999.

SHAPE OF THINGS TO COME? : *How the statue may look.*

NELSON'S COLUMN?

much of his time while alive to securing support for the project, and one of the leading black British newspapers, *The Voice*, took up the campaign in November 1999.[127]

But it is not just international acclaim that has cemented Nelson Mandela's image as redemptive icon. A number of accounts published in the national press by former fellow ANC prisoners on Robben Island have publicly asserted his key role as a wise leader.[128] Mandela's eightieth birthday in July 1998 was the occasion of a number of tributes in the South African press (as one would expect), and similar tributes appeared in the British press also.[129]

No one could question the extraordinary power of Mandela's life story or his charismatic role in the negotiations that led to the government of national unity, although he would be the first to insist that the outcome was not due to his negotiations alone but to the work of many of his comrades over a long period. Despite the persistent growth of a cult of personality, Mandela has constantly worked to dismantle it. Nixon provides some useful early examples, citing Mandela's first public address after his release from prison, when he addressed the crowd as "not a prophet, but as a humble servant of you, the people."[130] Similarly, on his first U.S. tour in June 1990, rather than playing into the American obsession with the "first," the "new," and the "unique," Mandela constantly invoked historical precedents in other (particularly black U.S. civil rights) leaders and their shared political and human rights agendas.[131] As a result, as Nixon points out, "From his first day on American soil, Mandela found himself represented simultaneously as a visitor from the historical past, a guardian of future hopes, and a redeemer of mythic dimensions."[132] Anthony Sampson (one of Mandela's most prominent biographers and an individual with formidable political credentials himself) was early moved to write about Mandela's ability to turn the prison experience into a positive, formative disciplinary training for the future. But significantly the thrust of Sampson's article, which was written on the occasion of the sixth anniversary of Mandela's release from prison, was to emphasize that "It is not just Mandela's island." Pointing to some of his younger former inmates, Sampson concludes: "These prison graduates, with their discipline and tolerance, offer much reassurance for a future SA [*sic*] without Mandela. Like him they do not need to prove their heroism with macho postures to their followers; they have learnt the secrets of self-reliance and building a community in the strictest school of all."[133] Likewise Ahmed Kathrada has been scrupulous in drawing attention to the differential treatment meted out to black and Asian prisoners on Robben Island. Such discriminatory conditions effectively perpetuated the apartheid system and attempted to set prisoners against each other. Kathrada has also taken care to highlight the importance of the support of women and family members for those imprisoned on the island.[134]

Nevertheless, as we have seen, a point of contention during the debates on the future of the island was precisely the sense that the ANC had highjacked the island narrative as *the* narrative of the liberation struggle. In a bizarre incident that could only fan the fire of this contention, in 1996 a full-sized replica of Mandela's Robben Island cell was reconstructed in the foyer of the National Assembly building in Parliament. It was part of an exhibition put on by the Department of Correctional Services (to coincide with the department's budget vote) presumably and oddly as an exercise in promoting the work of the prison service past, present, and future.[135] More seriously, in 1995, at a four-day conference on the future of the island to an audience of over thirteen hundred former political prisoners (some from Namibia and Botswana), PAC Deputy President Motsoko Pheko dismissed concerns over whether the island should become a tourist venue or a peace studies institute and argued instead that more attention should be paid to accurately recording the history of the island, especially the extent to which incarcerated members of political organizations other than the ANC had played a crucial role in the resistance.[136] Contention over the perceived elimination of the role of PAC and other political leaders from the official narratives of the liberation movement and the silences regarding their imprisonment on Robben Island was still rankling in 2000. At this time Pheko was moved to write a piece for the *Sowetan*. The "True History of Robben Island Must be Preserved" was concerned to elaborate the range of political resistance represented by those imprisoned on Robben Island since at least the seventeenth century. As we might expect from the deputy president of the PAC, Pheko details PAC experience on the island, insisting that it became known as "Poqo prison" in 1963, when a large influx of PAC prisoners arrived, and "Sobukwe university" after PAC leader Robert Sobukwe.[137] Pheko goes on to argue that ANC treatment in prison was nothing like as bad as the treatment of Sobukwe and his colleagues and that it was the Poqo uprising in 1960 that put Robben Island on the international map as "a symbol of national resistance against apartheid and colonialism."[138] His message is clear: "The history of Robben Island must not be desecrated. Africa and the world owe it to African posterity to tell the truth about Robben Island as it is; not to manufacture tales intended for political misinformation and the mutilation of the history of Robben Island."[139]

Interestingly, the official tours of the island notably downplay any tensions that existed between, for example, the younger influx of prisoners after the 1976 Soweto uprising and the older generation and the fact that, as Fran Buntman points out, there was considerable competition among different political factions to recruit the youth, frequently resulting in physical violence.[140] However, a number of extracts from various biographies and autobiographies published in the national press tended to open up this conflict to public scrutiny. One of the most prestigious extracts was from Anthony Sampson's biography of Mandela, which carried the banner headline in the *Sunday Independent*: "In this edited extract from *Mandela: The Authorised Biography*, Anthony Sampson shows that "the university of the left" was more divided than it appeared."[141] But such contentions and fissures remain primarily the subjects of local rather than international consumption. Indeed in 1997, in answer to Mogamad Allie's interview question, "Do you tell the same stories to all the groups you bring over?" Ahmed Kathrada replied: "I've suggested to André [Odendaal] that a group of us who've been on the Island should independently record things so that in the end we can have a uniform story to tell. After so many years our memories are differing on detail. It's important to present to the public one message of our Robben Island experiences."[142] The Robben Island Reunion, in February 1995, was another occasion where tensions erupted, in this instance due to the notable absence of wives and family members of the two thousand former political prisoners who had been invited. Marcus Solomon, from the Trotskyist Workers' Organization for Socialist Action (WOSA), voiced regret about the constant focus on the leaders: "I think the greater roles were indeed played by the ordinary people, and it is these people that we need to focus around mainly."[143] I remember watching Adam Low and Claudia and Jürgen Schadeberg's 1994 film, *Voices from Robben Island,* and being impressed by June Mlangeni's description of her visit to her husband, Andrew Mlangeni (one of the Rivonia defendants, on the island with Mandela). Such experiences and voices of the island story were missing from the tourist route; they graphically conveyed the poignancy of loss and separation in a way that the heroic stoicism of the official tour narratives failed to deliver. Mlangeni recalls:

> When the permit came to visit Andrew, I borrowed money for a third class ticket to Cape Town. The train took two nights and I arrived at seven in the morning. I had to be at the docks at one, which was when the boat left. I walked from the station to the harbour, which is a long way, got onto the boat and arrived at Robben Island. There were a lot of police and I was escorted to a waiting room. I was then taken to see Andrew, who was standing at the end of a long passage. There were many other families and everyone was shouting at one another over the noise. . . . Sometimes I couldn't hear what he said. We were only given thirty minutes. He looked terrible, in short pants, a canvas jacket, with sandals . . . and the weather was so cold. I didn't want to show him how hurt I was.[144]

Indres Naidoo's autobiographical account of his sentence on Robben Island, *Island in Chains,* describes in similar terms the thirty-minute visiting time in a chapter aptly called "Chaos": "We had to yell and scream to be heard on the other side, and the din was so great that as we begged our neighbours to lower their voices they begged us to do the same, but in no time we were all shouting at the tops of our voices again, repeating ourselves over and over, desperately trying to communicate. Those of us who could not speak English, Afrikaans, Xhosa or Zulu, the four permitted languages, were particularly hard hit—they struggled above the noise with their limited English, shouting to family members who frequently knew even less of English than themselves."[145]

The details in both Mlangeni's and Naidoo's accounts conjure up the callousness and emotional cruelty of the system. They also run counter to the usual filmic and televisual versions of prison visiting hours, which represent intense, one-to-one contact summoning a degree of intimacy, despite the glass barrier between the protagonists and the presence of the watchful warder. These accounts of the excruciating frustration of not being able to make oneself heard above the din of one's fellow inmates and their visitors, all clamoring to communicate in various languages, convey a far more devastating alienation.

An early project that was part of a series of creative workshops held on Robben Island attempted to explore some of the dynamics of the prison visit and to provide some idea of the experience of those on the other side of the visitor's grille. *Thirty Minutes* is a series of installations by nine artists who took over the bleak visitors' block. The artists produced individual installations in each of the visitor booths on the corridor. The "thirty minutes" of the title refers to the length of time allowed with the prisoner. How often these visits were permitted depended on what category the inmate was designated by the prison authorities.

Lionel Davis, himself an ex-prisoner and now one of the island personnel at RIM, confirms both Mlangeni's and Naidoo's accounts of visiting times on the island:

> My art piece is from personal experience as a political prisoner on Robben Island [see figure 37]. The visiting booth, a confined impersonal space, gave no privacy. Bouncing off the walls all over that passage with its open visiting booths was a cacophony of sound—everyone shouting to be heard in different languages and very little to be heard. Every word spoken was carefully monitored by prison warder [*sic*]: a language not understood was summarily stopped and so was anything political. We had to confine ourselves to family matters and mundane affairs. In that booth every political prisoner appeared to be impotent—not the person the visitor had known yesterday. This, however, was deceptive. Every word spoken by a political prisoner was carefully calculated because a wrong word spoken or an angry outburst could mean the end of a long-awaited 6-monthly visit. Beyond the prison walls the fight against the atrocious treatment and appalling prison conditions continued unabatedly.[146]

Appropriately, Davis's work recalls the babel he, Mlangeni, and Naidoo all describe as the precious thirty minutes they were able to spend in view of their loved ones.

For Cape Town artist Willie Bester the opportunity to participate in the *Thirty Minutes* exhibition was a moving and painful experience. Although his father had been imprisoned in Montague and had suffered similar abuses to the ones perpetrated on Robben Island—unable to wear long trousers, wearing sandals in winter, no bread or sugar to eat, and forced into unproductive labor—Bester's own experience of Robben Island was as a visitor to a common-law prisoner in 1975.[147] Bester's installation (shown in figure 38) consisted of a Bible wired as a bomb, with a white child's shoe in the center of the "semtex" base. He explains the hypocrisy of a religion claiming to be based on brotherly love between equals but systematically deployed to shore up the racial segregation that apartheid kept in place: "The

37. Lionel Davis, *Untitled*. 1997. Mixed media. Photo by Michael Hall. Courtesy of the artist.

Below 38. Willie Bester, *Die Bybel*. 1997. Steel, rubber, glass, found objects, resin, paper, 370 × 450 × 90 cm. Photo by Michael Hall. Courtesy of the artist.

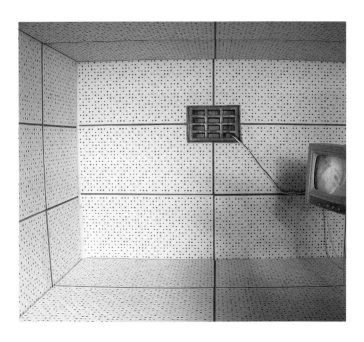

39. Sue Williamson, *Is Anybody . . . ?* 1997. Acoustic tiles, wood, air-brick, monitor, camera, sound. Photo by Michael Hall. Courtesy of the artist.

bible was used to keep the aspirations of black people at bay—instead of praying for the downfall of this vicious government, you have to pray to give them strength, to run the country. . . . The fact that the system was so cruel, so public, so open, reinforced my belief that it was a time bomb that had to go off some time."[148]

Another Cape Town artist, Sue Williamson, focused on the destructive and demoralizing effects of constant surveillance, not just as part of the prison system but in the minute details of everyday life: "Knowing that the police were trying to make you nervous but that what they were doing to those who weren't white and middle-class went far, far beyond that. Feeling rage. Feeling watched."[149] Her installation consisted of a small television monitor in the booth that played back the visitor's own image (figure 39).

These small but provocative installations go some way toward opening up the issue of what it might have been like for both the prisoner and the visitor on the island. The booths set up a series of questions that might profitably set the tourist thinking about "other" stories that are not part of the official tour narrative. More important, the installations provide a point of reference for family members, friends, and comrades and offer some acknowledgment of their vital and difficult role in supporting the prisoners. But alas, none of this is actually available on the tourists' "island experience." I was extremely lucky to see the installations and was able to do so only after I had obtained special dispensation and requested that the installations be switched on (since many of them required multimedia equipment) and because Sue Williamson and Les Witz were kind enough to facilitate this for me.

WOMEN IN THE STRUGGLE

The focus on Robben Island as the preeminent site of struggle encourages more serious omissions and amnesia, however. After the former political prisoners' reunion in 1995 its coordinators were berated by women from the ANC and other organizations for forgetting the role of women in the liberation struggle altogether. Thandi Modise's angry speech in front of over one thousand former political prisoners at the Peninsula Technikon was reported substantially in the *Sowetan*.[150] Indeed one of the difficulties presented by the exclusive focus on Robben Island (a prison for black male political prisoners) is that it eclipses many other prison experiences during apartheid, particularly those of black and white women in places like Nylstroom, Kroonstad, Pretoria Central, and Boksburg. The only time any women were mentioned on any of my tours to the island was in December 2000, when it was briefly remarked that women and white men were also imprisoned in the cause of the liberation struggle. This lacuna seems particularly perverse given the extent to which women's autobiographies and narratives of women's prison experiences and writings from prison are every bit as prominent in the literature, and were often available earlier than those of their male comrades.[151] At a celebration for the publication of Jean Middleton's prison memoirs in London in 1998, the author also expressed her disappointment that so little recognition was given to women's role in the struggle.[152]

Serious implications follow from these absences. The historical record of the liberation struggle is skewed through the exclusion of the crucial role of women (many of whom kept alive the underground network of resistance and the public visibility of the cause) and through silencing the memory of women's prison experiences. On another level, these absences perhaps register the difficulties involved in adequately representing the psychic dimension of relations under apartheid in any public forum—the embodied experience of a museum display, for example. How can material culture signal the texture and complexities of courage, compromise, and denial that comprise the lived experience of juggling the demands and desires for a private and domestic existence, on the one hand, with the daily terrors and slow erosion of personal dignities involved in working for social change in a fascist police state on the other?

Given the enthusiasm for commemorative projects and the drive to establish heritage sites relevant to the new dispensation after 1994, the lack of acknowledgment of women's role has often struck me. Perhaps it is no accident that a projected film series, *Women in the Struggle,* never made it beyond the treatment stage. Directed in 1993–1994 by Barry Feinberg (ANC activist and cofounder and former director of the Mayibuye Centre) a ten-minute preview was produced for a much longer project on women in the liberation struggle, but the series has never found the funding for completion.[153] In the preview, Liz Abrahams, Elizabeth Mafekeng, Dorothy Mfaco, Ray Alexander, Nyami Goniwe, and Nomaindia Mfeketo speak movingly of their experiences as union activists and political organizers during apartheid and of the particular challenges, frustrations, and devastating emotional and personal consequences of juggling domestic life with the public demands of the struggle and imprisonment.

There have been a few other notable attempts to reinscribe women's contribution to the liberation struggle as part of public culture. In December 1995 there was a proposal to relocate seven busts of former premiers (including Strijdom, Verwoerd, and Vorster) from their positions in the Parliament buildings in Cape Town and replace them with a series of sixteen portraits of women activists by Sue Williamson. These would have included Winnie Mandela, Nokukhanya Luthuli, Albertina Sisulu, Helen Joseph, Jenny Schoon, Mamphela Ramphele, and Lilian Ngoyi. Although never permanently replacing the apartheid premiers, Williamson's portraits were at least temporarily exhibited in Parliament. Interestingly, in 1995, there was no suggestion that the premiers' busts should be removed but rather (in nineteenth-century salon terms) "skied"—that is, elevated (usually to a less prominent position), in this case to niches above their original location in the gallery.[154] While the decision to move the former premiers had apparently been taken in August that year, implementation was slow because of fears about whether their new "home" would be able to support the weight of their granite pedestals, each of the men's busts weighing about one ton![155]

The millennium year was (or should have been) significant for women in South Africa. Phase One of the project to commission a women's monument (part of the newly established search for appropriate heritage sub-

40. Aerial view of Union Buildings in Pretoria marking proposed location of the Monument to the Women of South Africa. Entry form for the competition for the monument. DACST.

jects), the Legacy Project, began on 9 August 1998 at a Women's Day celebration at the Union Buildings. The deputy minister of arts, culture, science and technology, Brigitte Mabandla, renamed the amphitheater of the Union Buildings Malibongwe Mbokodweni (the place of women) and at the same time opened an exhibition dedicated to the role of women in the fall of apartheid.[156] In August 2000 the first such monument to commemorate women was ceremoniously unveiled. The monument was located at the site of the historic women's march of 9 August 1956, in which a multiracial crowd of about twenty thousand women converged on the Union Buildings in Pretoria to protest the extension of the detested pass laws to black women (the proposed site is shown in figure 40).[157] The protest marked acknowledgment of the power of women's strategic organization by both the ANC and other political organizations associated with the liberation movement as well as the ruling National Party. At a time when many have felt that women's vital role in the overthrow of the apartheid state has been sorely neglected in favor of a more monolithic representation of the liberation movement, this monument has come none to soon.

As the women waited to deliver petitions to Prime Minister Strijdom on that August day in 1956, they sang the hymn "Nkosi Sikilela iAfrika," which has since become South Africa's national anthem; it was followed by a rallying call now indelibly associated with women's struggles of all kinds in South Africa: *Wathint 'abafazi Wathint 'imbokodo Uzokufa* (You have tampered with the women. You have struck a rock. You will be crushed). The "rock"—the "imbokodo" of the refrain—is in fact a grinding stone, and the centerpiece of the new monument is indeed a grinding stone (figure 41). This is placed where the two wings of the Union Buildings meet at the top of the amphitheater, where the historic gathering congregated in 1956. Wilma Cruise and Marcus Holmes's winning design is intended to be an interactive sculpture. Once at the top of the steps (whose risers bear steel phrases from the women's petitions—figure 42), the visitor activates a tape of women's voices chanting the rallying call in the eleven official languages of the "new" South Africa. As the visitor moves around the columns supporting the small, domed antechamber between the two wings of the Union Buildings, a roving projection of the same words in the eleven languages meanders across the structure. In daylight the visual effect is muted but the audio component is heightened, giving the impression of suddenly finding oneself surrounded by quiet but insistent voices from the past. Rayda Becker, one of the judges of the commission, discusses this component of the monument in terms of a search by the artists to find an equivalent for the tradition of orality in many African cultures.[158] Intimate and paradoxically diminutive in scale, the monument's centerpiece invites the action of kneeling and recalls the specifically gendered (women's) labor of grinding.

As is the case with most commemorative structures worth their salt, the Monument to the Women of South Africa is no stranger to controversy and has been widely criticized as well as praised.[159] Mostly it is precisely the intimacy of scale that comes in for attack. A number of women participating in the inauguration of the monument criticized what they felt to be its lack of monumentality. Some suggested more conventional markers of respect— for example, statues of the leaders of the women's march.[160] ANC Women's League members opposed the grinding stone as too small and insignificant.[161] On the other hand, Luli Callinicos, chair of the judging committee, recalled that during the unveiling ceremonies one of the original marchers, wearing her ANC Women's League gown, removed it and knelt beside the imbokodo, miming the action of grinding. Becker also mentions veterans from the march being photographed "laboring" at the grinding stone.[162] Others felt that the symbolism of the imbokodo gave the piece a rural focus that did not adequately represent the technical and material advances since

41. Wilma Cruise and Marcus Holmes, detail from Monument to the Women of South Africa. Mixed media. Pretoria, 2000. Photo by the author.

Below 42. Detail from Monument to the Women of South Africa showing the steps inlaid with stainless steel lettering, with the words from the women's petition. Photo by the author.

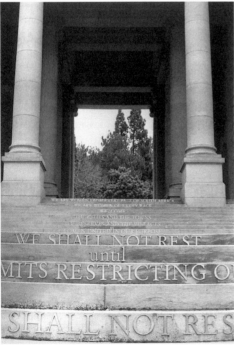

the march. In his opening address, however, Mbeki praised the monument as an important acknowledgment of rural women's struggle: "Only with the contribution of women in our rural areas can we bring an end to the poverty of our people."[163] Another difficulty, acknowledged by the judges, was the unevenness in the applications for the commission and the need for more careful training opportunities so that a broader range of art students and artists could be represented. (This was despite DACST's provision of some training workshops at the Pretoria Technikon in June and July 1999 for disadvantaged art students and artists who did not have access to useful technological developments.)[164]

In most cases there is considerable care to consult with the constituencies that would in any way be represented by such a monument or memorial. In this case, at least one of the judges on the committee was a veteran of the 1956 march, so at some level, consultation had certainly taken place. However, in March 2000 the mothers of the Guguletu Seven were extremely angry when a monument was erected to their sons, who had been brutally murdered by the police. The mothers claimed that not only had they not been consulted, but they also felt that the monument was inappropriate and—more to the point—incomprehensible to them. One of the mothers, Cynthia Ngewu, reported that she and the other mothers were thinking of ways to generate funds to erect their own monument.[165] A spokesperson for the Institute for Justice and Reconciliation, one of the bodies involved in discussing appropriate reparations for victims of apartheid, said that the issue of appropriate memorials was of critical importance but one that was very hard to resolve with many parties feeling inadequately consulted. The other problem they faced was a lack of experience in honoring the survivors and victims of apartheid.

More disturbing perhaps is the issue of access to the Monument to the Women of South Africa. When I was planning to see the new monument, I received the news that I would have to get ministerial clearance to visit the first "public" monument to mark womens' role in the liberation struggle. Luckily contacts in the Ministry of Arts and Culture were extremely helpful, and a date was set. In Pretoria I contacted the DACST office for the visit. The first difficulty came when, on the advice of Luli Callinicos, I mentioned that I understood the monument was a multimedia sound and light installation and that I was looking forward to experiencing it. This was to prove an almost insuperable request, and it looked likely that I would have to make another appointment at some unspecified time in an increasingly distant future. The key to switch the installation on was apparently too difficult to obtain from the Office of Public Works in Pretoria, and my contact would consequently have to make time in a busy schedule to go to Johannesburg to get another copy! I explained that since the monument was designed to be seen and heard in a particular way, I felt that it would be unfair to the artists if I were to write about it under less than optimal conditions. As unforeseen as the problem of the absent key had been, its resolution came as swiftly. On to the next hurdle.

When I arrived at the Union Buildings with my contact from the ministry, the policeman at the foot of the steps leading to the amphitheater refused us entry. Notwithstanding the protestations of the DACST representative, it looked as if we were destined to share only a virtual experience of the monument. However, the fortuitous presence of the head of security and a number of intense phone conversations produced the desired effect. We were on our way. With only one other minor complication and elaborate prohibitions against our taking photographs that might also glimpse a section of the Union Buildings, the visit passed off extremely pleasantly, with the additional benefit of the knowledgeable insights of Alicia Monis, my guide and facilitator.

If this is the way an official "public" monument is understood in a democratic South Africa, it inevitably raises some questions regarding the role and function of any such commemorative structure. The question of access has been such an issue that it was felt necessary to provide an official response in the national press. Consequently, Rob Adam, then director-general of the DACST, stated that "There would be structured access as you have, for example, at the White House."[166] Tour buses would be able to visit between, for example, 8 A.M. and noon, and might need special appointments.

This Byzantine procedure for gaining access to a "public" monument was also remarked on by a number of the artists submitting proposals; some of them were driven to abandon the prospect of designing anything in the so-called preferred location of the amphitheater in the Union Buildings simply because they could not get in there.[167] In some instances, this led to creative uses of city space and metaphors of travel and journeys that the memory of the march encourages. Indeed further phases of the project aim to incorporate two such "runners-up" in the future. Both are notable for involving women from all over the country: one to make mosaic pathways, with the intention of disrupting the formal classicism of the official structures of the Union Buildings, and the other in having women hand in their passbooks so that they can be encased in resin blocks and set in the paving that makes up Strijdom Square, thereby (in the words of the artists who conceived the project) "symbolically presenting their case to Strijdom in perpetuity. This should also reinterpret this space to render it acceptable to the broader community."[168] In fact the existing monument to Strijdom (seen in fig. 2) is one of the best justifications for the intimacy of scale of Cruise and Holmes's monument. Its gargantuan dimensions render it completely invisible to the passing crowds. Disinterest is the order of the day.

The significance of the 1956 women's march for the construction of a meaningful national history was further undermined during the inauguration of the Monument to the Women of South Africa. Journalists and politicians inevitably used the occasion to discuss other contentious issues that they deemed specifically "women's issues." Violence against women and women's relationship to the HIV / AIDS pandemic were the two most frequently cited. AIDS and HIV have of course become controversial topics, especially in the wake of Thabo Mbeki's various public statements, which many have interpreted as a denial of the link between the HIV virus and AIDS. (Similarly Mbeki's reluctance to invest in relatively economical drug regimes that could protect unborn children from HIV infection has been widely criticized.) Consequently, the inauguration ceremonies diluted what should have been at the center: the importance of women's activism in the history of the liberation movement and the valuable example of their extraordinary bravery for the youth of contemporary South Africa.

It is interesting that the only other contemporary memorial or monument to a South African woman is the memorial park and "wall of hope" dedicated to the memory of Gugu Dlamini, who worked to further AIDS awareness in various local communities in Durban (figure 43). As the dedication plaque in the park states, "She publicly revealed her HIV positive status on radio and television, as part of a campaign of Acceptance and Disclosure. Her statement was resented and she was brutally assaulted by a mob, resulting in her death on 14 December 1998." The park was renamed on World AIDS Day, 1 December 2000, in her honor. The wall (figure 44), designed by artists Jeremy Wafer and Georgia Sarkin, was conceived as a focal point for the rededication of the park, and the project was led in part by Rooksana Omar, director of the innovative KwaMuhle Local History Museum, who had in mind the Vietnam War Memorial and the Wailing Wall in Jerusalem as models.[169] The wall is in effect a fairly intimate ritual space, offering small niches for individual or group acts of commemoration or prayer offerings. Like the women's monument in Pretoria, it is deliberately understated, providing a more contemplative space than another AIDS monument

43. Grave of Gugu Dlamini on the day of its unveiling. Red Hill Cemetery, 14 December 2000. Photo by Nicholas Thomas.

Below 44. Jeremy Wafer and Georgia Sarkin, Gugu Dlamini Memorial Wall. Glass and concrete. Gugu Dlamini Park, Durban 2000. Photo by the author.

45. AIDS monument in Gugu Dlamini Park, Durban. Mosaic by Clive van den Berg. Photo by the author.

in the same park, a huge AIDS ribbon arching above a gloriously flamboyant mosaic (figure 45).[170]

This chapter began with an analysis of the debates concerning the future of Robben Island as a national heritage site for the "new" South Africa, as a means of introducing some of the complications arising out of attempts to provide accessible accounts of a liberation movement when this is also a foundational narrative of a "new" national history. It ends with another "public" commission to commemorate what many historians have argued was a crucial turning point in South Africa's liberation struggle—the women's march against the extension of the pass laws in 1956. One of these is a thriving international and national "heritage" tourist destination, and the other is virtually impossible to visit.

As we have seen, South Africa is not the only country where the actual or perceived desires of an international audience might conflict with the desires of both a projected national audience and a local constituency that itself is highly differentiated socially and politically. The pressures of international tourism, political expediency, or the ubiquitous tyranny of the "sound bite" can all result in the collapse of more nuanced and dialectical accounts of historical experience. Furthermore, the examples discussed in this chapter demonstrate the fissures that develop as soon as there are attempts to integrate personal with national history, private with public memory, and the small stories of everyday refusal to comply with the apartheid state with the grand narratives of heroic resistance.

3

DISTRICT SIX

The Archaeology of Memory

Language shows clearly that memory is not an instrument for exploring the past but its theatre. It is the medium of past experience, as the ground is the medium in which dead cities lie interred. He who seeks to approach his own buried past must conduct himself like a man digging. . . . He must not be afraid to return again and again to the same matter, to scatter it as one scatters earth, to turn it over as one turns over soil. For the matter itself is only a deposit, a stratum, which yields only to the most meticulous examination what constitutes the real treasure hidden in the earth: the images, severed from all earlier associations, that stand—like precious fragments or torsos in a collector's gallery—in the prosaic rooms of our later understanding.
—Walter Benjamin, "Berlin Chronicle"

And pale faces slept with black faces in District Six. They didn't feel, sense and permeate that difference, or the idea that they were different.—Anwah Nagia

If one of the legacies of the apartheid era is the alienation of individuals and communities from their own histories—so much so that aspects of those histories are either ignored through disinterest or willfully exploited for other ends and in the process destroyed—then the case of District Six is an important exception. More than almost any other site, this area of denuded land in the heart of Cape Town's prosperous downtown has been the locus of public debates on the abstract concepts of history, heritage, commemoration, memory, and nostalgia. Like its neighbor, Robben Island, District Six has assumed an iconic status, taking it beyond the local register and moving it into the national league so that in a sense it has become metonymic of all those dehumanizing instances of forced removals that were an integral part of apartheid's master plan from the 1950s onward.

It is worth considering the District Six story in the aftermath of apartheid in comparison to that of Robben Island. Both symbolize different aspects of the liberation struggle; both have different kinds of significance at the local, national, and international levels and for different audiences, which require various and not always compatible acts of commemoration. Both have also spawned a small industry of autobiographical accounts—by inmates in the case of Robben Island and by residents of the once thriving, culturally and ethnically diverse area known as District Six. In some notable cases, inmates of the former were also residents of the latter.[1] My aim in this chapter is not simply to counterpose one site against the other in order to rank them in some kind of moral meritocracy, but rather to look comparatively at these two extraordinary sites as a way of exploring different forms of embodied, difficult, and contested memory attached to locations with a heroic and iconic status.

As Vincent Kolbe, member of the Board of Trustees and a founder of the District Six Museum, has observed, "The connection between the two places, so central to the history of our country generally, has never been coherently documented." In relation to District Six, he has said, "There were too many 'clevers' there. It represented non-racial cosmopolitan living, everything the apartheid regime feared—and it was a prime piece of land worth stealing."[2] It is worth noting that from the start many different constituencies considered the apartheid government's policy with regard to District Six controversial; some of them were residents in the area, but the potent mix also comprised local government bureaucrats, councillors, and liberal intellectuals. It is the way this mix held particular tensions in place that largely accounts for the unprecedented success in blocking the business development of the area, unlike District Six's counterparts in Sophiatown, outside Johannesburg, and Cato Manor in Durban. In particular, the wholesale removals represented a slap in the face to the principle of local government autonomy. Such tensions were palpable in the 1980s during the state of emergency, when Prime Minister P. W. Botha stated in no uncertain terms that "District Six is a blot which the government has cleared up and will continue to clear up."[3] Brand, the Cape Town city engineer and a representative of the provincial government, held quite a different view, however: "The decay of District Six was not so much a blot on the City's scape, but a blot on the City's conscience."[4] Backed by the former city engineer, S. S. Morris, Brand advocated, instead of removal, subsidized housing close to the city center for city workers "in order to inject new life into the economically depressed central area."[5]

While District Six represented a particular set of anxieties for South Africa's apartheid government, such mixed areas have historically often been the locus of moral panics elsewhere—in Britain and the United States, for example. Ports in particular—sites of constant international comings and goings—conjure up the specter of irreversible change and the dissolution of imagined "fixed" and stable identities to those of a xenophobic cast of mind. Cardiff's Tiger Bay, London's Docklands, and Liverpool 8, a district in one of Britain's largest port cities, have all, like District Six, been the seats of intense anxiety owing to the perceived "threat" of miscegenation. The language of progress adopted by the various governments of the day to "deal" with the "problems" such areas represented was the same rhetoric of slum clearance and public hygiene that the apartheid government deployed in District Six. As a result, whole communities were displaced, dispersed, and "resettled" in more "suitable" accommodations. This shared history is another reason why District Six, with its persistent protests, resistance, and resilience against all odds, has assumed an iconic status both in South Africa and with a wider international public.

Another "problem" represented by District Six is intimated by Kolbe's remark and concerns issues of class as much as color. The port areas I have mentioned were all working class in origin. They also all became thriving cosmopolitan districts of their respective cities. And this, I think, goes to the heart of the "problem": since the areas were both working class and cosmopolitan, many of the people in them were seen as "having ideas above their station." Certainly many individuals from such "hybrid" communities have transcended the limitations of their origins to become significant contributors in literature, the theater, music, and art. More to the point, under apartheid what was construed as the problematic conjuncture of working-class origins, cosmopolitan aspirations, and being African or "colored" has left a complicated legacy. This means that the memory of District Six is not easily accommodated in the "new" South Africa either. The uneasy positioning of the memory of District Six within the new dispensation is most visible around the setting up and maintenance of the District Six Museum.

Despite the overwhelming evidence of local, national, and international interest, the District Six Museum (which is essentially the public face of the District Six story) receives a minimal government grant, whereas Robben Island snapped up 80 percent of the government grant for "arts, cultural and heritage institutions" in 1998.[6] In 1996 the museum received

R 200,000 from DACST and was told that this was a one-off grant. This was at a time when the government was spending R 1.5 million on the Oorlogs-museum van die Boererepubliek (the War Museum of the Boer Republics) in Bloemfontein; R 801,000 on the Afrikaans Language Museum; and R 1.2 million on the Voortrekker Monument Museum. Such a situation was bound to fuel resentment—particularly when hopes were especially high following the election of Mandela's government—and a number of the national papers picked up on what seemed to be a discrepancy in the kind of heritage projects in which the government was prepared to invest.[7] As a result of poor government funding, the museum has relied heavily on funding from external foreign agencies to survive as an institution.[8] While a greater degree of autonomy from state funding perhaps enables a critical distance and independence, this "freedom" inevitably comes at a cost.

A relatively new government initiative has given national recognition to fifteen museums and heritage sites in and around Cape Town. These now form part of a government consortium called Iziko, which means "a hearth" in Xhosa and which, according to the promotion leaflet, also means "the centre of cultural activity."[9] Furthermore, the leaflet proclaims itself "a comprehensive guide to museums of Cape Town."[10] Neither Robben Island nor District Six is included in Iziko (also known as the Southern Flagship). In the former case RIM opted out of the Southern Flagship and acquired the exceptional status of a third flagship or national museum, despite the fact that the government was publicly committed to having only two flagships, in the north and south of the country. The District Six Museum, on the other hand, has always been keen to gain recognition as a national institution, but by 2001 it had still not managed to wrest such acknowledgment from the government.[11] It has, however, received considerable recognition outside South Africa. For example, it has been voted one of the world's nine "Historic Site Museums of Conscience," together with the Lower East Side Tenement Museum and the National Park Service in the United States, the Maison des Esclaves in Senegal, the Liberation War Museum in Bangladesh, the Pamatnik Terezin in the Czech Republic, the Workhouse in the United Kingdom, the Proyecto Recordar in Argentina, and the Gulag Museum in Russia. The shared belief of this group is "that it is the obligation of historical sites to assist the public in drawing connections between the history of our sites and its contemporary implications. We view stimulating dialogue on pressing social issues and promoting humanitarian and democratic values as a primary function."[12]

For the tourist to South Africa with even a modicum of curiosity about the political histories of the country, Robben Island and District Six are two of the indispensable items on one's itinerary. It is certainly true that out of a number of sites / sights all equally significant for such histories, these two are likely to be the most consistently packed with eager visitors. Given District Six's prominence in the national and international memory, it is odd, therefore, that the government is so reticent about providing financial support to the museum. Partly because of the striking distinction between the status of these two prominent heritage sites, I became interested in the differences and similarities between RIM and the District Six Museum as commemorative projects for the emergence of the new nation.

In some senses, both museums are about finding ways to embody and to speak the unspeakable—about trauma, imprisonment, separation, and loss. Both share the need to reanimate particular spaces—the empty prison and the empty city center. They are also insistently about finding a way to incorporate an acknowledgment of trauma in a form of commemoration that is also a means of recovering memory for the construction of a better future. Kathrada's now famous words at the opening of "Esiqithini" are a forceful reminder.[13] Similarly, when the District Six Museum was opened, a banner proclaimed: "In this exhibition, we do not wish to recreate District Six as much as repossess the history of the area as a place where people lived, loved, and struggled. It is an attempt to take back our right to signpost our lives with those things we hold dear. . . . The exhibition is also about pointers to our future. We, all of us, need to decide how as individuals and as a people we wish to retrace and re-signpost the lines of our future. Such a process is neither easy nor straightforward. It is not predictable either."[14]

While both Kathrada's address and this proclamation are intentions to look to the future, the differences in the way such an agenda is phrased are important here. The first seems an appeal to a universalizing notion of abstract values of humanity, courage, and honor while the second is mediated by qualifications, doubts, and the recognition of the tensions that will inevitably be involved in such a mission.[15]

COMMUNITY

Both sites present versions of "struggle" history, but they offer very different ways of embodying it. In particular, the concept of "community," which is so favored in the rhetoric of transformation and reconstruction and which has been mobilized by both the District Six Museum and Robben Island, is interpreted distinctly. The most important distinction is that the Robben Island version of "community" is allowed to stand for the "nation," while the District Six version is systematically relegated to an idea of "community" that remains intractably local. Robben Island's "community" was not voluntarily on the island, of course, but was bound together unwillingly. Although it shared some aspects of a political agenda, tensions evidently existed among a number of different factions—for example, between the political and the ordinary criminal; among PAC, ANC, and Non-European Unity members; and between younger and older generations. Despite such friction, the overwhelming impression from any tour of the island is one of unity against adversity, thus giving the sense of a coherent "community" cemented by common values and shared politics—namely, those of the ANC.

Certainly the commemorative language and pictorial and material narratives suggested by the displays at the District Six Museum are similarly productive of myths and fantasies, but they are also structurally distinct from those constructed by RIM. The unifying myth here relies on nostalgic reminiscence about the rich diversity of the communities in District Six before the forced removals, begun in 1966 and continuing until 1981 and resulting in the displacement of about 55,000–65,000 people. The "zone" is metonymic of any subversion of the apartheid regime's attempt to implement a policy of "separate development." In the words of one commentator, District Six "proved" that all creeds and colors could live together in harmony.[16] The museum's curator, Sandra Prosalendis, summarizes District Six's significance for urban history: "District Six is remembered by many who had lived there as a place where they were able to cross religious, class and social boundaries. As a place where they were able to share their everyday experiences and to live not as 'coloured', 'whites', 'Africans' or 'Indians' but as South Africans, District Six occupies a special place in the history of South Africa."[17] It was a fundamental embarrassment to the apartheid government, as were the similarly "mixed" areas of the East End in Port Elizabeth and Vrededorp and Doomfontein in Johannesburg, which Prosalendis takes care to mention.[18] District Six was not, after all, the only instance of forced removals. Cato Manor in Durban and Sophiatown outside Johannesburg are two such instances that have also lived on in the national memory.[19] The museum marks this with a plaque at its entrance:

> Remember Dimbaza. Remember Botshabelo / Onverwacht, South End, East Bank, Sophiatown, Makuleke, Cato Manor. Remember District Six. Remember the racism which took away our homes and our livelihood and which sought to steal away our humanity. Remember also our will to live, to hold fast to that which marks us as human beings: our generosity, our love of justice and our care for each other. Remember Tramway Road, Modderdam, Simonstown.
>
> In remembering we do not want to recreate District Six but to work with

its memory: of hurts inflicted and received, of loss, achievements and of shames. We wish to remember so that we can all, together and by ourselves rebuild a city which belongs to all of us, in which all of us can live, not as races but as people.

The concept of "community" invoked here seems, then, to embody the "rainbow nation" of Mandela's first government. This makes exclusion from the nationally recognized heritage trail even more remarkable. It may not be insignificant that many of the key figures involved in the museum were not affiliated with the ANC but were members of the Non-European Unity Movement or (as Lionel Davis and Neville Alexander, for example) were members of the Trotskyist National Liberation Front.[20] Such a history of political alliances—coupled with a desire by some of the more prominent spokespeople to recall a "community" that is neither predominantly "colored," "white," or "black," nor Christian, Muslim, or Jewish, but rather a hybrid melting pot of all these constituencies—makes the "remembering" of District Six a highly volatile and controversial activity in the Western Cape. This is mainly because District Six cannot be "claimed" by either of the parties of government in the province. The ANC cannot claim it as wholly its own, but neither can the National Party, who controversially courted a separatist "colored" vote in the Western Cape in the 1994 elections and was returned as the party of local government largely, some would argue, on the basis of this sector's support.[21]

Robben Island and District Six, then, offer fundamentally different narratives of a history of an apartheid city. As we have seen, the Robben Island narratives largely exclude women's contributions to the liberation struggle, not necessarily willfully but by virtue of the fact that the Robben Island story (a story whose primary protagonists are black male prisoners) is so often promoted and received (abroad) as *the* paradigmatic South African liberation history. In addition, as noted, the tours tend not to allow for any elaboration of the fissures and tensions that did exist. The island is hampered, of course, by the perceived need to "process" a large number of visitors each day and deal with the logistics of ferrying and moving them through the site in a limited time.

The District Six Museum, on the other hand, has the benefit of both a dedicated building and the possibility of animating a much larger area of the city. Both aspects are deployed in such a way as to promote a space for contemplation, which inevitably opens up a number of stories for consumption. There is no prescribed order, no linear narrative, but rather a series of spaces that facilitate reflection. These spaces are constantly "in process" through the interaction of ex-residents and other visitors. Steven Robins, a lecturer in the Department of Anthropology and Sociology at the University of the Western Cape, noted another distinctive aspect of the District Six Museum experience. Robins argued that the TRC, by focusing on the worst crimes committed under apartheid, could unwittingly encourage amnesia about the more insistent and continuous aspects of human rights violations under the regime. Thus for him the District Six Museum is distinct from the grand heroizing commemorative project of Robben Island in one crucial regard: "It recollects what Hannah Arendt has called the every day 'banality of evil.'"[22] For Robins the museum performs an important function by helping to guard against the amnesia that enables many to "forget" their part in sustaining apartheid by shifting the blame onto notorious individuals often presented as "aberrations": "The museum suggests to me that apartheid was not exclusively about psychopathic killers such as De Kock. It was largely the result of a 'rational' and modern bureaucracy armed with a sophisticated technology of surveillance and social control."[23]

In addition, in many ways the District Six Museum initiative ideally fulfills the criteria debated in January 1997 in a series of workshops organized by the NMC and the International Council on Monuments and Sites (ICOMOS) with the aim of drawing up a South African charter for heritage conservation.[24] The workshops took as their starting point "the fact that until recently conservationists, architects and planners have looked at places and objects and judged their significance in terms of factors associated with their physical qualities, the physical remnants of our collective past, like authenticity, intactness, stylistic purity. Now we were going to think about the issues of representing and reflecting the intangible culture, memory, the hidden history, values, experience, the social and cultural fabric of communities and find ways to celebrate them."[25]

The District Six Museum has no permanent "collection" as such but rather relies on the testimony of ex-residents and the fragmentary remains of their possessions, often literally unearthed from the debris of demolition. Theirs are the intimate histories of (extra)ordinary lives lived in an apartheid city, and not only are they the strength of the museum, but they also helped to bring it into existence. Where better to test the NMC and ICOMOS agenda than in a site dedicated to a location that to all intents and purposes no longer exists in its former physical form, but that as a memory and a concept embodies all the attributes of a vibrant "community" that refused the "logic" of the apartheid state? Freud's insistence that the unconscious needs to be understood topographically delivers a useful and by now familiar metaphor for the way repression hinders the processes of memory and how we understand its effects on the unconscious. For Freud the analyst and patient are involved in a joint project of excavation.[26] It is hard to resist seeing the District Six Museum project through the lens provided by Freud's metaphor.[27] More than this, the museum, the site of the old District Six, and the memory work that is taking place are paradigmatic. As Peggy Delport, the chief curator, has argued, "Above all, the name District Six retains its role in contemporary South Africa as a symbol of the will to remember."[28]

There are inevitably problems with any reminiscing that tends toward an idealistic nostalgia, reproducing the experience of living in District Six as an idyllic, harmonious environment immune to political tensions and personal antagonisms. Indeed this aspect of the representation of the District both within and beyond the museum has come under criticism from some ex-residents themselves.[29] Looked at another way, however, a nostalgia that produces this image of District Six also serves to undermine the bureaucratic langauge of sanitation and public hygiene deployed by the apartheid demolition teams that so ruthlessly and effectively masked the more positive human aspects of the cheek-by-jowl existence that was the District Six experience of the poorer inhabitants. It seems, then, that a certain kind of nostalgic memorializing may serve important and productive functions given the reconstructive and transformative South African context.

Nostalgia has been theorized by some as the search for an "impossible object." Susan Stewart's psychoanalytic analysis characterizes the "prevailing motif of nostalgia" as "the erasure of the gap between nature and culture, and hence a return to the utopia of biology and symbol united within the walled city of the maternal. The nostalgic's utopia is prelapsarian, a genesis where lived and mediated experience are one, where authenticity and transcendence are both present and everywhere."[30] She continues: "This point of desire which the nostalgic seeks is in fact the absence which is the very generating mechanism of desire. . . . The realisation of re-union imagined by the nostalgic is a narrative utopia that works only by virtue of its partiality, its lack of fixity and closure: nostalgia is the desire for desire."[31] Others have attempted to move beyond this "impossible object," which at some level is also inevitably a denial of historical processes and complexities. Debbora Battaglia discusses the importance for urban Trobriand Islanders of nostalgia for the gardens of "home" (the Trobriand Islands), as opposed to the houses that have been their actual homes over the twenty years that they have been working for cash in Port Moresby (Papua New Guinea).[32]

Her analysis is particularly pertinent when considering the roles nostalgia might serve in the remembering of District Six. She offers a "practical or active nostalgia," characterized as "transformative action with a connective purpose, and the affective and aesthetic quality of an indulgence," as an alternative to an understanding of nostalgia solely as a form of regressive historicism.[33] She observes: "It is in this variety that nostalgic connection may also be imagined toward a past object without necessarily being the enemy of unformulated future relationships. Indeed, nostalgia for a sense of future—for an experience, however imaginary, of possessing the means of controlling the future—may function as a powerful force for social re-connection. In permitting creative lapses from dominant realities, it is such a nostalgia that enables or recalls to practice more meaningful patterns of relationship and self-action."[34]

Svetlana Boym, writing about forms of nostalgia in post-Soviet Russia, attempts "a typology . . . of some of nostalgia's mechanisms of seduction and manipulation" that similarly provides some insight into the possible uses of nostalgia in relation to District Six.[35] In particular, she suggests a distinction between what she calls "restorative" and "reflective" nostalgia:

> Restorative nostalgia . . . attempts a transhistorical reconstruction of the lost home. Reflective nostalgia thrives in . . . the longing itself, and delays the homecoming. . . . Restorative nostalgia does not think of itself as nostalgia, but rather as truth and tradition. Reflective nostalgia dwells on the ambivalences of human longing and belonging and does not shy away from the contradictions of modernity. Restorative nostalgia protects the absolute truth, while reflective nostalgia calls it into doubt. Restorative nostalgia is at the core of recent national and religious revivals; it knows two main plots—the return to origins and the conspiracy. Reflective nostalgia does not follow a single plot but explores ways of inhabiting many places at once and imagining different time zones; it loves detail, not symbols.[36]

Indeed, this distinction may aptly characterize the memory work being done via the museum in District Six. The remembering here shares many of the characteristics of a reflective model of nostalgia, especially in its tendency to explore contradictions and tensions in the historical memory of the place.

Given the specific context provided by the TRC of a very public remembering of loss, separation, and violation, it is easier to understand the way that District Six has come to serve what we might appreciate as a "necessary" paradigm of prelapsarian wholeness—a concept of "community" that not only denied apartheid, but also presumed, at times, an (impossibly) harmonious and unified population prior to apartheid and possibly colonialism. The museum proposes nothing less than a utopian moment and, by implication, future. Perhaps also nostalgia is a necessary stage in the "owning" of painful and difficult memories that may involve collusion with the apartheid bureaucracy or other smaller and larger betrayals. In this sense, it is useful to think about the District Six Museum project in terms of three concepts that can also in this case be used as metaphors: reminiscence, excavation, and reconstruction.

The first "exhibition" in the Central Methodist Church in Buitenkant Street, which has since become the permanent home of the District Six Museum, was opened on 10 December 1994. "Streets: Retracing District Six" consisted of displays of a series of reclaimed street signs from the old District Six (figure 46).[37] The story of their reclamation assumes the shape of a wonderfully ironic fairy tale. Some of the museum staff had got wind that David Elrick, the apartheid bureacrat responsible for supervising the demolition of District Six, had, perversely, kept the street signs of the area he had reduced to rubble. While the district's houses, cinemas, and music halls became landfill to support the Duncan Dock extension in Table Bay and the map of the cultural landscape was literally demolished, the signposts that proclaimed their existence were secreted away by the very man responsible for their demise. Sandra Prosalendis's account of the negotiations to procure these signs is indicative of the conflicting interests involved in restoring "memory" to the site: "Negotiations were difficult: He [Elrick] was anxious about meeting us, scared of being prosecuted for 'war crimes.' Some of our members were bitter and resented him, wanting no dealings with everything he stood for. However, the power of this remaining concrete evidence of District Six was stronger than both fear and anger."[38]

The Central Methodist Church was well known as a sanctuary for political opponents and victims of apartheid. A plaque set into one of its outside walls in 1979 is an apt introduction to the District Six Museum: "All who pass by. Remember with shame the many thousands of people who lived for generations in District Six and other parts of this city, and were forced by law to leave their homes because of the colour of their skins. Father forgive us."[39] The building takes the form of a large central hall with a balcony and balustrade running around the sides and held up by decorative ironwork pillars. For this first exhibition the street signs were dropped hanging in ladder formations from the balcony to the ground at both ends of the main hall, and individual signs were supported by the ironwork pillars around the sides. At the bottom of three such ladders were wooden trays with glass

Top 46. Installation view of "Streets: Retracing District Six." Opening exhibition, District Six Museum, Cape Town, 1994. Photo by Jean Brundrit.

Bottom 47. Fragments and objects unearthed from 75 Horstley Street, District Six. Exhibit at the base of the ladder of street signs in "Streets: Retracing District Six." District Six Museum, Cape Town. Photo by Jean Brundrit.

48. Detail of fragments and objects unearthed from 75 Horstley Street, District Six, showing the house plan etched onto the glass lid. District Six Museum, Cape Town. Photo by Jean Brundrit.

lids holding dust, dirt, and the shards and remnants of a daily life that had been salvaged from oblivion, excavated from under the rubble (figure 47). One lid had a floor plan etched onto it (figure 48)—the skeletal remains of a family home, the analogue map of a family life vacated by force. In the bays created at either side of the hall behind the pillars were archive photographs of life on the streets recalled by the signs. Hanging from the upper balcony were large portrait prints of key individuals (civic leaders, artists, and others) associated with the district's history.

Peggy Delport describes the main concerns behind the "Streets" exhibition and the research that went into its making. Many of these concerns remain central to the museum today: "The focus included the notion of accessibility, the creation of a generative arena for historical retrieval and interpretation and the interrelationship of historical method and aesthetics. These concerns were exemplified in the way in which the oral history was given form through the active engagement of narrators in assembling and interpreting their own materials within the museum space. The exhibition was constructed to provide a framework that led viewers into an interactive relationship with the contents."[40] One of the most immediately visible invitations to interact is a long bolt of unbleached calico that scrolls down one corner of the church hall. Every inch of the cloth is covered with signatures and comments. Begun at the time of the opening of the museum, by December 2000 the cloth had over six thousand signatures from former residents (figure 49). The texts are witty, poignant, or simply a statement of being. For example:

> Happy Days
> District Six
> Living was cheap
> Life precious
> Now in Hanover Park
> Living's expensive and
> Life is cheap
> 29 De Korte Straat
> Distrik Ses
> Ronnie Cloete

Or: "Mr. and Mrs. Willie Alexander owned Kinema Cafe, noted for their smoked snoek and boiled eggs. I am Val Moodley [nee] Lawrence. Those were the happiest New Years days where our families picnicked waiting to see the coons." Written in pen directly onto the calico, these have since been embroidered by women from local prisons and unemployed women's embroidery circles. Some of the cloth now provides the curtains in the memorial hall adjacent to the main museum space.[41]

A simple but extraordinarily effective mnemonic device covers the central floor space. Spread over almost the entire surface is a large, laminated map (7 m × 5 m) that reproduces the District Six of the street signs (figure 50). It represents an inhabited network of housing and civic activity that no longer exists. As Prosalendis explains, "The map is a fitting memorial, since, in an attempt to erase District Six from the map of local history [and, one might add, local memory], many of the street names, even the grid itself, were changed to make way for the white suburb of Zonnebloem and the development of the Technikon."[42] The map also recalls Walter Benjamin's observations on Berlin, the city of his childhood.[43] Seeking to account for "insights into [his] life that came in a flash, with the force of an illumination," he insists that it is the space of the city that provided the mnemonic key. An afternoon in Paris "made so apparent what kind of regimen cities keep over imagination, and why the city . . . indemnifies itself in memory, and why the veil it has covertly woven out of our lives shows the images of people less than those of the sites of our encounters with others or ourselves."[44]

Most important, the museum floor is another interactive space where

49. Detail of the signed and embroidered calico cloth. District Six Museum, Cape Town, 2000. Photo by the author.

Below 50. Section of the laminated street map covering the central floor space at the District Six Museum. Cape Town, 1994. Photo by Jean Brundrit.

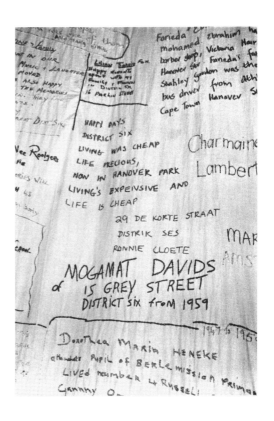

ex-residents put themselves back in the picture by inscribing their names and returning their houses to the map and writing comments, descriptions, poems, and stories. By so doing, they actively reconstruct District Six. One commentator, in an interesting analysis of the ways in which the map works, compares the actions of the ex-residents who write on the map to the walkers in de Certeau's *The Practice of Everyday Life,* who reclaim the city space simply by walking through it in ways that disrupt the intended logic of the urban planners.[45] The analogy with the French Situationists and what they had earlier termed "*détournement*" is curious in one sense, since the acts of inscription in the museum actually reconstruct rather than deconstruct the physical and—perhaps more importantly—the psychic spaces of the old District Six. The disruption that does occur, however, is that the intentions of the apartheid planners are thwarted by this act of recall.

This ritual has recently been extended in the form of a "District Six Walk." A former District Six resident, Stan Abrahams, is the narrator for the self-guided tour, the text of which is in *The District Six Museum Foundation,* the museum's brochure. Abrahams describes himself as part of a "family of nine [living] at 7 De Villiers Street until the 1970s when our family home was bulldozed. We were forcibly removed to various parts of the peninsula."[46] *This* is the kind of walk that radically revises the official view of the city but in an oddly subtle way and one that encourages reflection. These kinds of walks are familiar to the consumer of public history as "heritage trails." One of the features that makes the District Six heritage trail so distinctive is, of course, that the district in its former shape no longer exists. In its place is a landscape of razed, bulldozed rubble stretching into the distance, peppered with resiliant weeds and brave mosques and churches whose congregations refused to have them deconsecrated. This is what is called "salted earth"—the final protest of the departing District Sixers to stop new building on the land until democratic government arrived in South Africa. Amazingly, 35 percent of the original area that was District Six remains as it was when the apartheid government demolished it—a feat in no small measure due to the efforts of the Hands Off District Six Committee (HODSC) and the Ratepayers and Residents Association, whose members were also part of the founding board of trustees that set up the museum, along with the Roman Catholic Church and the Methodist Church.[47] As a result of the history of wholesale destruction and resistance, the District Six version of a heritage trail becomes especially poignant.

The District Six Walk has much in common with historical city walks that reclaim the hidden or, more specifically, masked histories that lie dormant and unremarked in the civic institutions of an otherwise familiar cityscape. This is particularly so where there are embarrassing histories of complicity and degradation upon which the wealth of the contemporary city rests. In the United Kingdom, for example, Bristol and Liverpool share the ignominious notoriety of being Britain's two major slave ports during the transatlantic slave trade. In Liverpool the Merseyside Maritime Museum's guide, the *Transatlantic Slavery History Trail*, is an attempt to redress this past by "owning" it. The port's history is not always evident to the contemporary eye because of the ways in which the city has transformed over time and because of the endemic amnesia that requires forgetfulness for such a shameful past, so the guide enables the walker to see the city in a new light, sometimes subtle, sometimes more obvious:

> Stop and look behind you. Over the roofs of the bungalows you can see the tall narrow Liverpool warehouses. This is the view that would have greeted ships in the Port at the beginning of the nineteenth century. . . . The homes [in Rodney Street] were constructed at the height of the slave trade for the merchant elite of the town. . . . The source of the wealth that flowed into Liverpool is shown by the decoration on the Town Hall. All around the building runs a frieze representing the wealth of Africa to European eyes—lions, crocodiles, elephants and ivory and black Africans. . . . The impressive Barclay's Bank was built next to the Town Hall in 1927 as the head office of Martin's Bank which incorporated Heywood's Bank. Heywood's was founded by Arthur and Benjamin Heywood who had owned slaving vessels such as the Phoebe in 1752.[48]

Against all odds, the District Six Walk reconstructs a sense of place out of far fewer physical remnants, although, as many commentators have noted, the emptiness of the scarred landscape speaks with a special eloquence. At Clifton, Arundel, Richmond, and Horstley Streets we are exhorted to "Try to imagine the terrace of small three-roomed houses that once stood on either side of this cobbled street. If you look closely you can still see the remains of some of the pavement stones."[49] Further on, at number 7 on the map (marked "vacant lot"), we are told, "The area is scarred with many vacant lots where houses once stood. If you look carefully you will be able to see the foundations of the front *stoeps*. From these, people all over the District watched the activities of the street pass by."[50] Outside the old Central Methodist Church (now the museum) at the start of the walk Abrahams introduces us to "his" District Six: "This church which was once the spiritual home of my family, baptised, confirmed, married, and buried us. . . . It has always represented hope to my family and community."[51] His narrator's voice serves to authenticate this view of the district, but more than this, it makes us aware that this is one view among many; it might well be shared, but it could equally be very different. This, then, is another attempt to make the consumer aware that all histories are mediated and that various voices might have a tale to tell. This walking tour is not *the* tour of the district; it is, after all, a personal memoir. Most important, both the slave trail in Liverpool and the District Six Walk defamiliarize the urban landscape, not in the incidental and serendipitous détournements of the Situationists or the Surrealists before them, but in the more deliberately dialectical sense of the Brechtian model.

The District Six Walk is a kind of archaeology in both the Freudian sense of the term noted above and more literally. In February 1996 a ceremony took place to mark the thirtieth anniversary of the first forced removals from District Six after its declaration as a "White Group Area." A component of the ceremonies involved a walk through the streets of the ghostly district and included a visit to the foundations of a family home in Stukeris Street—the recent "finds" of an archaeological excavation. As Martin Hall observed in a report on the work of the community archaeological unit (RESUNACT) at the University of Cape Town, through this walk, "From the church to archaeological site, to mosque, the community was asserting a right to both its history and its monuments. Whether these monuments be a few buildings that have survived demolition, or the foundations of the ordinary house in Stukeris Street."[52] This, then, is a new kind of monument that, while not replacing the "lost" subject it celebrates, nonetheless revives and rearticulates memory through the act of walking itself.

Other attempts have been made to repopulate the old District Six area, to recall the ghosts of the past, to exploit the absent presence of the "cleared" land. *The District Six Public Sculpture Project* gathered together ninety-six artists in September 1997 for a project revolving around several key sites in the former district: the area between Eastern Boulevard and Kaizergracht Street (the apartheid name for Hanover Street, one of the liveliest thoroughfares in the old district); the area around the controversial Technikon, one of the few buildings put up after the forced removals (see below); and the area above Constitution Street. Renate Meyer, one of the initiators of the project (along with Kevin Brand, the curator and an artist himself), describes the larger principle: "Participants had no restrictions placed on the work they produced other than that it had to be sensitive to the issues around District Six. If they weren't from District Six we asked that they consult with ex-residents and spend time at the District Six Museum archive."[53]

The project took place in the wake of the District Six land restitution case and just prior to what people felt would be the onset of a new wave of "development" because compensation had been granted to many of the former residents whose claims had been put through the courts.[54] The resolution of the claims had been one of the motivating forces behind Brand's insistence that the project go ahead at that time. Also debates about heritage and appropriate forms of commemoration were in full swing, and it was no accident that the date chosen for the opening of the project's exhibition was National Heritage Day.[55] The artists' awareness of the imminent redevelopment of the area made their choice of ephemeral commemorative structures even more significant. As Emma Bedford and Tracey Murinik observed, "No vertical static monuments were produced. On the contrary, the works made for this project were without exception anti-monumental, many of them being intentionally transient—destined to disappear or be removed, like the former residents and homes of District Six."[56] Many of the works were, in a vein similar to the museum's own policy, interactive and collaborative, focusing on process rather than a predetermined outcome.

The effect of encountering these scattered and sometimes elusive sculptures was akin to stumbling upon someone's personal shrine to a long lost and dearly beloved friend or relative. Cairns of rough stones, pathways of broken glass, torn paper; Roderick Sauls's bright satin strips, recalling the "strokies" or "colors" denoting the competing minstrel bands of the once famously anarchic "Coon Carnival" (figure 51); Randolph Hartzenberg's salt (as opposed to sand) bags, muffling the familiar timekeeping of St. Mark's church bells, stopping time (figure 52).[57] Nicola Jackson's chalked phrases inducing the senses to perform their memory work: "Fill your nostrils with home"; "Share the same view"; "Lick the taste of salt" (figure 53). The simplicity of Brett Murray's "memory" stickers beside a plaque with the injunction, "Mark a place on District Six that brings back memories." The ephemerality of the materials, the emphasis on found objects and interactive participation, together with the pervasive archaeological metaphors, complimented the museum's representation of the district. The scarred landscape became repopulated with ghosts from the past.

The idea of the area as "haunted" by presences no longer visible but visceral nonetheless is exploited in other ways in the museum itself in two exhibits opened after the museum's refurbishment in September 2000. Roderick Sauls, one of the former residents who had participated in the public sculpture project, constructed a space that he called *A Personal Memory* in 1999. This space is a kind of embodiment of the process of remembering. For a viewer conversant with recent trends in international contemporary conceptual art Sauls's space (known as *Rod's Room* in the museum—figure 54) bears comparison with Rachel Whiteread's *House* (1993), a poignant re-

Above 51. Roderick Sauls, *Moettie My Vi'giettie.* 1997. Wood, metal, silk, 8 m × 2.5 m × 3 m. Photo by P. Warne. Courtesy of the artist.

Left 52. Randolph Hartzenberg, *Salt Tower.* 1997. Bags of salt, 1.1 m × 1.1 m × 1.8 m. Photo by Randolph Hartzenberg. Courtesy of the artist.

Above 53. Nicola Jackson, *Six Senses.* 1997. White dust-free chalk. Photo by Nicola Jackson. Courtesy of the artist.

Right 54. Roderick Sauls, detail of *Rod's Room.* 2000. Mixed media. District Six Museum. Photo by the author. Courtesy of the artist.

55. Rachel Whiteread, southwest view of *House*. 1993. Poured concrete.
Bethnal Green, London. Photo by Nancy Jachec.

minder of the casualties of another case of so-called development, in London's East End (figure 55). The capitalist boom in Margaret Thatcher's 1980s
Britain resulted in an attempt to move the financial center of London to the
site of the old London Docklands. A large-scale building project (unplanned
and without consultation in the local communities) created a spate of new
business premises and middle-class housing estates for the yuppie entrepreneurs who were the envisaged employees in Canary Wharf. It resulted
in the demolition of tracts of long-established working-class and immigrant
housing in London's East End, a densely peopled and historically mixed
area whose populations were consequently displaced from their homes and
communities.

Whiteread's *House* was created in what would now be recognized as the
sculptor's trademark technique of inverted casting, so that what remained
was a block cast of an interior of a Victorian terraced house. Impenetrable
and inviolable, presenting the inside of the house as its exterior and thus
leaving the traces of once-inhabited domestic spaces visible but essentially
redundant as occupiable spaces, Whiteread's *House* was a poignant hymn
to the unremarkable but vital domesticity of the communities who were
forced to make way for the developers. As a sculpture, it gained notoriety
because of the controversy over the local authority's decision to tear it down,
rather in the same vein that the original terraced house had met its fate.
The irony—particularly since Whiteread had meanwhile won the coveted

Turner Prize for her *House*—was not lost on her supporters or on those who wished to interpret her sculpture in the terms I have set out above.[58] I bring in Whiteread's *House* at this juncture not simply to make the usual suggestions about conceptual and formal influence in relation to Sauls's room. This would be a banal and uninteresting exercise. But it seemed to me worth considering the two pieces together as a way of better understanding different but related strategies for producing embodied memory. Both are also monuments of a kind; indeed the controversy over Whiteread's piece could also be seen as a debate regarding the appropriateness of her sculpture as a permanent monument.

Rod's Room has a lot of work to do. Sauls describes what the project means to him:

> I have many memories of the place itself, some vague though tantalising, others more vivid. However, I have a lasting legacy; the objects / artifacts and oral histories of relatives, ex-residents and friends at home. This exhibit explores what memory means to me and also those who experienced nostalgia and loss within our country. In my determination to remember I am constantly reminded of Milan Kundera's famous dictum from the *Book of Laughter and Forgetting*, "the struggle of man against power is the struggle of memory against forgetting." The objective of the exhibit is to restore my lost identity, my African heritage, my culture and memories.[59]

Unlike Whiteread's piece, Sauls's is not a clean inversion of inside / outside, absence / presence, where the interior, while exposed, still resists the viewer's curious gaze. Sauls's room mobilizes a different metaphor. Here the plaster takes on a similar property to the lava that smothered the ancient streets of Herculaneum and Pompeii. It refers to the job of erasing rather than to the work of bringing form into being that Whiteread's cast suggests. The traces of real objects, which are embedded in the plaster walls of Sauls's room, have the quality of breaking through the plaster despite the density of the coating and its attempt to contain and erase the character of the families or individuals whose lives it witnessed. The shoulder of a coat edges its way out of the plaster, and the brim of a hat escapes its tacky grave. The spines of files and books are discernible on what might have been a shelf once, and further around the room the handles of mugs poke through alongside the spout of a half-submerged teapot (figure 56). Like the walls of a cell whose occupant has run out of time, every inch is covered with words—in this instance, terms that have historically been used by the colonizers and by apartheid to define and categorize the various populations of South Africa.

56. Roderick Sauls, detail of *Rod's Room*. 2000. Mixed media. District Six Museum. Photo by the author. Courtesy of the artist.

Nothing is quite as it seems in this room: the Bible resting on the quilt turns out to be an embroidered lexicon of moral and Christian values and even virtues but ends in a litany of discrimination and prejudice. The quilt is a series of screen-printed images of pages from books apparently defining terms and categories that became the basis for justifying the discriminatory practices of apartheid (figure 57). The linoleum floor is a patchwork of scenes of life in District Six—both negative and positive. The signs of domesticity breaking through the plaster begin to seem like the signs of an everyday life escaping the prison of apartheid's skewed logic. This then also seems to be a poignant plea for the quotidian in a context where everything conspired against it. And this is another strength of the District Six Museum: the grand narrative of enforced removals is always mediated by a recognition of the heroism of the every day, of the domestic, of the street. The quotidian is acknowledged, in other words, as an integral part of the grand narrative.

Nomvuyo's Room (figure 58) is entered by an unassuming door from the main hall of the museum. In many ways its museological strategy is related to the rooms in Museum Africa discussed in chapter 4. There are some notable differences, however. *Nomvuyo's Room* is a "real" space—it is a room one chooses to enter and leave, so the visitor gets the feeling of entering someone else's domestic interior. Nomvuyo Ngcelwane, a Xhosa woman,

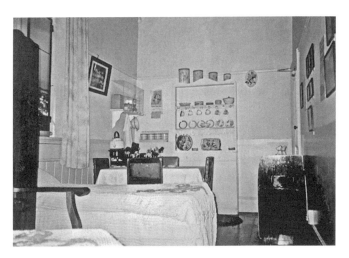

Top 57. Roderick Sauls, detail of quilt and cloth Bible with "immorality" embroidered onto the page. *Rod's Room*. 2000. Photo by the author. Courtesy of the artist.

Bottom 58. Nomvuyo Ngcelwane, *Nomvuyo's Room*. 2000. District Six Museum. Photo by the author.

supervised the organization of the room and donated materials and objects, and consequently it is a memory work itself.[60] It exactly fits the description in Ngcelwane's autobiography, *Sala Kahle, District Six,* where she details the room in 22 Cross Street, which was her family home.[61] Out of the window in the museum room the view that greets us is "the yellow Muir Street Zainatul Mosque, the Foreshore and Table Bay."[62] The voices we hear on tape, as if coming over the airwaves of the old radiogram, are those of former residents of the district, reminiscing. Here, then, is a reflective space where the voices of those who once peopled it animate the room and whose authority is reinforced by the presence of their autobiographies in the museum bookstore. Because of this authorial presence and despite its being in a museum, the room is somehow less of a spectacle—a box with one side exposing its contents to the curious voyeur—than the rooms in Museum Africa.

Nomvuyo Ngcelwane pointedly begins her autobiography as a dialogue between herself and her brother in Guguletu, a township outside Cape Town. In the scene she sets her brother has just been to a meeting where it has been revealed that Africans who had been the victims of the Group Areas Act and had been moved out of District Six in the 1960s were eligible for compensation. She reports her surprise at this news: " 'This move is surprising, dear brother,' I said, 'really surprising, since it is seldom if ever acknowledged that Africans, too, used to live in District Six. People only know of the experiences of their former Coloured neighbours.' " Later on in the passage she muses, " 'I sound racist, don't I?' I said. 'But I'm not. It's just that it is often forgotten that we hold the same sentiments about the place as them. Don't we? How on earth can I be expected to forget twenty years of my life? That's ridiculous!' "[63]

It is not insignificant that the one reconstructed domestic interior represented in the museum is the family room of a Xhosa woman. This is another example of the museum's deliberate engagement with some of the more controversial aspects of the "memory" of District Six and its effort to guard against a romantic nostalgia from within a certain constituency of former District Six residents themselves.[64] Two prominent ex-residents, Dullah Omar and Richard Dudley, have explicitly addressed what Omar terms the "distortion of history," where descriptions of District Six "as an area inhabited by 'Whites,' 'Coloureds,' 'Malays' and 'Indians' " is premised on a denial of "the large number of 'Africans' who lived there and who were forcibly removed."[65] Despite such supporting evidence for the museum's efforts, it has not been without its critics, and this is one of the tensions to which Prosalendis referred in her statement about the museum's work.

Peggy Delport has argued that "The content of the Museum is located not in what is seen but in what happens within the space. Once the Museum stops being a live, generative space and becomes an object, to be consumed, merely looked at and left behind untouched, its function as a living space will end. Its visual form would have turned against itself, and become unproductive and closed."[66] The fact that the museum was transformed into a Land Claims Court in one of the landmark cases establishing the protocol for land claims and restitution in South Africa is yet another instance of how the institution fulfills its role and of its status within a broader community beyond District Six.[67]

In April 1997 the *Sunday Times,* a national broadsheet, sent out a notice: "The District Six Museum, one of the few original buildings still standing since the forced removals, is to be the August 5th venue for a court ruling that could pave the way for one of the country's biggest land claims. The session is to ratify the transfer of land rights from the managers, the Cape Town municipality and the provincial government, to a community beneficiary trust representing former residents—a major step towards land restitution."[68] This announcement came at the end of long and tense negotiations. As might be expected, the issue of restitution and compensation for the forced removals in District Six was a fraught affair. The tensions that erupted during this process are instructive and worth outlining here because they highlight the political stakes in the district of various and sometimes competing interest groups. An account of the debates concerning restitution also has the virtue of demonstrating in graphic terms how apartheid's divisive strategy of "separate development," cemented through the Group Areas Act, is a tenacious legacy and one that to a certain extent has been internalized.

The controversy also serves to clarify the personal investment in the "memory" of District Six and helps us understand the complicated balancing act the museum performs as the public face of the memory of District Six and (in this instance) as the symbolic and actual venue where the transfer of power from state to community was enacted. More than any other events, the land claims demonstrate the extraordinary role played by the museum and its trustees as brokers among the state, local government, and a "community" that the museum staff acknowledges as both diverse and fractured but that simultaneously lays claim to a version of the concept that has more to do with the "imagined" coherence of Benedict Anderson's thesis than with the diverse and sometimes antagonistic polity that it actually represents.[69] This is the uncompromising tightrope that the museum has chosen to walk in the interests of "community."

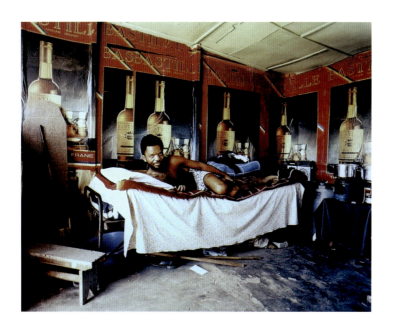

Top PLATE 1. Zwelethu Mthethwa, *Untitled,* 1996. Color photograph.
Courtesy of the artist.

Bottom PLATE 2. Zwelethu Mthethwa, *Untitled,* 1996. Color photograph.
Courtesy of the artist.

PLATE 3. Zwelethu Mthethwa, *Untitled,* 1996. Color photograph.
Courtesy of the artist.

Facing page PLATE 4. Chart by James Drury indicating skin tones and
colors to be matched when painting the body casts. The bottom segments
of the chart are the colors ascribed to the skin of body parts belonging to
the "Hottentot Woman" whose anthropological measurements chart is in
figure 69. Courtesy of the South African Museum. Iziko Museums
of Cape Town.

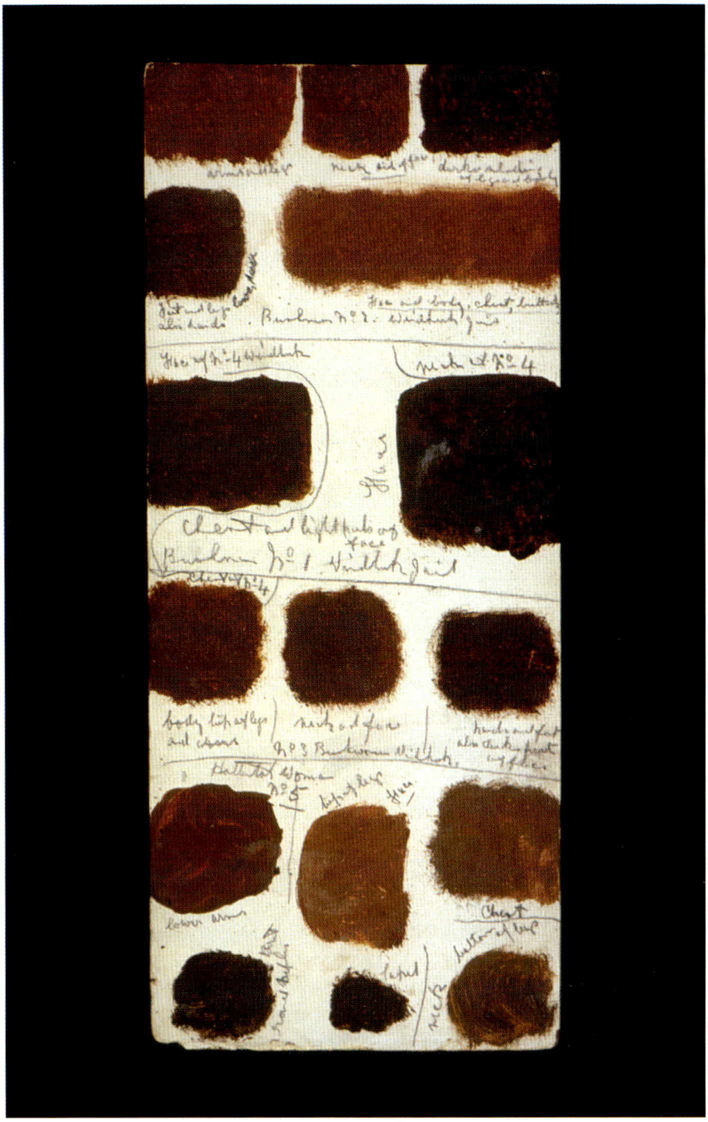

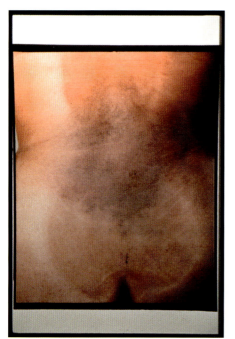

PLATE 5. Berni Searle, Installation view of *The Palms of the Hands, the Small of the Back, the Nape of the Neck, under the Belly, the Soles of the Feet*. From the *Discoloured series*, 1999. Digital prints, photographs, wooden shelves, henna. Photo by Jean Brundrit. Courtesy of the artist.

PLATE 6. Berni Searle, detail from *The Small of the Back*. From *The Palms of the Hands, the Small of the Back, the Nape of the Neck, under the Belly, the Soles of the Feet*, 1999. Digital print, photograph, henna. Photo by Jean Brundrit. Courtesy of the artist.

PLATE 7. Berni Searle, Installation view of *A Darker Shade of Light*. From the *Discoloured* series, 1999. Digital prints installed in light boxes. Photo by Jean Brundrit. Courtesy of the artist.

PLATE 8. Berni Searle, detail from *A Darker Shade of Light*, 1999. Digital print installed in light box. Photo by Jean Brundrit. Courtesy of the artist.

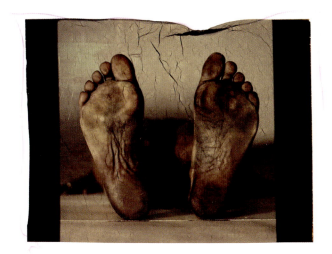

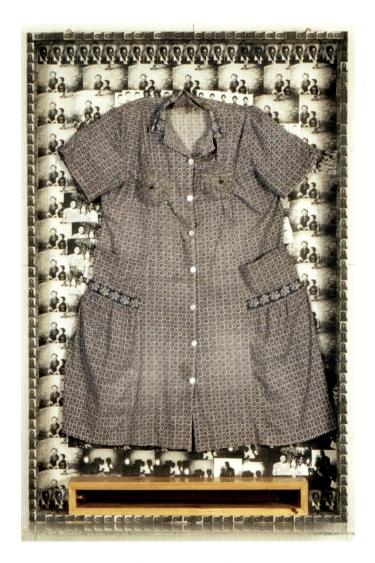

PLATE 9. Senzeni Marasela, *Our Mother,* 1998. Dress, pins, police baton, photocopies. Courtesy of the artist.

PLATE 10. Penny Siopis, *Tula Tula I*, 1993–1994. Photocopy, photograph, steel wool, found object (Victorian frame), oil on board. 111 cm × 67 cm. Photo by Jean Brundrit. Courtesy of the artist.

PLATE 11. Mural in "Zulu Room," 1933. In hallway of the fourth floor, South Africa House, London. Murals by Eleanor Esmonde-White and Le Roux Smith le Roux. Photo by the author.

In 1995 two exhibitions dealing with District Six opened in Cape Town. One, "District Six: Image and Representation," was held at the National Gallery and was a joint venture between the gallery and the District Six Museum. It ran until 2 February 1996 and comprised an eclectic mix of paintings, prints, photos, and other documentary archive materials. The other, "Texture and Memory—the Urbanism of District Six," was put on by the Cape Technikon's Urban Housing Research Unit. Unit members described the exhibition as one that traced the urban development patterns of the district before its demolition so that future development could be informed by this history.[70] It too contained important archive materials and many of the photos taken in the heyday of the district's existence prior to the forced removals. In defense of the exhibition, Marco Bezzoli, a member of the research team, felt compelled to emphasize that the unit, while housed in the Technikon, was independent of it.[71] Such a qualification fell on deaf ears, however, and the District Six Museum refused to lend support to the exhibition. Neither the museum nor the District Six Community Land Trust was represented, and the trust's chief executive officer, Basil Davidson, declined an invitation to deliver an address at the opening of the exhibition.

The Cape Technikon, the institution hosting the exhibition, is almost universally reviled by former residents and their supporters.[72] When community pressure in the 1970s had incredibly succeeded in keeping property developers from exploiting the razed land, the apartheid government flew in the face of such opposition and erected the Cape Technikon. It did so despite both an array of professional research providing evidence that the location made no sociological, technical, or economic sense and the availability of alternative sites. In fact even the City Council objected to the siting of the Technikon in District Six—partly on economic grounds, since removing the remaining families off the site to make way for the Technikon would end up costing the council about R 206,000 a year in lost rates.[73]

At the time it was built, the Technikon provided educational opportunities for whites only, and this legacy has been hard to shake off. The soulless buildings still have the power to rile former residents and have become symbolic of the mindless bullying of the apartheid state. Events in the mid-1990s heightened their ire. In June 1995 it became evident that despite a voluntary freeze on the sale of land in the area, plots had already been sold to private developers, and the Technikon was aiming to create new sports facilities.[74] To add insult to injury, when rubble was cleared for this venture, a commemorative cairn begun by former residents and their supporters around the time of the opening of the museum was nearly completely obliterated.[75]

The case of the Technikon and its continuing controversial status provides a neat insight into the baroque alliances and tensions among competing political entities that make any decisions concerning land claims in District Six particularly fraught. The fact that the museum's absence from the opening of the Technikon exhibition was worthy of note in the national press suggests that the institution carries considerable weight as a moral arbiter in the affairs of the district and therefore nationally, since District Six continues to have a rather privileged status as an instance of forced removals.

On the eve of the first democratic elections many political commentators expected the outgoing government to go out on a morally magnanimous note and pave the way for the development of District Six. (More cynically, such a move would have increased the National Party's "colored" vote.) However, just as the Community Land Trust was about to be ratified as a legal entity charged with coordinating the development of the site, objections to (among other things) the extent of ANC representation on the trust resulted in holding back the agreement.[76] The creation of a land trust was intended to provide a representative body for overseeing and negotiating the redevelopment of the area and was envisaged as comprising 50 percent community members and 50 percent local and other authorities. Its formation had been approved by Cape administrator Kobus Meiring.[77] More specifically, the trust was to be a ten-member body comprising a Cape Town City Council member; a member of the ("colored") Management Committee's steering committee; two representatives from the CPA (one of whom had to be a tax expert); two from the business community; one from the ANC; one from the Cape Housing Action Committee; one from the South African National Civic Organisation (SANCO); and one from the West Cape United Squatters Association.[78] A nonprofit utility company was to be formed to deal with the development of the area in conjunction with the trust.[79] When the Community Land Trust was eventually ratified, Western Cape housing minister Gerald Morkel insisted that no applicants for rehousing in District Six would ever again be assessed on the basis of the color of their skin: "We must never, ever look at a person's colour or race when he applies for accommodation in District Six. If a person is a South African and qualifies in terms of the prescriptions of the Trust, they should be allocated accommodation. Anything else would be unconstitutional."[80] But deciding the criteria for the right to restitution became precisely one of the biggest obstacles to the process.

Who indeed should be the rightful beneficiaries of the 1994 Restitution of Land Rights Act?[81] This was especially problematic in District Six, where about 60 percent of the property before the forced removals was owned on paper by white landowners. Africans and others were largely tenants. This situation was due to the fact that in order to get around the prescriptions of the Group Areas Act many "colored" landowners had paid "key money" to white friends and associates so that the land was registered in the white associates' names and technically "rented" to the actual owners.[82] Consequently the Community Land Trust argued that the community that had been destroyed and needed compensating was the community of *tenants*, not landlords. It applied for District Six land to be exempted from the Land Claims Court's jurisdiction so that "owners" could be given land of equivalent value elsewhere and individual claims would be ceded to the trust, who would be responsible for parceling out the land under what was hoped would be a controlled development plan.[83] The trust's solution was controversial, and some former District Six residents still wished to claim land on an individual basis.[84] The District Six Residents' Association, which represented about fifty former residents and was chaired by Anwah Nagia, was particularly opposed to the idea of a group claim: "[It] smacks of the same tactics the government and the council used when they declared District Six white."[85] Davidson and the trust believed, on the other hand, that it was the only way to enable more of the former tenants to move back to the area under the existing terms of the act.[86]

Matters were expected to come to a head in October 1996 with a court case to decide the issue. The fact that the Community Land Trust was prepared to take the issue to court escalated the antagonisms among different factions of the former residents of District Six since this would likely cost them around R 300,000 in legal fees. Meanwhile, other groups of former residents entered the fray. Ebrahim Jacobs, the secretary of Concerned Ex-Residents of District Six, representing about nine hundred ex-residents and part of the District Six Development Forum, expressed his concern to get the redevelopment of the district on the road as soon as possible. According to him, the opposition of the District Six Residents Association was the primary cause of delay in the resettlement of tenants back to the district. (His family had been rehoused in Mitchells Plain, some twenty-five kilometers from the city center.) He supported the trust's application to the Land Claims Court because he felt it was the best way to enable tenants to return to District Six, even if this meant that they could not be rehoused in their exact old locations.[87]

By October 1996 Nagia, now also a leading figure of the newly formed District Six Restitution Front, was reported to have called for a postponement of the court hearing: "Many potential claimants are worried that the court application could take away their chances of regaining land in District Six without any guarantees of compensation. We asked that the court hearing be postponed as a prerequisite for negotiations to resolve the acrimony around the question of land restitution and objections to the court case."[88] Western Cape land claims commissioner Wallace Mgoqi stated that although not all claimants would be able to return to the district, all legitimate claims would qualify for other state land, financial compensation, or priority access to state housing schemes.[89] Finally the court case was postponed, and it looked likely that the deadline would be extended to ensure that further claims could be made by District Six claimants. The priority now became the resolution of differences among competing interest groups in District Six and the assurance of a broad-based consent from all parties concerned for the method of conducting restitution.[90]

This was recognized as a victory for the District Six Restitution Front. Land Affairs chief Geoff Budlender noted: "The people who were dispossessed should be as fully involved as possible in the design of alternative forms of restitution, including decisions about the manner in which the land should be used and the selection of beneficiaries. If these matters are not satisfactorily addressed, it is inevitable that claimants and other people who were dispossessed will feel aggrieved by what will be perceived as a second act of dispossession."[91] Two facilitators, Neville Alexander and Elaine Clarke, were duly appointed by the court to help negotiate among the factions. By July 1997 Alexander and Clarke had produced a report recommending a beneficiary community trust to oversee the redevelopment of the area, with all claimants becoming associate members of the trust and the province and municipality ex officio members of the board of trustees.[92] "The report proposed that restitution take place on the basis of 'just and equitable' compensation. Those wishing for restoration of their homes would be accommodated in the integrated development plan where possible, while those opting for compensation would receive equivalent land or accommodation elsewhere. A baseline amount should constitute the foundation to which all other due amounts can be added, the report said. This amount would be determined by the length of claimants' residence in District Six."[93] The District Six Beneficiary and Development Trust was duly founded under the chairmanship of Anwah Nagia. On 5 August 1997 the Land Claims Court, sitting in the District Six Museum, finally approved the withdrawal of the Cape Town municipality and the provincial government's application.[94] This meant that individual claims could be submitted.

Victory was short-lived, however.[95] In February 1998 Land Affairs minister Derek Hanekom stated that some of the "key" stakeholders had expressed dissatisfaction with the conduct of the beneficiary trust, claiming that they were being marginalized by the trust and that the trust was unconstitutional.[96] The aggrieved parties included the Cape Town municipality, Cape Technikon, and an organization known as the Voice of District Six. John Oliver, the rector of St. Markus Church and deputy chairman of the District Six Development Forum, was reported as insisting, controversially, that current residents such as the hated Technikon should be considered qualifying stakeholders in the final restitution package. Indeed the Cape Technikon's registrar, Jacques van Zyl, issued a public "apology" in the District Six Museum: "[The Technikon] is truly sorry that it moved into this highly sensitive area. . . . The technikon realises that it cannot operate in isolation. [It] is desirous of becoming involved in the community in which it finds itself and is prepared to share, wherever possible, its resources with the community. The technikon commits itself to fully working with whichever structure this court creates or puts in place."[97]

In a controversial move, Hanekom dismissed the two prominent activists, Alexander and Clarke, intending to employ two new facilitators who would be accountable primarily to him. This was interpreted as "political interference" by some, and the trust insisted that Hanekom offer an unconditional apology to Alexander and Clarke for "questioning their integrity."[98] The trust's concern centered on the ways in which Hanekom and the municipal government seemed to be equating the claims of business enterprise with those of ex-District Six residents and the provision of working-class housing in the redevelopment scheme. Clarke was quoted in the national press saying that she had a "terrible message" for people pinning their hopes on returning to District Six: "Hanekom says business has the same status as them and they'll have to stand in line."[99] By November 1999 no claims had yet been settled.[100]

In the end, after a seven-year struggle to set up an equitable process for land restitution in District Six, a complicated set of settlements and options was finally thrashed out by November 2000. In a special ceremony, former residents and their descendants were finally given some official compensation for their losses, either by way of relocation to the area or financial compensation.[101] Thabo Mbeki presented the certificate officially handing over the land to Anwah Nagia.

The District Six Museum had been the ground for many disputes and debates. Finally it was the ground upon which resolution was negotiated. My relatively brief account of the complexities of the negotiations makes it clear that the museum is one of those very rare institutions that is capable of supporting initiatives that are more likely to expose problems and contradictions than to smooth over dissent. Nowhere is this more evident than the Land Claims Court proceedings that took place in its main hall. Moreover, the remnants of District Six and the embodied memory provided by its museum may offer a productive space to preserve and explore those other liberation narratives at present occluded in the Robben Island story.

4

NEW HISTORIES FOR OLD

Museological Strategies

> Fundamentally dialectical, the museum serves both as burial chamber of the
> past—with all that entails in terms of decay, erosion, forgetting—and as site
> of possible resurrections, however mediated and contaminated, in the eyes
> of the beholder. No matter how much the museum, consciously or uncon-
> sciously, produces and affirms the symbolic order, there is always a surplus of
> meaning that exceeds set ideological boundaries, opening spaces for reflec-
> tion and counter-hegemonic memory.—Andreas Huyssen, *Twilight Memories*

In 1988 a conference on the conservation of culture was held in Cape Town,
focusing on the theme of "changing contexts and challenges."[1] The gathering was jointly organized by SAMA, the NMC, the Department of the Environment, the Humanities and Social Science Research Council (HSRC),
and the South African Society for Cultural History. Described by Denver
Webb as "a landmark" conference, it was unusual in bringing together interested professionals across the political spectrum, with participants from the
right-wing FAK sharing sessions with members of the radical, multiracial
United Democratic Front (UDF).[2] This was a fair achievement in itself and
one of the first times such organizations had cooperated. However, it was
also clear that the compromises of such a collaboration more often than not
resulted in a stalemate where the polarities of positions were maintained
rather than breached. Papers ranged from woolly sentiments expressing the
general need for change to suggestions representing little more than outright political opportunism. Nonetheless, some cogent critiques of the museums and heritage sector were backed by concrete proposals. In sum, the

conference was an important event at a formative period, raising issues concerning "truth" and history, diversity or unity, with some careful analyses of the impact of South Africa's political legacy for the development of policy decisions in the museums sector.

One of the grievances that facilitated this gathering was the apartheid state's division of museums into "own affairs" (white) and "general affairs" (all other) institutions. This division was one of the results of the 1983 tricameral constitution, ostensibly a bid by P. W. Botha to win over Indian and "colored" support for the government by giving voters in these categories minimal representation through separate parliamentary assemblies while continuing to deny any African representation and maintaining white monopoly over power.[3] The concomitant segregation policy as applied to museums was opposed from the start by SAMA, and this opposition was cemented at the 1988 conference. One session at the conference, "Culture Conservation and the New Constitutional Dispensation," was in fact devoted to a discussion of the implications of this policy for museums. This seems to have been a rather fraught affair, with representatives from the Department of Education and Culture House of Assembly promoting the logic of the tricameral parliament as the basis of a cultural policy, to the evident distrust and irritation of many of the other participants. The absurdity of the policy was summarized neatly in the proceedings of the conference; the summary is worth repeating in full here to give the reader a flavor of the Byzantine restrictions and proscriptions with which cultural institutions were under pressure to comply. Many have interpreted such restrictions as a last ditch attempt to maintain power by the outgoing apartheid government. The synopsis also gives the reader a taste of the specific conditions and difficulties that beset those South African museum professionals who genuinely wished to transform their institutions:

> Perplexity was voiced as to how museums are to separate their collections and activities in terms of general and own affairs as prescribed. Logically it could mean that certain museums would have to be dismantled and their collections separated. How was the cultural history of a mixed community to be depicted by the museums? Is a white own affairs museum now required to ignore the contribution to the cultural history and life of a community made by blacks, Indians, Koi, etcetera? What was to happen to all the sub-groups and sub-racial classifications? As yet not a single museum administered by coloured or Indian administration exists. Instead a Malay cultural museum (the Bo-Kaap Museum) is an integral part of a white own affairs museum, the South African Cultural History Museum [in Cape Town].[4]

The exasperated tone of this resume adequately conveys the chaos generated by the ludicrous scheme and its disingenuous attempt to present as a
coherent "scientific" principle a discriminatory racist practice with no logic
other than the basest opportunism on the part of a flailing and increasingly
isolated government.

While some participants reiterated the ideal of the museum as a "neutral" space, others clearly felt that "In a society where everything is so
highly politicised, culture (including visual cultural statements) cannot be
divorced from politics: *Culture is in politics and politics in culture.*"[5] Other sessions attempted to articulate an adequate intellectual critique of the structural problems in most museums in order to develop some concrete strategies. One of the most confrontational and hard-hitting critiques of what
was perceived as the woolly liberalism underpinning the conference agenda
and the current museum structure itself was by Keyan Tomaselli (professor
and director of the Contemporary Cultural Studies Unit at the University
of Natal) and Mewa Ramgobin (national vice president of the Congress of
South African Writers). Entitled "Culture and Conservation: Whose Interests?," it advanced the case of "conservation as liberation"—that is, "a liberation from apartheid and the conservation and development of the em-
bryonic grassroots democratic structures that have developed to contest
apartheid."[6] The authors argued "for a dynamic, inter-active, consultative
and educative use of buildings and spaces which will alert all South Africans
to the institutionally preferred readings which have shaped our consciousness for so long. Monuments, museums and other cultural spaces should
embody the history, experience and values of different groups and classes
from *their* perspectives, not only those of the previously or currently dominant."[7] In a dense and detailed argument Tomaselli and Ramgobin challenged the ways in which ethnicities were being marshaled to support op-
portunist power mongering. Focusing on the mobilization of a form of Zulu
cultural nationalism by the chief minister of KwaZulu Natal, Mangosuthu
Buthelezi, they aired a criticism that was gaining ground in a number of
quarters (Buthelezi's presence as a speaker at the conference made their
attack particularly volatile):

> It is not without irony, for example, that Chief Minister Mangosuthu
> Buthelezi will be talking about the *black perspective* in cultural conservation
> later today. He and his National Cultural Liberation Movement, Inkatha,
> seem to have adapted early Afrikaner nationalist strategies to seek a slice of
> power in a reformist, but class-divided, authoritarian South African state.
> When people are *forced* into *group loyalties* through appeals to ethnicity, cul-

ture / nation and membership cards / passports / *citizenship* documents, and job opportunities, only violence can ultimately sustain such mobilisation. . . . The struggle is *not* cultural, neither is it ethnically motivated. It is caused by politics mobilised through cultural, ethnic and historical symbols.[8]

Instead of an ethnic nationalism based on a divisive and artificial "tribalism," Tomaselli and Ramgobin argued for the importance of conserving what they identified as the hybrid and dynamic culture of urban city dwellers and the "township culture [that] gave birth to the Mandelas, the Tambos, the Sisulus, the Tutus, the Gumedes, Hector Petersens, the Bikos, the Boesaks and the youth of today—whose culture has overcome feelings of temporariness and tribalism."[9] The Freedom Charter of 1955 was hailed as a "blueprint for the future" and a socially cohesive, peaceful strategy for democratic change.[10] Museums were enjoined to "embrace the dynamic of history" with "blacks as makers of history" rather than "blacks as makers of pots" and to encourage "a reflexive approach where visitors to museums are exposed to debates rather than clear cut single issue answers and where they become aware of the processes which shape popular memory."[11]

Not surprisingly, "grassroots" interests in conservation issues were deemed virtually nonexistent. Consequently, discussion focused on how to get both urban and rural communities involved and committed to the conservation of their own cultures.[12] In "National Monuments in the Ciskei," Denver Webb addressed the issue of community involvement and the disparities among local, national, and international interests. Webb's research in the Ciskei confirmed a situation shared by many historically marginalized and disenfranchised groups: "Over-population, inadequate education, insufficient healthcare, shortages of housing, unemployment, soil erosion, deforestation and the lack of an infrastructure are all very real issues. These take priority over national monuments, especially ones that reflect unflatteringly on one's ancestors."[13] Most Ciskeians were either unaware of any monuments that might be of national significance or simply saw those that received attention by the state as promoting white histories and values and consequently of little interest to them. As a result of such apathy, many structures of historic interest were often vandalized and sections were sold off to visitors or indeed museums. Some materials were simply reappropriated; for example, wire fencing around historic cemeteries and wooden floorboards were pressed into more urgent service around the home or as firewood. Webb reported on a particularly inventive form of what he called "recycling" in the case of the Peddie Cavalry Barracks: after corrugated iron from the roofs and bricks from the walls had been expropriated, squatters moved into the remaining ruins "using mud bricks and recycled material from the old buildings to convert them into fairly comfortable houses, in an attempt to alleviate the acute housing shortage in Peddie."[14]

A feature of the conference presentations—and one that was to become increasingly prominent in discussions concerning progressive developments in museum practices in South Africa—was a case for awareness of the ecological impact on both the structure and maintenance of society. Arguments for the development of tourism based on an exploitation of the natural environment are always complicated by the often competing and diametrically opposed claims on the land by various groups. In particular, tensions come to the fore among developers, capitalist entrepreneurs, and local people, who may have scant regard for land or livestock outside their immediate need to eke out an existence, be it legally or illegally (in other words, via "poaching" of protected wildlife). These tensions are further complicated by other factors in the equation. Conservationists, genuinely concerned for the preservation of the resources in their care, have daily battles with local communities who might see conservation as a waste of potential livelihood or simply as life support. Conflicts can result in difficult choices that end up privileging either animals or humans but rarely accommodating both.

In the wake of various museum conferences in the late 1980s, some of the more liberal South African museums concluded that four major areas needed attention in order to redress some of the imbalances and absences of the past. First, since "culture" was uniformly represented by white settler experience in historical museums, it was felt that the resilient contributions to cultural and political history represented by the township experience of the majority black cultures needed to be acknowledged. Second, many commentators keenly felt that the cultural and social history of the working environment and conditions of employment—especially for the black majority, whose labor was a decisive factor in the economic and cultural wealth of the country—was a crucial component of any new national history. Third, the virtually hidden history of slavery, which had made so fundamental a contribution to white settler wealth (especially in the Western Cape), was similarly recognized as critically important. Fourth were the extraordinary beauty and wealth of the natural environment and the diversity and rarity of the flora and fauna, which had always played a significant role in promoting the country as an international tourist venue. Unlike the first three aspects, the environment issue was less one of absence than of translation— in other words, how to transform perceptions of the landscape as either a playground for the rich or as one of the few raw materials for indiscriminate exploitation by the poor into a democratically available and ecologically managed resource for all. It is with this last issue that I want to begin, in part because it exemplifies one of the structuring foci of this chapter: the complications that arise when the concept of "community" is invoked as a way of uniting a new nation.

LAND

Government publicity materials produced to entice the European tourist to South Africa from the mid-1920s provided an image of a vast landscape populated almost entirely by large beasts, with not a black figure in sight. Humans of the white variety, when visible in this apparently virgin land, were represented as genteel consumers profiting from the meticulously conserved natural environment provided by the new drive to turn game reserves into national parks.[15] Such careful (on the one hand) and entirely unconscious (on the other) editorial work reached its heyday under apartheid, but it was a feature of most tourist publicity up until the mid-1990s.

There is a long and interesting history to the development of nature reserves on the African continent.[16] In many ways, it can be characterized as a shift of emphasis from specialized, big-game-hunting safari tourism to big-game-viewing safari tourism—from shooting with a rifle to "shooting" with a camera. As Ciraj Rassool and Leslie Witz suggest, "Instead of guns, these tourists came armed with cameras, seeking to capture an image of 'Timeless Africa' to adorn their walls like animal trophies."[17] In the South African context, such developments have taken place within the framework of both colonialism and apartheid, and this carries with it certain ramifications for future developments in this area.

In a fascinating article on the contradictory relations between the nature reserve and the labor compound in South Africa in the late 1920s, and the fantasies embedded in the development of both, David Bunn has written of "the emergence of such notions of enclaved, 'primitive' space—the space of the 'reserve'—as an imaginary repository of value forms lost in the process of modernisation."[18] The transformation of the Sabi and the Singwitsi Game Reserves into Kruger National Park and the founding of the National Parks Board of Trustees in 1926 coincided with the emergence of Afrikaner nationalism and the various constructions of a Voortrekker culture and "tradition" as a national heritage.[19] One component of this "invented" tradition was the concept of the Afrikaner as by nature and tradition a nature conservationist, a myth promoted in a series of publications by the National Parks Board after 1948.[20]

The consolidation of Afrikaner nationalism was accompanied by rapid economic, industrial, and agricultural development, which effectively and radically altered the natural environment. Consequently, "Two entirely contradictory maps of ethnically conceived space came about: that of railway tourism for whites, emphasizing the picturesque experience of tribal domains; and that of state labour organization, which attempted to prevent African urban populations from becoming settled, by holding them in segregated Native Locations, or by enforcing migrancy to and from rural Reserves."[21] Bunn argues that Kruger National Park helped sustain this contradiction by providing the compensation for urban whites of a "primitive" and "wild" environment untainted by either the encroachment of industry or the perceived threat of black "hordes" (except as contained tribalism). The park had the additional advantage of being literally next door to the expanding industrial sprawl of Johannesburg. Jane Carruthers has argued, in addition, that the so-called national parks in South Africa, rather than fostering national unity when they were founded, were highly "divisive institutions."[22] She also makes the point that by refusing hunting rights to the majority black communities who had previously used the land for subsistence, Kruger National Park played a role in creating a cheap labor pool just at a time when expanding industrialization required a proletariat to service the new economy; without the prospect of hunting, there was little means of surviving outside the capitalist economy.[23] This complicated legacy has left some difficult obstacles, not least of which, as noted above; are the competing claims on the uses of land. Any attempt to recast this legacy in terms of an inclusive eco-tourism would be a gargantuan task, particularly when so many of the affected parties have a greater concern for housing and employment than for participating in devising a coherent strategy for developing an ecologically sound tourist industry—no matter what the potential long-term gains.

We saw in the chapter on Robben Island how eco-tourism can effectively support campaigns to preserve a location from large-scale entrepreneurial development. However, arguments for eco-tourism can just as easily fall prey to the representations so familiar throughout the apartheid years—of South Africa as a landscape uniquely populated with large game and entirely devoid of human life (other than privileged white tourists). The dilemma is similar to the challenge of acknowledging cultural diversity without reproducing apartheid's policy of "separate development." Consequently, one might be forgiven for cynically interpreting this penchant for eco-tourism (coinciding as it did with the lead-up to and the wake of the first democratic elections) as providing an alibi to carry out only limited reforms that involved the fewest confrontational changes, particularly since the thorny issue of representing the past could be left to one side. Given this legacy, coupled with the understandable exploitation of resources by an often impoverished population, any argument for prioritizing the conservation of the environment is a complex business in South Africa.

Terence Ranger, in an article that takes a comparative view of the development of two tourist sites—the Matapos Hills in Zimbabwe and Uluru (known also by its colonial name of Ayers Rock) in Australia's Central Desert —provides perceptive insights into some of the contradictions that might arise from attempts to engage diverse communities with sometimes competing political, historical, and religious investment in specific sites that have become the focus of eco-tourism.[24] (In keeping with Ranger's personal research preoccupations, most of the historical material in this analysis focuses on the changing significance of the Matapos Hills.) One of the differences Ranger suggests between the histories of the developments of the two sites is that in Australia, the Anangu, the term that Pitjantjatjara and Yankunytjatjara people who form the main groups laying claim to the site use to refer to themselves, have systematically relied on establishing historical continuity of land ownership and occupation.[25] The residents of the Matapos Hills make less recourse to what Ranger sees as an essentializing discourse. He points out that they were only too well aware of the way in which the site was constantly renamed and reappropriated, not only by white settlers, but also by various African groups such as the Ndebele, the Banyubi / Kalanga, and the Shona even before the advent of European colonization.[26] Thus President Robert Mugabe's use of the same essentialist argument for "indigenous" as opposed to settler claims to the land was revealed as opportunistic and disingenuous by the very peoples he was supposedly supporting. Ranger cites a San correspondent to the *Zimbabwe Herald* "who wrote tongue-in-cheek to say that he was glad to hear that his people were soon to get their hunting grounds back from Ndebele and Shona usurpers! The acute sense [continues Ranger] of white Rhodesians in 1980 that they had 'lost' the Matapos was not balanced by a sense among local people that they had 'regained' them."[27] This anecdote serves to usefully complicate the concept of "community."

In addition, in the Zimbabwean example, "the modernist doctrines of international conservation are embraced by the Zimbabwean state, which in the interests of the 'whole community' does not allow locals to collect plants, or hunt, or visit holy places within the park. The imperatives of international tourism have ensured that the park still presents much the same symbolic face that it did under settler rule."[28] In other words, long after independence was achieved in 1979, international tourism has encouraged a predominantly "settler" historical significance for the region, with a visit to Cecil Rhodes's tomb a mandatory feature of any visit and a relative disregard for any African historical and religious significance for the area. Both Ranger and Edwin Wilmsen alert us to the dangers of an essentialist view of history and tradition as a means of legitimizing land claims. In relation to the Khoisan claims to "First Peoples" status in South Africa, Wilmsen argues that "The discourse reifies its subjects not only beyond race but paradoxically, given its intentions, beyond humanity. The image of the 'First Peoples' leads in the wrong direction, feeding a spurious traditional / modernity divide."[29] And Ranger makes the same point in relation to Australian Aboriginal land claims. While this is undoubtedly an important caution, the strategy has nevertheless proved invaluable for gaining a political platform and considerable capital by those claiming "First Nation / Peoples" status in Canada, Australia, and South Africa.

One of the crucial features of the legal process over the management and ownership of Uluru has been precisely that once the Anangu land claim was accepted, their involvement in any decision making regarding the site became an absolute given. Despite complications and compromises, they have, since 1985, been acknowledged as the owners of the land surrounding Uluru. Consequently any other stakeholders must negotiate a partnership with the Anangu and lease their operations from them.[30] Given the extent to which Uluru has achieved an iconic status in relation to constructions of Australian national identity, this must be seen as a significant political victory, notwithstanding any setbacks in Aboriginal rights and status under John Howard's government.[31] Indeed, the transfer of power and title to the Anangu may well be a useful model of how organizations can work in tandem with local groups who identify themselves both as belonging to a larger body that is in a politically marginal position nationally and also as a specific group with particular claims and traditions within this larger body.

During the early 1990s in South Africa there was considerable debate about the best ways to develop and transform a tourist industry that had clearly been dwindling (partly due to the representation of South Africa in the international media as a hotbed of political unrest and violence and partly under the increasing pressure of international criticism during the 1980s).[32] The concept of "community" figured large in these discussions, as did the importance of capitalizing on the extraordinary natural beauty of the country. In 1994 the National Tourism Forum, under the chairmanship of Peter Mokaba (a former ANC youth activist who became deputy minister of environmental affairs and tourism in Mandela's government), concerned to develop the tourist potential of both cultural and natural resources, proclaimed the importance of a "community driven tourism."[33] Certainly it may be pertinent to remain skeptical of the appeal to "community" in the development of certain tourist initiatives in the early period of the first government of national unity; this is clearly the tone of the engaging and lively article by Rassool and Witz. But it is worth looking in some detail at the government's serious attempts to draft a new environmental conservation policy since such attempts not only have important implications for producing a viable public face for eco-tourism in South Africa, but they also address communities that have so far had no reason to cooperate in such initiatives.

In 1996 two "Green Paper" drafts of an environmental policy for the "new" South Africa claimed an imperative supported by Agenda 21 of the UN program for globally sustainable development, as well as what was then the *Draft Final Constitution of the Republic of South Africa.* The drafts declared:

> Everyone has the right:
> (a) to an environment that is not harmful to their health or well-being; and
> (b) to have the environment protected for the benefit of present and future generations,
> > (i) through reasonable legislative and other measures that prevent pollution and ecological degradation;
> > (ii) promote conservation; and
> > (iii) secure ecologically sustainable development and use of natural resources while promoting justifiable economic and social development.[34]

Both Green Papers were careful to historicize environmental issues in terms of the long-term damage incurred by apartheid policies. One noted the following: "The black majority were denied the vote, disempowered and dispossessed. They were forcibly removed from commercial farming land to overcrowded and under serviced rural and urban settlements. Often they had to live close to industrial areas and waste dumps, exposing them to environmental hazards. And, crucially, survival sometimes demanded unsustainable and environmentally damaging patterns of resource use."[35] The document goes on to state explicitly that "Nature conservation areas were developed at the expense of local communities. The system led to forced removals and exclusion of communities from the management and benefits of conservation."[36]

The other Green Paper, on the conservation and sustainable use of biological diversity, emphasized that there is a widely held perception that protected areas are playgrounds for a privileged elite, and that biodiversity conservation is exclusive and irrelevant to the majority of South Africa's people."[37] As a corollary, there had been a tendency to erroneously equate environmental issues with nature conservation alone, and one of the reasons for this had been the "lack of human, financial and organisational resources to enable civil society, and community based organisations in particular, to participate in environmental management and policy development."[38] It is significant that in their analyses of current environmental awareness, both documents were concerned to establish a precolonial tradition of nature conservancy in South Africa:

> Evidence suggest[s] the application of elaborate natural resource management systems by indigenous African peoples, such as the San, Khoi and Nguni prior to the country's colonisation. Because most traditional African societies were for the most part dependent upon natural resources, including the wildlife that surrounded them, political systems generally included a set of rules and procedures designed to regulate the use of natural resources. Examples include the setting aside of hunting preserves for Zulu royalty, soil conservation methods of the BaTswana people, and totemic protection among people such as the BaSotho. A rich folklore reflected the close relationship between traditional societies and nature, and linked people to the environment through an ethic which was strongly spiritual and cultural.[39]

One of the important outcomes from the framing of a national environmental policy in terms of a recognition of land management *before* colonization and apartheid is the acknowledgment that the legacy of this earlier knowledge can be found *today* in the work of traditional healers and others whose ecological know-how was curtailed and suppressed by apartheid policies.[40] Indeed references to "traditional knowledge" come up repeatedly in the environmental policy document:

> Past policies also resulted in the banning of traditional medicine, despite the fact that over 80% of South Africans depend upon traditional herbal remedies for their primary health care.
> An issue of particular contention relates to the fact that the considerable benefits which modern society has gained from the traditional knowledge and innovations of South Africa's people have resulted in few, if any, of such benefits being returned to the people from whom knowledge was derived. Indigenous knowledge of plants and their patterns of use assisted

colonial botanists in South Africa to identify species of commercial potential, the benefits of which were reaped solely by foreign companies. There is currently substantial interest from foreign companies in the genetic resources of South Africa, and firm evidence that sampling guided by traditional knowledge substantially increases the efficiency of screening plants for medicinal treatments. However, there is no legal protection in South Africa for traditional knowledge, which is often not confined to a single community or person. Furthermore, conventional intellectual property right regimes do not correspond well to the innovations of traditional cultures.

There is therefore a clear need to strengthen traditional and customary knowledge, practices and cultures by protecting and recognising the value of such systems and preventing their loss. This may be achieved by ensuring that benefits arising from the innovative use of traditional and customary knowledge of biodiversity are equitably shared with those from whom knowledge is gleaned, and also by incorporating traditional knowledge and practices into biodiversity research and conservation programmes.[41]

The document also recognized the need for government incentives beyond what the authors termed the "command and control mechanisms" of most legislation governing the use and conservation of natural resources in order to encourage people to change their behavior rather than simply be confronted by a series of punitive measures.[42] The historicizing of environmental use and abuse also resulted in a statement that the government was committed "Through the Land Restitution programme, and in accordance with the Constitution of South Africa and the Restitution of Land Rights Act 22 of 1994 [to] facilitate the settlement of land claims, taking into account the intrinsic biodiversity value of the land, and seeking outcomes which will combine the objectives of restitution with the conservation and sustainable use of biodiversity."[43] The Green Papers were important policy documents that offered a number of incentives to any organization wishing to take up the call for an ecologically responsible use of the environment. It was clear that private landowners might benefit from adherence to the principles they laid down. In addition, the Tswaing Crater Museum decided to launch an initiative that responded to these directives.

The argument in favor of a holistic, ecologically minded museum practice that would develop a South African variant on the open air museums of the Scandinavian model was discussed in a conference jointly organized by the National Cultural History Museum in Pretoria and the Mayibuye Centre. The conference, "Museums and the Reconstruction and Development Programme (RDP)," held at the Willem Prinsloo Agricultural Museum outside

Pretoria on 8 November 1994, was one of the first forums after the election of Mandela's government to devise concrete policy proposals for bringing museums (as national institutions) into line with the government's Reconstruction and Development Program, an initiative for establishing an "achievable, sustainable [program to meet] the objectives of freedom and an improved standard of living and quality of life for all South Africans within a peaceful and stable society."[44] It was an exciting event to be involved in, particularly since it was an early platform for the new ministers from the DACST to air their views. These included Mongane Wally Serote, chair of the Standing Committee on Arts and Culture; Richard Chernis, director for Arts and Culture; Rupert Lawlor, chair of the Tourism Liaison Council; and Mary Metcalfe, minister for Education in the Pretoria, Witwatersrand, Vaal triangle (PWV). Case studies of their own institutions by Udo Küsel (National Cultural History Museum), André Odendaal (Mayibuye Centre), and Brian Wilmot (president of SAMA) followed discussions concerning new government structures, processes, and potential partnerships with educational institutions and tourist initiatives. The final session was devoted to workshops around various themes with the participants at the conference (academics, administrators, teachers, NMC representatives, and museum professionals).

The workshop organizers outlined the objectives of both the conference and the workshops in "Revitalising the Nation's Heritage": "Museums are an integral part of the principles and key programmes of the RDP. They are there for the people, and their principal mission is to aid in the protection and sustainable utilisation of our country's natural and cultural heritage. . . . This document discusses the paradigm shifts museums have to make in order to make a meaningful contribution to the transformation of South African society. Furthermore, it synthesises possible ways for museums' commitment to the RDP principles and participation in the key programmes."[45]

What strikes one on reading the document is the proposition that ecotourism and environmentalism are presented as not one but *the* way forward for museums. The authors express this in terms of the need to "start addressing our country's environmental problems ('green' issues) and the basic needs of people ('brown' issues) [in order to break] down the barriers between 'natural' and 'cultural' history."[46] This is followed by the proposal that "The whole natural and cultural heritage of the nation is in fact a collection. Much of this cannot be moved, but needs to be protected and utilised as site museums. Museums should dismantle the walls of their traditional buildings, and adopt the concept of the museum without walls, where the whole environment in which people live (or used to live) is in fact a museum. Also, no longer should museums concentrate on the visiting public. The community has become the new client."[47]

The action plan in the document lists suggestions on how museums could put the principles of the RDP into practice and articulates some interesting proposals, as well as reiterating some more predictable ones regarding "community" empowerment and consultation. Some of the proposals are worth considering in relation to later developments and also because they remain controversial strategies both within South Africa and also beyond the immediate confines of the South African context. Under the RDP heading of "nation-building," for example, the document suggests that groups wishing to retain their cultural identity should be accommodated but that museums should rather focus on the common ground and shared aspirations: "History museums should concentrate more on the history of common challenges and solutions, and less on the history of conflicts. Let us forget about the battlefields, and concentrate on the ploughed fields!"[48] This poses problems for any representations of the past and begs the question of how far such histories might end up simply reinforcing the silences imposed by apartheid. It also raises the issue of how far such a strategy might encourage a convenient amnesia about the struggle for democracy and the sacrifices made during the liberation struggle. And these were exactly the kinds of qualified criticisms made of Mandela's government of national unity.

One other aspect of the action plan worth mentioning here is that museums are promoted as institutions that have the potential to provide both the knowledge and research necessary to resolve disputes and debates regarding land redistribution and restitution; moreover, museums should play a part in facilitating other basic rights such as housing and education.[49] The museum research program could provide ecological and geological information, as well as assist with "animal breeding, food gardens and agro-forestry and permaculture programmes."[50] Land reform, housing reform, energy efficiency and conservation, and developing medicinal and nutritional alternatives through increased awareness of plant and animal resources are just some of the ways in which museum-based research is promoted as indispensable to the RDP. Taking their lead (and headings) from the RDP document, museums are made to meet the needs of each objective outlined in the government paper. This is an ambitious agenda but one well suited to the euphoric ambience of the conference, coming as it did hard on the heels of the April election results. Although there is no reference in their paper to similar agendas elsewhere, museum professionals have been instrumental in resolving land rights claims and other politically sensitive issues in Australia, New Zealand, and Canada, and in other African countries. Indigenous rights groups have drawn on the expertise and research of historians, anthropologists, natural scientists, and geographers in order to establish the authenticity of their claims. More cynically, arguing a case for the indispensability of museums for implementing the RDP in the utopian but uncertain aftermath of apartheid was an important strategy for enhancing the appeal of museums for the new government and for gaining government funding.

The National Cultural History Museum in Pretoria undertook to set up the first eco-museum in South Africa by developing a meteorite crater site in the northeast of what is now Gauteng. The museum's name is a bit of a misnomer since it actually comprises nine distinct branch museums and heritage sites in and around Pretoria, its remit extending some distance beyond the city. It has attempted to expand the definition of "museum" in South Africa in order for such institutions to become more inclusive phenomena in terms of the kinds of material preserved and conserved, the institutional models available, and the extent of the consultative process. The museum has also been in the forefront of various initiatives that have a bearing on the development of a more holistic approach to environmental protection and on negotiation with and participation of constituencies not previously consulted.

One such initiative was the opening on Heritage Day 1996 of Thulamela, an archaeological site in the northern part of Kruger Park. Thulamela is understood to have been occupied between A.D. 1400 and 1700 and is thought to be part of the Zimbabwe culture responsible for the building of Great Zimbabwe, mentioned in chapter 1. Udo Küsel made the point that archaeological sites are often the casualties when countries are in the process of developing an economic and political infrastructure because of a lack of resources and the imperatives to develop the surrounding area. He noted that an estimated ten thousand prehistoric rock art sites in South Africa were rapidly being destroyed through careless tourist or land use. Consequently the museum had established a rock art owners' conservation group "in the belief that when landowners with rock art sites assume responsibility and manage them as an asset, the sites can be protected and conserved."[51]

Another significant initiative is the Tswaing Crater Museum, which attempted to bridge the chasm between "community" and institution and to

59. Tswaing Crater. Photo by the author.

redress the legacy of inequities reinforced by the development of national parks and reserves to which I referred earlier.

The Tswaing Crater Museum, forty kilometers northwest of Pretoria, was officially opened on 30 March 1996 by Minister of Arts, Culture, Science and Technology Ben Ngubane. The first "eco-museum" in South Africa was an enterprise "characterised by its integrated management of cultural, natural and human resources. It is geared towards the conservation and utilization of these resources and focuses on environmentally directed education."[52] Two of the staff of the National Cultural History Museum most involved with the project from the outset were Helen van Coller (at the time planning officer of the Historical Studies Research Division) and Robert de Jong (at the time head of the Historical Studies Research Division). (De Jong was also one of the key organizers of the 1993 SAMA annual conference, which prioritized the environmental theme for the first time in the organization's history.)[53]

Tswaing ("place of salt" in the Tswana language) is a crater formed by meteor impact about two hundred thousand years ago (figure 59). A number of studies have supported this contention; no traces of volcanic rock have been found in any of the geological studies that have been undertaken to establish the construction of the crater. Nearby is a smaller, shallower crater, which, if it were found to be a satellite of the main crater, would "represent a unique phenomenon on a world-wide scale."[54] Tswaing is filled with a shallow brine lake supplied by granitic groundwater that contains dissolved bicarbonates and carbonates (mainly sodium), and deposits of soda and salt are left on the rim of the crater in the dry season. In 1993 and 1994 the National Cultural History Museum acquired portions of two existing farms, Zoutpan and Uitspan, on which the crater was situated, so that the total area envisaged for the Tswaing site was just under two thousand hectares.[55]

Museum personnel stressed that not only the geological features, but also the flora and fauna were important natural resources and a unique eco-environment.[56] Human settlement of the area was established through archaeological finds as going back to at least the Middle Stone Age (50,000–100,000 years ago). Since then the area has been settled by successive waves of people. During the Iron Age (some thousand years ago) these included the Tswana-Sotho, who possibly assimilated with the Ndebele. In the 1820s came white settlers and ultimately the Voortrekkers, who "claimed most of the Transvaal by right of conquest . . . and used this claim to dispute the rights of refugee groups to their original homelands."[57] In 1876 the Transvaal government formally took over ownership of the crater and the farms on which it stood, eventually leasing the land to a series of salt-making companies (among them the Pretoria District Salt and Soda Company, the Johannesburg Consolidated Investment Company, and finally South African Alkali). In 1953, with its supply of salt and soda virtually exhausted, the Zoutpan was taken over as an experimental cattle-breeding enterprise by the state agricultural department until 1992.

As a result of this interesting history, Tswaing and the surrounding area have been the site of a series of migrations and forced removals and consequently the establishment of "artificial" or "new" communities. Thus, "By the beginning of the 20th century there were a number of African villages in the Tswaing area. Whilst some of these were consolidated by the 1913 Land Act, others were moved. Three 'locations' were created in the area: Makapan Zwartbooi, and Mamogalie, and more to the east Mabane. The Native Trust and Land Act of 1936 incorporated these locations into areas, some of which bordered on Zoutpan and Uitspan, and which generally constituted the Odi and Moretele districts of the later Bophuthatswana."[58] As a consequence, in 1994 the two farms bordered on a number of large settlements, both formal and informal, to the north, west, and east (Nuwe Eersterus, Kromkuil, Winterveld, Klippan, and Mabopane, for example), and to the south they bordered on Soshanguve (among others). According to de Jong, "These local Black communities form part of the population of the "Greater Pretoria Region" and are of crucial importance when developing the Soutpan Environmental Resource Centre."[59] By October 1994 there were an estimated two million people living in and around the vicinity of the new museum.[60]

As a result of the special circumstances, community negotiation and participation at every level were the watchwords during the development of the site. The Tswaing Mission Statement makes this clear: "Tswaing Museum is a non-aligned independent people's project for the conservation and utilisation of the environmental (natural, cultural, human) resources of the Tswaing area. Resources will be provided for environmental management and education, training, research, tourism, and recreation. This is done in a democratic, participatory manner in order to enrich the quality of life of people in a healthy environment."[61] From the start the slogan for the museum was "By the people, for the people."

In early documents setting out the economic and development rationale for Tswaing, community involvement was a crucial aspect of the justification for the project. This position also helped to promote the museum as an integral part of the RDP. The National Cultural History Museum was careful to make the connection between its work and the RDP explicit early on (as noted above), and it was only opportune to do so since the project might well be eligible for RDP funding.[62] The six basic principles of the RDP laid out that projects should form an "integrated and sustainable programme," be "a people-driven process," further "peace and security for all," aid in "nation-building," "link reconstruction and development," and provide a means of consolidating the "democratisation of South Africa."[63] To a very large extent the museum's ability to promote itself as the helpmate of the RDP was dependent on its declared concern to work in tandem with the local groups surrounding it. As Nomvuso Tembe, public relations officer at the National Cultural History Museum in 1994, reported, "Research has shown that many African people don't visit museums because they don't feel part of them. They don't think that museums preserve their past. We wanted things to be different with this museum. We wanted local people to accept it."[64]

Even under the most auspicious circumstances such objectives would pose a considerable challenge. In the Tswaing region, the legacy of apartheid had created almost intractable difficulties for any attempts at community collaboration and liaison. Recent research has provided a much clearer understanding of just what the museum team was up against in 1994, particularly in relation to Winterveld, one of the largest sectors bordering Tswaing. Winterveld is an informal settlement close to what have been described as the "decentralised formal 'black' towns of Mabopane and Shoshanguve."[65] After the reclassification of white farmland as "Bantu only" following the 1936 Native Trust and Land Act, Winterveld became one of the first private black freehold areas in South Africa.[66] In the 1950s the Group Areas Act augmented the population of Winterveld after black constituencies were forced to leave the newly declared "whites only" inner urban areas in and around Pretoria and Johannesburg. Such widespread displacement resulted in a heterogeneous community of Africans from an unusual variety of ethnic and cultural backgrounds, including Tswanas, Shangaans, Sothos, and Zulus. As Francine de Clerq demonstrates, this apparently peaceful coexistence was complete anathema to the apartheid government.[67] It was, however, a short-lived thorn in its side. After the government gave nominal "independence" to the neighboring "bantustan," Bophuthatswana, in 1977, it encouraged the Bophuthatswana administration to incorporate Winterveld within its jurisdiction. When this was accomplished, the majority Tswana-speaking population instituted legislation that effectively took all rights of business and land ownership away from Winterveld residents, ensuring the region's economic and political demise and turning it into a center for the homeless. This legacy has created intense rivalry and mistrust between Winterveld and the surrounding communities and has ensured that since democracy "Winterveld has represented the challenge of socio-political empowerment, and reconstruction and development."[68]

Given the complications posed by the area's history of pre-colonial and colonial migrations, forced removals, and shifting geographical boundaries, the museum's appeal to "community" and that term's association with some ideal of continuity and homogeneity might seem an impossibly hubristic strategy. However, it is precisely the history of engagement with the surrounding groups that provides the most compelling aspect of the Tswaing story. In addition, if one goes beyond the bland managerial tone of the later public relations documents to the earlier rationales for the project, it is clear that "community involvement" was in part driven by a concern to inculcate a sense of investment in the environment and in the benefits accruing from careful management of natural resources. In other words, the larger agenda was driven by concerns similar to those voiced by Denver Webb when he noted that more people needed to feel invested in conserving rather than pillaging local heritage sites. The Tswaing team quickly recognized that in order for such changes in attitude to take place, it was necessary to provide material incentives, particularly among economically deprived groups: "By involving the communities in the planning, development and management of a conservation area like Tswaing, the communities would eventually attain co-ownership of the project, thereby ensuring its continued protection."[69]

As a means of implementing community involvement, on 9 October 1993 a meeting was called to establish what later became the Tswaing Forum, consisting of representatives from the Mabopane, Soshanguve, Nuwe Eersterus, Winterveld, Stinkwater, and other areas surrounding Tswaing. ANC and PAC representatives who were active in the area were also invited to join, as well as individuals from other institutions who could offer specific professional expertise to further the objectives of the project.[70] Three shareholders were represented on the forum: the National Cultural History Museum, the Geological Survey, and the Transvaal Museum (a natural history as opposed to cultural history museum). At the time of its launch, membership on the Tswaing Forum was open to any individual or organization expressing an interest in and a willingness to contribute to the development of the museum. Küsel seems to have felt that since "no financial or political gain can be achieved by joining the Forum," with only "[involvement] in a very special project as compensation," membership would be unlikely to suffer from oversubscription![71]

The Tswaing Forum was "To serve as a general advisory body comprising all individuals and representatives of organisations concerned with the development of Tswaing Museum" and "To constitute working groups for specific tasks."[72] Four working groups or committees (fundraising; planning; scientific and technical; and tourism, education, and training) were set up at the meeting, all reporting back to the Executive Committee. An indication of some of the possible complications of working with the various groups around Tswaing surfaced at this initial meeting, where evidently representatives from the local civic associations had problems deciding about which of the working groups they should join: "Mr. Bacus Mahlanga informs the Tswaing Forum that working groups to serve the community have already been established by the Civic Associations and that members of Civic committees might be appointed to the Working Groups of the Tswaing Forum. He requests that a period of two weeks be allowed to consult with the Civic Association. They will join in the Working Groups as soon as the necessary consultations have taken place."[73] These were not then simply "local communities" but local communities who already had in place a number of structures that operated as a de facto local government to coordinate and effectively run the formal or informal settlements that were their homes.

Civic associations had played a crucial role in organizing and coordinating black urban resistance to apartheid. Developing from the ground laid by the Black Consciousness movement of the early 1970s and the growth of a labor movement, many grassroots civic associations drew upon the organizational structure and style of the UDF when it was founded in 1983 and became affiliated with it.[74] The first democratic elections posed something of a crisis for civic associations since historically they had always operated independently of local and national government structures to undermine the apartheid regime. With the ANC in government from 1994, much debate focused on whether they should remain independent of government funding to retain some autonomy from centralized power structures. This in turn generated discussion around the nature of "civil society," the role of civic associations within it, and civil society's potential contribution to the new democracy.[75] Such uncertainty surrounding the future role of these historically vital grassroots organizations meant that negotiations with the civic associations around Tswaing were politically delicate operations from the outset.

Nevertheless, people from the surrounding areas were encouraged to participate in the Tswaing project and in the discussions about the way the development should proceed with the incentive that once the museum was up and running, they could be employed as guides and education officers for the site. A number of initiatives provided a minimal income for those willing to participate in the experiment. For example, locals were paid for cutting and binding sickle bush into bundles. Another scheme investigated the possibility of a brick-making program "to help small businessmen who are looking at possibilities to build houses with minimal capital outlay."[76] Recognizing that the crater was of ritual significance for some local groups who apparently believed it was "a site with supernatural connotations [occupying] a prominent place in myths and legends," the project team established a nursery for indigenous plants that "have been used traditionally for wood fuel, construction material and medicinal and religious purposes."[77] Selling arts and crafts in an open market at Tswaing was another anticipated money spinner for locals, as were literacy classes to train disabled people locally. A recycling project "to facilitate environmental education awareness" was also mooted as providing employment opportunities. Confusingly, however, the term "volunteer" is often used in conjunction with these suggestions, raising questions about the financial arrangements.[78]

In February 1994 a workshop was arranged by the Tswaing Forum's Tourism, Education, and Training Committee in order to try to determine some of the educational needs of the local communities. The findings were passed on to the Planning Committee for consideration, along with other findings by the other committees.[79] Some suggested the promotion of "African art" and "African music" as potential tourist attractions, as well as archaeological training so that "women from the community could be taught to instruct the visiting groups on pottery, etc."[80] Finally, at the meeting of the forum on 11 June 1994 a needs list was presented by the Planning Committee from submissions made by "the community as well as experts and based on the Mission Statement of Tswaing Crater Museum."[81] The importance of prioritizing the items as either short- or long-term objectives was emphasized; a particular point was made to include the Homeless People's Association in the deliberations of the Tswaing Forum and incorporate twelve members from the association onto the various committees.[82] The inclusion of the Homeless People's Association is indicative of the attempts by the initial museum project team to involve the local community.

Some indication of dissatisfaction in museum-community relations is evident in the minutes of the Tswaing Forum of 15 January 1994. By this time it was clear that security at the museum was becoming an issue, with fencing, cattle, and other museum property having been stolen. Moreover, environmental awareness had obviously not struck a chord with the surrounding communities, who were reported to have cut down trees and damaged the vegetation.[83] A contributing factor may have been that the Homeless People's Association had not been included in a social function organized by the museum on 8 January. The museum's politically nonaligned stand may have been perceived as compromised by this oversight, and minutes record that "every possible precaution would be taken to prevent a recurrence of the problem."[84]

At first the solutions suggested for the security problems were more draconian than the measures actually adopted: "Finally it was decided that the main tasks of the Forum would be to educate the community and to teach them to respect the property that would be developed mainly for their own good. The community would also have to be taught to take responsibility for the preservation of the environment."[85] The support of community leaders, referred to in the minutes as "tribal chiefs," was to be sought, and it was decided to step up information to the surrounding communities about the aims of the project.[86] In the same January meeting the security issue was brought up again, with an explicit emphasis on the "large informal settlement" adjacent to the museum.[87] It is hard not to infer that the residents from this settlement were perceived as largely responsible for the vandalism and damage. Nonetheless, Küsel was careful to explain this kind of vandalism as partly the result of local alienation when the state had run a research station at Tswaing. The policy of exclusion, then, had increased local suspicions and led to complete noncooperation. Fences and cattle started disappearing, and trees were chopped down for building and firewood. "By the end of 1992 the problem was so severe that the State decided to give up the farming, demolish all buildings, pull up the fences and leave the area for the squatters to occupy."[88]

To the museum's credit, its approach was to make sure that the people in the informal settlement were properly informed about the project: "It was also suggested that all communities be involved in the project and that they should work together in its development and so make it their own."[89] By February 1994 it was clear that the problems of unsatisfactory community involvement had not been resolved. At a meeting that month in the council chamber of the National Cultural History Museum the agenda was solely a discussion on "where Tswaing Museum stood on community involvement since Mr. Johannes Mabetwa, community and education officer for Tswaing Museum, has come upon some problems."[90] Mabetwa then proceeded to give an account of "community involvement": "It was however evident that the squatters on the southern side of Tswaing Museum as well as the villages of Moeka, Mmotla and Ratjiepane were not fully informed about the project."[91] Mabetwa suggested the establishment of a community development organisation, "a formal structure and mechanism whereby the community can participate directly in the process of improving the living conditions and quality of life of the total community."[92] The minutes indicate most of all that it is extremely hard to get a clear sense of the tensions and conflicts that necessitated such a meeting in the first place; such is the obfuscation created by the managerial public relations tone.

In March 1994 Abe Damaneyt was appointed official curator of the Tswaing Crater Museum and was formally introduced to the Planning Committee on 13 July. Damaneyt had already worked for the National Cultural History Museum as training officer for black museum personnel (and had been appointed with the aim of improving productivity in the workplace). He had also been involved in voter education for black workers during the run-up to the 1994 elections.[93] His account of the tensions that erupted between the Tswaing communities and the museum management sheds some light on the situation. However, by this time conflicts had arisen between Damaneyt and Mabetwa, so any version of the story is bound to be affected by the experience of difficult personalized animosities.

The main protagonists in the ensuing drama were individuals from the Homeless People's Association, which Damaneyt described as a dispossessed, unemployed, informal labor force. Part of the problem seems to have been the lack of cooperation between the Shoshanguve Civic Association and the Homeless People's Association. The problem was exacerbated by the association's feeling that it had not been properly consulted over the plans for the Tswaing project. In April 1994 the Homeless People's Association wrote to Küsel announcing that it was taking over the museum and installing Mabetwa as curator in place of Damaneyt. Members of the association apparently forced security to open the gates at Tswaing, *toyi-toyied* down to the crater, and only finally dispersed after the intervention of the police.[94] A representative from the South African Parks Board (who had initially recommended the education officer for the post) was called in to mediate among the parties. Agreement was finally reached concerning the protection of museum lands and cattle and the necessity of forming a properly representative committee that would include the Homeless People's Association.[95] By 11 June 1994 Mabetwa had left his post as education officer, and no replacement had been appointed. Consequently it was recognized that "General education and training for people from the community for involvement in the projects must get priority attention. A programme consisting of modules for training people must be considered and a time frame is most urgent. The first trainees must be ready to take groups through in August 1994."[96] By September Mabetwa's replacement had still not been appointed.[97] Presumably any training initiatives were also on hold over this period.

By November 1994 an architectural landscape zoning report incorporated the wish lists of the various groups invested in the museum project. The report makes it clear that the priorities of the museum professionals were not necessarily compatible with those of the surrounding communities. At a meeting of the Tswaing Forum Planning Committee in July, attention had already been drawn to the potential problem: "There is a big contrast between the communities' needs and the museum's needs; some of the communities' needs are practically impossible according to the data collected on land use."[98] Nonetheless, it seems that all the parties' wish lists were incorporated into the zoning proposals report. The communities prioritized a community hall, a picnic area, and a swimming pool. They also specified health care provision, a church, and an education center (including a library), as well as a shopping complex, bank, and post office.[99]

It is perhaps significant, given the difficulties recounted above, that the authors of the zoning report felt compelled to mention that "Closeness to surrounding informal settlements leads to people destroying the assets of the site to provide their basic needs" and that "Personal safety on the site cannot be guaranteed at this stage, should persons venture into the veld unaccompanied."[100] The latter does not necessarily mean that the threat to safety was perceived as human; it could equally well be a threat from the physical environment. But it is interesting that these two "constraints" were listed together under "location." It is also interesting that the drawn zoning plans incorporated a number of features that were not in the minutes of the various committees of the Tswaing Forum but that correspond to a more traditional concept of "tourist" development. These include a "display of African settlement and other cultural aspects," which, roughly translated, means a mock village of tokol huts with arts and crafts manufactured by individuals wearing "traditional" attire, as well as an "accommodation" area showing a group of white visitors seated around a bush fire outside a thatched structure.[101]

I am not interested in making judgments about the integrity of the original museum team's motives regarding the involvement of the surrounding settlements. Rather, what concerns me here is that the museum is a useful example of an institution that evidently recognized the importance of being seen to make an address to an ideal of "community" (from which by implication it absented itself), even going so far as to couch the project for the new museum within the framework of the RDP. At one level the attempt clearly did involve setting up managerial and committee structures designed to accommodate the participation of groups other than museum and academic experts, but it foundered on the fractured loyalties and desires of the surrounding groups, who had not in the past been in any way encouraged to see each other's interests as part of a shared investment. It is in the end fairly remarkable that despite the best efforts of apartheid legislation to divide and rule through its policy of "separate development," it was still possible for people who had otherwise been compelled to compete with one another for dwindling resources to have any capacity for working together at all. Certainly in 1996, Udo Küsel was optimistic about Tswaing in this regard, claiming that it had been a tremendous learning experience for both the museum professionals and the participating locals. For him one of the clearest signs of the success of the venture (at that date) was that "the Homeless People designed their own notice boards and erected them all around the boundaries of the farm to tell people to keep out. In the last two years not a single head of cattle has disappeared and the chopping down of trees has stopped. In comparison, at the Irene Agricultural Research Station, south of Pretoria, some 50 cattle have disappeared during 1994."[102] Nevertheless, as we have seen, apartheid's divisive strategies had left in place some intractable antagonisms that are dramatized on occasions such as the Tswaing experiment.

In 1994 the doors opened on a new museum, the Museum Africa, in Johannesburg's Market Square, next door to two institutions made famous during the apartheid years as windows of hope and defiance in the face of oppression: the Johannesburg Market Theatre and Kippie's Nightclub. The new museum was the postapartheid successor to a civic institution originally intended as a museum of South African history.[103] In one respect at least the new museum shared a priority with its predecessor, the old civic museum, established in September 1935 and known as the Africana Museum. According to R. F. Kennedy, one of its early directors and writer of a semi-official history of the museum, the Africana Museum was primarily conceived as a resource for "popular education and not for research: all exhibits were for display. It was therefore essential that the layout, description and display of exhibits should be both popular and informative."[104] Likewise, the new Museum Africa lays claim to a pedagogic emphasis in its displays. This, however, is probably where any similarity between the two institutions ends.

A number of criticisms about the Africana Museum set the agenda for its revamping. Up until the 1970s it is clear that the museum's idea of "popular and informative" displays concerning South African history was a focus on the European settler experience. Its acquisitions policy stressed the importance of the written word (books) and visual material that usually formed part of colonial / settler representations of "native" life.[105] Any material culture from groups other than these was usually acquired by accident, rather than by design, through a bequest or loan.[106] "Anything that fell under the rubric of 'tribal' history or culture was displayed separately in the Market precinct—the Museum's present location, previously Johannesburg's fruit and vegetable market, acquired in 1974—while its premises in the Library building housed the 'history' exhibits."[107] In 1970 Hilary Bruce was appointed as the first ethnographer to the Africana Museum, and any consistent interest in the social and historical aspects of African cultures dates from this period. When Museum Africa opened its doors to the public in August 1994, she became the first director of the Africana Museum in its new guise.

As with Tswaing, Museum Africa was also an experiment in engaging a broader public—specifically a public more fully representative of South Africa's newly acknowledged electorate. Accordingly, in 1993 the mission statement for the new museum was rewritten: "To be a dynamic museum of the community where a diverse history and heritage of Southern Africa is

explored and presented; to be an educational force for unity and reconciliation."[108] The mission statement for the new museum's education department was even more explicit: "The goals of the new department would be to
attract the broadest possible audience, to communicate with the community
and to accommodate their needs."[109] As a means of implementing this mission, the museum embarked on a number of consultative projects: a postal
survey and traveling exhibition; intensive discussions with Luli Callinicos
and Cynthia Kros of the University of the Witwatersrand social history research group, the History Workshop; consultations with faculty from the
University of the Witwatersrand history department; a number of temporary displays soliciting reactions from the visiting public (this last being
suggestive rather than making claims to scientific representativeness). As is
so often the case with museums, it is not always the grand public statement
that is the most effective or inventive.

The 1990 postal survey was sent to 106 groups, including women's,
youth, and educational organizations; organizations for the disabled; cultural associations (Afrikaans, Indian, and Chinese, among others); and the
educational and tourist sectors.[110] From the responses a list of ten historical topics emerged that it was felt the museum should prioritize. The first
five in order of priority were: "black protest and township unrest, including
Sharpeville and the Soweto riots of 1976"; "the origin and history of black
tribes"; "the release of Nelson Mandela"; "the great trek"; and "the Anglo-
Boer war."[111] Other suggestions were later incorporated into the museum
displays—in particular "early Johannesburg and the discovery of gold." The
postal survey also established the visibility of the museum: "In addition to
the many who refused to visit the museum because it did not fit into their
framework of reference, there were those who were simply oblivious to the
museum's very existence. It was also evident from the findings that the majority of the community felt that while education was the most important
task to be fulfilled this function was being neglected."[112]

Although based on a relatively small sample, the survey results show con-
sistencies within each of the groups of respondents, defined as black, white
(subdivided into "English" and "Afrikaans"), colored, and Indian. For example, in response to the question "Why do you visit or not visit museums?," no black, colored, or Indian respondents answered that they went
to a museum "to learn more about [their] own people" or "to discover how
all South African Communities live." When black respondents gave negative answers, it was mostly because they found museums "irrelevant," or
because "museums are biased; are not representative of all South Africans,"

or they had simply "never been exposed to museums." And the largest proportion of negative responses came from respondents classified as "black" in the survey.[113]

In March 1994 a report was commissioned by an independent body, Integrated Marketing Research, ostensibly to discover to what extent the original name (the Africana Museum) was a contributing factor in dissuading the constituencies who rarely went to or had negative impressions of the museum. Essentially the objective was to establish a new name that would help to promote a positive image for the institution to these groups. The firm conducted two types of qualitative research: a brainstorming workshop of a group of fifteen (including three representatives from the museum) and a questionnaire to leaders of major civic, political, labor, and community organizations in South Africa.[114] The questionnaire, though targeting somewhat different groups, asked questions basically similar to those in the postal survey, and it got the same results. The participants of the workshop recommended unanimously to change the name of the museum. As an indication of the general feeling of the group, one participant noted, "I think it is important that they change the name—everything starts with a name; if we don't change the name it will be the same—even if everything else changes."[115] The report also emphasized the need for the museum to be "democratized" and "that steps be taken to ensure that the board, directors, staff, advisers, consultants, tour-guides, and supporters reflect the complexion of the total South African population."[116]

A temporary initiative that yielded fruitful results by imaginative means was Ronit Ben-Guri's traveling exhibition to not only inform "the community" about the existence of the museum and its change in direction, but also to get it "involved in the transition through the monitoring of [its] responses."[117] The project was outlined by a team from the museum at a visit to the Funda Centre in Soweto, where it conducted workshops with young people from an organization called the Inspiration Centre. (The center finds work and provides an educational program for matriculants, university dropouts, and young unemployed professionals.)[118] Students from the center were asked to consider such questions as "Why are museums important in society?" and "Why and how should we study history?" The workshop ended with a number of improvised performances based around selected museum objects, with the aim of drawing "the objects into their historical context."[119]

The ultimate objective was to get members of the group who felt enthusiastic about working with the museum to help write the "script" for the traveling exhibition, which would also involve animating specific objects through a series of dramatic performances and audience participation. Once completed, the exhibition was intended for the Soweto College of Education, Vista University, and a number of high schools in the Johannesburg area. The initiative offered training for four members of the Funda Centre who wished to continue working for the museum. The use of theater, improvised by the young people themselves, was an inspired method for promoting interest in the museum with wit and humor. It had already been used to considerable effect in other African states for educational purposes, especially in relation to AIDS and HIV awareness. Just prior to the museum's opening in March 1994 another project was devised with schools and "aimed at primary school children, and in particular those who have not traditionally visited museums . . . which will give the children, parents and teachers knowledge of what a museum can mean in their community, to encourage them to become part of museum collecting, preserving and educational activities, and to do this by using appropriate means to reach out into the community."[120] The goal was to get children involved through a competition to design a poster advertising the opening of the new museum.[121]

After members of the History Workshop at the University of the Witwatersrand had read the drafts of scripts for the proposed "chronological history" section of Museum Africa, Luli Callinicos (a long-standing member and the prime mover behind an initiative for a workers' museum in Newtown) met with the museum staff and provided detailed suggestions. These included the importance of linking "themes of women, land and dispossession, labour and migration."[122] Two other aspects were stressed: the importance of including oral histories and other forms of historical narrative and performance and of providing a view of history as perceived by those experiencing it within the country rather than from the colonial / settler perspective.

Consultations with other Witwatersrand historians foregrounded one of the longest running debates among museum staff members—whether or not to structure the historical material in two simultaneous strands: a macro history (referred to in the debates as a chronological history) and a micro history dealing with the lived experiences and stories of individuals (referred to as the cultural history strand). It is worth detailing some of the discussions around this issue because they shed considerable light on the nature of producing a relevant revisionist history in a South African public museum. The problem was summed up in an article by Hilary Bruce and the museum's history curator, David Saks: "Critics of the chronological / cultural history split have expressed concern that a Cultural History Gallery might come to perpetuate the much-discredited apartheid policy of breaking up South African society into mutually exclusive 'cultures,' for many South Africans a distorted and ideologically repugnant interpretation."[123] This comment refers to the *volkekunde* school of anthropology's emphasis on the explanatory power of "ethnicity" as the primary structuring category of society and culture and the ideological uses made of it by the apartheid state.[124]

A discussion paper circulated among the museum staff involved in conceptualizing the new displays outlines the difficulties in the South African context and more broadly with the use of the term "culture." The author, Eric Goodwin, summarized: "The tribal categories of culture which assume the existence of primordial identities [are] not acceptable. As I have pointed out, 'cultures' is a politically loaded term, and its use tends to encourage a distorted view of history. On the other hand, 'Culture' is a somewhat fuzzy term with a specific historical baggage, encouraging a Romantic, organic view of social processes. Sharp's [this should read Thornton's] re-definition of culture as a resource, or set of resources, is quite promising. Rather than attempt to say what culture is, we should concentrate on showing what it does."[125] In other words, Goodwin's allusion is to Robert Thornton's synthesis: "An understanding of culture, then, is not simply a knowledge of differences, but rather an understanding of how and why differences in language, thought, use of materials and behaviours have come about."[126] Further objections followed from the chrono-cultural split as a structuring principle for the new displays: "In our north gallery, we have a display of chronological history and an ethnological display of "culture." Chronological history is white, and culture is black. This represents a very basic ideological division which has been perpetuated in the proposals for a hall of chronological history and a hall of cultural history in the new museum."[127] Goodwin continues: "The main problem facing us in the hall of 'cultural' history seems to be how to display culture as something dynamic, open-ended and changing."[128] The proposed solution was to substitute the term "social" for "cultural" history, to be free "from the endless intellectual agonising that is inevitably associated with attempting to say anything relevant or true about culture."[129]

David Saks defended and finally won the case for the chrono-cultural division while acknowledging that his views were not shared by many of his colleagues: "It is unrealistic to group an ordinary event (e.g., a *nagmaal* [or First Holy Communion gathering]) with an extraordinary one (e.g., Xhosa Cattle Killing). To do so would lessen the impact of the latter example whose revolutionary nature and profound short- and long-term consequences would come to look almost typical or run-of-the-mill."[130] Interesting here is that the chronological history galleries (and therefore the macro histories) were evidently not conceived of simply in the usual terms of great white men, wars, and high finance. For example, Saks was at pains to defend a display that later aroused considerable controversy—"Birds in a Cornfield"—in the chronological (macro) history section despite the objections of some of his colleagues, who considered it to belong with the cultural (micro) history section. The exhibit consisted of a series of informal houses acquired by the museum from the families who had actually lived in them. Saks's impassioned defense sheds light on the structural differences that can be made when hitherto marginalized events are incorporated into a narrative presenting them as part of major historical forces:

> I am dismayed that there is controversy over the destination of the Shack whose inclusion in Chrono. I thought had been settled long ago. The Shack simply makes too many powerful statements about the period within which it is to be included: Forced removals, black poverty and homelessness, cheap labour etc. To included [sic] it in Cultural where the emphasis is less on politics than on lifestyle would be a frightful waste since the above messages would be subliminated [sic]. The Shack is not a statement about how people lived but a stark and visceral indictment of callousness and legalised suffering. It must be emphasised that the very existence of the shack is *Extraordinary,* a product of unusual and deeply unsettled circumstances. It will give essential punch to an area of the display that, perhaps more than any other, really needs it (i.e. "Apartheid and Resistance 1948–1963").[131]

It is to the "Birds in a Cornfield" exhibit that I want to now turn. In some senses a controversial exhibition, this section of the museum dealt with an aspect of housing in and around Johannesburg, described in an early document at the time of its conception as follows: "The display . . . focuses on squatters and aims to show that people living in enforced unsatisfactory conditions transform their environments according to their needs, desires and aspirations. The figures for people living in informal housing in the Johannesburg region range between 1.4 and 2 million: this provides the justification for dealing with the aspect of housing."[132]

In September 1991 the museum was offered the chance to buy a squatters' shack in Thokoza, a township in the East Rand.[133] Referred to in a museum design brief as the "Nyambose family zinc shack" at the time of the curators' visit to the township, the structure (figure 60) was located in the yard of the Nyambose family's permanent house and was being sublet "to generate extra income. It was eagerly occupied by those to whom poverty, a housing

60. Nyambose family zinc shack beside their new concrete house. Thokoza, 1991. Courtesy of MuseuMAfricA.

backlog and residential restrictions offered little other choice."[134] The museum, recognizing the necessity of the structure (to both the Nyamboses
and the current occupiers) replaced the shack with what was described as "a
new prefabricated hut." The museum design brief records that "The Nyambose family have lived an unstable life in Thokoza on the East Rand since
1967, moving from one back yard shack to the next. They finally acquired a
permanent home in 1991."[135]

The selection of Thokoza is not incidental. Thokoza is infamous to many
in the Johannesburg area, and certainly to most black locals, as the site of
violent clashes between IFP hostel dwellers and residents of Thokoza, Katle-
hong, and other nearby townships who were mostly ANC supporters. The
violence reached its height during the run-up to the 1994 elections. Over
six hundred victims from both sides died in the fighting, including women
and children, journalists, photographers (including Abdul Shariff and the
award-winning *Star* photographer Ken Oosterbroek), and political leaders
such as ANC leader Sam Ntuli and the lawyer Thabo Molewa. Later Thokoza was to be the site of a monument to the victims of this very violence: a
granite block, in a form reminiscent of memorials usually associated with
world wars, inscribed with the 688 names of those killed. The monument
was erected in the infamous no-go area, Khumalo Street, which formed
a natural boundary at the time of the clashes between the IFP-supporting
hostel-dwellers and the ANC township dwellers, and it was clearly intended
as a symbol of peace between the two factions. Moreover, the timing of the

initially scheduled unveiling was clearly designed to provide both Mbeki and Buthelezi with the opportunity to stage another kind of reconciliation during the lead-up to the 1999 elections. In the event, the opportunity was missed, reputedly because of tensions between the Thokoza Monument committee and IFP members, who claimed that the funding for the monument was not transparent enough. Mbeki's speech at the unveiling, which was almost a year late in coming, focused on the cause of African unity: "We are all Africans.... We must agree that we will never allow the apartheid ideology of separate mentalities to play its sinister part in fuelling animosity, hatred and violence amongst our people."[136]

One other dwelling, constructed with corrugated iron, wood, and newspaper, was acquired by the museum from Alexandra Township. Like the Nyambose family zinc shack, it had a personal history attached to it, having actually belonged to a named individual, Charles Mbubana, rather than being a reconstructed model of informal housing. Mbubana was already employed by the museum prior to the construction of the exhibition and was later to animate his home for the visitor. "Charles Mbubeni [sic], a member of the museum staff, was born in Alexandra.... When he reached secondary school he was sent to family in Venda (in the northeast of the country) in order to get a better education than was available in Alexandra. He returned to Johannesburg to work, found the family home no longer available and built himself a shack in a vacant lot where 13 other homes and at least 60 people live."[137]

The area in Museum Africa dealing with informal housing is called "Masekeng," or "the place of shacks." It is introduced with a historical section on the Orlando squatters' movement. Begun in 1944 by the increasingly frustrated and desperate homeless in the area, the movement was led by James Sofasonke Mpanza, a member of the Orlando Advisory Board, who is famously reported to have said, "Very well then, we shall go and sit down on municipal land and wait for the Municipality to come and put a roof over our heads."[138] What began with 250 shacks in March 1944 gained momentum to become a mass movement involving over twenty thousand people. The display brief continues: "By October 1945 Shantytown still existed under extremely unsanitary conditions and 4,042 breeze block shelters were finally constructed to house the people under slightly better circumstances. Since this time the extreme shortage of housing available to African people has continued and squatting and other forms of informal housing have only multiplied dramatically."[139] The brief also describes the reconstruction of "two hessian shacks" erected under the direction of individuals who lived in the Orlando squatter camp in the 1940s. Information

on the families involved and the "office" from which Mpanza ran the operation were intended to be on display with photos of the events surrounding
the squatters' movement.

The whole Masekeng area, including the two contemporary examples of
informal housing, uses sound to animate the displays. In the case of the
Nyambose home, given a night-time setting by the curator, the sounds are
of a lullaby and snoring from a sleeping family. In the case of the Mbubana
house, "A tape of friends chatting and laughing in the kitchen with all the
other sounds of life in an overcrowded yard has been made and will be playing continually." [140] For the Orlando section the sound track was intended to
be *Mzulu, Mxhosa, Msuthu hlanganani* (Zulu, Xhosa, Sotho must all stand
together): "This and other songs sung at the time [were to] be played continually, with a background of hammering, calling out, and shouts that
Mpanza and others would have made in calling people together for meetings and community discussions, or reminding people to pay their levy." [141]

The design brief, produced by curator Kerrie Shepherd-Nkosi, is concep-
tualized around a set of political and social circumstances and makes no
bones about laying the blame at the door of apartheid. "When the mining camp of Johannesburg began in 1886 it was made very clear that black
people were only wanted in the city as single working units. Their need for
family life and homes was actively ignored. From this early beginning until
very recently the state and Municipality [have] put considerable effort and
resources into controlling the number of black people entering the city and
where they may live." [142] The broader aims of the display are to highlight
"the need for a home as one of the most basic of human needs" and "To
give some living examples of how some black families have acted upon their
given situations, resisted the limitations placed on them and lived out their
God given right to a home." [143] Ultimately the display was also intended to
touch on "the current crises in the Witwatersrand of homelessness and the
plans under way to address this problem." [144]

It seems then that the museum was very careful both to provide a historical context for the squatters' movement and to see it as a form of resistance
against apartheid—in other words, both an oppressive set of circumstances
imposed on black South Africans and the occasion for creative and organized agency on the part of this same constituency. The evident importance
of this aspect of the new exhibitions was signaled during the grand opening
events of the new museum. The owners of the shacks were advertised as
being there "to welcome visitors to their old homes." A performance by the
Sofasonke Party Choir (named after Mpanza) was followed by a talk from

Mpanza's daughter, recounting how her charismatic father had led the first squatters' movement.

The "Birds in a Cornfield" display raises many interesting questions, not least about constituency. The curator responsible for it, Kerrie Shepherd-Nkosi, explained: "Everyone knows how white people live. But only black people know how black people live."[145] Certain critics were quick to pick up on this as a sign of a deeply paternalistic attitude. Ivor Powell in the *Weekly Mail and Guardian* conceded that "The museum, as the press releases insist, is a museum for all. In one sense this is manifestly true: the launch exhibition does record a lot more than the white Johannesburg construct of the colonial and apartheid past."[146] But he added some scathing commentary on the shack exhibit: "Mbubana is the Alex resident whose home has made the journey—and note the irony: in South Africa it is a geographical one, not historical—of about 10 kilometres. In the course of that journey it is magicked from shelter into ethnography—for whites, that is. For a whole lot of the 'all' the museum is aimed to serve, it's a lived environment."[147] Of course, to a white viewer, liberal or not, this is inevitably the effect. Other coverage on the new museum simply reported the display with little positive or negative comment but often stressed its uniqueness and that it was the first time such an exhibit had been shown in a South African museum.[148]

The story, however, is a little different once various black views are solicited, including those of the people whose very homes are on display. One report suggested that with the money Charles Mbubana got for the shack from the museum, he was able to build a brick house. When asked how he felt about the museum buying his former home, he said, "I am very happy to see my shack at the museum. History is not Jan van Riebeeck or Nelson Mandela. What we are doing here is for our children. Maybe in 20 years' time we will be having houses and not shacks anymore, and my home will be part of history."[149] Another report was misleadingly headlined, "Welcome to Our Humble Home . . . Step Inside—and Take a Trip Back in Time" (while the accompanying photograph of the inside of the Nyambose family home carried the more pertinent caption, "We are free, but we still live in shacks"). Mbubana emphasized that "This will show people what living in a shack is like," and "I hope they will learn that most of us did not choose to live in these conditions. We had no choice."[150] Sam Nyambose was reported as initially horrified at the museum's request to buy his shack: "What do these white people want to do—laugh at us? I didn't know what a museum was."[151] He then went on to say, "You can't hide from the truth. It's where I come from. I can't lie and say I lived in Sandton."[152] The text of his family's story is on the outside of the shack (figure 61), and Nyambose was a familiar presence at the exhibit, explaining the circumstances and conditions of life in Thokoza to visitors.

In December 2000 both Charles Mbubana and Sam Nyambose kindly agreed to be interviewed. Mbubana's story is interesting for what it tells us about conditions in the townships prior to and just after the 1994 elections and about his own expectations from the exhibition of his family home, and for additional information it provides about the museum's role in relation to Mbubana in the construction of the exhibition itself. For Mbubana the most important visitors are black children from middle-class families who have no knowledge of the living conditions represented by his shack and the others in the "Birds in a Cornfield" exhibition. It is clearly crucial to him that the next generation grow up aware of the housing crisis and the conditions in which people were forced to live. He is aware that participating in such a personal capacity leaves one potentially vulnerable; he related that his brother and sister were not happy about having their home exposed to view, particularly to more privileged children.

A sound track with the busy chatter of his mother's clients drinking her home-brewed *umbumbote* (beer) and the goings-on of the street outside forms an integral part of the three-room Mbubana exhibit. Charles recorded these himself with a tape recorder provided by the museum. Likewise, the museum gave him a camera to take photos he considered relevant—again, his mother's income-generating beer business and scenes of her clients drinking figure prominently and are on the wall of one of the rooms. Unlike most reconstructions, whose aim is to reproduce a seamless fantasy, the tools of the trade are displayed on the walls: while listening to the sounds of clients drinking and joking we see Mbubana's photograph of the tape recorder leaning nonchalantly against a wall, picking up their voices (figure 62). The kitchen items in the exhibit belonged to Mbubana's mother and were replaced with new ones by the museum.

The house itself was bought by the museum, and the money was used by the Mbubana family to construct a single room out of concrete breeze blocks. Mbubana emphasizes that it is not a great house and certainly not the best in Alexandra, but it is better than before. He talks of the construction of the shack and the relative warmth provided by cardboard (as opposed to corrugated iron) but notes the solidity provided by iron. (Mbubana's reconstructed bedroom is in figure 63.) He mentions the freezing cold in the winter and the blistering heat in summer and emphasizes the importance of the door, which seems to have a significance way beyond its use value. Despite the fragility of the cardboard walls, thieves rarely if ever choose to

Top 61. Nyambose family zinc shack reconstructed in Museum Africa.
Photo by Jean Brundrit.

Bottom 62. Clients drinking Mrs. Mbubana's home-brewed beer. The tape
recorder lent to Charles Mbubana is leaning against the wall to the right.
Photo by Charles Mbubana. Courtesy of MuseuMAfricA.

63. Charles Mbubana's bedroom in his reconstructed shack in Museum Africa exhibit. Photo by Jean Brundrit.

enter a shack via the walls. According to Mbubana, an unspoken protocol makes the door the unimpeachable / indisputable threshold. Such is the symbolic and actual significance of the door that its presence is underlined with a photograph of it *in situ*, barred for additional impermeability beside the reconstruction.

Mbubana spoke vehemently about the demoralization and danger of living in such conditions and noted that rural townships were even worse. He said that everyone had high hopes that the situation would change after the elections; although things were certainly better, changes were too slow in coming. He was aware that the exhibition might be misleading in that it might encourage "outsiders" to think that such conditions could be consigned to the past. He also felt that if he were in the education department of the museum, he would be able to avert such misunderstandings. As it stands, his family story—the story of the house—is written in the Venda language on the walls of the reconstructed shelter.

When the Nyambose home in Thokoza was obtained by the museum, Sam Nyambose was also given recording equipment. He chose to record

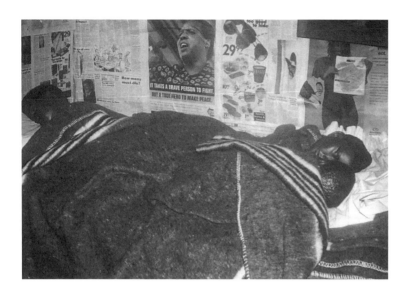

64. Bedroom inside the reconstructed Nyambose family shack in Museum Africa showing details of the newspaper lining the walls. Photo by Jean Brundrit.

his mother singing a traditional lullaby, "Tula Tula," and a child crying. As the visitor walks into a room that serves as a bedroom, he sees the figure of a mother rocking a child in her arms by the light of a paraffin burner; the sound of the song and the child fill the tiny, darkened space. In our interview Nyambose draws my attention to the newspaper that lines the cardboard walls and remarks that the carbon deposits from the stove necessitated changing it often (figure 64). He repeats this later and underlines his point with the comment that you "don't have to have money to be clean." For him, as for Mbubana, the door into the shack is important. He indicates the damage to the door and explains that it is the original door that they had in 1969, which was kicked in by two men with knives just before Christmas that year. They stole the family's Christmas food, as well as money that they had put aside for school fees. He recalls how nervous the family was after the attack, and he reiterates the importance of safety. People get dangerous, he says, when they are hungry. No one should have to live like this. When the museum first approached the Nyambose family, Sam was skeptical about the project. But his mother convinced him that it was important for foreigners to see their living conditions, and one of the museum curators insisted that the display would be informative. She took it upon herself to convince Sam of the significance of having his home in a museum, especially since he was unfamiliar with such an institution. She apparently took him around the transport museum and offered by way of explanation that a museum was "where we keep history."[153]

For Nyambose the exhibition was valuable as a spur to disadvantaged communities to show them another way to change their circumstances. He also felt that it was an important educational tool for people who were ignorant about such housing conditions and thought the shacks simply signified "a place where thieves lived." When taking tours around the exhibition, Nyambose noticed that children who were from Thokoza and lived in shacks were very quiet around the exhibition, whereas those from more privileged families—and even those who were also from Thokoza but who lived in concrete houses—would treat the display very differently, displacing the dummies and other objects and playing with them. For them it was only a set in a museum, not a part of their lives. Sam was adamant that the exhibition was experienced very differently by those who actually shared such living conditions.

When the exhibit first opened in 1994, I quizzed an old friend, Pitika Ntuli, about his feelings on the shack exhibit, and his response was similar to Mbubana's. He too felt that such exhibits were useful for his young sons' generation. For him too there was a strong sense that his sons might grow up never knowing the realities of informal housing settlements. In some sense this may seem an odd response and one that also suggests a willful disavowal of the continuing homelessness of many black constituencies in contemporary South Africa. On the other hand, perhaps it is also indicative of the aspirations of a new black middle class. How far might such a response be born from the need to consign such representations (perhaps too quickly) to the past? It is evident from the design brief and also from interviews that this was not the aim of Kerrie Shepherd-Nkosi, who "wanted to show how nothing has really changed and that the African housing problem has only deteriorated."[154] In other words, her clear intention was to get across the message that very little had changed since the days of the squatters' revolt in Orlando in the 1940s.

Since the stir they caused at the opening of the museum, scant attention, controversial or otherwise, has been paid to the shacks. This is perhaps only to be expected. Any museum would consider itself extraordinarily lucky to get constant coverage for a permanent display. But it would be interesting to know what kind of response there would have been if such an exhibit had been put up more recently rather than in the wake of the euphoria generated by the first democratic elections. In 1994 an exhibit foregrounding not only the historical circumstances that resulted in the proliferation of informal housing, but also the continuing growth of this unacceptable situation in the present, seems to have been acknowledged as well intentioned and even progressive. Perhaps crucially, the exhibit's opening corresponded with a moment when most individuals living in informal settlements felt optimistic about the prospect of finally getting decent government housing and even, in some cases, settling land claims or getting compensation. How such an exhibit is viewed today by individuals living in informal housing, when it has become clear that homelessness is still a nationwide problem of growing dimensions and when most land claims are yet to be recognized, is an important contingency to consider when thinking through the kinds of meanings produced by such displays. Would this mean that the cynical criticism of an Ivor Powell (that the display simply produced an "ethnographic" subject for white edification) might be more appropriate today? At the time of the opening, on the other hand, Powell could (and possibly should) have been exposed as having fallen prey to his own critique by reading the exhibit solely from the perspective of a white liberal rather than considering that there may be a perspective to which he (precisely *as* a white liberal) had limited access and knowledge—responses that some reporters took the time to elicit from the "ethnographic subject" of Powell's article.

In order to explore further the ways in which such images are embedded in complex and contradictory meanings, it may be instructive to compare these museum reconstructions with another group of images of informal housing interiors and their occupants. One of my reasons for doing this is to explore how far the institutional setting constrains and produces the meanings of such displays.

Zwelethu Mthethwa has become well known since 1994 on the international art circuit and within South Africa. Initially he achieved a reputation through his work in pastels, but in 1996 he began to produce a series of posed photographic portraits of individuals in the interiors of their informal dwellings. Mthethwa is by no means the only photographer to focus on informal housing in South Africa, but he is one of the few to do so exclusively in color, and this factor alone is a major component of the quality and appeal of his work. His are not the only representations of township life which could just as easily be understood in terms of the interior as metonymic of the individual or group. His photographs clearly embrace the creative ways in which individuals extend the limited means at their disposal for expressing individuality (limited through either the restrictions of social control or economic constraints) by projecting an ideal personality via the small spaces that do remain in their control—in this case their shacks. It would also be true to say that especially to a European not exposed to the conditions of life on informal settlements, these interiors represent a compelling and appealing combination of invention driven by necessity.

Consequently, one of the difficulties with Mthethwa's work, compounded by its primary locus of consumption in the contemporary international art market, is that the decorative surfaces and often incongruous juxtapositions immediately aestheticize the interiors to a viewer susceptible to the ironies of Surrealist disjuncture.[155] There is in the end, however, something different about Mthethwa's images and the other documentary photographs of township life. If we compare Mthethwa's interiors with, for example, Rashid Lombard's *Remember Our Women No. 5* (1990) and Jolene Martin's *The Ndewesu Household, Guguletu* (1996) (figures 65 and 66) it seems to me that Mthethwa's combination of dense color printing and the compositional focus on the individuals in their own space allows an element of agency not usually present in the more familiar documentary photographs of township life. The fact that both Lombard's and Martin's images are shot in black and white and that they share the snapshot "moment in time" quality usually associated with documentary photography means that ultimately these moments are "stolen" from the subjects, who also inevitably become objects of sociological scrutiny, "representative" of a life situation. Consequently the primary agency here is that of the artist / photographer. This is despite the fact that the women in the Martin image are evidently looking straight at us and despite the fact that there is no attempt to pursue the conceit of "snapshot" to the extent of making it seem as if the subjects in either of these images are unaware of the camera. It is interesting that Lombard and Martin come from different generations but that, on one level, they illustrate a continuous tradition. The classic construction of "incidental" juxtaposition, which belongs to the documentary mode and which is historically already embedded in the South Africa context within the narrative frame of the photojournalism of the "liberation struggle"—a difficult legacy to shed—ultimately acts as a distraction from the possibility of the subjects being able to represent themselves.

Whatever the problems of Mthethwa's work, something else is going on here. His work may effectively aestheticize poverty—albeit in the mode of kitsch or global invention rather than the usual romantic narrative of victim / hero(ine). Notwithstanding this qualification, it seems to me that it is possible to argue that his subjects are represented in such a way that they "own" their space. They are neither defined primarily as the "victims" of apartheid, nor are they necessarily oblivious to the limitations of their environment. Perhaps this reading is elicited by the combination of the often dramatic seriousness of their facial expressions and the extraordinary

65. Rashid Lombard, *Remember Our Women No. 5*, 1990. Black-and-white photograph. Courtesy of the artist and the South African National Gallery.

66. Jolene Martin, *The Ndewesu Household, Guguletu*, 1996. Black-and-white photograph. Courtesy of the photographer.

vibrancy of the surface decoration of walls, tables, cloths, and floors that make up the distinctiveness of these interiors. Indeed it is significant that these "portraits" are seen and mostly reproduced as a series rather than as individual photographs (at least in catalogs and books). Their representation as a series reinforces the creative capacity of the individuals to customize their interiors despite the limited resources at their disposal. This alone tends to emphasize the sense of agency in a way that remains ambiguous in the Lombard and Martin images, although it is also true that in Mthethwa's series this issue is complicated by the fact that none of the individuals are ever named; they are all "Untitled."

Mthethwa explains his antipathy to the use of black and white and his preference for color photographs:

> When I view some of these [black-and-white] photographs I cannot help but think of these people who have been photographed as victims of abuse. The choice of photographing in black and white by most photographers gives an acute political angle of desertion and emptiness. I do not believe that poverty is equal to degradation. For me, colour restores people's dignity. I ask myself why we, as photographers, should deny these people colour while it plays such an important part in their lives. I cannot start to imagine how drab the photographs I am currently taking would look in black and white; how desolate their state would be to the viewer's eye. I think these photographs preserve and show a humanness of the occupants in their private spaces. They restore their pride and affirm their ownership.[156]

It is hard to refute the optimism of this statement when looking at Mthethwa's series of photographs taken in 1996 at the famous Crossroads settlement outside Cape Town. Here, surrounded by billboard-scale advertisements for Bastille brandy, a man reclines on his bed, facing the camera, while his broom (a sign of his self-conscious concern for his interior) is propped against the wall of the shack and a row of gleaming cooking pots and a music system are prominently included in the shot (plate 1). Another man reclines on an aging sofa in a corner of a room whose walls gleam in checkered splendor from the all-over papering provided by the red squares of Lifebuoy Soap packaging. Tables are covered with pristine tablecloths and carefully placed ornaments (plate 2). A priestess from a Zionist church sits unmistakably regally on a bed, staff in hand, dressed in officiating robes; the walls are covered in newspaper overprinted with a plaid design that picks up on the pattern from her bedspread (plate 3). Another series that Mthethwa completed in 1999 continues the theme begun in 1996. Some photographs

67. Percival Nkonzo, *Siphiwo Stalking a Dog at No. 42, NY 70, Nyanga*, 1996. Black-and-white photograph. Courtesy of the photographer.

from this group have the effect of emphasizing the inventive construction of the space itself and the care and precision with which items are placed within it.

Of course, one might argue that while the color and format of Mthethwa's portraits with no name may certainly diminish the usual desolation portrayed in other photographs of informal settlements, not all black-and-white images necessarily fall into this category. Some manage to break the mold of the medium's association with "struggle" documentary. As part of a project of picturing South Africa after the first democratic elections, a group of young people was selected to work with Gavin Younge to produce images of what they considered to be the truly representative landmarks of their city, Cape Town.[157] One particular image shot by Percival Nkonzo offers us a new vision of the township. *Siphiwo Stalking a Dog at No. 42, NY 70, Nyanga*, shows a young man crouching with his back to us, reenacting a fantasy of a hunting ritual complete with so-called traditional weapons (a shield and spear) (figure 67). But the irony of his actions and Nkonzo's representation of them are immediately evident, for his "prey" is someone's pet dog—or perhaps just a domesticated stray. His actions are emptied of the ritual significance attributed to them by colonial fantasy or touristic enthusiasm determined to place the "native" in his "authentic" ethnic setting. The sharp lines of the photo pick up on the variety of building types and materials: the carefully constructed clapboard house with corrugated iron roof on the right; the less regular segments of housing reconstituted from motley materials to the left; the brick patio—laid but uncemented; the fence—functionally organic. The township is not the usual setting for such ritual stalking reenactments, and Nkonzo knows this all too well. We share the joke with him. His image is both humorous and serious in that such juxtapositions may well also remind the viewer of "the experience of dislocation and relocation that is the everyday for hundreds of thousands of South Africans."[158] As Jane Taylor points out in her introductory essay on the project, Nkonzo's title, with its elaborate coding in place of street or house name, draws attention to the dehumanizing and regulatory aspect of worker housing provision under the apartheid state.[159]

Now that we have seen a number of representations of urban township living and informal settlements by artists from different generations, different class backgrounds, and different experiences of township living, ranging from firsthand to thirdhand, it is possible to appreciate more fully the possibilities and limitations represented by the museum reconstruction (for this is the most accurate description) of informal settlements. Certainly in a prestigious new institution such as Museum Africa, which claims greater accessibility and an appeal to a more representative public and which also claims to be dealing with a revised account of the history of not only Johannesburg, but also the nation, it is a "great leap forward" to document the struggle of ordinary (and extraordinary) people for their right to a home; moreover, an account is offered that informs the viewer not only of the struggle, but also of inventiveness and resilience in the face of violent state opposition. Perhaps the rich texture of the different forms of agency available to individuals and groups that is so suggestive in the humor and irony of some of the photographs we have explored may be missing from the "Birds in a Cornfield" exhibit. Perhaps also without direct animation by Mbubana or Nyambose the displays risk becoming simply a poorer version of the images offered by black and white "struggle" photographers. Nevertheless, it seems to me that such an exhibit serves a useful purpose in attempting to contextualize informal housing as a necessity, a form of resistance, *and* a disgrace but certainly an integral part of life in Johannesburg for thousands of black families at one time or another.

It is also important to see the "Birds in a Cornfield" exhibit in relation to two other displays that introduced the public to the new museum in 1994, since together they present a more multidimensional representation of life in the outlying townships surrounding Johannesburg. "The Sounds of the City" focuses on the musical culture of *marabi*, which thrived in the unpromising environment of the slumyards of Johannesburg in the 1920s and 1930s. Marabi became one of the sole forms of recreation for the hundreds of thousands of migrant workers who were virtually forced into wage labor in the mines, driven from rural areas by high taxes and legislation such as the 1913 Land Act, which reserved huge tracts of land exclusively for white farmers. This section also recreates a *shebeen* (an informal nightclub) environment from 1950s Sophiatown. The walls here are plastered with posters and photographs from the pages of the famous *Drum* magazine—photographs of township jazz musicians, many of whom went into exile and became household names abroad, such as Abdullah Ibrahim, Hugh Masakela, and Miriam Makeba. The whole recreated environment fairly hums with the sound of township jazz produced during a period in Johannesburg's history that saw "developments in indigenous jazz, the introduction of radio and the start of the record industry."[160] We leave this display via an exhibition that leads us summarily through some of the "rhythms of resistance"— instances of music used to protest against the apartheid regime from the 1960s to the 1990s. Such upbeat (literally) historical and contemporary representations of township living and the rich texture of cultural expression that emerged from it provide other and perhaps more positive images of black working-class life, as well as of an emergent middle class, that offer productive complications to the more homogeneous image of poverty and struggle represented by the shack display.

LABOR

Johannesburg's fortunes have always been closely tied to those of the international gold standard. The huge red mine dumps that announce one's entry into the city are an indelible reminder that the wealth of this sprawling, riverless city is founded on gold mining. It is fitting, therefore, that a new museum highlighting local history should have some kind of exhibition dealing with the impact of this industry on its citizens. In order to fully appreciate the kind of intervention represented by Ann Wanless's curatorial plans for the "Work" section of the exhibit "Johannesburg Transformations" at Museum Africa (part of the opening exhibit for the museum), it is worth considering one of the only other representations of "labor" available in the city prior to the opening of Museum Africa or the Newtown Workers' Library and Museum in April 1995.[161]

Heralded in its publicity as being a mere eight kilometers from the Johannesburg city center, Gold Reef City has been part of the tourist itinerary since its opening in the late 1970s. It comes as no surprise to discover that out of the 75,000–85,000 visitors per month—certainly up until 1990—who were paying for the privilege of "experiencing" a working gold mine, among other attractions, a third of these were foreign tourists.[162] Owned initially, by the appropriately named Empire Amusement Park Company, Gold Reef City presents a reconstruction of industrial life and labour that lives up to the company name and offers the visitor all the fun of the fair and a neatly sanitized version of history, "a past without compounds or segregation."[163] There is no mention, here amid the fun of the fairground atmosphere, of the migrant labor system or the gruesome living and working conditions for the black workforce: "the blacks of Gold Reef City are mostly happy songsters, music-makers and dancers."[164] Even the reconstructed Victorian mining cottages have been transformed into more acceptably spectacular environments, filled with a hodgepodge of Africanalia and the ever-expanding souvenir opportunity. Mark Gevisser, in a report on the attraction, interviewed a number of white and black families with historical connections to the location. It seems that neither were any the wiser about their familial histories after a visit: "A doctor, Sibusiso Nkono, and his daughters also came looking for their past, but they had less luck than the (white) Brand family. 'My father grew up right here,' said Nkono, pointing at some Victorian Coffee Shoppe or other. 'I have to ask myself, what really went on?' "[165] As Cynthia Kros wittily observes in her sharp analysis, "In a wonderful colonial transposition, the Europeans come to trade their currency for beads and baubles. Gold Reef City has become a trading post on the frontiers between an imagined Africa on the one hand, and a sentimental Europe and the newer, less environmentally tactful, colonial powers on the other."[166]

Nonetheless, Gold Reef City retains some pretensions to serious educational value by being one of the few places where one might find some of the earliest examples of headgear and electronic hoists from the history of the mining industry. The visitor is treated to a gold pour and, for an additional fee, can experience going down a mine shaft in a mine cage guided by ex-miners or mine officials.[167] My own tour of the mine shaft was indeed informative and clearly critical of the conditions to which the men were subjected. But this veneer of historical realism becomes more of a problem than a solution in a context where the majority of what is on offer is so patently an entrepreneurial fantasy. Furthermore, as Rassool and Witz have pointed out, Gold Reef City as a model for putting an acceptable public face on an otherwise unacceptable industry with an extremely poor record of labor relations and health and safety provisions has clear historical precedents in South Africa. It has more than a little in common with the attempts of the Chamber of Mines, particularly in the 1940s and 1950s, to "clean up" its public image as a means of countering escalating criticisms abroad and at home. Part of this drive involved increasing public access to carefully vetted and elaborately prepared areas of the mine compound and organizing tours down the "modern" mine shaft and to the "scrupulously clean and pleasant" mine workers' housing and kitchens.[168] As with Gold Reef City, mine dancing displays were often a feature of such tourist encounters. Rassool and Witz argue that in the 1940s and 1950s such performances fostered the fiction of a fit and healthy workforce efficiently "at home" in a modern industrial setting yet never abandoning its own "traditions"—apparently benefiting from the best of both worlds.[169]

By 1990 it was clear that any acknowledgment of industrialization as part of the history of Johannesburg—or indeed of South Africa more broadly— in what was still the Africana Museum was relegated to three display cabinets. One purported to be about "Chinese Miners" and consisted of opium pipes, a pair of embroidered slippers, and two photographs with a brief caption informing the visitor that most Chinese were repatriated in 1910.[170] Another concentrated on Randlords and the last on strikes. More to the point, by 1992 the Africana Museum was clearly not exactly proving hot competition for Gold Reef City, whose visitors were more than four times the 19,152 per annum at the museum.[171]

Consequently the new exhibit prepared by Ann Wanless represented an attempt at both a total transformation from the old Africana Museum and a radical alternative to other public representations of the history of labor on offer at venues such as Gold Reef City. The visitor is introduced immediately to the power of gold, both in aesthetic terms as a commodity and also in terms of the stock market and the development of capital as the structural economic foundation upon which Johannesburg is built. The exhibit takes us down a simulated mine shaft. This aspect of the display cannot compete with the actual experience at Gold Reef City, but another aspect of the small display compensates somewhat by providing a scale model of a worker's hostel, with cement bunks, opposite a scale model of a room in a manager's house—a juxtaposition obviously placed to elicit unfavorable comparison. Texts indicate the ways in which the hostel system was designed to minimize the "risk" of unionization by African workers and a further exhibit gives the visitor some idea of how workers managed to organize themselves despite management attempts to block such activism. This display links to the formation of the Domestic Workers' Union and the experience of African women in the urban labor force.[172]

This section also deploys a strategy similar to that in the exhibition of informal housing. Here Martha Paya, at the time a domestic worker

68. Martha Paya sitting in her "room" in Museum Africa, 2000. Photo by the author.

in Yeoville, Johannesburg, was invited to help supervise the organization and interior of a domestic worker's room. Unlike the exhibit on informal housing, however, the visitor is not invited into a space but rather remains on the outside looking in (figure 68). The text beside Martha Paya's room tells the visitor the following:

> This room belongs to Martha Paya. She and her husband, Johnson, rent the old coal shed in a block of flats in Yeoville for R 200 a month in this year of 1994. Martha came to Johannesburg to look for work in 1979; before that she had worked as a domestic servant on a farm in the Northern Transvaal for about ten years. She did not have a pass to work in Johannesburg and always ran the risk of being arrested. In 1981 Martha began to do 'piece work.' She cleans houses and does laundry for three different people and earns about R 420 a month. Martha has four children who live with her mother in the Northern Transvaal and go to school in Pietersburg. She gets home to see them two or three times a year. Martha and Johnson belong to an independent church in Alexandra and sing in the choir there.

Martha went to school for three years. She thinks it is very important for her children to get a good education.

Martha Paya was asked to give everything in her room to the museum. The museum in turn bought her replacement objects. She kept back only some special items of personal value. In the tiny room there is space only for a single bed and a side table and very little else. Martha's Zionist robes hang along the back wall, and on a string suspended above a corner of the bed hang her husband's work shirt and trousers and her dress. The bed is carefully made up (in fact she makes it again while we talk) and elaborately arranged so that the triangular edge of a sheet, painstakingly embroidered by Paya with flowers and butterflies, is revealed down one side. Beside the bed under a table are a few cleaning implements, and on the table is a Bible in Paya's first language, northern Sotho. A photo board has color snaps of her and her family and contains her passbook. In an attempt to histori-cize domestic labor, the museum has added other photographs of domestic workers going about their business in earlier periods. Martha and her hus-band commiserate over the fact that things have been stolen from "their" room. The radio by the bed has gone, and so has her hairbrush, the plastic bucket they used to fetch water, and the cereal bowls, knives, and forks. Paya points out that when she gave her room to the museum, it demonstrated exactly how it was possible to live in such a space. Now it is no longer accu-rate, and this distresses her. It is evidently important to her that the visitor see "exactly" how she and others like her live. Similarly the "authoring" of this space and the fact that the museum needs her knowledge are points of pride.[173]

For Paya it is especially important that the international visitor see her room. One of the considerations that convinced her to give her room to the museum was the idea that this act of display would transform her everyday life (and that of others like her) into "history," and thus many more people would have the chance to see what her life has been like.[174] At the open-ing of Museum Africa, Martha sat in her room to answer questions. She remembers Ben Ngubane, at that time minister for arts, culture, science and technology, talking to her. But unlike either Charles Mbubana or Sam Nyambose, Martha Paya never takes tours around her room. Ann Wanless explains the importance of Martha's room for the museum: "They [domes-tic workers] are the hidden supports of white family life, caring for the chil-dren, cooking, cleaning, gardening, and in some cases nursing the sick and elderly and even chauffeuring. We will try to convey the wide range of tasks that they perform and that they *used* to perform in the early days."[175] Despite the fact that at the time of its opening the Museum Africa display probably constituted one of the first serious attempts to integrate a critical history of labor relations into a national museum, very little attention was paid to this aspect of the new exhibitions in the press.

In April 1995 another museum in Johannesburg involving the representation of the history of labor relations opened its doors to the public. The Workers' Library and Museum in Newtown virtually opposite Museum Africa (at the Newtown Workers' Compound) was a long-term project nurtured by Luli Callinicos and Public Service International secretary Roshnie Moonsammy (among others). The museum is housed, appropriately enough, in an early-twentieth-century building designed to accommodate electricity workers employed by the Johannesburg municipality. A feature of the building is that it retains the alienating environment to which workers would have been subjected. Not simply a reconstruction, the building still contains the original dormitories in which migrant workers had to live, with concrete bunks; narrow, barred windows; and ablutions area. At the time of its opening, Labour Minister Tito Mboweni, in an emotive address that claimed that the initiative was "an important act of historical recovery," stressed that South Africa's manual workers received scarcely a mention in many history books and were notably absent from museums and public monuments.[176] In a damning reference to Gold Reef City he added, "The main public theme park which records the early days of the mines, pays next to no attention to [the workers] at all. Certainly there is no mine compound there to visit."[177] The museum was intended at the time of its opening to be more of a resource center that included objects of importance donated by the workers themselves. Pat Craven, the museum's administrator, explained, "The museum on its own would obviously concentrate on the past, but the library helps workers arm themselves for the future, to get some of the education they were deprived of."[178] The project was clearly driven from the outset by those who had been subjected to the cruelties of the migrant worker regime. Its board members included South African Municipal Workers' Union president Petrus Mashishi, unionist Humphrey Ndaba, ex-unionists Moses Mayekiso and Marcel Golding, and Ahmed Kathrada.[179]

Despite the support from various sections and individuals (MPs, trade union leaders, academics, and workers), the venture very nearly foundered because some city councillors evidently thought the revamping of City Hall was a more important project and one that could be funded by cutting the budget allocated for the library/museum project.[180] Although the museum and library proved successful and were well used as a resource by schoolchildren, other interested researchers, and the workers who had set it up, by 1999 the facility had to lay off security staff and its two full-time workers went without salaries because of a shortfall in cash. Earlier funding from the Ford Foundation, the Friederich Ebert Stiftung, and the European Union through the Kagiso Trust had been vital in setting up the project, but these organizations were unable to commit to running costs. By 2000 the museum and library had lost both their paid workers and were existing on volunteer staff. As Luli Callinicos, one of the founders and trustees of the project, commented disconsolately, the future of the project was threatened because on the one hand workers were now "out of fashion," and on the other hand, because of mounting unemployment, workers understandably had more pressing concerns than ensuring that a museum be kept running.[181] Lucky Ramatseba, the oral history project administrator, in a plea for funding in the national press, had emphasized the importance of the project: "It is when people forget the past, or allow themselves to forget the past, that history repeats itself."[182] The project was an important means of keeping alive the memory of the inhuman conditions of the migrant worker system. Sadly, many of the initiatives that thrived in the early days of the new democratic dispensation and that addressed issues identified as imperatives for postapartheid museums have folded, and it looks likely that the workers' library and museum may be yet another casualty.

SLAVERY

The final area identified as a crucial concern for those wishing to redress the historical imbalances of the previous regime was the thorny issue of slavery. In an important article outlining some of the difficulties of producing histories of slavery in South Africa, Kerry Ward and Nigel Worden discuss how such histories have been systematically suppressed and that almost all constituencies, including liberals and progressives, have colluded in this suppression.[183] They make it clear that slave histories have not become canonical heritage fare in South Africa (as they have in the United States), not least because of the particular nature of slavery in the Cape. Unlike the transatlantic slave trade, slaves in the Cape were transported *to* Africa *from* other areas of the Indian Ocean. Three institutions most obviously central to an investigation of the public history and visibility of slavery remained until very recently steadfastly silent on the issue. The South African Cultural History Museum in Cape Town (a state-funded institution) had actually been the lodge for the slaves of the Dutch East India Company. The Bo-Kaap Museum, in an area of Cape Town historically populated by Malay peoples, many of whom had entered South Africa as slaves, has only recently integrated slavery into the museum's accounts of the history of the area. Finally, an obvious local industry that depended on slave labor (until recently unacknowledged) were the now thriving tourist venues of the surrounding vineyards, including Groot Constantia.[184]

Ward and Worden argue that one of the reasons for the lacunae of any revisionist histories of slavery postapartheid in any of the drives for new subjects for public histories in the "new" nation is that many of the constituencies most affected are concerned to deny this part of their own familial past. In the first decade of the twentieth century some Cape "colored" elite were concerned to differentiate themselves from black Africans as a way of claiming a privileged status and cementing closer identifications with whites.[185] Ward and Worden emphasize that in the 1940s and 1950s Cape Town Muslims of South East Asian descent attempted to cement a distinctive Cape Malay identity, further dividing the communities in the Western Cape by splitting the colored constituency—a move that also fostered a further distinction and hierarchy between artisan slaves and unskilled field laborers, who were predominantly non-Muslim. They argue that further obstructions to owning a slave past were provided by the radical NEUM's insistence that a focus on a slave past was politically divisive because it would necessarily draw attention to the differences between the Cape and the rest of South Africa in the context of building a political platform on the basis of a common "settler" enemy. The land claims of the 1990s also made Khoisan or "indigenous" ancestry much more appealing than slave ancestry since slaves were necessarily immigrants and consequently "claims" associated with them would be difficult to prove.[186] Ward and Worden end by suggesting that there have been some moves to reintegrate a history of slavery into school curricula and some museum displays but that many of the public appeals to a slave past have been misleading and only serve to further exacerbate the misrepresentations of slavery in South Africa.[187]

Nevertheless there were some early expressions of interest in UNESCO's international Slave Route Project, which aimed to trace the historical passage of slaves both inside and beyond the African continent. In July 1998 the first issue of the projects' newsletter from the South African Chapter was published. It was heralded rather ambitiously as the *Newsletter of the South African Chapter Sub-Commission: Nation-Building and African Renaissance.* Apparently "born under the guidance of Dr. Mongane Wally Serote," the South African Chapter was also described as "an active group of subcommissions—Tourism Education, Museums and African-Renaissance."[188] All the projects mentioned as under way were in the Western Cape and included a project to design and research historical slave routes for tourists in

Cape Town and the Western Cape by history students at the University of the Western Cape. On the back page of the four-page newsletter are sundry points of information regarding the history of slavery generally; on page three is a list of items concerning relevant sites in Cape Town and information about surnames that might indicate a slave ancestry—as well as a comment about the first written exemplars of Afrikaans being in Arabic script. The second newsletter, published in August 1998, defines the aims and objectives of the South African Chapter, and these are expanded in the third issue:

> We investigate, commemorate and promote part of the "forgotten history" of our country. For 150 years settlers and officials in the Cape Colony imported slaves from countries bordering the Indian Ocean. They come mainly from India, Sri Lanka, Indonesia, Madagascar and Mozambique. By 1834, when slavery was abolished in British colonies, there were approximately 38,000 slaves at the Cape. This may seem a small number in comparison to the millions of slaves in places like Brazil and the United States of America, but slaves at the Cape made up a significant proportion of the total colonial population. Until 1795, slaves outnumbered the free population. Many South Africans, especially in the Cape, are partly descended from slaves.[189]

The newsletter also pointed out that in South Africa slavery had been mainly treated as "peripheral to the 'real' events of the colonial era" or had been viewed primarily from the perspective of the slave owners rather than the slaves.[190]

Most of the second newsletter was devoted to a report by Farieda Khan, one of the project directors of the history of the Elim Mission Station in the Bredasdorp district.[191] The mission station, set up in 1824 by Moravian missionary Hans Peter Hallbeck, was built and first maintained by runaway slaves and by emancipated slaves after 1838. The results of the oral history section of the project are particularly interesting. Interviews with older inhabitants of the mission station confirm Ward and Worden's remarks on denial among many constituencies in South Africa: a number of the elderly residents were not only reluctant to concede that they might have slave ancestry in their families, but were also reluctant to admit that slavery ever existed in the Western Cape.[192]

The next newsletter focused on the Heritage Day commemorative ceremony of renaming the National Cultural History Museum (or reverting it to its original name) as the Slave Lodge. The newsletter outlined the history of the slave lodge and included a copy of the only known plan of the lodge, produced in 1798.[193] Two other items are of interest here. The center pages contained a map of the city recast as a series of twenty slave sites, which suggested a walking tour. And on the final page was the itinerary of the "Slave Route Walk" conducted as part of the Heritage Day celebrations in Cape Town on 24 September 1998; it included four main stops, with attendant activities and dramatic interludes by (among others) a group aptly called "Living History Productions," who also performed at the museum itself.[194] The fourth edition of the newsletter recounted these events in more detail, included some further sites of significance for the history of slavery in the Cape, and contained two articles, one by Farieda Khan and the other by Worden; both sought to complicate and open out the history of slavery and emancipation in the Western Cape and the various political alliances commanded by both (and comparatively, in the case of Worden, with Jamaica and Mauritius).[195] In 2000 the historical research into slavery in the Western Cape resulted in an initiative whereby individuals and students interested in tracing slave ancestry (and with a Standard 7–8 education level) can now go to the archives of the National Cultural History Museum and make use of the database, compiled by Worden and his students, of slaves held by the Dutch East India Company.[196]

Unravelling the complexities of a slave past that has obviously had an impact on the lives of so many contemporary South Africans and making the findings both rich and accessible is extremely important work in a context where reconciliation and remembrance are uppermost in many minds. However, by December 2000 it was clear that the South African Chapter of the UNESCO Slave Route Project had foundered, even though the local initiatives in the Western Cape, largely through the efforts of Worden, Sue Newton-King, Farieda Khan, and other local historians and academics, were still producing significant findings and creating new opportunities for collaborative work in the public sphere.[197]

Because of the stakes in the history of slavery and the complicated political claims and refutations made by competing factions, it has been seen by a number of politicians as running counter to a political agenda promoting national unity.[198] Consequently government responses to the UNESCO Slave Route Project have been marked by reticence. Worden summarizes the reasons:

> Local researchers and tour guides saw the "Slave Route" as a public commemoration of the specific institution of Cape slavery, particularly designed to empower local communities of slave descent. However, central government representatives insisted that slavery be seen as part of

a broader "South African nation-building exercise" and that it should include "such issues as indentured labour, forced migration, convict and farm labour." . . . The current stress of the South African government on "nation-building" means that any heritage which is only local could be anathema, particularly when it might be interpreted as an evocation of "Coloured" ethnic identity which is widely believed to have led to repeated ANC electoral defeats in the Western Cape.[199]

By the end of 2000, according to Worden, the state was still reluctant to support an initiative to acknowledge slavery and those taken as slaves as part of the commemoration celebrations of the four-hundredth anniversary in 2002 of the founding of the Dutch East India Company, although a privately funded exhibition was being planned in the Castle in Cape Town that was intended to include material on Cape slavery.[200]

This investigation into strategies adopted just prior to and following the 1994 elections ostensibly in an attempt to redress the distortions and absences in the representation of South African history in national museums is partly about the difficulties of marrying the official pronouncements of government policy with the physical and material requirements of the museum environment. It has also highlighted the particular conditions confronting museum professionals over this period, to give the reader a clearer idea of the challenges they have faced. Museums did not uniformly enthusiastically embrace these challenges, but those that did, whether out of expediency or a genuine desire for change, were met at every stage with an apartheid legacy that, while not completely eradicating alliances and accommodations that could be described as "community," nevertheless complicated irrevocably the ways in which this concept could be thought and imagined.

5

WHAT'S IN A NAME?

The Place of "Ethnicity" in the "New" South Africa

> We think that a lot of the trouble in the world comes from the fact that people don't stay in their own place. . . . We think that everything would be much simpler if people stayed where they came from and took good care of their land and did not invade other people's land. — Kiwiet

Evidently, despite the entrenched conservativism of most museums in South Africa, in the lead-up to the April 1994 elections there was a considerable struggle over this terrain as a potential staging post for the reinscription of public history. As we have seen, some of the key concerns emerging from the debates on how to effect progressive transformation of heritage sites and museums focus on redressing the perceived imbalances of hegemonic historical narrative so that those voices and histories previously occluded could be represented.[1] Strategies included challenging the often exclusive focus on white settler histories (a common feature of many older institutional versions of "national" histories in both New Zealand and Australia) and illuminating precolonial histories, as well as later liberation struggles and conflicts.[2]

A related dilemma that surfaces in the South African debates is what the ideal role of the museum should be: to educate for transition and for a new model of national unity or to be a venue that eschews a conciliatory role in favor of exploring the contradictions and tensions of a more dynamic model of history and society. In other words, how much should shared histories and common goals be foregrounded rather than emphasizing the ethnic, cultural, and political particularities of different sectors of society and the tensions among them? Such an issue has special implications in South Africa because ethnic particularity was a structuring principle for apartheid segregation. The concept of the "rainbow nation," promoted under Mandela's government of national unity, was designed to mediate such a legacy and to foster national solidarity while accommodating ethnic diversity. Dubbed by some as the "Benetton effect," the strategy was subject to similar charges of willful exclusion and naive idealism and was not without its contradictions.

In this chapter I am concerned to evaluate the extent to which the language of current discussions on the function and nature of public culture as a repository of history and as constitutive of "community" can effectively "travel" between the local and global contexts and, in the South African case, between the postcolonial and postapartheid contexts. While the terms used in these debates may seem similar, they are significantly transformed in translation from one geopolitical situation to another.[3] As we have seen, "cultural diversity," "pluralism," and "multiculturalism" are all loaded terms in South Africa, making their meanings far from transparent. Consequently it is difficult to deploy them as part of a liberal or progressive discourse without considerable mediation. The idea of an "indigenous" or originary ethnicity or people is another concept that occupies a special place in attempts to redefine a national history.[4] Here too the term evades easy translation and is not necessarily commensurable across national boundaries.

On a number of visits to Australia I have noticed that many progressive Australian academics regularly deploy "indigenous" as a way of describing the black majority cultures in South Africa. It has always seemed to me highly inappropriate, but it set me to wondering about the differences in the use of the term on the two continents. "Indigenous" has clearly become a term of empowerment in Australia for many Aboriginal peoples precisely because they have successfully managed to redefine the label as a useful political tool for getting more or less recalcitrant white governments to acknowledge their prior claims to land and resources before white settlement and colonization.[5] Some might interpret such a move as a perfect example of what much postcolonial theory would see as strategic essentialism.

It is a miserable indictment of the colonial process in Australia that the Aboriginal population was massacred by the thousands and literally hunted like wild game immediately following settlement of the continent by white immigrants. Later in the early twentieth century the much reduced Aboriginal population was subjected to the further indignity of an "assimilation project" which forcibly removed from their mothers young children up to the age of four years and placed them in the care of white families in an attempt to "breed out" their Aboriginal origins. The policy, which lasted (officially) up until the 1960s, has resulted in some important work on what progressive historians and Aboriginal activists now refer to as "the Stolen Generations."[6] One of the far-reaching effects of this gruesome legacy is that the Aboriginal population is now down to about 1 percent of the total population of Australia. Given this history, it is easy to understand how the claim to originary status—to indigeneity—can be a powerful vindication of legal rights (though it is also true to say that it is only through the tenacity and ingenuity of Aboriginal spokespeople and supporters that any gains have been made at all).

Vocal criticism of government policy and discrimination were much in evidence during the 1988 bicentenary celebrations of the founding of the penal colony and the beginnings of white settlement in Australia. In fact, bicentennials and quincentennials have tended of late to become the focus for contesting the assumptions of *terra nullius* upon which such celebrations of colonial settlement are based.[7] Many of these demonstrations are staged by those with a stake in indigeneity.

In South Africa the use of "indigenous" as a marker of self-identification has become increasingly complex since the first democratic elections. Although the term is completely inappropriate for describing the heterogeneous majority black population in South Africa, there have been very public instances where claims to indigeneity and originary authenticity have been played out in the full media glare of South African political and cultural life. These are worth exploring for what they tell us about the ways such concepts can play a central part in the reconstruction of national history during periods of political and social transition, when such categories are being redefined, not least through the drafting of new constitutions, where the very notion and terms of citizenship are being recast.

One of the clearest cases where complications of terminology are exemplified has been in the representation of and by the Khoisan peoples in South Africa. There is considerable controversy surrounding the correct appellation for San or Khoikhoi peoples of southern Africa. Historically the terms "Bushman" and "Hottentot" were used by Europeans to denote those who lived primarily by herding, hunting, and gathering in southern Africa, "Bushman" often being the misnomer for the San and "Hottentot" for the Khoikhoi. Research has demonstrated that these terms are ridiculously reductive and inadequate to the task of describing the complex kinship patterns of diversified and heterogeneous communities with different political and geographical affiliations but whose peoples and economies have necessarily become intermingled over time. I use the term "Khoisan" in this chapter as a means of signaling the now hybrid "identity" of peoples in southern

Africa whose existence may historically have been primarily pastoralist or hunter-gatherer.[8]

Khoisan histories are some of the most well worked over in the research of academic anthropologists, and, as many scholars have observed, they have found their way into numerous contemporary novels, films, and plays, largely as representative of a prelapsarian moment when man supposedly lived in total harmony with his environment. Obviously the Khoisan are not the only indigenous peoples to have been appropriated in this way (nor, it should be added, are they the only indigenous peoples who have capitalized on such romantic projections in order to win support for their own political agendas). Various Native American peoples have similarly fallen prey to such appropriation, but, again, this has not been without more progressive outcomes.[9] Of course, idealized narratives have often been intended as a corrective to the much longer history of grotesque descriptions and images of the Khoisan as bizarre living remnants of a European prehistory the likes of which we are so familiar with from seventeenth- and eighteenth-century travelogues or voyage literature. The culmination of these myths is found in the infamous fascination with male and female Khoisan genitalia of Cuvier's and others' anatomical dissections in the early nineteenth century and the traffic in Khoisan skulls and skeletons (often procured before the flesh had even disintegrated) that was fueled by the needs of physical anthropology and the growing collections of human remains that were the necessary staple of the discipline.[10] Indeed collecting skeletal remains was acknowledged as a good earner in South Africa, where considerable sums changed hands for the remains of Khoisan body parts obtained largely from prisons, frontier war battlefields, and what can only be described as the "culling" of what were considered to be "wild" men.[11] The conflation of nature and culture implied by the appellation "wild man" has continually dogged the ways in which Khoisan cultures and histories have been presented in South African museums. In its most obvious manifestation such a conflation is reinforced by the fact that both the extraordinary rock paintings and other archaic and contemporary products of Khoisan material culture have historically been exhibited in natural history museums rather than in cultural history or art museums. This is an anomaly that has only very recently been addressed.

There is now a wealth of research charting the proclivity for exhibiting various colonized peoples in those staged spectacles of colonial power that took place primarily in Europe and the United States, at world fairs and international and colonial expositions.[12] Countries with Commonwealth and Dominion status within the British Empire were not immune from this practice. And in South Africa the peoples most frequently subjected to such public scrutiny were the Khoisan. In the early part of the nineteenth century groups of Khoisan variously described as "earthmen," "Bosjesmans," "Hottentot," or "Bushmen" were popular crowd stoppers at many European traveling "freak" shows, as well as exhibitions with more serious pretentions.[13]

Crucially, however, the Khoisan were also incorporated into exhibitions intended as significant way-markers in the political history of South Africa as an emerging country with its own particular cultural and economic contribution to make within the British Empire. I am not suggesting that these appearances were necessarily less demeaning than in the earlier spectacles, but rather that the representation of the Khoisan was clearly used as a sign of a specifically "South African" indigeneity at sensitive times when the construction of an image of the country as more than just another outpost of the British Empire was part of a bigger political agenda. Thus in the Union Pageant of 1910 the Khoisan make an appearance as part of a battle re-enactment. Again in 1936 a group of scientists from the University of the Witwatersrand mounted a highly publicized scientific expedition to find a group of "purebred" Bushmen from the Kalahari to feature in what became advertised as the "Bushmen Camp" at the 1936 Empire Exhibition in Johannesburg.[14] Saul Dubow makes the point that there was a public campaign to set up a Bushman "reserve" in the Kalahari Gemsbok Park at exactly the time of the Empire Exhibition.[15]

In 1952 the Khoisan were also on show in a special enclosure as part of the Jan van Riebeeck Tercentenary Festival.[16] By this time, apartheid was already coming under considerable criticism, and consequently certain nuances emerge in the display of "Bantu life" (in other words, aspects in the daily life of the black majority) as opposed to specifically "Bushman life." Leslie Witz provides an illuminating and detailed analysis. As he points out, with increased international criticism of the South African government's discriminatory racial policies and its violation of the terms of the UN mandate, it was in the interests of the Department of Native Affairs to promote an image of how the "White race" had been largely responsible for "the upliftment of the Bantu in all spheres—spiritual, physical and economic."[17] It is worth recounting in detail some of this change in approach in order to understand what might have been at stake in the "preservation" of the Bushmen by the very groups who had been responsible for their demise and to shed some light on the complications opened up by this initiative. It is through an understanding of this historical legacy that we can better comprehend some of the difficulties that might arise through the deployment in the present of the misleading notion of the Khoisan as a people closer to nature and threatened with extinction by the incursions of the modern world.

By 1952 a commissioner for the preservation of the Bushmen had been instituted in the person of the anthropologist and game ranger P. J. Schoeman. Schoeman's intellectual trajectory formed part of the volkekunde tradition that had been the basis of much anthropological training in South Africa and that had risen to prominence in the 1940s through the work of anthropologists from Stellenbosch and Pretoria Universities. The basis of their research, which would serve the apartheid state well in the coming years, was that "mankind is divided into *volke* and that each volk has its own particular culture."[18] Consequently, by segregating the "races," or "volke," each would be free to develop its own way of life without the "problem" of miscegenation creating undesirable "impurities." This would also ensure, of course, the strengthening of the "white" (and the specific concern here was with the Afrikaner) race. The "Bantu races" at the Van Riebeeck Tercentenary Festival were shown in "productive labor" and benefiting from the "clean" and "modern" conditions provided for them in the Transvaal Chamber of Mines pavilion, thus emphasizing the apparently "progressive" changes wrought by the South African government—an important sop to international criticism of the regime. The Bushmen, displayed as a primitive people on the edge of extinction, served to cement a different aspect of the benevolence of the South African regime in what initially might have seemed a distinctly contradictory representation. Constructed as a "dying race" in need of safeguarding, they were presented as being under the care and "protection" of their self-appointed interpreter and guardian, Schoeman, and the state.

As Witz points out, the presentation of Bushman culture and history at the festival was highly selective and omitted the history of dispossession and extermination by settlers in Namibia in the late nineteenth and early twentieth centuries. "By silencing the processes of genocide, and casting the knowledge of the bushmen in the mould of a curious unchanging society which was in danger of extinction, and therefore had to be saved, Schoeman was situating the bushmen into a discourse of nationing. In these terms the 'solution' to the 'problem' of the 'wild bushmen' of Namibia, was to maintain their 'purity'—and the 'purity of Africa'—by setting up reserves."[19] Significantly, even the popular Afrikaans journal *Die Huisgenoot,* an organ that had been instrumental in inventing a homogeneous Afrikaner "tradition" and "culture" at a formative moment in the development of Afrikaner nationalism, now reported a newfound concern and understanding of the Bushmen; their presence at the festival had made *Die Huisgenoot* nostalgic for what they now represented—a "pure and ancient Africa."[20] It is clear from Witz's research that while the organizers of the festival took great pains to promote this idea of the Bushmen as a means of complementing the image of a modern and progressive new nation with that of a caring protector of indigenous peoples, they were not entirely convincing. The Bushmen themselves were disgusted and offended by the gawping of the crowds and their constant interference, touching them and lifting up their clothes to check the appendages beneath. In a neat inversion—picked up on by various sections of the liberal press, who slated the representation of the Bushmen at the festival—the inhabitants of the Bushman enclosure likened the white spectators to baboons and refused to perform on demand for the crowds, eventually leaving the festival early, irritated by the treatment to which they had been subjected.[21] Thus "The bushman display, instead of highlighting the 'progress of the nation,' or indeed the need 'to preserve the bushman,' was . . . beginning to raise questions about the fundamental assumptions of the 'white nation's' claim to modernity."[22]

I found it instructive to look back to the opening speeches delivered at the inauguration of the Voortrekker Monument in 1949 on the eve of the apartheid state, to see the ways in which the Khoisan were continually inscribed as an integral part of an originary account of the history of South Africa. It seems to me that this example demonstrates the extent to which such an account was deliberately promulgated in the broader public domain as part of the promotion of a legitimate Afrikaner nationalism and the emergence of the new state (republic). It was an account popularized as a public history for the new nation extending way beyond the narrow confines of the more circumscribed intellectual and academic concerns of anthropology and ethnography, and it clearly indicates how such knowledge may serve an ideological and political purpose not necessarily intended by those whose research it mobilizes.[23] The narrative demonstrates how the apparently positive inscription of the Bushman presence in South Africa (on the occasion of the inauguration of one of the major monuments to Afrikaner nationalism) could be reconciled with the racist politics of apartheid.

In "The Great Trek and Its Problems," published in the commemorative volume from the inauguration of the Voortrekker Monument, I. J. Rousseau discusses what he calls South Africa's greatest problem, "The Native."[24] The place he attributes to the Bushmen is telling and graphically illustrates the justification for Dutch colonization:

> The [Dutch] expansion eastward encountered but little opposition; the stone-age, bow-and-arrow, artistic Bushman, the real aborigines of Southern Africa, as witnessed by their cave paintings from the Cape to the Zam-

besi, were regarded as little more than human and were hunted down by both Hottentot and European, the former, in turn, to be dispossessed of his land. . . . In fact, he ceased to be an obstacle to the White Man's advance from the outbreak of smallpox in the first half of the Eighteenth Century. Home defence [became] a different proposition when towards the close of the Century the trek Boers and elephant hunters reached the banks of the Fish River, where they came in contact with the vanguard of the Bantu in his age-long migration down to eastern shores of Africa, therefore as much an intruder as the "White Man." Thus the popular phrase, the "Black Man's country," is hardly ethnographically correct.[25]

In this rehearsal of the popular historical myths that formed the foundation of apartheid, the Dutch had every bit as much right to the land as those other "intruders," the Bantu. And the Bushmen, who were "no longer a threat" and could be safely lauded as "the real aborigines of Southern Africa," "artistic," and "hunted down by both Hottentot and European," were also conveniently no longer able to call the colonizer to account for his dispossession and destruction. Thus, the Khoisan could be safely claimed as both the legitimate inhabitants of South Africa—the first South Africans—and a primitive version of early man, which necessarily gave way to the superior civilization of the European but whose historical and anthropological significance also lent status to the new republic in scientific terms.

During the period just prior to and after the first democratic elections in South Africa a series of events and exhibitions attempted to restage the received myths surrounding the Khoisan and provide an alternative revisionist account. At this time the Khoisan were also the focus of other projects by contemporary artists, historians, and museum curators. The most controversial of such attempts were hosted by two major public institutions in Cape Town, the South African National Gallery and the SAM. Both institutions have long histories, with the SAM boasting the status of the oldest museum in the country. What follows is an analysis of these attempts and some of the responses to such revisionist tactics. This chapter considers the implications of the often volatile reactions they provoked in terms of the broader questions thus raised for curators attempting to exhibit the complications and contradictions of difficult histories, where apparently authenticating ethnicities are being claimed and forged anew as a prelude to a new national history. As we have seen, the Khoisan occupied a central position in the writings on "race" and its intersections with nationhood in the early twentieth century in South Africa. The traces of this sometimes idiosyncratic intellectual legacy are still present in the complex debates around origin and authority in contemporary South Africa.

The SAM was founded in 1825 by Lord Charles Somerset, with Andrew Smith, an army surgeon and graduate of Edinburgh University, appointed in a directorial capacity as superintendent. It was not until 1855 that a board of trustees was formally constituted and the first curator, Edgar Layard, a naturalist with legal training, was appointed. Established as a general museum and housing both natural history and what were described as "articles of human manufacture" from local and other groups further afield, the development of the museum, as Patricia Davison, the assistant director, makes clear, followed the move from a motley collection of trophies (of either the animal or human variety) to a more systematic organization and classification in line with the evolutionary models prominent in Europe and the United States in the nineteenth and early twentieth centuries.[26] Davison cites a passage from one of Layard's *Annual Reports to the Trustees*, which gives a graphic account of the early displays: "On arriving at the head of the lower flight of stairs . . . the visitor will have on his right hand the large Mammalia. . . . Overhead are placed a fine collection of horns of South African antelope. . . . Against the wall are arranged, as trophies, various implements of war and the chase, belonging to different nations. . . . Crossing the end window by the Aquarium, which now holds a Burmese Alligator, and still confining his attention to the wall, the visitor has before him some wonderful specimens of savage ingenuity."[27]

An archive photo of the interior of the museum gallery from about 1882 shows a scene that could easily have been unearthed in the archives of any museum established in the late nineteenth or early twentieth centuries in Europe or the United States that began life as a natural history collection and later incorporated material culture from the colonies in what became identified as the ethnographic collections. It shows a stream of taxidermied beasts from various colonial heartlands marching up the central aisle of a typical Victorian museum gallery; they are flanked by display cases containing specimens of local and exotic flora and minerals, with two further galleries above. The uppermost walls are plastered with decorative "trophy" displays of the human equivalents of the specimens below—the implements of "war and chase." Thus the stage was set for encouraging the notion that very little divided the animal world—the focus of the domain of natural history—from the human subjects who became the objects of ethnography and anthropology.

As we saw in chapter 4, such a confusion was clearly perpetuated up to the 1990s in South Africa through the policy of reserving museums dealing with cultural history for the exclusive display of settler histories and consistently consigning material culture from any other communities to natural history / anthropology museums. Further developments in anthropology, archaeology, and philology in the early twentieth century did little to dispel this confusion. Since the Khoisan were seen to reside on the very lowest rung of the evolutionary ladder—the closest to nature, being the closest to the highest form of ape, and thus understood to be living remnants of "civilized" man's prehistory who were also (thanks to the incursions of successive waves of colonialism) fast disappearing—they became the focus of intensive research. Mathias Guenther, writing on European misconceptions about the Khoisan, cites a number of explicit nineteenth-century examples equating the Khoisan with animals, specifically the orangutan, believed to be the highest form of ape.[28] Indeed, as Stephen J. Gould points out, there is some evidence to suggest that the earliest term for the Khoisan used by the Dutch in the seventeenth century—"Bosmanneken," or Bushman—was a "literal translation of the Malay word 'OrangOutan' or 'man of the forest.'"[29] By the latter part of the nineteenth century it was clear that autochtonous peoples resisting the onslaught of white settlement had been violently quashed and many of the survivors had been pressed into (indentured) farm labor or were living on the fringes of urban settlements.[30] The people known then as the Bushmen and Hottentots featured in the early collecting expeditions of the SAM's first supervisor, Andrew Smith, but it was not until Louis Peringuey took up office as the director in 1906 that they became a virtual obsession and remained a primary research area for the next two decades.[31] And it is this period in the museum's history that lays the bedrock of scientific fallacy against which later revisionist strategies have reacted.

By about 1905, and in line with the widespread belief in the European scientific community in the direct correlation between physical type and evolutionary status (and consequently intellectual, cultural, and social status), physical anthropology became a dominating intellectual force in South Africa, particularly in relation to the development of the country's prehistory.[32] It is significant that 1905 was also, as Saul Dubow points out, the moment at which "modern theories of racial segregation began to be discussed at a political level."[33] Coincidentally 1905 was also the year when the British and South African Associations for the Advancement of Science decided to combine forces and hold a joint annual meeting in South Africa. Discussions around the significance of South Africa's aboriginal peoples featured in the proceedings. A. C. Haddon, the British anthropologist responsible for transforming London's Horniman Museum from a glorified curiosity cabinet to a paradigmatic example of the typological evolutionary classification so in vogue at the time, and F. Von Luschan, the director of one of the largest ethnographic museums in Europe (the Museum für Völkerkunde in Berlin), are both recorded as insisting on the imperative of gathering as much data as possible on what were considered to be the last remnants of prehistoric man.[34]

The fact that these prescriptions from such prominent members of the scientific community coincided with the shift to physical anthropology in South Africa determined to a large extent the nature of the "data" that would be accumulated. Peringuey responded with a project that would preoccupy him for over seventeen years, from 1907 to 1924. In a fascinating article, Patricia Davison outlines his thinking on the subject. She cites a letter Peringuey wrote to the under colonial secretary to the Cape in order to get support for his project from the Cape government: "Sir, Owing to the rapid disappearance . . . of the pure specimens of the Hottentot and Bushman races the Trustees of the Museum are endeavouring to obtain models from the living flesh which would enable the exact physical reproduction of the survivors of these nearly extinguished races."[35]

Peringuey's request is interesting in that it also makes clear the extent to which the majority of the surviving Khoisan population was by this time incarcerated in jails up and down the country, very often for petty crimes, which were largely the result of the dispossession and displacement and consequent vagrancy to which they had been reduced by the settler rush for farming land that had been their traditional foraging and hunting grounds. Peringuey was keen to have unconditional access to the country's jails and prisons and to have the governor's authority "in the case of men and women in jail to have the casts and necessary photographs and measurements taken by experts."[36] He ends his plea with a reassurance that could not have been further from the truth: "The process is not a long one; it is very simple and absolutely painless."[37]

Anyone familiar with the anthropological questionnaires produced from the mid-nineteenth century by the Royal Anthropological Institute in London will recognize the thinking behind the minutiae of physiological detail that Peringuey demanded of the museum modeler, James Drury, when he was sent out to do this "simple and absolutely painless" task of casting from living Khoisan.[38] The express purpose of such questionnaires was to elicit detailed information from travelers and government officials in the field. It was a method particularly popular during the period of "armchair" anthropology, when documentation gleaned by amateurs in the field was crucial for the academic anthropologist compiling texts from the comfort of his (since most academic anthropologists of note were usually male during this period) university office. The questionnaires gave detailed directions for obtaining specific photographic views, hair texture and color, eye color, and precise measurements of each body part, all of which were designed to provide the anthropologist with the physical data to be able to determine (as it was believed at the time) the intellectual, moral, and evolutionary status of the individual involved. (Charts are shown in figure 69 and plate 4.)

Sander Gilman, Stephen J. Gould, and others have also drawn attention to European obsession with the dimensions and positioning of the genital organs of both Khoisan men and women.[39] Over the period of the cast project it is clear that such a prurient fascination had not abated. As Davison points out, Peringuey was explicit in his directions to Drury that "purebred" women of the group would exhibit steatopygia and an enlarged *labia minora* (the so-called *sinus pudoris,* referred to by Cuvier in his report on the dissection of the body of Saartjie Baartman as her *"tablier"* or "apron"). More specifically Peringuey stated in a memorandum to Drury in 1911: "Men are desirable; women more so. You will be careful to take all their peculiarities including the 'apron.' A special moulding of the same to be added to the statue is very much wanted."[40] The men, Peringuey had apparently been reliably informed, were identified as "pure specimens" by the fact that even in a resting state, their penises would be semi-erect. Therefore "the purity of the race was denoted by the angle at which the penis stood normally."[41] Obtaining precise measurements of such physical attributes involved, as the reader can imagine, a hideous degree of humiliating scrutiny and manhandling. Both Davison and Pippa Skotnes have attempted to ascertain through their research on the casting project whether such activity might have been considered unacceptably invasive and to what extent the Khoisan involved were cooperative or coerced. Letters in the SAM Archives from Drury, as well as from the linguist / ethnographer Dorothea Bleek, who was simultaneously attempting to get photographic documentation of the Khoisan for her own anthropological purposes, reveal the difficulties of getting the Khoisan to cooperate when they were asked to undress. In an article coauthored by James Drury and M. R. Drennan for a medical journal, the description of the method employed for obtaining such "data" leaves one in no doubt at all about the excruciating shame and evident pain that were involved: "On asking a woman of these tribes to remove her loin cloth or apron, one could not at first detect any difference between her and an ordinary woman. . . . On separating the lips of the vulva it was easy to grasp the *labia minora* with a pair of forceps and pull them out for examination. This increased exposure gave rise to a distinct accession of shyness on the part of the women."[42]

On several occasions between 1907 and 1924 James Drury traveled the

SOUTH AFRICAN MUSEUM, CAPE TOWN.

Anthropological Measurements.

Taken at Windhoek 7—9 Dec. 1920 / Drury

All measurements to be expressed in millimetres. —7

BODY AND LIMBS.	mm.
(a) From the ground	
1. To vertex of head. (Height)	156.3
2. To middle of ear-hole	160.7
3. To point of chin	133.
4. To the top of the shoulder-blade	126.
5. To the top of the breast bone, in the depression between the collar bones	124.5
6. To the elbow, *i.e.*, to the top of the radius	96.7
7. To the wrist, *i.e.*, lower end of radius	73.5
8. To the tip of the middle finger	57.
9. To the top of the thigh-bone	87.
10. To the inner side of the knee-joint, *i.e.*, to top of tibia	42.7
11. To the ankle, *i.e.*, to bottom of tibia	5.3
(b) 12. Length of foot	22.
(c) 13. Maximum breadth across shoulders	36.
14. Maximum breadth between outer sides of tops of thighs	22.
In the above, (a) can be taken with a graduated scale supplied with a plummet and a sliding bar set at right angles to the scale. (b) and (c) should be taken with callipers.	
HEAD.	
15. Maximum length	25
16. Maximum breadth	13.5
17. Upper facial height or naso-alveolar height (measured from deepest part of depression between nose and forehead to edge of gum between two upper central teeth)	8.1
18. Naso-mental height (from root of nose, as in 17, to point of chin in middle line)	9.2
19. Total facial height (root of hair on forehead in middle line to point of chin)	15.
20. Height of head (from upper border of opening of ear to top of head)	12.2
21. Maximum bizygomatic breadth (measured across face between outside points of cheek-bones)	15
22. Maximum bimastoid breadth (measured across mastoid processes from behind)	15
23. External orbital breadth (measured between outer margins of the long processes around the eye)	11
24. Internal orbital breadth (measured between inner margins of the long processes around the eye)	3.
25. Nasal height (from root of nose to angle between nose and upper lip)	4.
26. Nasal breadth (greatest diameter between wings of nose unexpanded)	4.
27. Maximum length of ear	5.2
28. Orbito-Nasal Curve (measured with tape from points mentioned in 23, tape being pressed lightly over root of nose)	12.

Chest 27

Len (?) ... 25

Tip lips 22

nipples 33

lapel 34

neck(?) 1.9m of leg. 28.

Sex... *Hottentot ♀ Windhoek Jail no 5 [white figure stout]*

Age... *about 30*

Locality... *Bettany*

3904

♀

70. Photograph of Drury's casts of Khoisan in the SAM, circa 1911. The angle of vision of the museum photographer's shot clearly emphasises the women's steatopygia. Courtesy of the South African Museum. Iziko Museums of Cape Town.

length and breadth of the country seeking out "pure specimens." He made sixty-eight casts, which were later painted in the museum studio, and a further twenty that were not produced as figures until the 1980s.[43] Some of these casts were displayed in the museum in 1911. One photograph in the SAM Archives shows a group of casts taken from an angle that itself accentuates the physical attributes so prized as indicators of "pure" Bushmen. In the foreground of the photograph documenting the display of the casts in the Museum, two casts of older Khoisan women stand in profile so that their steatopygia is the most visible aspect to the viewer (figure 70).

Davison makes the point that the display of Khoisan casts in the museum was consistent with the emphasis on physical anthropology and remained so even when this was being challenged in anthropological circles in South Africa in the late 1920s. No attempt was made to see the figures in any way as part of a complex social and cultural network, nor indeed to see them as they were at the time of the casting. In fact these aspects were explicitly denied. While the people who were cast were often recorded in Drury's notes by name, the casts are recorded by registration number, racial type, sex, and location in the museum records; the displays focused on the individuals as representatives of a "racial type."[44] Consequently they were described for the museum viewer in the following way:

CAPE BUSHMEN:
The Bushmen of the Cape appear to have been the purest-blooded representatives of the Bushman stock, much purer than those of the Kalahari and other more northerly districts. They are now practically extinct. They were light in colour and of small or medium height; the prominent posterior development (*steatopygia*) of the women was a characteristic of the race. To anthropologists the Bushmen are one of the most interesting races in the world. There are strong grounds for suspecting that they are of the same stock as the remote Upper Palaeolithic period. This cannot yet be definitely asserted but recent discoveries in North and East Africa have tended to strengthen the probability considerably.[45]

There are a number of things that one could draw to the attention of the reader here, but one of the most striking is that despite the fact that *at the same time that this label was written and for some years hence* a museum employee was actively spending his days in the company of numerous groups of Khoisan from every part of South Africa, the label persists in describing these peoples consistently in the past tense and consigns them to inevitable (and possibly convenient) extinction.

THE DIORAMA

It was only much later, in the 1950s, that plans were laid to incorporate Drury's casts into a display still known today as the "Bushman Diorama," which was produced as part of a related but nevertheless somewhat different narrative in what was intended as a more contextualized setting. It is interesting that such an arrangement should have been initiated during the first decade of apartheid, a coincidence that may suggest more about how the diorama fitted into received popular conceptions about the Bushman than telling us anything about the explicit intentions behind the dis-

71. "Bushman Diorama" at the SAM. Taken in 1994. Photo by Jean Brundrit.

play. As Davison points out, Alfred Crompton, the director of SAM under whose supervision the diorama was constructed, insisted on keeping the museum open, in principle, to all South Africans at a time when the Separate Amenities Act was being implemented nationwide.[46] (It is also the case that 1957 was the first year that entrance fees were charged, and this would certainly have had an effect on the numbers and constituency visiting the museum.)[47] According to Davison, the diorama was loosely based on an aquatint by Samuel Daniell from his 1805 collection, *African Scenery and Animals 1804–5*, although there are additional figures present in the diorama in order to accommodate more of the casts (figure 71).[48] Evidently a certain kind of naturalism was the goal here, with a great deal of careful attention paid to the integration of certain items of material culture and also to the painted Karoo scene behind. Yet the diorama resembles nothing so much as an ethnographic studio photograph from the late nineteenth century, with all participants in suspended animation against a tasteful backdrop. The new arrangement necessitated a new label, and accordingly one was appended to the display case:

> A CAPE BUSHMAN CAMP IN THE KAROO:
> This diorama shows some activities of hunter-gatherers. The viewer should imagine that a large flock of birds has flown overhead and attracted the attention of the group.
>   With the exception of a few in Gordonia, there are no Bushmen living in

the Cape. The figures shown here are PLASTER CASTS of living people aged between 18 and 60, excepting the man making fire who was alleged to have been about 100. They were nearly all living in the Prieska and Carnarvon districts. The casts were made by Mr. James Drury, modeller at the Museum from 1902–1942.[49]

Despite what is evidently an attempt at providing a cultural context (however flawed)—to the extent of setting the moment of the scene for the viewer by the use of an imaginative temporal scenario!—the insistence again on framing the whole within a narrative of extinction and the lack of specific historical temporality do little to relieve the problems of the earlier display. That the exhibit existed and continues to exist in the context of a natural history museum, coupled with the emphatic attention to the fact that the figures are not merely imaginative renditions but actual casts from living people, makes it hard to avoid an association with the art of taxidermy, which after all was (and is still) the staple of most natural history galleries all over the world.

While many obvious misunderstandings and misrepresentations result from such a display and have extremely damaging implications for any peoples wishing to establish recognition for their history and heritage, what I want to suggest here is that it is the single fact that the figures in the case have such proximity to actual human bodies, that they are the physical traces of human contact and the flesh of individuals who have since died in often demeaning and distressing circumstances, that poses the greatest difficulty. I believe that it is this visceral association with death and dissection generated by the fact of the casts that Drury made all those years ago that constitutes the real problem of the diorama then as now.[50]

This focus on the diorama at the SAM is not due to some idiosyncratic whim. My reason for analyzing this display in the context of a discussion on the creation of public histories of the Khoisan in South Africa is because the diorama has such a tenacious presence in the public psyche. Two cartoons will give the reader a sense of how familiar the SAM display is. Both rely absolutely on the viewer's familiarity not only with the diorama, but also with the controversies surrounding it. In 1960, on the occasion of British Prime Minister Harold Macmillan's visit to South Africa, the *Cape Times* ran a cartoon by David Marais showing Macmillan and Verwoerd striding past the diorama with a dinosaur behind them (figure 72). Through the vitrine the viewer can read a sign, "S. A. Museum—Europeans only," and the caption that synthesizes Verwoerd's anticipated defense of apartheid in the face of Macmillan's opposition, exemplified one week later in his famous "Winds

★ "Often maligned and misunderstood, South Africa's racial policies are actually designed for the *preservation* of each racial group as a separate entity, with its culture intact."

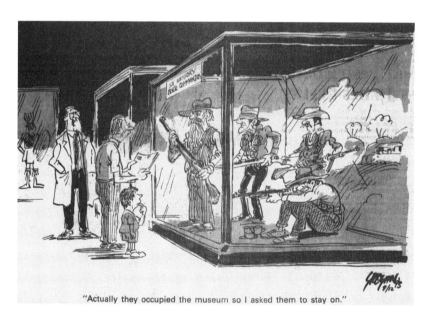

"Actually they occupied the museum so I asked them to stay on."

Top 72. David Marais, cartoon. *Cape Times,* 26 January 1960. Courtesy of Independent Newspapers. Copyright David Marais.

Bottom 73. Tony Grogan, cartoon. *Cape Times,* 9 December 1993. Courtesy of Tony Grogan. Copyright Tony Grogan.

74. One of a series of postcards showing details of the cast figures from the "Bushman Diorama" at the sam, produced originally in the 1970s and still in circulation in Cape Town in 2000.

of Change" speech (in which he cautioned Verwoerd about the irresistible rise of African nationalism and the need to change with the times): "Often maligned and misunderstood, South Africa's racial policies are actually designed for the preservation of each racial group as a separate entity, with its culture intact."[51] In December 1993, an unmistakable reference to the diorama figured as a way of consigning the Pretoria East Boere Kommando, the far right wing Afrikaner group that took over the Schanskop Fort opposite the Voortrekker Monument, to "prehistory" along with the "Bushmen" by putting the group in the vitrine (figure 73).[52] In the 1970s the diorama was evidently considered so synonymous with the tourist view of Cape Town that one enterprising company produced a series of postcards depicting individual cast figures in the diorama setting. On a trip to St. George's mall in downtown Cape Town in December 2000 I came across the same series being sold in a souvenir shop, along with postcards of Robben Island and the waterside (figure 74).[53]

In 1988 Davison and her colleagues at the sam took the first steps in mediating the diorama and the assumptions that they felt it perpetuated since, as she said, "through researching the history of the casts, it became apparent that the diorama, as an artefact in itself, could be used to heighten public awareness of museum practice and to create a more active response among viewers."[54] Accordingly the first thing that was altered was the label describing the diorama. It now read:

> In the early nineteenth century /Xam hunter-gatherers lived in the semi-desert Karoo. From hilltop camps they could watch the movements of game on the plains and spot the approach of enemies. Their way of life was shaped by the seasonal availability of edible plants, water and the movements of game. To avoid overusing food and water supplies /Xam bands ranged widely within hunting territories which were defined by recognised landmarks. By the mid-nineteenth century most hunter-gatherers in the Karoo had been killed in fighting with advancing colonists and displaced Khoikhoi. The survivors were drawn into colonial society as labourers and servants.[55]

Next the title of the diorama was changed so that it reflected a historicized moment, in this case around 1800. But the deconstructive turn revolved around a later initiative by Davison and her colleague Gerald Klinghardt specifically designed both to reveal "that there was a contradiction between what was known by Peringuey and Drury and what was shown in the Museum" and to make explicit the constructedness and artifactuality of the diorama as a product of its time.[56]

The intervention took the form of a series of storyboard panels set up beside the diorama in a structure that deliberately invokes a feel that this is a "work in progress" rather than a completed project, as if to suggest that the "myth" of the Bushman is continually in the process of evolving as different representations both by and of them circulate. By 1994 the display contained a photographic representation of the diorama itself beside a cast figure of a Khoisan woman who, unlike her counterpart in the diorama, was fully clothed in the headscarf, long skirt, and shirt in which Drury would have met her over the period of the casting project (figure 75). While one of the storyboard panels contained printed material that provided a selection of prominent literary tropes figuring the Khoisan from different genres (from novels to ethnographic treaties), the most striking materials that provided the visual rival to the diorama were the cases and panels that dealt with the casting process itself. These contained archive photographs of the actual named individuals who had been waylaid by Drury and his team, taken at the time of the casting (figure 76). They are in many ways the clearest indictment of the process since they personalize the casting, as well as temporalize the scene in a way that the diorama explicitly disavows. Another panel plunders the museum's archive to show how the casts were used in the mu-

Above 75. Cast figure of
Khoisan woman. Part of
SAM exhibition critically
deconstructing the myth of
the Khoisan represented
by the "Bushman
Diorama." Photo by
Jean Brundrit.

Right 76. Archive photographs of individuals cast
by Drury. SAM display.
Photo by Jean Brundrit.

seum, with Drury and Peringuey in the modeling studio. In addition, in a display case that has the effect of understatedly parodying the ethnographic cabinet, an exhibition takes the viewer through the technical stages of casting from the human body and makes undeniably explicit the discomfort and intrusion that such a practice necessarily involved (figure 77). Since 1994 more material has been incorporated that looks at the practice of ethnography and anthropology in the early twentieth century. It all focuses on the Khoisan, but by exploring the linguistic research of Lucy Lloyd and Wilhelm Bleek, it suggests another model of ethnographic fieldwork driven by rather different motives than the emphatic evolutionary typologies of physical anthropology that initiated the casting project (figure 78). In other words, the scrutiny of museological anthropology and its implications for any representations of the history and culture of the Khoisan are complicated by versions that resist a monolithic representation of anthropological fieldwork itself and of the possible relationships between the anthropologist and his or her subject / informant.

In some senses, then, the changes Davison and Klinghardt instigated in the anthropology gallery were responsive to the challenge Davison identified as finding "new ways of displaying objects, a new display vocabulary, so that the visual rhetoric will encourage an awareness of multiple views and not reduce the complex presence of an artifact to a single, authoritative interpretation."[57] However, Davison, in a typically self-deprecating comment, felt, in 1991 at any rate, that the "attempt to raise awareness of museum practice and to stimulate critical responses to the diorama through the display about the diorama seems to have been largely, although not entirely, unsuccessful."[58]

Pippa Skotnes, reminiscing about research she carried out in the sam in the 1980s, writes of the popularity of the diorama with local and foreign visitors and the kinds of comments that were so often part of the tour guide's narrative.[59] Her impression was that almost every description focused on the physical appearance of the figures, often rehearsing the kinds of preoccupation with the genital areas so familiar from earlier accounts. She draws attention to the ways tour guides' narratives of the hunting and gathering lifestyle "frequently characteris[ed] Bushmen in the same way as they might predators such as lion or leopard, or omnivores such as baboons" with one guide reporting that "the Bushmen were nocturnal, and slept in hollows in the ground during the day, coming out at night to hunt."[60] Ciraj Rassool, describing his impressions of the diorama at a conference organized by the sam to discuss how to broaden the visitor base of the museum in November 1993, recounts, "As I came in this morning, I joined a

77. Details of the casting process. Display case at the SAM. Photo by Jean Brundrit.

Below 78. Display at the SAM historicizing the linguistic research of Lucy Lloyd and Wilhelm Bleek. Photo by the author.

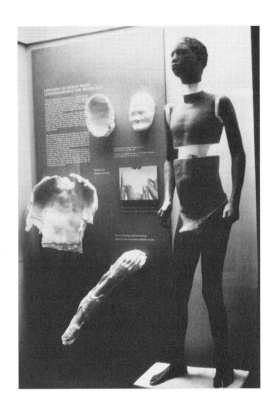

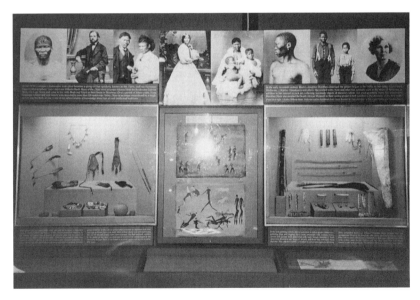

guided tour through the Bushman display. Tourists were told about crinkly bodies, nakedness. There were references to the height of people and their habits. All this discussion took place in the present tense with some references to ecological questions. As the group progressed, reference was made to the national languages of South Africa and tribal tongues and dialects. No reference was made to the accompanying written material that pointed to possible controversy. Discussion was couched in terms of tribes and tribal habits."[61] In contrast, sam assistant education officer Damasani Sibayi (appointed in 1989 and one of whose strengths is that he is a native Xhosa speaker) reports in 1994 of his strategy to begin any school visits to the museum with a trip to the "Bushman Diorama" precisely because it illicited strong responses from his young charges.[62] This confirms a position I have long upheld: the ethnographic or anthropological collection has the potential to provide critical and disruptive narratives of cultural contact, exchange, and difference precisely because it is so difficult to read as a neutral space today—unlike the art museum, which still so often persists in claiming some kind of autonomy for cultural production and for the institution itself. Once the visitor is aware of a historical relationship between anthropology and the colonial process, even in the most general terms, the potential for a dialectical and dialogical reading against the grain is enhanced rather than mitigated by the very fact of the ethnographic or anthropological museum as marked by its formation as a colonial institution.[63]

From October 1989 to January 1991, sam conducted a survey of visitor responses to the "Bushman Diorama," partly as a way of gauging how far the deconstructive intervention had challenged the viewer's perception. Unfortunately the survey seems to have been fairly unproductive, and it is difficult to deduce broader conclusions from it partly because of the very limited number of responses. However, some of the documented responses correspond to the poles of opinion that others have catalogued in a more speculative mode. Also evident is the fact that notwithstanding the intentions of the curators, it is always difficult to control the ways an exhibit may be animated by others outside the institution (or sometimes within it) and may consequently take on a life completely at odds with the original plot or design!

From the feedback to the sam survey, four comments encapsulate the debate around the diorama. One response read, "[The diorama conveys] a picture of the life of the Bushmen as it was—simple, with its own dignity— a folk who had their own ways of surviving despite the vicissitudes of the terrain and the attacks they endured at the hands of others. The diorama has its own integrity. To change it would be to impose transitory viewpoints /

issues which seek to rewrite history in the image of current ideologies. By all means show the present life of the Bushmen but do not interfere with an exceptional depiction."[64] A second, by someone described in the survey as "a professional art historian," commented, "Confusion generated . . . engaging excellence of display but discomfort at presentation of people in this fashion. Case detailing history and controversy goes some way towards contextualising issues but insufficient. . . . I find the juxtaposition of displays of dinosaurs and *some* people alarming and irresponsible as regards the dangers of entrenching problems of attitude such as paternalism, racial superiority and discrimination."[65] Third, an informant described as a "Xhosa-speaking man studying in Cape Town," reported, "It represents the old way of life of these people without showing any change. The transition from that kind of tradition / culture should be displayed. . . . The Dutch must also be shown here to show how change occurred."[66] Finally, a "young woman student" commented, "Why do whites first exterminate indigenous populations and animals and then afterwards try to 'preserve' them behind glass cases. . . . Why don't you say that people were *exterminated* / and [what about] their resistance?"[67]

"MISCAST"

Partly on the back of the Davison-Klinghardt experiment and the interest it generated and because of the evident notoriety of the "Bushman Diorama," Pippa Skotnes, a practicing artist and lecturer at the Michaelis School of Fine Art (part of the University of Cape Town), put on an exhibition that was the culmination of a long-standing research commitment. "Miscast: Negotiating the Presence of Khoi and San History and Material Culture" was shown not at the SAM, but at its neighboring institution, the South African National Gallery. Opening in April 1996, "Miscast" was hugely controversial and the subject of a number of long and mostly critical reviews locally and internationally. However, as is so often the case, it was the very controversial nature of the exhibition that made it a valuable, if painful, experiment in envisaging a revisionist history.

The exhibition was intended as a critical engagement with the ways in which the Khoisan were pathologized, dispossessed, and all but eradicated through colonialism and apartheid. But it was also intended as an exposition of the epistemological violence that provided the justification for such acts. In other words, "Miscast" was also devised as a provocative disquisition on the ways in which science, religion, and literature had been responsible for promulgating a series of highly contentious and actively destructive myths around these people. In this sense the exhibition shared a similar agenda with the SAM display, with one significant difference. "Miscast" was constructed as an experiential installation that focused on the complex ways in which vision and visibility produced their object historically. Part of the aim was to make contemporary viewers aware of how one might become complicit in this process by involving them in compromising viewing positions. As an exhibitionary strategy there are many aspects of this much smaller enterprise that recall the grander project of the Holocaust Memorial Museum controversially situated in the Mall in Washington, D.C. There too a traumatic history is exposed through a carefully constructed viewing space, which similarly mobilizes the technique of a suggestive and complex installation work, combining more didactic textual displays with poetic iconic representations without explanatory text, and the visitor is intentionally isolated in a space that necessarily encourages a reflexive and intensely personal response to what inevitably takes on a more metonymic emphasis.

The deconstructive turn in "Miscast" is flagged immediately by a quotation running around the top of the walls of the main room. It is taken from Greg Dening's *Mr. Bligh's Bad Language:* "No-one can hope to [act as] mediator. . . . Nor can anyone speak just for the one, just for the other. There is no escape from the politics of our knowledge, but that politics is not in the past. That politics is in the present" (figure 79).[68]

At either end of the room were black-and-white archive photographs of the Khoisan—at the 1952 Van Riebeeck Festival, the 1936 Empire Exhibition in Johannesburg, and other historical instances where they formed part of a spectacle. Set into the same walls, however, were recessed display cases with artifacts related to specific individuals who had played a part in the narrative of scientific inquiry that Skotnes wished to foreground as a counterpart to the other displays recalling the focus on physical anthropology— that is, the activities of the philologists Lloyd and Bleek. The tactic of using glass cases that spotlit the contents of Lucy Lloyd's personal effects side by side with the contents of a divining bag that might have belonged to !Kabbo or another Khoisan informant was intended to represent both sets of artifacts as equally valuable and the owners as equally significant participants in the construction of history, and it deliberately invoked the genre of display associated with the "treasures of the collection" mode in either art or ethnographic museums. Such displays also effectively produce a dialogue with the photographic archive surrounding them so that they highlight the differences in the forms of objectification—the homogenizing effects of the spectacle of colonial exhibitions as opposed to the individual agency called up by the personal effects. In South Africa, such a valorizing display of Khoi-

79. Installation view of "Miscast" with Dening quote. South African National Gallery, 1996. Courtesy of Pippa Skotnes.

san artifacts has been rare. Indeed this lacuna in South African museums, particularly the lack of attention to the extraordinary Khoisan rock art, has been the topic of many a tirade by the two scholars most responsible for bringing new interpretations of such work to light, Thomas Dowson and J. D. Lewis-Williams.[69]

In another section of the "Miscast" exhibit thirteen casts of body parts, made from Drury's molds, were arranged in a semicircle. Truncated and fragmented remnants of headless bodies, these casts, lit from beneath and glowing in the low light of the gallery, bear an uncanny and disturbing resemblance to the ghostly remains of those frozen in time after the volcanic destruction at Pompeii. Confusingly caught between references to the scene of an innocuous life-modeling class and the scene of untimely and sinister death, they refer to the living but are literally emptied of life. Beside the casts were stands with texts relating incidents of violence against the Bushmen, borrowing a method deliberately invoking the narrativizing strategies familiarly used by art galleries and other museums. In the center of the same room, a circle of rifles supported a flagpole, the base of which was a gray brick structure containing windows found in a blockhouse defense, a jail, and a church, and beside it a "garden" contained a half-buried box with a collection of cast human remains, cacti (generally considered indigenous to South Africa but actually all "aliens"), and five books, half buried, with the spines collectively spelling the word "truth" (figure 80).

In another section of the room a tall glass cabinet displayed various anthropometric implements associated with early-twentieth-century scientific research concerning the Khoisan. Among these exhibits was a letter from a Dr. Fischer, dated 13 November 1913, detailing the procedure amateurs should follow when obtaining body parts in order to ensure maximum use-value for scientific research. A bank of empty cardboard archive boxes leaned against one wall of the room, labeled not with contents, but with significant events in the recorded history of the Khoisan, often with two dates—the date of the event and the date of its recording in historical narrative. It was intended as a self-reflexive commentary on the constructed nature of the archive, and this was cemented by the strategy of placing mirrors so that the viewers' own reflections were cast as they looked at the so-called evidence. The casts made another appearance here as a pile of unlit body parts jumbled together on a table in front of the archive boxes (figure 81).

One of the most contentious aspects of "Miscast" was in the second display room, where the floor was covered with vinyl, screenprinted pages taken from nineteenth- and early-twentieth-century illustrated journals, anthropological and medical journals, police records, and other ephemera advertising shows and spectacles that featured the Khoisan; almost all the articles were clearly derogatory (figure 82). Yet here too the dialogue was intended to be between the images on the floor and the photographs on the walls of the room. These photographs were scenes of daily life, taken by Paul Weinberg between 1984 and 1995 with the cooperation of Khoisan peoples from Botswana, Namibia, and the southern Kalahari, and they bore little resemblance to the pathologizing representations on the floor.[70] Indeed many of them explicitly undermined any attempts to produce the Khoisan in some timeless vacuum and instead showed them putting various consumer commodities to good use (an example is in figure 83). In the same room there was an attempt once again to introduce a self-reflexive device intended to draw attention to the act of looking: video cameras were placed on the floor as if recording the viewers' actions.

The last room of the exhibition was set aside as a different kind of contemplative space, with a selection of the research materials that went into the making of the exhibition available to the visitors. Around the walls were copies of Khoisan rock paintings produced by various researchers over time. Skotnes records what the rock art in this room represented for her:

Top 80. Circle of rifles in "Miscast." South African National Gallery, 1996. Courtesy of Pippa Skotnes.

Bottom 81. Archive boxes and pile of cast body parts in "Miscast." South African National Gallery, 1996. Courtesy of Pippa Skotnes.

Above 82. Floor printed with newspaper and illustrated press cuttings in "Miscast." South African National Gallery, 1996. Courtesy of Pippa Skotnes.

Left 83. Paul Weinberg, *Weekend, Bushmanland, Namibia*, 1984–1995. Black-and-white photograph. Courtesy of the artist.

the only place where the various unique views of the Bushman world expressed by the Bushmen alone reached across time and into the present. This is the only place from the colonial period and before, where Bushmen spoke entirely with their own voice. This voice belongs to the paintings and the landscape where the paintings were made but the tragic truth is that there is no one left to interpret the paintings. No painter was ever interviewed, no unbroken painting tradition survives, and the multiple copies, drawn or photographed, with their accompanying interpretations, represent the impressions of others. At best, there is a kind of "cooperation" between the painted images and their researchers, where the Bleek and Lloyd archive and the other ethnographies inform the interpretations. At worst, the paintings outside of their own environment are silent, bearing witness, in the museum or gallery, only to the act of tearing them out of the landscape and possessing them for museum collections.[71]

What interests me about "Miscast" is that this reflection on a traumatic history took place at a critical time in the emergence of the new democratic nation. Yet again, the Khoisan and their representation figure as a central mediator at a moment of nation building, just as in 1952 they had figured as a mediator for the apartheid state at the Jan van Riebeeck Tercentenary Festival, which I mentioned at the beginning of this chapter. This time, the historical moment necessitated a mediator between that apartheid state and the young democracy of Mandela's government of national unity. At the same time, another crucial event was taking place in South Africa. The TRC held its first hearings in April 1996. This extraordinary tribunal raised many questions, but in relation to the complicated histories of Khoisan representation in South Africa, it immediately foregrounded for me the issue of how one can adequately represent a traumatic past and the images and objects associated with it without subjecting the victims of this past to the same violence all over again. In the television transmissions of the TRC proceedings, one of the most striking aspects of the coverage is the extent to which the pain and terror to which individuals were subjected under apartheid is necessarily relived in the courtroom. One of the most graphic instances among many such examples was when the mothers of the Guguletu Seven were shown the news footage of the police killing their sons. One particularly distressing scene films a policeman who, having attached a long rope around the body of one of the young men—rather in the same vein as a cowboy lassos his bull—pulls the rope from a distance to roll the body over for the cameras, as if the body were just so much dead meat. The timing of "Miscast," then, had an impact on its reception. This meant that the attention it received and the burden of representation it was made to bear were possibly far beyond the expectations of the organizers.

In what ways did the installation strategy deployed in "Miscast" offer different possibilities to both the more didactic and perhaps, we might argue, less imaginative counterexhibition at the SAM and the traumatic personal testimonies of the TRC? And what were the risks of such a strategy, particularly in the South African context at that moment? How, for example, do the horrifying images of grotesque scientific experimentation in the Holocaust Memorial Museum and the equally devastating reportage on the death camps escape the criticisms of prurient voyeurism and accusations of reinforcing rather than challenging such violence—the very criticisms that were leveled at "Miscast"? How does its location in the South African National Gallery impinge on the reception of the material exhibited?

It is obvious from my sympathetic description of the exhibition that "Miscast" was clearly intended and carefully constructed as a self-reflexive archaeology of the historical and scientific misrepresentation of the Khoisan. Yet it somehow missed its mark. Even among a viewing public familiar with either conceptual art practices or museological strategies for engaging a critical eye, many of the clues were unappreciated. One of the difficulties is that in order to understand the conceptual framing, the viewer has to already be well versed in the histories that are being deconstructed and to have perceived them as somehow problematic. In fact, one would need quite a detailed grasp of these. Some typical misunderstandings are outlined by Steven Robins, an anthropologist at the University of the Western Cape; in a series of interviews Robins asked a number of South African visitors their views on the exhibition in order, as he puts it, to see what "a heterogeneous and culturally differentiated public" made of it.[72]

Michael, whom Robins describes as "a 24-year old colored student of history at the University of the Western Cape," was adamant that most visitors would simply have their prejudices reinforced of the Khoisan as an exotic and primitive people. He found the display of archive boxes, labeled with both historical incidents and taxonomic categories, "disgusting" rather than seeing them as a critique of museological and scientific practice. Sally, described as "a white woman in her twenties," thought that Skotnes had exhibited the resin casts to "make the Bushmen look more human so that we would know how these people looked and that they actually existed." Other visitors failed to grasp the critique of what Skotnes and others believe is a paternalistic and essentialist view of the Bushmen as a primordial people carrying on a way of life close to nature and untouched by modernity and colonialism. This misunderstanding surfaced particularly in relation to Paul Weinberg's photographs. Sarah, described as a forty-year-old teacher, irritatedly comments that Weinberg's work "spoils" this cherished image of the Bushmen: "There's a picture of a bushman sitting in the bush in his little hut with a tin of coffee. I can't understand this sort of exhibit. If I was to have a display I would put the bushmen in their natural environment. That is how they live. They are masters in their own environment."[73] At the other extreme, many of the Khoisan representatives who spoke the day after the opening saw the exhibition as a "dehumanising portrayal" of their people and an insensitive means of absolving white South Africans of their complicity in the history. Mansell Upham, the legal representative of the Griqua National Conference (GNC) made no bones about his feelings: "While we welcome all attempts to help expose the devastating colonial impact on the Khoisan, and are even impressed by the layout of Skotnes' book [which accompanied the exhibition], we are saddened by the non-indigenous people's persistence in hijacking and exposing our past for their own absolution."[74]

One of the other difficulties with this kind of exhibition lies not only in the extent of the brief and the complexity of the relationships that Skotnes intended to expose, but also in the range of conceptual strategies she devised to carry this out and the familiarity with different registers that the visitor then requires. This has been one of the problems with the inventive and polyvocal displays at one of my favorite museums, the Museum of Sydney, for example, where the range of interpretative registers required of the visitor can sometimes make the experience resemble more a cacophony than a symphony. More importantly, given the highly sensitive nature of the images and histories being scrutinized in "Miscast," there was a need for a reflexive and private space or set of spaces. This is particularly the case where evidence of trauma is concerned, especially if the exhibition is not to become a distant, voyeuristic experience. This is a precaution that the Holocaust Memorial Museum was so careful to take. Its models were often drawn from conceptual artists' suggestive juxtapositions, and they were designed to exploit the one-on-one viewing experience, which is the presumption of much contemporary art.

Yet obviously a limited constituency was clearly horrified and moved by the kinds of relationships and detailed evidence suggested by the putting together of objects and images that would otherwise be kept apart as discreet histories informed by discreet disciplines. Paul Lane, a lecturer in archaeology at the University of Botswana, in one of the more perceptive and informed reviews of "Miscast," writes of how his own practice as an archaeologist was challenged by the exhibition. In connection with the display of archive boxes, some of which deliberately draw attention to the storage and classification of human remains, he writes, "The specific technicalities of the display also challenge and subvert the anonymity to which such human remains are normally assigned, and the rationale for keeping and examining them. In place of site codes and catalogue numbers, the labels provide glimpses of real people whose lives and deaths became part of a collective history. Thus the need to acknowledge that history, how it has been written and how it could be written differently is immediately foregrounded."[75]

While the SAM exhibit is arguably far more pedestrian and less ambitious in its remit, one of its strengths is that it focuses on one specific instance of the misrepresentation of the Khoisan and one in which the institution itself is clearly implicated. There is a kind of integrity to the deconstructive display on the making of the Bushman Diorama that seemed lacking in "Miscast," precisely because the history of the museum itself is at the heart of the critique. The distance required to fully appreciate "Miscast" is a gap that is deliberately closed through the SAM exhibit. In a sense—and this is crucial—the curators at SAM were producing the exhibition for themselves and about themselves as much as for a putative public. Their own discipline was at the center of the interrogation.

The American anthropologist Meagan Biesele, who acted as translator for a group of San at a forum held at the National Gallery for Khoisan representatives to air their views, provides a particularly moving and measured response to the events around the time of the opening of "Miscast." One of the problems she foregrounds is specifically the issue of distance. She speaks of the long and sophisticated tradition of layers of self-reflexive critique that enables some viewers to distance experience from themselves, and she notes that not enough consideration had been paid to the possible responses of people who might come from a different viewing perspective, particularly if the experiences represented were historically their own.[76] Biesele remarks that the Khoisan representatives were outraged and shocked at the way in which they were "forced" to walk on the pictures of their ancestors in the room with the vinyl floor and dismayed that body parts of men, women, and children were on open display. She explains that the Khoisan are not squeamish or coy about bodily parts or fluids, and indeed their folklore is littered with references to both. But complex rules govern who may speak of what, how, and to whom. In the forum held at the National Gallery, while many expressed unequivocal anger, others made suggestions to remedy the faults of the exhibition. For example, one Khoisan representative suggested separate viewing areas for men and women and for younger and older initiated individuals.

Such consternation from Khoisan representatives inevitably raises issues concerning levels of consultation. Notwithstanding the use that was made of the exhibition for political grandstanding by various (and sometimes competing) Khoisan rights groups, there was clearly a problem of communication at some level. Although the organizers of "Miscast" followed some consultative protocols, many of the criticisms might have been averted if more systematic consultation with various representatives had taken place regarding the details of the display.

There are other reasons why the critical distance necessary to an appreciation of the dialectical intention behind the use of images and objects that show trauma and violence was not possible for the Khoisan visitors to "Miscast," while it has apparently not posed similar difficulties for the Jewish visitors to the Holocaust Memorial Museum. The Khoisan are still a dispossessed minority in the "new" South Africa, whereas most of the various Jewish constitutencies in the United States are a powerful political lobby with access and influence in many state and federal institutions. Perhaps given such conditions it is a tall order to expect a Khoisan visitor to view with dispassion documents, photographs, and the instruments of a colonial process that has systematically reduced the Khoisan to a set of dispersed, disenfranchised, and economically vulnerable communities throughout southern Africa.

Other important conjunctural factors make the particular use of body parts in "Miscast" especially controversial in the South African context (although they also meant that the debates it stimulated were politically potent and even empowering to the very constituencies that were its strongest critics). Some months before the exhibition was launched, in April 1996, Saartjie Baartman was again making headline news. The GNC demanded that Baartman's remains be returned from the Musée de l'Homme in Paris to South Africa for proper burial. In a memorandum submitted to Nelson Mandela in December 1995, the GNC called for the recognition of the Griquas as "an indigenous or a First Nation of South Africa."[77] At the same time, the organization addressed a letter to the French Embassy in Pretoria invoking the Universal Declaration of Human Rights and the Draft Declaration on the Rights of Indigenous People to enforce its claim for the return of Baartman's remains.

It is clear that by this date Saartjie Baartman had become an iconic symbol of the dispossession of the Khoisan peoples, and the return of her remains became a rallying point not only for the Griquas, but also for other Khoisan groups. Ben Ngubane, then Arts, Culture, Science and Technology Minister in Mandela's new government of national unity added his voice to the

Khoisan demands for the return of Saartjie Baartman in a statement that lent a new twist to the controversy: "The return of South Africa to the international community marked the beginning of the process of healing and restoring of our national dignity and humanity. The process would not be complete while Saartjie Baartman's remains were still kept in a museum."[78] Baartman consequently became an icon not only for the Khoisan, but also for the nation—a development that incidentally also lent credibility to the Khoisan demands for recognition as a special ethnic group within the "new South Africa."

In February 1996 Ngubane held talks with the French minister of co-operation, Jacques Godfrain, in an attempt to secure the remains from Paris. That same month Patricia Davison told the *Weekly Mail and Guardian* that the SAM had a policy of being "entirely open about our holdings and to work together with relevant stakeholders in the process of negotiating a curatorial policy that is both sensitive and responsible."[79] She went on to say that "It is recognised that policies regarding human remains must be developed in partnership with relevant institutions and community groups" but that "the historical importance of the collection should not be overlooked. Collections from the past are powerful reminders of the ideas that contributed to the shaping of cultural identities and thus have an important educational and cultural role to play in the present."[80] At the annual conference of SAMA at Kimberley in April 1996 (the same month as the opening of "Miscast") members adopted a formal resolution expressing support for the return of the remains of Saartjie Baartman. They also arranged a workshop in May that year in Cape Town to develop "a professional framework, for South African circumstances, within which the heritage sector can negotiate more widely on issues of sensitive collections and foster an atmosphere for open, constructive and international cooperation."[81] Brigitte Mabandla let her personal views on the subject be known when she mooted the idea of creating a cemetery "with an on-site museum where collections [could] be kept in a way that allows academic access subject to rules and ethics drawn up in partnership with indigenous organisations."[82] Martin Engelbrecht, the researcher for the Khoisan Representative Council (KRC), suggested that it might be difficult to get the consent of his members if the remains of their ancestors were not buried in the traditional way but added, "We also know we are only a community if we can get enough knowledge about what happened to our people. We want to know about the study of our skeletons. We need to benefit from knowledge."[83] Given the escalation of demands around the potent symbolic figure in death as in life, of Saartjie Baartman and the political pressures raised by the specter of human remains in many South

African and European museums, the vacant spaces of the resin cast body parts exhibited in "Miscast" became metonymic—too close a resemblance to the very human remains that were the focus of so much political and emotional investment to enable an intellectualized response from some constituencies (although evidently for many others who were not Khoisan, it was *both* a shocking *and* an enlightening experience).

"Miscast" unwittingly demonstrated yet again that it is not enough to simply exhibit signs of creative cross-cultural exchange and modernity—as, for example, Paul Weinberg's photographs were clearly intended to do—as a strategy for countering a history of pathologizing objectification. It is necessary to demonstrate a sense of peoples as subjects with the agency to be able to effect their own history—sometimes through resistance and, as in the Khoisan case, through political organization.[84] In a painful but constructive turn of events this is exactly what the Khoisan demonstrated at the National Gallery forum, organized partly by way of acknowledging this very point. Here, in an unprecedented gathering of many Khoisan from all over southern Africa, they voiced their concerns, and often competing demands, for the very land from which "Miscast" had so inventively charted their historical dispossession.[85]

6

NEW SUBJECTIVITIES FOR THE NEW NATION

> The stories of the TRC represent a ritualistic lifting of the veil and the vali-
> dation of what was actually seen. They are an additional confirmation of the
> movement of our society from repression to expression. Where in the past
> the state attempted to compel the oppressed to deny the testimony of their
> own experience, today that experience is one of the essential conditions for
> the emergence of a new national consciousness. These stories may very well
> be some of the first steps in the rewriting of South African history on the
> basis of validated mass experience. — Njabulo Ndebele, "Memory, Metaphor,
> and the Triumph of Narrative"

Media coverage of the TRC more than any other event in South Africa's recent history has highlighted the debate around what is and is not repre-
sentable through visual culture. In particular the televising of the Amnesty
Commission (AC) and the Human Rights Violations Commission (HRVC)
brought into sharp focus the incommensurability of the means of representation with the actual pain, suffering, and other complex emotions lived by
the central protagonists of these poignant and horrifying narratives.

Established in 1996 as an essential component of nation building and the
peace process, the TRC was overburdened from the start by the expectations
of those who needed a visible material and symbolic form of reparation for
the crimes committed under apartheid rule. The commission's brief (in the
words of its chair, Desmond Tutu) was to "unearth the truth about our dark
past, to lay the ghosts of that past so that they will not return to haunt us and
that we will thereby contribute to the healing of a traumatised and wounded
people, for *all* of us in South Africa are wounded people, and in this manner to promote national unity and reconciliation."[1] In a sense the TRC was

presented with an impossible mandate. Yet it has been demonstrated historically that something productive can nonetheless ensue from such national confessionals.[2] One significant aspect of the South African example (in sharp contrast to its Latin American counterparts) is that out of the nineteen instances of international truth commissions, the South African TRC was the first to be held as a form of public hearing.[3] Another crucial dimension is that the TRC was turned into a media spectacle.[4] The lies, the deceptions, the brutality, the tears, the weaknesses, and the strengths were transformed into theater via the representations, which were broadcast regularly on SABC and national radio and reported in the national press.

A number of implications follow from such a public representation of pain and shame. While one might be able to argue that such media coverage made the TRC process available to larger numbers, it is also true to say that, as with all media representations, the coverage was always only ever necessarily a series of edited highlights. Thus while transparency and access were invoked as the main benefits of media coverage, there were nevertheless yawning gaps and deafening silences.[5]

Ironically it is the very public nature of what inevitably becomes spectacle that sets limits on the means by which multifarious forms and levels of personal pain and experience can be made explicit to the viewing public. These limitations are partly the result of the tribunal process itself because of the narrow repertoire of performative gestures available for exhibiting personal trauma in this type of forum—speech (usually narrative), tears, aggression, withholding, and hesitation. Ultimately, then, the visibility of the TRC process has contributed to the frustration of recognizing the difficulties of representing the "truth" and of an adequate representation of the anguish of the victim. More than this, the inadequacy of representation of the complexities of personal lived experience of such pain also has repercussions for the ways in which such pain can be made to serve as representative for the larger ideal entity of "national pain" or "collective guilt."

It became clear to me on a number of visits to South Africa that one of the areas where the inadequacies of representation might be being addressed was in the realm of fine art. This is particularly so in relation to issues around trauma and violence, but also in relation to those gray areas often involving a complex acknowledgment of guilt, complicity, and compromise relating to the experience (most obviously) of being white—or indeed *any* color—in apartheid South Africa. In the TRC hearings the individual was always staged in one of three ways: victim, perpetrator, or hero(ine). I became interested in the possible ways in which one might represent a more differentiated notion of subjective experience without losing sight of the larger political significance of each individual case. If the most widely disseminated and apparently most visible medium was inadequate to the task of representing the trauma of South Africa's past, in what specific ways could fine art (a set of practices bound by their own limitations) offer different means of articulating this past?

In many obvious ways the chosen repertoire of the artists whose work I discuss in this chapter has resonances beyond the boundaries of the South African context in which they live and work. Their work with video, photography, performance, and installation could, and does, establish a dialogue with artists in any international art arena. However, it is also the case that the terms "postmodern" or "postcolonial," which currently describe such practices, often operate as glib smokescreens for those too lazy to map the rich texture of political and cultural exchanges and appropriations that complicate such terms and render them meaningful.[6] In the cases of all the artists discussed below, it repays the effort to analyze the work not only in terms of its wider appeal, but also in terms of its engagement with themes particular to the South African context. One of the strengths of their work is the articulation of broader issues within this specificity.

I want to suggest that there may be ways in which the drawbacks of fine art—its ambiguity, its recuperability as a screen for personal projections, for example—may also be its strengths in this context. For those artists who attempt to do more than simply document or represent the effects of trauma or guilt and who try to tackle the gray areas in between complicity and victimization, fine art, unlike the mass media, offers a smaller theater in which their work may be consumed more intimately on a one-to-one basis. Indeed this might well be one of the reasons that fine art can sometimes more successfully juggle both the big spectacle of apartheid and the insistent personal intrusions and degradations so often invisible to others but that were such destructive features of some individuals' experiences of living under apartheid.

There are a number of reasons for analyzing the work of the artists in this chapter. The first is that their art is characterized by a dialectical relationship between past histories and lived experience in the present. Rather than deny history, they mobilize (and in some cases invent) historical memory as a tool for dealing with the contradictions of life in contemporary South Africa. Secondly, as individuals they also usefully span the generational divide. They also represent a range of constituencies, marked out ethnically according to the discriminatory logic of apartheid, and much of their work is evocative of the ambiguities of the TRC. Most importantly their work engages the complications of inhabiting subject positions that are riven with conflictual, inherited histories but out of which they attempt to fashion new subjectivities appropriate for the new nation.

Between 11 June and 9 July 1999, the History Workshop at the University of the Witwatersrand, together with the Centre for Violence and Reconciliation, organized a conference entitled "The TRC: Commissioning the Past." Five artists were commissioned for an exhibition around this theme, "Truth Veils," at the Gertrude Posel Gallery (on campus). One of the most resonant pieces in the exhibition was by Cape Town artist Berni Searle, who produced an installation entitled *The Palms of the Hands, the Small of the Back, the Nape of the Neck, under the Belly, the Soles of the Feet* (plate 5). The work consisted of five large color photographic details of the parts of the body named in the title. These were hung, unframed, from a shelf so that the ends of the print rested on the floor in a scroll. Black Egyptian henna was sprinkled on the shelf and on the scrolled ends of the prints. Above the shelf were much smaller framed photographs that related directly to the larger segments represented in the prints. This multifaceted work, which in any viewing context would operate on a number of levels, in addition to the South African context, engages very specific issues readily resonant for a local (Western Cape) and national (South African) audience.

The body in Searle's prints in *The Palms of the Hands, the Nape of the Neck, under the Belly, the Soles of the Feet,* is her own, although this is never explicit in the work, and her face and head are never available to the viewer. The use of the body of course has a long history, particularly in feminist art practice since the extensive performance and time-based work of the 1970s, where it was so often deployed as an act of reclamation.[7] But in the context of a society that was systematically oppressed on the basis of "evidence" apparently writ large upon the body, such an emphasis is immediately charged with another political dimension. Searle has commented on a number of occasions on how the racialized classification system that formed the basis of apartheid has shaped her work. Since 1998 she has elaborated these complex identifications through two series of photographic installations, *Colour Me* and *Discoloured,* of which the piece commissioned for "Truth Veils" forms a part.

The effectiveness of this work stems partly from the fact that it both repels and seduces the viewer. Searle calls up the process of classification and the pseudo-scientific racial categories of apartheid through both the kinds of images she produces—the focus on skin and the attention drawn to color by the henna—and the method she deploys to make the large color prints. After being stained with henna, the chosen section of the body is pressed up against transparent glass. This produces various effects. Because the body is pressed hard against the glass, it is distorted so that the flattened surface takes on the quality of a specimen between glass slides offered up for microscopic inspection—held up for view, almost opened out, but not quite (see detail in plate 6). As with a sample or specimen, the body is a living organism, and in this instance the signs of life are eerily present as condensation against the glass owing to heat coming off the body's surface. But we are never offered the whole body. It is always fragmented and faceless. In addition, the conditions under which the process has been completed are ambiguous. These are alluded to but never explicitly revealed. Each of the five much smaller framed photographs set above the shelves compounds the association with the concept of "evidence" generated by the other aspects of the installation, for these relate in particular ways to the larger prints below. Every smaller frame seems to promise further elucidation by either magnifying a detail of the bigger prints or by providing, paradoxically in miniature, more of the whole to which the part relates—the entire back rather than just the "nape of the neck" or the "small of the back." And yet it is clear that once again, despite all these details posturing as conclusive "evidence," more is withheld than elaborated.

There seems to me to be a dialectical relation established between the component parts of this installation and the assumption of verifiable racial hierarchies promoted through apartheid legislation and the so-called scientific scrutiny that underpinned it. By on the one hand appropriating (visually) the language of science assumed as an elucidating discourse designed to make the "truth" visible but on the other hand only hinting at rather than stating ways in which such "evidence" could be read, Searle draws attention to the spurious "visibility" and "transparency" (objectivity) of scientific investigation—in this case where it specifically relates to questions of race and ethnicity. In other words, this is not just some witty "po-mo" indeterminacy at work here but a more attentive mobilizing of different kinds of visual metaphor and particular properties of certain media in order to provoke a critical engagement.

As with all of Searle's work, at some level these prints are also the "evidence" of actions—the remnants of another time and an undisclosed location. Just as the body parts of the title refer to the most vulnerable areas of the body—those least exposed to view—so the reference to activity becomes, if not sinister, then certainly anxiety provoking. We do not know what has taken place, and the signs available to us are giving off mixed messages. The Egyptian henna has a disturbing propensity to stain the skin to the color of bruising. This, together with the knowledge that the chosen areas of the body are all "hidden" vulnerable areas not usually exposed to view, cannot but generate an association with torture.

In 1998 the University of the Witwatersrand hosted another conference, this time on the subject of violence and women in Africa. In South Africa rape is a major concern among many women. In addition, in war zones, where women and children are often deployed as human shields or made to pay for the deeds of their absent menfolk, violence against women is endemic. Neither of these scenarios takes account of the considerable domestic violence that is also often a corollary of unemployment and social inequality. These conditions make the topic of sexual violence a familiar concern. Under apartheid, torture involving sexual and other violence was a feature of many prison regimes. It is no surprise, then, that Searle's sequence of photographs also recalls evidence of a different kind to the pseudo-scientific taxonomies instituted under apartheid. They recall the kinds of forensic evidence so often denied by the regime.[8] In September 1999 Searle exhibited another version of the work shown at the "Truth Veils" exhibition as part of "Staking Claims: Confronting Cape Town," an exhibition organized by the senior curator at the South African National Gallery, Emma Bedford.[9] The location for the show was integral to the efficacy of Searle's piece. Much of her work is site-specific and draws its power from the relations she invokes between the histories of the location and the components of her installations. The Cape Town exhibition was no exception.

The Granary, which was the venue for "Staking Claims: Confronting Cape Town," is a building that has had a number of uses in its lifetime, including a magistrate's court and police station incorporating a prison dedicated to what were euphemistically referred to as "problem city women." Searle's reworking of the "Truth Veils" piece as *A Darker Shade of Light* had the effect of refining some of the associations suggested in the earlier piece. In particular, those more sinister readings of the work, which conjured up forensic evidence and torture, were cemented by the surroundings. For her installation Searle used a large, bleak room in a decrepit state, with peeling paint and damp walls showing traces of the paraphernalia of bureaucratic occupation—for example, stained areas of wall previously housing noticeboards— and fluorescent lighting overhead (plate 7). In one view of the installation, a barred window adjacent to the light box containing the images of the "soles of the feet" produces a particularly poignant conjuncture (figure 84). In other words, the exhibition space had none of the niceties of the modern gallery but was already charged with a discomforting past.

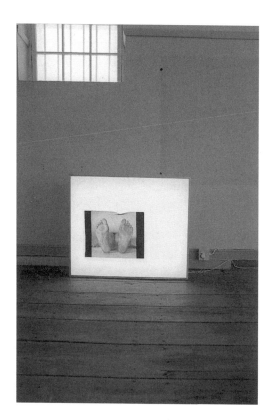

84. Berni Searle, detail from
A Darker Shade of Light,
1999. Digital print installed
in light box. Photo by Jean
Brundrit. Courtesy of the
artist.

   Into this environment were installed large light boxes with the same body
details as in "Truth Veils." This time, however, they were given a different
treatment. Taken as Polaroid photos, the images were then floated off the
backing by submerging the photographs in hot water so that the images
then seemed to reproduce the same qualities as skin itself—creasing, folding, and wrinkling. Finally, this delicate texture was scanned, digitally enlarged, and reproduced on translucent paper, laminated between sheets of
perspex, and boxed. The resultant images, seen through the light boxes,
recreate the sensation of medical investigation, but instead of a negative
image that reproduces the shadowy interior of the body through x-ray, the
positive visible through the light box captures every detail of the body's surface (example in plate 8). In addition to the other readings, they become
analogues of the traces left by life. Paradoxically these intimate details of
the body's surfaces are a more accurate "map" of an individual than any portrait, while at the same time they refuse the limits of representing just a
singular being.

On the other hand, the sites of the body that Searle has chosen to work with are also those that recall snatched phrases of love poems. They refer, after all, to a lover's knowledge and a lover's touch. The fragility and intimacy of this "naming of parts" compounds the voyeuristic experience of being invited to look while feeling rebuffed by the uncertainty of what is on show. Gender is a crucial component that foregrounds a (nevertheless ambiguous) vulnerability, successfully enticing the viewer while challenging the shockingly naturalized relations between sex, violence, and death. The somatic experience of these images, their proximity and scale, encourages the contemplation of loss and trauma in relation to the viewer's own body—unlike the distance maintained by the spectacle of pain in media representations of the TRC proceedings.

Much of Searle's work has focused on challenging the ways in which the inscription of color on the body was used as a technology of apartheid. A trademark feature of many of her installations is the manipulation of substances and pigments already resonant with colonial referents and the tropes they reproduce, such as the spices of the *Colour Me* series (which evoke discovery, exploration, exoticism, sensuality, and slavery) and the Egyptian henna of the *Discoloured* series discussed above. One of the effects of using such highly charged materials in conjunction with her own body is to highlight the more arbitrary significations of color and its relation to constructions of "race."

Unlike many artists who authenticate their work with claims to one or other originary identity, Searle's work is about the limitations of such essentializing positions and about the necessarily messy and complicated mixings that have produced all contemporary societies. At a time in South Africa's history when various constituencies are making competing claims to originary status, it is important that those with a public voice are seen to resist the temptation of buying into an all too appealing identity politics as a means of justifying their practice. Searle has expounded on the difficulties of the term "colored," and her qualification goes to the heart of the matter: "I use the term with reservation, as a way of indicating a resistance to the imposed hierarchical racial classifications under apartheid. Interestingly enough, there are tendencies by various groupings in post-apartheid politics, particularly in the Western Cape, to claim the term 'coloured' in reference to an ethnic minority which I find problematic. Apart from many concerns, one of the problems within this 'ethnic minority' framework, is that identity is often viewed in static terms which reinforce stereotypes about who we are."[10] Searle's own family history reinforces the fallacy of such assumptions. It spans a network of colonial encounters and migrant desires

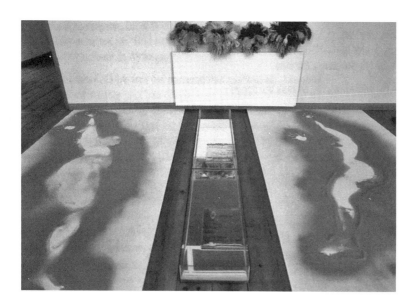

85. Berni Searle, *Julle Moet Nou Trek*, 1999. Mixed media. Photo by Lien Botha. Courtesy of the artist.

from Mauritius to Saudi Arabia, Germany, England, and South Africa. As she points out, the apartheid context has made such histories even more difficult to map effectively: "Tracing this heritage is an ongoing process, often hampered by a reluctance of relatives to talk about where they come from, especially those who were re-classified white. Often, amongst 'coloured' people, tracing this heritage is avoided because of the negative stereotypes surrounding indigenous people and slaves that were brought to the Cape. A further complication is the lack of official documentation such as birth, death and marriage certificates which forms an essential part of this process of 'tracing.' "[11]

Indeed much of Searle's work explicitly invokes the absences of conventional histories and the limitations of the archives that traditionally supply their sources. In 1999 fellow artist Lien Botha curated "Bloedlyn" as the culmination of an experimental dialogue between visual artists and writers. Searle, in collaboration with the poet Anoeschka von Meck, produced *Julle Moet Nou Trek* (You must move away) (figure 85). The installation was a kind of treatise on language, visibility, and power. It was also an indictment of the kinds of essentializing versions of cultural heritage that ignore the mutability of identity.

In *Julle Moet Nou Trek* the ghosts of ecstatic female bodies rise out of red clay dust, the characteristic color of so much of the South African soil. These figures flank glass cases at floor level that have the words of one of Von Meck's poems, "Trekslet," on their surface. As viewers read the verses, their own images are reflected back at them via minerals (oil and water) lining the bottom of the cases. Von Meck's poem uses the rich double entendre of the Afrikaans vocabulary to conjure up an image of the language itself as a promiscuous woman—powerful, vulnerable, abused and abusive, everywhere and at all times insinuating herself between man and land but damaged and ultimately transformed by those (men) in control of that same land. Searle explains the title as "likening the Afrikaans language to a cheap woman *(slet)* who moves around the land. To 'trek' is not just to move around though—it involves taking everything with you. Within the South African context, the word has a strong reference to the Great Trek."[12] While the viewers' eyes read the Afrikaans, their ears hear the distinctive sounds of a Khoisan language. It is a recording made in 1936, when a group of ǂKhomani and |'Auni Bushmen were brought to the city for the Johannesburg Empire Exhibition.[13] The speaker, ||Khaku, recounts the story of a hunt. When he returns he is told by a farmer that he must leave because his activities are chasing the farmer's gemsbok away. It is a story of displacement and disenfranchisement.[14] The two languages interrupt each other in the installation until they become part of the same sight / sound track. While the corporeal presence of the clay figures is absent, their traces in the red dust take on a monumental quality. Refusing to vanish, they become indelible imprints. And this is the point. While the installation reminds the viewer of the almost "lost" languages and culture of the Khoisan, whose survival has been continually threatened by successive waves of colonization and subsequent displacement, it also provides an image of resilient return in the residual actions of the leaping female bodies whose "shadows" dominate the piece. Searle's commentary is useful here: "Apart from the rather stark contrasts between Afrikaans and indigenous languages, there are also, however, connections. Survival, for the Khoisan people, involved abandoning their cultural and linguistic identity, many of whom, if not the majority, shifted to Afrikaans, bringing dynamic variations to the language."[15]

Once again, location is important to the effectivity of the installation. The Klein Karoo Kunstefees (arts festival) at Oudtshoorn is a particularly appropriate venue for a work that engages with the ways in which Afrikaans as a language is historically imbricated in different power structures and competing definitions of cultural heritage. The festival has gained a reputation as an event intended to challenge right wingers' exclusive ownership of Afrikaans as the language of apartheid and of Afrikaans culture as necessarily

86. Berni Searle, *Off-White: Back to Back*, 1999. Digital prints and flour. Photo by Jean Brundrit. Courtesy of the artist.

that of the oppressor. Searle's work, then, is also about the complicated trajectory of different kinds of exchange (cultural and political), the outcomes of which are not always easy to anticipate.

If *Julle Moet Nou Trek* foregrounds the vicissitudes of language to signal the elisions of historical memory, Searle's own body frequently calls attention to other, more ambiguous absences. In both *Red, Yellow, Brown: Face to Face* and *Off-White: Back to Back*, references to her own body recur repeatedly (figure 86). Both familiar and alien, the doubling of the human form takes on a spectral quality, enhanced, in the one, by the absent center formed by removing her body from the red, yellow, or brown spices, and, in the other, by the effective "white out," accomplished through the use of pea flour. Freud's *unheimlich* (uncanny) resurfaces. The repetition of the body in these installations performs an insurance against death while simultaneously anticipating it through the spectral double of the silhouette or shadow.[16] The concept of the *uncanny* works to further complicate that other dimension of these installations, which engages the ambivalences of how color (specifically skin color) both constructs and negates visibility and being.

While Searle's 2001 Venice Biennale video commission *Snow White* and the *Monument to the Women of South Africa* in Pretoria are both testimony to the persuasive power of women's collective action and to the unsung provision of life-sustaining food, Searle's constant use of her own body shares something in common with another form of protest specific to women (and, research suggests, specific to African women).[17] In 1990, after a desperate and protracted fight to procure decent housing, a group of women stripped naked in the face of police and municipal officials who had moved in with dogs and bulldozer to dismantle the shacks of the informal settlement that was their only shelter. This extraordinary event occurred in Dobsonville, Soweto, and was captured on film in a controversial and moving documentary, *Uku Hamba 'ze—To Walk Naked,* made by Sheila Meintjes, Jacqueline Maingard, and Heather Thompson.[18] As Meintjes explains, "The visual impact of the remarkable action of the women, and their subsequent evocation and explanation was profoundly moving."[19] There is a long tradition of women from many different African states resorting to naked protest in the face of official (usually male) reluctance to listen to their grievances and address their demands.[20] It seems to me that we could understand Berni Searle's insistent use of her own body as also belonging to this tradition, for it is in her work's capacity to resist the facile consumption of woman's body as commodity that she reminds us of the confrontational power of that same body, in which so many myths, desires, and necessities reside.

HAIR

If Searle's work operated during this period partly through foregrounding the dialectical relation between "scientific racism" and the lived experience of apartheid, Tracey Rose's early installations were concerned to foreground relations between the legal apparatus of apartheid and the contradictions it produced for those living under apartheid rule. In some senses her work created a taxonomy of how apartheid ideology was internalized. For her, hair was the key signifier: "Hair is significant in coloured communities. It marks you in certain ways, towards blackness or whiteness. On the one hand, it's about the 'privilege' of having straight hair as opposed to *kroes* [kinky or frizzy] hair, but on the other hand, having straight hair meant you were often insulted for thinking you were white, for pretending to be white."[21] Rose works through installation, performance, and video, and, as with Searle, her own body is a crucial mediator.

87. Tracey Rose, installation view of *Span II,* 1997. Mixed media. Courtesy of the artist.

Two performance pieces that received a lot of critical attention in South Africa and abroad are *Span I* (1997) and *Span II* (1997), both performed for the first time at the National Gallery in Cape Town as part of "Graft," a show curated by Colin Richards for the second Johannesburg biennale in 1997.[22] *Span II* involved Rose sitting naked in the kind of glass cabinet more usually associated with nineteenth-century ethnographic museums. More specifically, it recalls the dioramas in the neighboring SAM (figure 87). Given the demography of the Western Cape and Rose's own preoccupation with the contradictions of living with the label "colored," her gesture, intentionally or serendipitously, resonates with the "Bushman Diorama," which has, as we have seen, achieved a certain notoriety. It is hard to avoid associations with the kinds of anthropological scrutiny that resulted in the diorama and was responsible for authorizing so many of the racial theories that underpinned apartheid.[23] The point, however, is not that Rose's actions reproduce this historical relationship but that the association reinforces its inversion—or at least raises the possibility of a more ambiguous power relation. No longer a passive recipient of the gaze of others, Rose is lost in her own world and actions, intent on the "work" she is doing and apparently oblivious to the stares of visitors. In this way the glass case is transformed from a containing display device to a protective barrier that enables her to continue undisturbed.

The viewer becomes almost incidental. Rose's self-containedness ensures that her action functions as an affront rather than an invitation for voyeuristic pleasure. In this sense it acts as a riposte to the passive consumption that was encouraged by the "Bushman Diorama." Rose herself insists that the piece is "more a generic statement about the emotional and physical domination of women by men," while she acknowledges that it has wider ramifications than her own personal motivations.[24] Certainly in the generic sense it is about looking and power, and this articulation is in part dependent on assumed gender relations. In addition, however, the specific contextual conjuncture of Cape Town, the National Gallery, and its proximity to the SAM lends other resonances that work particularly powerfully on both national and regional levels in South Africa.

In her glass case Rose is engaged in knotting a mass of dark hair while sitting on a television monitor. In the same way that Manet's *Olympia*, to the shocked nineteenth-century Parisian viewer, paradoxically drew attention to her sex by covering her pudenda with her hand, the pile of dark hair falling from Rose's lap conjures immediate associations with pubic hair while also effectively covering her own. As we know, European tradition has historically associated any quantity of pubic hair in a woman with sexual appetite and an unbecoming and discomforting virility. (This tradition of the nude offered up any number of desexed nubile bodies for easy and undemanding consumption.) From this perspective Rose's nude is distinctly uncomfortable. The monitor on which Rose sits plays back a video of her own naked body. The video is filmed from a vantage point to which (in the National Gallery installation) the viewer is deliberately denied access—a full frontal pose. On closer inspection we can see that it is a film of the action that we are witnessing in the glass case, the frame focused on the area between her breasts, where her hands are knotting. The monitor is upended on its side so that the image becomes a witty inversion of the European tradition of a "reclining nude."

Because Rose is not only naked but shorn of all body hair, we assume that the hair she is so intent on knotting is her own. Since hair is traditionally one of the trappings of femininity and female sexuality, it becomes a perverse and challenging gesture for a young woman to shave it off. In the context of the Western Cape such a gesture from a young "colored" woman instantly draws attention to the arbitrariness of this signifier as a marker of identity— in the same way as Searle's use of henna or spices. As Rose says, "In terms of coloured identity the texture of the hair is layered with connotations that are racial and sexual. There is a racial saying that goes straight hair / light skin is more attractive. On a racist level straight hair has a positive interpretation compared to kinky hair. I would like to remind you here about a test referred to as the Pencil Stick Test. This test was used under apartheid in order to ascertain people's identities if they looked like whites naturally."[25] In addition, for women a shaved head has many other disturbing associations, which cut across cultural boundaries but are intensely gendered, of mourning, shame, penance, and incarceration. In a 1996 video, *Ongetitled* (Untitled), Rose exploited some of these other associations. She filmed herself shaving off all her body hair, cutting her long hair, and finally shaving her head in an austere tiled bathroom with a sound track of the buzz of an electric razor—an implement usually identified with male bathroom ritual. The video, which is shot from a high angle down onto the shadowy figure of Rose, obscured by the deliberately grainy print of the film, has a disturbingly claustrophobic feel to it. The sinister register is cemented by the viewpoint, which, together with the quality of the film, invites an association with surveillance cameras.

The companion piece to *Span II*—*Span I*—is a work that in the National Gallery exhibition was "performed" by an ex-prisoner who was employed by Rose to etch a text onto the wall of the gallery in front of the glass cabinet where Rose sat mute but similarly "at work" knotting her hair. This "art work by proxy" mobilizes language and narrative in an act that recalls the testimonies being given to the TRC at the time of its making. Rose describes the wall text as a confessional: "The text is a series of personal memories, the secrets that you don't tell during a confession. As against the 'white lies' I've told priests."[26] The narrative is in the style of an oral history, presented as a "stream of consciousness" that gives the impression of being unedited and unmediated (figure 88). It tells of the experiences and contradictions of growing up as a young "colored" woman, often expressed in sentiments that would have been difficult to articulate during apartheid because of their political "unacceptability." They are also expressions of personal and familial conflict around the fact of growing up "colored," which are not the staple of the narratives recounted in front of the TRC tribunals.

The "confession" on the wall has the effect of highlighting the silences of the tribunal testimonies. Where the latter present the grand narratives of apartheid experience, Rose narrativizes the quotidean. By doing so she draws our attention to the insidious ways in which apartheid discrimination could become internalized by constituencies who were themselves the object of this discrimination. In this way Rose also displays sentiments that are personally compromising and often involve her feelings toward her mother and other family members, she thus acknowledges how her own sensitivities to skin, hair, and eye color conditioned her responses to individuals even

88. Tracey Rose, detail of wall inscription from *Span I*, 1997. Courtesy of the artist.

among her own family and friends. Her use of autobiography enables her to tell of this secret complicity and to own it as "hers," but in addition, the device of employing a "proxy," who is physically responsible for the exposure of this complicity, ensures that this action (being once removed from Rose) also becomes an effective means of signaling a larger complicity. In other words, the autobiographical mode produces an air of authentic lived experience without simply being reducible to Rose's individual experience. The fact that the text is cut into the wall by a black ex-prisoner is also significant given the historical context of hierarchical racial politics, particularly in the Western Cape. That the chosen conduit for Rose's "confession," who consequently assumes the role of her redeemer and confessor, is a black man, who himself has already "done time" for some undisclosed misdemeanor, foregrounds the issue of power relations and ultimately also presents a challenge to some of the assumptions underlying these.

Other work by Rose has exploited these references to penance and the "confessional," and here too the use of autobiography has been crucial. In *Sticks and Stones* in 1998, Rose created a video projection of text that recalls the kinds of taunts children experience in the playground. Much of the text (as the title suggests) revolves around pejorative name calling, but again the main protagonists of the racial jibes are not what one might expect. One line reads, "The first time I said Kaffir Rachel was on top of me trying to grab a sweet out [sic] my mouth the word tasted bitter." As Rose explains, "They're memory-based recollections, thought and experiences from my childhood, a documentary of a 'coloured' person."[27] While the texts in both Span I and Sticks and Stones are readily legible to most viewers with any understanding of the history of apartheid as a "confession" of the unconscious complicity of children's own prejudices, Rose's deliberate use of "colored" slang makes the full impact of the work truly accessible only to "insiders." This strategy is partly explained by her concern that her work be relevant to constituencies outside the usual fine art groupies but to make this address nevertheless within a fine art environment.[28]

Rose is not the only one among a younger generation of South African artists who is unwilling to consign difficult histories to the past, but she is one of the few who actively questions her own complicity in apartheid at a moment when it would otherwise be only too easy for her to trade on her status (particularly abroad) as part of a constituency discriminated against during that period.

HEAD

Another artist of Rose's generation who feels the contradictions of her own familial context as a deeply compromised upbringing and who has chosen to address this in her work is Senzeni Marasela. The daughter of a police-man, she recalls the time during the 1980s when policemen's houses in the townships were targets for arson attacks. Unable, therefore, to go to school in the township, she was educated in a Catholic high school in what she describes as "a white, Afrikaner suburb."[29] While the privilege of this kind of education is undeniable, particularly in the context of the wholesale de-skilling that was the systematic agenda of the state "Bantu" education policy, for a young black woman from the townships it was evidently a complex and fraught experience at times.

These kinds of contradictions have marked Marasela's attitude to the re-cent past and the ways it has been painfully resuscitated by the testimonies before the TRC:

> I grew up in another world where these things didn't really touch me. For example, when Stompie Seipei died I was clueless. When someone was necklaced a few doors down from where I lived, I didn't even know. I

was kept away from the political struggle, packed off to the eastern Cape every time there was turbulence in the townships. Growing up I believed the security forces were doing the right thing, that they were on our side. As a result, there isn't really anything I can lay claim to. So my work is about me finding a place in my history, about reclaiming my history and re-inventing my identity.[30]

Consequently, as with Rose's work, there is an autobiographical element to some of Marasela's output. One particularly poignant piece, *Our Mother* (1998), used found objects from her own home framed on a background of Xeroxed black-and-white snapshots of Marasela and her friends taken in a passport photo booth (plate 9). Centrally placed onto this surface Marasela has put her mother's housecoat and below it her father's police baton. The combination of the smiling youthful faces overlaid by the worn and stained dress has the effect, in the best tradition of modernist montage, of emphasizing the disjuncture between the lived experiences of two generations. The police baton interrupts these familial references to foreground the intrusion of the state, while nonetheless suggesting an uncomfortable relationship to the domestic realm signaled by the dominant feature of her mother's dress.

Another piece that combines references to the domestic and familial environment while at the same time indicating the larger political context of state violence is *Stompie Seipei, Died 1989, Age 14* (1998) (figures 89 and 90). The technique here of repeating the image of the young Stompie by screenprinting his black-and-white portrait onto a series of fine calico handkerchiefs edged in white or gold lace has the effect of elevating his image to the status of an icon. Producing such an image on the handkerchief creates a disjuncture that forces the domestic and the private into the realm of the public. According to Marasela, the handkerchief is also intended to recall the grief associated with the death of Seipei. In addition, the choice of Stompie as iconic figure cannot be anything but controversial since his death in connection with Winnie Madikizela-Mandela's "football club" muddies the waters of the narrative accounts of the liberation struggle by emphasizing the conflicts and contradictions within the ANC during the late 1980s.

Rather than opting to glorify the figures already made canonical in the annals of the liberation movement, Marasela (like Tracey Rose) has deliberately selected incidents or references either from her own familial experience or from South Africa's recent past that foreground the difficult passages in the country's history. "In the popular media Hector Peterson

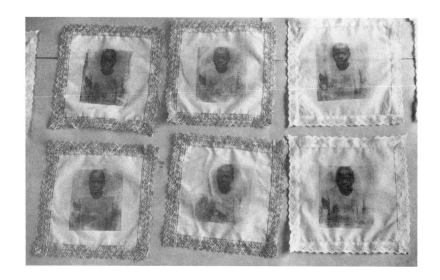

89. Senzeni Marasela, *Stompie Seipei, Died 1989, Age 14*, 1998. Silkscreen on calico, lace. Courtesy of the artist.

Below 90. Senzeni Marasela, detail from *Stompie Seipei, Died 1989, Age 14*, 1998. Silkscreen on calico, lace. Courtesy of the artist.

represents a certain kind of innocence, a defencelessness, that makes it easy for his image to be used to invoke feelings of disgust at the apartheid regime. The death of Hector Peterson also opened up more debate because it was seen as a slaughter of an innocent child. In the case of Stompie Seipei, however, we aren't encouraged to be sympathetic towards him. He was a different kind of victim."[31] The *Stompie Seipei* piece invites us to reflect on his vulnerability since the faint snapshot portrait presents an image of a child whose isolation is highlighted by the absence of any background environment in which to locate him as part of a social milieu and whose truncated life is suggested by the fine material upon which the image is reproduced, leaving a ghosted image, a barely legible trace.

Another strategy for dealing with the "silences" produced by even the most public kind of national tribunal such as the TRC has been to build on an existing historical archive and to "invent" the voices of protagonists who are not available through the usual channels of either written or oral tradition. Two artists who have successfully mobilized this conceit are Clive van den Berg and Penny Siopis, the one with regard to homosexual histories, the other with a view to exploring the desires and projections of diasporic experience.

HEART

Van den Berg has for some time now been concerned with what he sees as the anomalous way in which only certain highly selective spaces are deemed appropriate sites for the projection of collective memory and as the repositories of public history. His own work has deliberately sought out those naturalized spaces that have become almost invisible through overuse and that have often been associated with unsung activity, such as the migrant labor that created the huge mine dumps announcing the visitor's arrival in the historic gold capital of South Africa—Johannesburg. In a tactic reminiscent of the Black Audio Film and Video Collective's *Handsworth Songs*, Van den Berg conjures up the "ghosts of other stories" that inhabit that perversely majestic debris. For him such sites are also erotic spaces where entropy metonymically signals the dissolution of multiple forms of control, allowing the mine dumps to become scenes for the projection of phantasmagoric presences.

For the first Johannesburg biennale in 1995 Van den Berg created *The Mine Dump Project* on two of the largest dumps outside Johannesburg—one on the road to the airport and the other on the Soweto Highway. The installation consisted of a series of braziers filled with glowing coals. These were

91. Clive van den Berg, Installation view of *The Mine Dump Project,* 1995. Courtesy of the artist.

arranged so that together they produced shapes—a huge glowing human profile, an enormous flaming staircase. Each individual brazier was also pierced so that from close up small icons of bourgeois domesticity gleamed out at the viewer. Lamps, televisions, and armchairs created a domestic play of opposites with the monumental forms that the braziers produced collectively (figure 91). Times advertised for the ceremonial lighting of the braziers in the evening brought the art audiences, but the incidental viewer coincidentally passing on the highway provided an important serendipitous encounter with the work for Van den Berg.[32] In the daylight other domestic and daily life incidentals were visible from the highway, constructed in outline from whitened stones reminiscent of those used to delineate burial sites in otherwise unmarked land.

As Rose's work iconicizes the child's experience, so Van den Berg painstakingly memorializes the domestic and draws our attention to the discriminatory ways in which some experiences are clearly deemed inappropriate fodder for national remembrance. Just as those who made the physically demanding "pilgrimage" up the mine dump were rewarded with the knowledge that the braziers were repositories of other images "hidden" from those who watched from the comfort of distance, Van den Berg's deliberate exploitation of the differential viewing experience can be seen as a metaphor for the arbitrariness of the reification of certain acts or traces of acts as commemorable history while others remain invisible to the naked eye, depending on one's perspective and experience.

In a sense Van den Berg's method of working reinforces this interpretation. His installations are generally extremely labor-intensive, necessitating careful calculations to accommodate complex logistics, each installation being almost obsessive in its attention to detail. Another feature of his work is that the installations / performances often have an ephemeral dimension but one where a trace of the action that has just taken place is always left behind. The braziers may burn for only a limited time, but the scorched earth beneath them bears witness to this activity long after the glow from the last coal has subsided. The process is like memory, which attempts to consolidate fragmentary snatches of another time and place, only to transform both through the act of recall itself.

In 1996 Van den Berg produced an installation that developed the concept of memorial:

> In order to reform memory according to a different, mostly unwritten schema, I develop visual narratives or conditions of looking that attempt to fill in some of the gaps. . . . In them I try to insinuate that much more is needed for the recuperation of a nation's memory than the confessions and revelations currently being told to the TRC. I don't in any way wish to undermine or demean those narratives. A very important process is currently being played out in South Africa, but it is always going to be a fragment of the story—not just because only some of the people affected by apartheid will speak, or are able to speak. It is rather that the parameters of what should be legitimated still happen largely within hetero-sexist boundaries.[33]

In this instance, for an exhibition entitled "Faultlines," in a work entitled *Men Loving* (1996), Van den Berg chose to rearticulate a story from 1735. A white farmer, Rijkhaart Jacobsz of Rotterdam, and a Khoikoi prisoner, Claas Blank, were discovered to be lovers and were subsequently condemned to death on 19 August 1735; they were chained together, with their limbs weighted, and forced to walk the plank from a boat anchored off Robben Island. In a room inside the Castle in Cape Town Van den Berg constructed a huge, grassy mound almost reaching the ceiling. At the flattened apex of this trapezoidal structure was an area scarred with red oxide pigment (as if burned) and demarcated with small white stones (again recalling the memorial stones marking burial sites). In the center of this area were two plaster heads—of a black and a white male. Part of the effectivity of *Men Loving* lies in its dialectical engagement with the particular historical and contemporary resonances of the exhibition space, for—as with Searle's piece in the Granary—the Castle in Cape Town is another colonial building; it has a continuous association with the military and was still the headquarters of Western Province Command in 1996.

Speaking of the kinds of narratives of belonging usually commemorated in various official memorials, Van den Berg explains his stragegy: "Underpinning many of these narratives is a figure of the dutiful man, imagined on the sites of battle, those fissures of terrain that are another way of demarcating the nation. I appropriate sites venerated as proof of what the masculine body should 'properly' be used for, as places to figure a different usage of the body. I make these images as being other than the confirmation of 'productive' action, not the gains of a masculinist energy in the sacrifice for a cause, but rather as subjects that prompt investigation into some alternative life, I suppose a kind of Foucaldian heterotopia. This gives me the licence to memorialize in a different language, and to define purpose in a different way."[34] In *Men Loving*, then, Van den Berg disrupts the traditional model of "manly" behavior promoted by those military organizations billeted in the Castle. His work speaks not only of cross-racial alliances, but also of homosexual liaisons. To cement this transgression, he has further "contaminated" the safe and controlled environment of the military enclave by transporting wayward and unpredictable nature into the ordered arena of culture. To some viewers this was clearly volatile material, particularly in the context of Cape Town Castle.

Whatever cynicism one might feel about the transformative potential of fine art, there are certainly some subjects that continue to have the power to rankle more conservative constituencies. Consequently, the command at the Castle moved to close down Van den Berg's installation. However, the new constitution was invoked in defense of the piece, and the military was unable to censor the work. At the entrance to *Men Loving*, a text presented a brief account of the event that was commemorated through the sculpture. It was followed by the statement, "On Friday May 8 we adopted a constitution which forbids discrimination on the basis of sexual preference. Perhaps now loving will be easier." This is just one of a number of occasions when work featuring gay or lesbian themes has come under attack and has tested the solidity of the new constitution.[35]

In 1995 the first gay and lesbian art exhibition, "Gay Rights, Rites, Re-Writes," traveled across the country to Cape Town, Johannesburg, and Bloemfontein. As one might have predicted, in the more conservative Afrikaner heartland of Bloemfontein, there were attempts to shut down the exhibition, although ironically—and again predictably—the notoriety of the show meant that it was better attended there than in either Cape Town or Johannesburg.[36] In 1997, one year after the "Faultlines" exhibition at the Castle, a group show of students from the Stellenbosch Fine Art Department was threatened by the fundamentalist Christians for Truth (Christene vir die Waarheid), an Afrikaans group based in Kuilsrivier who took exception to a series of photographs by Jean Brundrit entitled *Does Your Lifestyle Depress Your Mother?* These are photos of various lesbian couples going about their daily business—a kind of "day in the life of . . ." snapshots of lesbian sociality in Cape Town (an example is in figure 92).

The vitriolic response of Christians for Truth paradoxically confirms the effectiveness of Brundrit's strategy of deliberately refusing a monumental or heroic scale that would have produced iconic images, setting the women up as somehow out of the ordinary. Instead she chose the more intimate and quotidian scale of a family album, reinforcing the sense that any one of these women could be one's sister, wife, or daughter. The black and white of the series recalls documentary photography and gives an up-to-the-moment quality that also helps to bring the series into the domain of daily life. Unlike the documentary tradition, however, particularly in South Africa, these images specifically record activities that are incidental and mundane, despite often being staged for the photograph.[37] It is precisely this staging of a lesbian "normality" that Christians for Truth found so threatening. They wrote a letter demanding that the Tygerberg City Council shut down the exhibition. The letter highlighted the particular offensiveness of exhibiting what they rightly identified as "a clearly positive commentary on lesbian life."[38] The city council responded by informing Brundrit that she had to take down her photographs or it would close the exhibition. When Brundrit and her co-exhibitors refused to comply with the city council's demands, the council, in a stunning act of iconoclasm, locked the images inside the exhibit space and forbade public access to the show. There was a further outcry when some of Brundrit's photo series was reproduced in a *voxpop* piece in the *Cape Times* on same-sex relationships across the religious spectrum as part of Cape Town's "One City: Many Cultures" project in February 1999 (figure 93).[39] The *Cape Times* was inundated with letters attacking the article's so-called promotion of homosexuality.[40]

Another example of the volatility of homosexual and lesbian subjectivities is the ambivalent response from both liberals and conservatives to the first of Clive van den Berg's series, *Memorials without Facts.* It was first shown in "Purity and Danger" (after anthropologist Mary Douglas's influential book of that title), an exhibition curated in 1997 by the Johannesburg artist Penny Siopis at the University of the Witwatersrand. This installation

Top 92. Jean Brundrit, *Does Your Lifestyle Depress Your Mother?* 1998. Black-and-white photograph. Courtesy of the artist.

Bottom 93. Lead page on same-sex relationships with Jean Brundrit's series *Does Your Lifestyle Depress Your Mother? Cape Times,* 17 February 1999.

94. Clive van den Berg, detail from installation of *Memorials without Facts*, 1997. Still from film projected onto grass mound. Courtesy of the artist and the Goodman Gallery.

represented both a development of some of Van den Berg's earlier work on history and memory and a new departure. Exploiting a similar device to the grassy mound of *Men Loving*, Van den Berg brought the audience into physical proximity with nature in a space designated as "cultural," imposing a visceral / bodily relation to the work through the deliberate use of smell and texture. Once again the artist made use of those trademarks of death and burial—the white cairns interspersed in the long grasses of the constructed mound. Onto this huge, sloping mound he projected a film composed of both found stills of familiar and iconic images from the period of the Boer War and other black-and-white footage of male actors wrestling or making love. Throughout the montage of images from different historical registers, a naked male figure recurs running through a field—through the mound and filmed so that the horizon shifts uncomfortably, as if through the eyes of the runner himself or his pursuer (figure 94). The sound track follows the runner with a menacing rumble that transforms into the popular Afrikaner folksong "And Yet the Mountains Are Still So Blue," while images of burning stencils of a house, a bed, and a pitched tent recall the British policy of slash and burn and the horrifying concentration camps the British set up for Boer prisoners. These iconic images are followed by a photo of one of two brothers well known to any scholar of the Boer War. (One of the brothers agreed to the compromise of the British terms at the close of the war, was duly treated as a traitor by his family of "Bitter-Enders" [Boers who fought to the bitter end], and was whipped on his return to the family farm.) We return to the vulnerable image of the running figure, now unmistakably hounded by an unseen assailant. The film loops around to repeat the images, which are initially ambiguous. Finally, through repetition a narrative clarity emerges speaking of freedom, illicit love, destruction, and flight. The film gradually becomes a paean to the pain of compromise and failure despite dedication and suffering. It is about human frailty, and the cipher Van den Berg chooses to carry this message is one usually made to bear the burden of invincibility or threat—the naked male body.

In his next film, *Memorials without Facts: Men Loving* (1998), Van den Berg returns to the theme of fraught and unspoken relationships and impossible intimacies. Here the materiality of film and the viewing experience it provides are fully exploited so that the audience becomes immersed in the sounds and images projected on the screen. Van den Berg stresses the importance of the dislocating effects of sitting in a darkened space, treated to a series of suggestive images, while being smothered in the sound of Isolde singing to Tristan's dead body before she finally takes her own life in Wagner's tragic opera *Tristan and Isolde*. Water, fire, and light are ciphers of transformation that carry the viewer through the different registers of time represented by the film sequences of found footage, contemporary shots of natural landscape features, and Van den Berg's trademark illuminated and perforated silhouettes of iconic objects. The recurring elements of water, fire, and light provide the connective tissue throughout the film. But there is no easy narrative framing here—just snatches of narrative logic that culminate in and mirror the momentary intimacies and tenderness between two men before their deaths, signaled by the cairns mapping a fictional grave site in which they lie down together. From the opening shot of Van den Berg's own disembodied face—covered in mud and filling the screen in a defamiliarizing strategy that culminates by closing in on his lips, silently mouthing some unspoken words—to the accompanying sound track of *Tristan and Isolde*, there is an uneasy relationship established between the visceral (one might almost say abject) and the sublime that the viewer is forced to confront and by which he or she is finally seduced. Just as the suggested relationship between the men was historically and until very recently illicit and is only very gradually becoming a visible part of South African sociality, so the poetics of the film gently entice us to share in the intimacies it offers.

In 1999 Van den Berg exploited more directly the concept of a partially invented history, already suggested in *Memorial without Facts: Men Loving.* In *Memorial without Facts: Love Story,* he attempts to reconstruct a putative liaison between a Boer soldier and a British army captain during the Boer War. The narrative sequence, introduced by intertitles (1901; 15 February, Meeting; 18 February, Loving; 23 February, Dying), and the logic of the interaction between these two protagonists provides us with the stuff of history—dates and (later) location. The further use of intercut images of punctured, backlit, silhouetted forms of men's heads in profile with bullet holes through the temples, or hillsides punctured by small, rectangular cairns indicating graves hastily dug after battle, enhances the narrative sense. The sound track is a breathless tune hummed by a panting male, ambiguously signaling hurried passion, anxious anticipation, or flight. Van den Berg initially considered using as voiceover a fictional diary he had written from the perspective of the British captain but decided to make the images themselves work to generate the story of the illicit encounter. Once again water is an important cipher, marking the passage from life to love to death. Various film qualities (grainy, sharp, dense, and diffuse) are exploited as a way of suggesting shifting temporal zones and emotional states so that by the end of the film, we have become immersed in the possibility of the encounter between Boer and British to such an extent that we no longer care if this was an actual event. The final text, over a hazy black-and-white landscape, captures the poignancy of the narrative and brings us back to the temporal space of history: "Two bodies were found at a river near the town of Dullstroom. James, the British captain, was buried on a hillside above the river. Stephanus was buried a short distance from the British dead. When the rest of the Boer remains were moved to a nearby monument for collective reburial, his alone were left in the field." The final image is of a backlit, stenciled hillside with stenciled cairns marking two rectangular grave sites with crosses as their headstones. The light behind the stenciled image strobes back and forth, giving the impression of a searchlight scouring the veldt. As I have noted, these cairns are particularly resonant icons in the South African context. In the same way that the chance discovery of prehistoric standing stones on the otherwise bleak expanses of Dartmoor or Exmoor in Britain is an eerie experience that has the effect of populating the landscape with the whisper of generations from a distant past, so it is not uncommon in tough terrain across South Africa, where Boer and British fought during the 1899–1902 wars, to stumble on rough mounds of broken shale and scree piled along the length of a body, sometimes with a larger

piece of rock by way of headstone. Unmarked in any other way, these discreet memorials are poignant reminders of the lonely deaths and bloody
encounters between the strategic and effective guerrilla action of the Boer
Commandos and the incompetent and inappropriately prepared but well-
resourced British forces. Precisely because they speak of such conditions,
the scattered cairns that liberally litter the veldt are a more potent memorial
than the predictable iconography of the formal obelisks and other figurative commemorative monuments that were erected in the aftermath of the
wars in areas where the fighting was fiercest. The loneliness, isolation, and
harsh realities of combat in such terrain is evoked more profoundly somehow by these makeshift grave sites, where bodies were necessarily buried
where they fell in order to escape the putrefaction hastened by blistering
summer heat. Van den Berg's insistent repetition of the image of the grave
site marked by a row of (sometimes) whitened stones is consistent with
his larger project to challenge the conventional notion of commemorative
monuments—not simply in terms of what is and is not deemed appropriate commemorative material, but also in terms of the ways in which different kinds of memory might be best served by memorials that perhaps take
on themselves some of the ephemeral, fleeting, and suggestive rather than
embodied qualities of memory.

For any kind of memory work film lends itself to the task particularly
well. In Van den Berg's work it facilitates a suggestion of narrative time
while simultaneously the text of the film is composed of a series of animated
images of inanimate material / objects that provide a constant backing and
forthing between historical and narrative time and space and produce the
sensation of an indeterminate liminal zone.

VOICE

Penny Siopis is another artist who has adopted film as the medium of preference, specifically in terms of its peculiar appropriateness for any engagement with memory. Siopis's work is at its best when it deals with the notion
and experience of "whiteness" in South Africa. Criticisms of Siopis for
putting herself and her "whiteness" center stage in her work entirely miss
the point. Siopis has long been concerned with the lived and historical relations between black and white women in South Africa and the ambivalent
and dependent relationships formed between white, middle-class women
and black women working in the domestic labor market during apartheid.
Through such an engagement, her aim is to explore how the appropriation

of black women's time, lives, labor, and bodies has shaped her own history. This was a primary theme in *Private Views,* a 1994 retrospective of her work in Johannesburg.

In a long interview in December 1994, some months after the first democratic elections, Siopis articulated the ways in which she was grappling with these complex relations and their aftermath for the main protagonists:[41]

> The experience of having a black nanny would have meant more to my brothers or to men and to my white male child. What's difficult is that the trauma that the white male suffers also in some measure afflicts the black woman because she loses, not only her voice, but her authority—little as it was—in relation to white women. She had something with this child. Then she loses the child. The child quite literally goes away to school and she is structured into a different relationship with it which involves rejection. That child becomes a person who calls her by a name that is not her name, that orders her around. He might even use her body sexually, and he becomes the boss, the master. The loss that she suffers is all the greater because she has experienced a genuine affection both from and for the child who has now withdrawn from her. And he must suffer some loss in relation to that black woman. And I suppose what I'm trying to work through is the nature of that loss, such trauma which occurred in the apartheid years—things that can't be spoken. I'm completely fascinated by this incredibly powerful constellation of relations and feelings as something that is just so much part of this society and cries for representation.[42]

One of the works that tries to resolve, in a representational form, the absent psychic dimension of such a "loss" is *Tula Tula,* a series of three works. In *Tula Tula I* (1993–1994) Siopis uses an enlarged negative from a photo of her brother sitting on his nanny's knee, with his hand resting on hers (plate 10). Despite the color reversal through the use of the negative rather than the positive image, it would be clear to a South African viewer that the child is white, and this identification is crucial. "I've tried to work up the negative spaces of the photocopy, particularly around her face and his face. Because it is a photographic negative, she's in fact white, if you like, colour-wise, and he's black, but his eyes are white. I've tried to invert value-laden colour. His eyes are in some ways absent or blank because in the original photograph they would have been black. Thinking psychoanalytically about vision and power the child's 'blank' eyes and the nanny's gaze become crucial details. She looks down at him and he looks out at the viewer."[43] In addition, the space occupied by the woman's knees and legs in profile is replaced by a Victorian gilt frame that contains, on a field of steel wool, a photograph showing part of an inscription on a now infamous monument in Pretoria. As Siopis explains,

> The monument was erected in the 1980s in honour of the "victims of terrorism." Obviously the victims were supposed to be white and terrorists assumed to be black. So I've used the inscription, *terrorisme,* an Afrikaans word, and juxtaposed it with the image. The word points to an actual historic monument in South Africa and has arisen from an identifiable historical period of oppression. In a sense it signals the idea of the split identities of black women as both "comfort" and "threat," as perceived by white people under apartheid. Black women were obviously seen as the people who would look after their children, love their children. But at the same time they're seen as the "enemy."[44]

Tula Tula I represents an attempt by Siopis to work more closely with the contradictions of her own familial experience by acknowledging the complicity of her own upbringing.

In 1992–1993 Siopis had also attempted to explore the complexities of the nanny-child relationship and the peculiarities and oppressions of how this was racialized in South Africa. In *Maids* she draws attention to the attempts at erasing the African identity of the black female domestic workers and suppressing their own familial relations in order to maintain the white family unit (figure 95). Framed by a series of newly bought pink domestic workers' housecoats, still folded and bearing their shop labels, is a central panel of rice paper with a laser printed image of a Voortrekker mother and child, complete with kappie, taken from the frieze of the Voortrekker Monument. Over the image are printed segments of verse from the English translation of *Die Stem* (The voice or The call), which was the South African national anthem under apartheid. The uniforms are all "embroidered" in cake icing with European name tags (often the names of Christian virtues, such as hope, mercy, and goodness), a gesture that refers explicitly to the erasing practice of forcing European names onto African domestic workers in place of their given African names. The piece attempts to draw out the hypocritical relationship between Christian virtues and the propagation of myths about so-called originary cultures that laid claim to superiority and primacy under apartheid (represented here by the Voortrekker woman) and the relations of exploitation and suppression that underpinned their ascendency.

In 1997 Siopis brought her work and the found images and objects that characterize her practice even closer to home. She attempted to conjure up

the experience of going to the early "picture houses" of the 1920s by reproducing a scaled-down version of a theater interior, complete with the kind
of battered velour folding seats we now associate with the oldest fleapits
(figure 96). This darkened, miniaturized version of early cinema was the
constructed setting for the screening of her film, *My Lovely Day*. Also an
excavation of gender relations, but this time among three different generations of women in the same family—her own—*My Lovely Day* succeeds in
offering a poetic archaeology of nostalgia that crucially manages to avoid
the usual pitfall of simple reproduction. Any sentimentalized and idealized
version of the past is constantly challenged by Siopis's insistence on the arti-
fice of the setting (a mimicry of cinema) and indeed of the film itself, which
is clearly found footage transposed as video.

One of the "voices" in the film is called up through the use of subtitles in a
typeface that recalls the old Underwoods and Remingtons that sent "home"
copy from the colonies. Through this device Siopis recreates a historicized
version of her grandmother's "voice," and it is this "voice" that narrates the
film; it is a narrative recreated through the imperfect and partial fragments
of Penny's childhood recollections of her grandmother, a fiction made up
of different times and places, imagined and experienced, in the fickle way
that only memory produces. The artist's mother provides the raw material
for the visual narrative by way of a "home movie" of family and friends in
the 1950s South Africa of middle-class, second-generation immigrants. The
final version is the finely crafted result of the daughter's (Siopis's) own intervention as editor of the "found footage" of familial video and the traces of
her grandmother's presence in the subtitles.

As well as a film about generations, *My Lovely Day* is also an exploration
of the effects of traumatic displacement. It may not be in the same register as the trauma recounted at the TRC hearings, but it is part of the
complex of difficult loyalties, nostalgic longings, misplaced desires, and internalized prejudices that make up any society that has a long history of
immigrant settlement. One of the narrative threads running through the
film is the story of Siopis's grandmother's flight from Asia Minor in the
wake of the Turkish invasion: "Arrived on the island from Smyrna. Had to
leave in a hurry. Lost everything. Nothing we could do. People were being
killed." The narrative shifts from Smyrna to what is referred to enigmati-
cally as "the Island" throughout (a device that helps to reinforce a sense of
the grandmother's alienation) and then to South Africa. But this is never
a simple chronology. Rather, both the linguistic and the visual narratives
create a ceaseless motion back and forth between different time zones and
locations, mimicking the fickle action of memory itself. Siopis exploits the

95. Penny Siopis, *Maids,* 1992–1993. Maids' uniforms, cake decorations, rice paper with laser print. 144 x 123 cm. Photo by Jean Brundrit. Courtesy of the artist.

Below 96. Penny Siopis, Installation view of *My Lovely Day,* 1997. Velour cinema seats, screen, video. Photo by Hannelie Coetzee. Courtesy of Penny Siopis.

disjunctures and disruptions achieved by the unlikely juxtaposition of dislocated temporal and geographical zones; cut adrift from their usual associations, these succeed in creating an odd congruence among the violence of Asia Minor, the alienation but relative safety of "the Island" (where the grandmother is a focus of local attention), and the savage quotidian of South Africa in the 1950s, at the height of Verwoerdian apartheid. So that over a long scene of black-and-white footage of a quasimilitary parade with scouts, nurses, and other local dignitaries in the streets of an unidentified town in the Northern Cape, the subtitles read: "Marching reminds me of so many terrible things. There were no marches on the Island, only religious festivals, saints' days. Quite a primitive place. The women called me 'Princess,' loved my clothes and 'jewels.' Stroking my hair and touching me as if I wasn't real. Had never left the Island, these peasant women. Listened with mouths open to my stories of London and Paris" (figure 97).

Interspersed with the discomforting associations—and reinforcing their uncanny quality—are scenes of domestic and familial pleasure, particularly of Penny and her brothers and friends cavorting around or swimming, "playing," in the fictionalized voice of her grandmother, "as if nothing is happening around you." Footage of young girls in frilly, white, "Sunday best"; of Penny and her brother paddling in the river or running across the wild grasses of a stretch of South African veldt; or of Penny sporting a large bow in her hair, rushing toward the eye of her mother's camera, is subtitled with the somewhat petulant "voice" of her grandmother marking the different experiences of other lives lived in other places at other times: "You live such charmed lives. I watch from the verandah! Charmed lives! Nothing to fear! What do you know of the real world?" (figure 98). Much of the film moves between the registers of public and private. Scenes of public life, represented through larger-scale, more ritualized (possibly national) spectacles (the street parade mentioned above or shots from the Vryburg or Kimberley agricultural shows and scenes of orchestrated gymnastic, eurythmic, and Afrikaner folk dancing demonstrations) are juxtaposed with more intimate familial and domestic scenes. The effect is to assert an unspecified connectedness between the everyday familial and the grand narratives of public government. This of course is a political point, and it is a subversive suggestion that insinuates itself at various stages of Siopis's film.

It is perhaps by now a commonplace observation, but one nevertheless worth repeating in this context, that film is a particularly appropriate medium for memory work since it has the capacity to reproduce a material equivalent of some of the qualities of the workings of the unconscious mind, as classically defined by Freud (condensation, displacement, and symboli-

97. Penny Siopis, still from *My Lovely Day*, 1997. Photo by Hannelie Coetzee. Courtesy of Penny Siopis.

Below 98. Penny Siopis, still from *My Lovely Day*, 1997. Photo by Hannelie Coetzee. Courtesy of Penny Siopis.

zation). In one obvious sense this is reproduced through the seamlessness of the film's movement among different geographical and temporal zones, so that a narrative clearly relating to Siopis's grandmother's experience on "the Island" may be juxtaposed with shots of Penny playing or her mother in South Africa. In another sense Siopis reproduces this through exploiting the materiality of her mother's old home movie to considerable effect. Despite the technology at her disposal, she has deliberately chosen not to digitally remaster the film. The handheld, handmade, "found" quality of the film and the hand-tinted quality of the color lend it a certain fragility. The crackle, hiss, and sometimes abrupt cuts from one shot to another or within the same shot lend an otherworldly dimension to the film that immediately takes us back in time. The subtitles serve a similar function. In addition, they lend a mesmerizing quality to our experience as we sit in the darkness listening to the crackle of the film and the sound track of Siopis's mother singing from an old recording she made of the eponymous song of the title. Scenes are interspersed with the haunting sounds of Greek bouzouki music or moderated by the lilting melody of early recordings made in Greek villages. The juxtaposition of scenes and music evokes tensions between "East" and "West," between Turkish and Greek influences. Part of the effect of the combination of these various components is to shake the viewer from his or her attachment to sequential narrative. It enables us to share in the film's own regime of truth if we accept that to work across these different generational registers simultaneously and through the deployment of fragments it is possible to reproduce a closer approximation of the contradictions and conflicts, the fleeting desires and frustrations, of lived experience.

Most importantly, perhaps, Siopis has, in common with Rose and Marasela, deployed an autobiographical mode to interrogate, in this case, not the contradictions of "colored" identity in South Africa but the conflicts and compromises of "whiteness," the uncomfortable prejudices but also the legitimate desires of an immigrant middle class scored through with the traces of migratory histories and dreams of belonging.

In each of the examples I have discussed here the artists have attempted to grapple with elements of their own histories that intersect with the larger iconic moments replayed in the testimonials of the TRC hearings. In some instances they have chosen to represent uncomfortable "truths" that may be autobiographical but that are also, implicitly, part of a shared experience of complicity or denial (Rose, Marasela, and Siopis). In some cases they have attempted to give visual form beyond spectacle in an attempt to defamiliarize the naturalized relations between sex, violence, and death (Searle and Rose). Other work has foregrounded shared histories that are still occluded despite the new dispensation of transparency, openness, and inclusion (Van den Berg and Brundrit). Each artist has mobilized different technical and formal strategies that all engage the ways in which viewing and vision are always already embedded in and part of a historical process that conditions their reception. It is partly the dialectical use of this knowledge that ensures that while the work discussed has a resonance beyond South Africa, it has a particular poignancy in the fragile context of the aftermath of the TRC.

EPILOGUE

Changing Places

Trafalgar Square, in the heart of London's chic West End and theater district, has a historical reputation as a center of political protest and mass gatherings.[1] It has been the final destination of many rallies and demonstrations since the nineteenth century. One of the longest-running protests was the vigil by the anti-apartheid activists who took up permanent residence on one side of the square outside the South African High Commission, effectively boycotting entry to South Africa House. Consequently, for many of us the building was out of bounds until 1994 (figure 99). The year of the first democratic elections in South Africa inevitably heralded a new era for the South African High Commission and nights spent tucked up in a warm bed rather than on the inclement street outside the building for the anti-apartheid protestors.

For most of us who had never seen the interior of South Africa House, setting foot inside the building was an extraordinary experience. One had the strong sensation of crossing a threshold in both the symbolic and actual sense of that word, for the building was a perfectly preserved representation of an idealized 1930s South African universe—idealized in that it produced with minute attention to detail the symbolic regimes of a nation on the cusp of an independence from its colonial ruler (Britain) but one that would also usher in the segregationist and racial supremacist ideology of apartheid. Clearly the new democratic dispensation in South Africa in 1994 would need to put another face on one of its key diplomatic missions, and by the year 2000 a refurbishment plan had been drawn up that was designed to be more representative of the ideals of the new government.

In many ways the tale of the two high commissions is the tale in microcosm of this book, for it both revisits some of the earlier history concerning the foundations of the apartheid state and takes us forward to a vision of the

99. Paddy Donnelly, Anti-apartheid rally outside South Africa House, c. 1980. Black-and-white photo. Courtesy of Paddy Donnelly.

future for the newly democratic South Africa. The search for an adequate means of representing the "new" South Africa in a building with such a strong legacy of both the colonial and the apartheid pasts synthetically dramatizes the debates around the nature of symbols and themes appropriate to the new dispensation that have taken place in South Africa over the last decade and that have been the subjects of the previous chapters. In addition, the inauguration of South Africa House at its ceremonial opening on 22 June 1933 marked a transition in the state of the nation in much the same way that the rededication of the building on 14 June 2001 by Thabo Mbeki marked a new phase in the representation of the public face of the reborn nation in one of its most symbolically loaded diplomatic missions.

By 1933 relations between whites of British descent and Afrikaners had already been seriously tested, and tensions between these constituencies were to increase over the next ten years. During the early 1920s the National Party under the leadership of James Hertzog did much to consolidate the cultural and political clout of Afrikaners, and in 1924 it had defeated the English champion, Jan Smuts, to form a coalition government (the Pact government) with the Labour Party under the leadership of Frederick Cresswell. The keystone of this alliance was the combined support of Afrikaner farmers, who resented what they felt to be the privileging of English industrialists under Smuts, together with a white proletariat (predominantly miners) who wanted to ensure segregated labor policies to secure their jobs against the possibility of being undercut by cheaper black labor, which the English mine owners (a crucial support base for Smuts) were intent on employing.

In addition to the fostering (or "invention," as Isabel Hofmeyr has suggested) of an Afrikaner cultural "tradition," Hertzog's other contribution was the institution of racial segregationist policies, key among them being the removal of the vote from Africans on the Cape in 1936. By 1934 Hertzog's National Party had formed a coalition with Smuts's South African Party, to become the United Party; this was known as the "Fusion Government." One of its guiding principles became the supremacy of "white civilization," although what was considered by some to be Hertzog's compromise away from the development of a more fundamentally separatist Afrikaner nationalist political project resulted in the establishment of the breakaway "Purified" National Party, which, under D. F. Malan, was later to lead the apartheid government. The reader will remember from chapter 1 the mass spectacle provided by the reconstruction of the Great Trek and the subsequent foundation of the Voortrekker Monument in 1938. Clearly by this date there was already considerable popular support for a form of Afrikaner nationalism. Through this historical sketch of the shifts in political power in South Africa, it is evident that even if apartheid proper was not fully implemented until the National Party won the elections in 1948, the seeds had already been sown by the time of the inauguration of the South African High Commission in London, and relations between British and Afrikaner were not entirely predictable.

Consequently, the building and decorative schema of the South African High Commission in 1933 represented a certain tension between incoming and outgoing regimes—just as it does today. In the 1930s this was exacerbated by the personal histories and political allegiances of the two individuals most directly connected with the new commission, the architect Sir Herbert Baker and High Commissioner Charles T. Te Water. Colonial architect par excellence, Baker already had a reputation as one of the British Empire's premier architects, with key public buildings in Rhodesia, Kenya, South Africa, and India (where he had designed the new, imperial Delhi with that other stalwart of imperial architecture, Sir Edwin Lutyens). Baker had lived in South Africa between 1891 and 1913, during which time he had designed and built the structures most symbolically resonant of South Africa's colonial relationship with Britain, the Union Buildings in Pretoria. His designs for the High Commission in London were carried out in collaboration with Te Water, whose task it became to negotiate a pathway between the waning imperialist interests of the British and the Afrikaner nationalists, whose ascendency required a very different interpretation of South African history. The new building received a great deal of attention in the international press, and this often focused on the paintings, sculptures, murals, and other aspects of the interior design. As a result, a number of art and design journals featured South Africa House. Inevitably the building's international profile contributed to the high stakes placed on any historical representations.[2]

One of the most striking features of the interior of the building and an aspect that makes it such an apt comparison with the other examples discussed in this book is the extent to which the building was clearly designed as a showcase for the arts, industries, and natural products of the country, much in the same way that the national pavilions in international and colonial exhibitions promoted the natural and industrial products of their nations. In fact, many of the items of furniture in the high commissioner's room were "specimen pieces which formed part of the timber exhibit at the British Empire Exhibition at Wembley, in 1924."[3] The floors, walls, and ceilings of the building are veneered in hardwoods especially imported from South Africa or clad in marbles, granites, and quartz similarly imported. Even slate from Robben Island figures in the manufacture of the building. The new building also boasted an exhibition hall with access to the general public, complete with dioramas depicting sites of special natural beauty (such as Victoria Falls, Kruger National Park, and the city of Cape Town) and industries such as citrus fruit growing and viticulture. In adjacent exhibition cases precious minerals were displayed as reminders of the mineral wealth of the country.

But it is in the decorative schema of the building that the visitor is still struck today by the constant references to an ideal of nation and indigeneity that is the overriding impression of Baker's design. Most crucially, the interior of the building narrativizes history with a persistence that is rare. Moreover, the paintings in South Africa House were understood by many at the time as accurate representations of passages in South Africa's history, to the extent that a number of publishers of school history texts requested copies of the images as illustrations of events for their books.[4] Given that the concepts of "nation," "indigeneity," and "history" are the very touchstones of the new polity, all so ardently debated in South Africa after the fall of apartheid, it is possible to see why the refurbishment of South Africa House is so necessary but also why the task is not an easy one.

Early on in discussions concerning the interior decoration of the building a list of relevant historical subjects was drawn up. The official aim behind the adoption of historical subject matter was to encourage "The hope of a wider Union—Africa federated and a bulwark of the Commonwealth of Nations, and in the van to free its peoples from all that enslaves the human spirit" and "To express also somehow the spirit which has always possessed South Africa, i.e. the yearning for Freedom—the Spirit of high adventure—the facing of difficulties in order to overcome them—the hope for the future."[5] The list included "the Kaffir Wars and the Kaffir menace to Civilisation."[6]

The decorative schema of the building accomplishes its objectives by essentially two means. Baker was determined that the structural components and furnishings of each room should remind the visitor of South Africa's "history and romance." Consequently the whole building is littered with iconographic details supposedly quintessentially resonant of South Africa. The markers of indigeneity in this complicated schema, however, are produced largely through references to flora and fauna—the proteas in the air vents and on the finials of the banisters and the springboks featured both inside and outside the building. Something akin to the "ethnographic realism" of the nineteenth-century French Orientalists surfaces in Baker's extraordinary devotion to botanical and historical "accuracy." The archives attest to frequent exchanges between the architect (by then in his seventies) and various "experts" at the botanical gardens at Kew (with regard to the many botanical specimens), Rhodes House in Oxford (in connection with the heraldic shields), and the National Library in Lisbon (with regard to representations of the explorer Bartolomeo Dias).[7]

Another marker of indigeneity, which consistently drew public attention and acclaim from the international press and which more than any other aspect of the interior was designed, I would argue, to mediate between both British and Afrikaner interests, was the "Zulu Room" on the fourth floor, in an anteroom adjoining the suite reserved for ministers and senior officials visiting London. Here a couple of young students (both twenty-one at the time they began their commission for South Africa House) completely covered the walls with egg tempera murals supposedly representing "the life and customs of the Amazulu—'People of heaven'—the paramount native race of Southern Africa. . . . On these walls an attempt has been made to represent the Zulu tribal life as it was before the effects of civilisation became apparent" (plate 11 and figure 100).[8] This is the only painting in the original decorative schema of South Africa House that made an attempt to

100. Detail of mural in the "Zulu Room," South Africa House, London. Photo by the author.

represent the particularity (however idealized and problematic) of any of the country's black constituencies. And it is no accident that the group chosen for this treatment were the Zulu.

If "black" South Africa had to be represented in any substantial way, the Zulu were the group most perfectly suited to mediate between the demands of the British (both at home and in South Africa) and the Afrikaners. The image that was promoted by the murals was eminently adaptable to either those requiring the ideal of an ordered and hierarchical society ruled by what in effect was a constitutional monarchy existing in Africa or to those requiring a distinct ethnic community that could fit easily with the segregationist view of separate development that later characterized apartheid thinking.[9] Between 1913 and 1933 there was a marked rise in interest in a distinct Zulu ethnic identity, promoted by both anthropologists within South Africa and Zulu nationalists themselves.[10]

Most importantly, the more complex and contradictory aspects of contemporary Zulu life and politics in South Africa in the 1930s were replaced by images that papered over any vexing conflicts of interest by representing the people in an idealized precolonial state. Furthermore, if Baker wanted to provide an image of the "romance and adventure" of South Africa to a British public, the Zulu were the most obvious candidates. Familiar to the British public since the Anglo-Zulu War in 1879, when they were vilified as a society of cruel and violent savages ruled by despots, they had nevertheless earned a reputation as fearless fighters and formidable military strategists. H. Rider Haggard had cemented their popularity through a series of colonial novels with Zulus as central protagonists; one of the novels had had a successful run as a stage adaptation in London in 1914.[11] Similarly, "Zulu" troupes had often been a high point of performances and reenactments at the various colonial and international exhibitions that toured the country.[12] By 1933 Zulus had also made an appearance as part of the spectacle at the 1924 Empire Exhibition at Wembley. As Carolyn Hamilton points out in her detailed study of the uses of the image of the Zulu Leader Shaka, there was also a growing ethnographic and linguistic interest in the Zulu by the 1920s, in both Britain and South Africa, and much of this knowledge circulated in the form of popular lectures to a diverse public, as well as in more academic spheres.[13] Thus the "Zulu Room" had something for everyone. Given the ambiguous political status of the IFP and of Zulu nationalism in South Africa today, it is perhaps significant that the "Zulu Room" is one of those aspects of the decorative schema at South Africa House that will remain intact.

The proliferation of heraldic shields on each floor rehearsed a repetitive canon.[14] The "canon" is, of course, highly selective; the coats of arms represent Henry the Navigator, the Dutch East India Company, Dias, Vasco da Gama, Jan van Riebeeck, Simon van der Stel, Sir George Grey, Earl Macartney, the 1820 British Settlers, and the Huguenots (among others). Van Riebeeck's ship, the *Geode Hoop,* makes frequent appearances throughout the building, and represented on a plaque in the high commissioner's room are the wagon, muzzle-loader, powder horn, and Bible described as the Voortrekkers' "mainstay in a land then wild and uncivilised."[15] The diversity of South Africa's black population is represented by one escutcheon for "the Native Races," which consists of a beehive tokol below two crossed assegais and shields, all surrounded by a wreath of mealie meal. With the exception of the "Zulu Room," this extraordinary "shorthand" is found in every instance where reference is required for South Africa's majority black populations.[16] (Figure 101 shows two of the escutcheons.)

If Baker's penchant for heraldry reinforced a set of historical precedents for South Africa that paid homage to the Portuguese, the Dutch, and the British, the numerous murals that were specially commissioned from South African artists (living in either Britain or South Africa) foregrounded the Dutch contribution to the country's history. The primacy of the Dutch legacy is also reinforced in one of the key reception rooms in the building. This was (and still is) a seventeenth-century period reconstruction of a

101. Heraldic escutcheons signifying the Dutch East India Company and the "Native Races" in South Africa House, London. Photo by the author.

Dutch *voorkamer,* complete with beamed ceilings and antique Cape Dutch furniture; the cabinets display the characteristic blue and white of delftware, and the window sills are tiled in blue and white heraldic emblems made to Baker's indefatigable specifications, sporting the Dutch East India Company acronym "voc" and three proteas bearing the date 1820 as a reference to the British Settlers (figure 102).

The South African artists were commissioned for murals in symbolically significant parts of the building, such as outside the high commissioner's room. Here, too, themes reinforce the importance of European colonization as the harbinger of civilization and of the Portuguese and the Dutch as the "discoverers" who brought South Africa into being. We might feel that these are common enough tropes in any schema devoted to a celebration of colonization. In 1933, however, they were also topics that were potentially highly controversial. Unlike the "Zulu Room," which passed off with little controversy, certain murals depicting Dutch colonization became the focus of acrimonious Afrikaner antagonism. A stream of vitriolic correspondence followed with the high commissioner, as well as a flurry of reporting in one of the main Afrikaans dailies, *Die Burger.*[17] The contretemps that broke out over the central panel of Jan Juta's triptych of Jan van Riebeeck's arrival in the Cape is exemplary.

The triptych was to be given a prime position on the corridor outside

102. The *voorkamer* in South Africa House, London. Photo by the author.

the high commissioner's office. It supposedly depicted incidents from Van Riebeeck's landing in the country. The original central panel showed Van Riebeeck having landed, with his ships off the coast, and a group of his followers kneeling under a large cross, which dominates the painting. Afrikaner nationalists objected to what was perceived as a representation that encouraged a view of Van Riebeeck as a Catholic. Since one of the historical justifications for Van Riebeeck's landing was to provide Protestant sanctuary during the religious wars in Europe, many Afrikaners roundly condemned the mural. After much resistance from Te Water, the mural was duly replaced with a less contentious rendition of the Dutch landing.[18] The controversy is symptomatic of the significance attributed to the creation of the High Commission in London as a key representative of South Africa "overseas," especially because of its location in the heartland of the once powerful British Empire. More to the point, the virulence of the criticisms is also indicative of the growing political tensions between the British and the Afrikaners and the growing status of elite Afrikaner opinion in the country.

Even more telling of the antagonism brewing between the British and Afrikaners over the representation of South African history in South Africa House was an attack on Herbert Baker by one of Afrikaner nationalism's favorite artists, J. H. Pierneef (who, like his arch rival Juta, was given substantial commissions in the new diplomatic mission). Pierneef held Baker to be ultimately responsible for any historical inaccuracies, accusing him outright of giving everything "an imperialistic taint."[19]

As a result of such controversies, subjects that were to become central to Afrikaner nationalism were given lengthy captions to eliminate any hint of ambiguity in their significance for the nascent South African state. Thus under Juta's painting of *The Voortrekkers*, the words of one of the Trek's leaders, Piet Retief, are inscribed: "Be it known that we are resolved, wherever we go, that we will uphold the just principle of liberty." Similarly, under Juta's controversial mural, *The Landing of Johan van Riebeeck, Table Bay, Sunday, 7 April 1652*, were inscribed the words, "That the interests of the East India Company may be promoted, justice maintained, and the true Reformed Christian Doctrine implanted and propagated amongst the wild and savage inhabitants of this land."

If Baker's professed and rather grandiose aim was "to get these cultural interests to lift people above racial and economic controversies" and "to help all who visit the building to think high above the material and disruptive obsessions which may hinder progress and unity in South Africa and the world today," then he had surely underestimated the signs represented in the historical tableaux that adorned his building.[20]

Given this brief account of some of the ways in which representations of the past were inscribed in the very structure of South Africa House at the time of its inauguration in 1933 and the fact that these images of South Africa, its peoples, and its land remain intact as an integral and unavoidable feature of the building, the refurbishment project takes on a greater significance. This synoptic history also spells out in no uncertain terms that the symbolic legacy inherited by the new diplomatic mission in 1994 asserted the Dutch as the founding fathers of "civilization" in South Africa, with individuated and named "heroes" lauded for specific colonial activities. The black majority, however, functioned as markers of "indigeneity," which had a certain use value for some in 1934 as a means of producing a unique and naturalized South Africanness. Crucially, this was partly achieved through the implicit relation between representations of the culture of generalized black South Africans (with the exception of the "Zulu Room") and the insistent repetition of indigenous South African flora and fauna. Both were designed to enhance the "authentic" South Africa by recourse to a concept of "nature" and "natural" that the one reinforced through an association with the other. Consequently the old obfuscation of nature versus culture worked to cement the familiar colonial divide, with Dutch colonialism representing the coming of "culture" to the "nature" of the black majority. The fact that such ideologies are literally embodied and embedded in the fabric of South Africa House—in every corridor, in every public reception room, in the walls and ceilings, in the floors and balconies—must have been experienced as a constant and oppressive reminder of recent histories to many of the incoming diplomatic team. For them the building's transformation from the symbolic universe of the apartheid regime to an adequate representation of the new democratic dispensation has come none too soon.

In 1933 challenges over the representation of history and modernity were clearly at some level about which constituencies had the right to represent the nation "overseas" and what image should prevail. Nearly a decade on from the first democratic elections the question of what kind of image the "new" South Africa should create abroad is even more vital than in the immediate aftermath of the 1994 elections. South Africa is no longer the flavor of the month in the international media, but the need for intelligent and informed international support is crucial as a means of sustaining the gains won by the elections. Now as in 1933 there is a need to acknowledge and negotiate complex and—as the chapters of this book make clear—highly contested investments in South Africa's past and present from diverse constituencies, from abroad as well as within the country. Now as then the new interior aims to provide a representation of the present that engages with the past while also signaling "a confidence in [the] future."[21] Now as then there have been some obstructions to the desires of those in charge of the project.

If those in post in the High Commission after the demise of apartheid had imagined that they had finally put their colonial oppressors to rest, the refurbishment process has been a rude awakening. In a final irony in this tale of two high commissions, the project manager, Lorna de Smidt, was informed by English Heritage (a historical conservation body) that because the building was part of *English* heritage, the South African government had no right to destroy or alter either its exterior or its interior. The result has been a neat and pragmatic solution that quietly but insistently will alter irrevocably the face of South Africa's "home" in London.

To this end the metaphor deployed is one of "transparency"; the aim of "the architectural design encapsulated within the submitted proposal is to contextualise the existing symbols and functions by way of increased transparency and layered portals bridging past, present and future."[22] Thus "Clear structural glass panels of precise measurements, pinned delicately and separated from and over existing identified murals, become separators and portals in dialectical terms."[23] This metaphor could be seen as extending to the newly commissioned artworks themselves.

Although many murals in the building were less ideologically controversial in 1933 than Juta's Van Riebeeck triptych, virtually all the murals cannot escape the charge today of either covertly or overtly representing a version of the past that has since proved to be the foundation upon which apartheid's discriminatory logic was cemented. Often it is as much the *absence* of certain themes within identifiable subjects that mirrors the lacunae identified by some museum professionals in debates about the representation of a new public history that I discussed in chapter 4. It is through these absences that many of the artists commissioned for the refurbishment have chosen to engage with the histories inscribed in the old decorative schema of the building.

Senzeni Marasela's proposal for South Africa House foregrounds the absence of an acknowledgment of women as the agents of historical change in South Africa's recent history. In a move that mirrors the Monument to the Women of South Africa (discussed in chapter 2), she has prioritized the celebrated 1956 women's march against the extension of the pass laws not only, as she says, "because of the monumentality of the event but because [she] believes it is one of the greatest turning points in South African history."[24] For her too the amnesia signaled in the missing and distorted histories represented in South Africa House is reflected more generally in the new dispensation: "The majority of us grew up with the perception that there were no gender issues in politics because that would be divisive of black solidarity. Yet I have discovered through the years that many women, both white and non-white, have participated and some died in anti-apartheid activism. Yet none of us see memorials commemorating those women."[25] In line with the metaphor of transparency outlined in the general refurbishment brief, which also appropriately has the potential to call up the idea of ghosting or haunting, Marasela's work, *Amakhosikazi,* is a series of line portraits of significant women activists in South Africa's recent history, with the leaders of the 1956 women's march in the foreground, sandblasted onto a mirrored surface. In this way viewers cannot fail to be confronted by their own reflections, filling in other more ambiguous gaps, as they contemplate the absent presences represented by the women's portraits.

Berni Searle's contribution to the new South Africa House, *On Loan: Acquired, Preserved, Transformed,* is an installation designed, as the title suggests, to draw attention to "the relationship between artwork / object / artifact and the places in which they are 'housed.' "[26] In particular, she is aware of the national significance of South Africa House in an international arena and the necessity therefore of providing some kind of dialogue with the representations of history in the building that she sees as embodying "the

103. Jan Juta, *Africa 1652*, 1933. Mural, 150 x 58 cm. South Africa House, London. Photo courtesy of Paddy Donnelly.

ideas and aspirations of a particular time in the history of South Africa."[27] Her challenge is "to try and unpack how these ideas and perceptions impact on our sense of who we are and how this may relate to individual perceptions about identity in contemporary South Africa."[28] Searle has selected two murals by Jan Juta on the mezzanine above the Exhibition Hall that precisely represent the generic indigeneity mentioned above. One depicts three black men represented as generic "warriors" in an unidentifiable landscape; the other depicts three black women bearing pots on their heads (figure 103). Searle's work consists of a transparent red acrylic box over the murals as a "counter-strategy to ethnographic practices of display." Playing on conventional framing and conservation methods, Searle notes that the murals are "simultaneously 'preserved' and 'transformed' into three-dimensional

104. Jan Juta, *Willem Adriaan van der Stel on His Farm, Vergelegen,* 1933. Mural, 150 x 262 cm. Lower ground floor gallery in South Africa House, London. Photo courtesy of Paddy Donnelly.

objects / installations" through the use of the boxes.[29] Thus Juta's works lose their "local color" through the economical device of the red acrylic; they are effectively neutralized and themselves become objectified as they once objectified others.

Paradoxically, at a time when labor disputes were at a critical pitch in South Africa, the representations of mining and other crucial national in-dustries in the newly opened South Africa House show idyllic, almost pas-toral scenes. Similarly in Juta's scenes of the Vergelegen estate, black sub-jects appear as either servants or decorative vassals and always in postures that emphasize their subservient relationship to a colonial master (figure 104). Slavery is of course never hinted at, although we know that the Groot Constantia vineyards of Gwelo Goodman's murals (shown in figure 105) and the farms in Juta's murals dedicated to Simon van der Stel and Willem Adriaan van der Stel were totally dependent on slave labor. Any references to bondage are evident only in its naturalized representation in the painter's un-self-conscious depiction of "harmonious" social relations between mas-ter and servant / slave, with each individual occupying his or her "rightful" place in the existing (colonial) social order. In Juta's murals this is under-

105. Murals by Gwelo Goodman: Siole panels— *South African Fruit and Vegetables*, 1933. 72 x 88 cm and 72 x 86 cm. Center panel— *Groot Constantia*, 1933. 149 x 110 cm. Ground floor anteroom, South Africa House, London. Photo courtesy of Paddy Donnelly.

lined by the insistent orchestration of the composition into a kind of rhythmic harmony where the action is marked by stylized poses of hieratic figures ranked in steady rows. In Goodman's *Groot Constantia* there is no representation of labor of any sort. The focus is rather on the "heritage" represented by the vernacular of seventeenth-century Cape Dutch architecture and the lush grounds surrounding the estate. There is no danger here of any ambiguous human intrusion onto the scene.

These are the absences that Sue Williamson has chosen to engage in her proposal for South Africa House, *The Profit and Loss Account of Simon van der Stel*. As Williamson points out, the caption to Juta's mural of Simon van der Stel ("Simon van der Stel at the Castle, Cape Town, 22 December 1681) refers to the exchange of pieces of copper. Her work involves "a different kind of exchange. I have researched the records for details of slaves bought and sold by Simon van der Stel and established that he was involved in over fifty transactions in the purchase of slaves, and fifteen sales transactions between the years of 1660 and 1688. In one case, he bought six child slaves aged between eight and fourteen for a lump sum of 120 Riksdollars."[30] She

106. Sue Williamson, Proposal for South Africa House: sketch for *The Profit and Loss Account of Simon van der Stel*, 2002. Engraved glass. Courtesy of the artist.

similarly employs the metaphor of transparency to considerable effect in her work by engraving a glass rectangle of the same dimensions as Juta's mural to represent the open pages of a ledger. On this surface are the accounts of Van der Stel's slave transactions, giving the "date, name, age, place of birth and price paid or received for each slave."[31] Through the now inescapable evidence of the ledger's accounts the viewer is forced to see Juta's painting through a very different prism (figure 106).

All of these artists, and others not mentioned here, who have received commissions for the new South Africa House are intent on understanding how different versions of the past inform the present and on somehow making such knowledge explicit in their work. Rather than deal with the past by literally obliterating it and destroying the murals and sculptural friezes, these artists—in a move recalling some of the earlier arguments put forward by the ANC against the destruction of apartheid monuments and in a deliberate dialogue with the existing artworks in South Africa House—create the possibility of a new set of meanings. Their efforts have the effect of literally "framing" the past and perhaps neutralizing it by objectifying its representations. Such a strategy might ironically have the salutary effect of symbolically putting an aspect of South Africa's past to rest while opening to scrutiny the very processes by which histories are embodied in the public domain.

NOTES

INTRODUCTION: MAKING HISTORY MEMORABLE

1 Interview with Max du Preez, Johannesburg, August 1999.
2 For an introduction to the histories of alternative media in South Africa under apartheid, see Tomaselli and Louw, eds., *The Alternative Press in South Africa,* and Tomaselli, Tomaselli, and Muller, eds., *Narrating the Crisis.*
3 Max du Preez, "I Am an African . . . an Afrikaner," *Star,* 17 June 1999.
4 Cited in Makoba, ed., *African Renaissance,* ix.
5 Makoba, ed., *African Renaissance,* is one of the most useful sources for coming to terms with the official definition of the concept.
6 Max du Preez, "I Am an African . . . an Afrikaner" *Star,* 17 June 1999; Thobeka Mda, "Can Whites Truly Be Called Africans?" *Star,* 24 June 1999; *Star,* 6 July 1999; Max du Preez, "Sisters, You've Got It So Wrong," *Star,* 8 July 1999; Lizeka Mda, "Max, Mind Your Own Baas Business," *Star,* 12 July 1999; John Matshikiza, "Trouble among the Natives," *Weekly Mail and Guardian,* 16–22 July 1999; *Star,* 15 July 1999; Thobeka Mda, "Whites Have the Right to Decide," *Star,* 20 July 1999; Max du Preez, "All It Needs Is a Word in Your Ear," *Star,* 22 July 1999. The debate is taken up again specifically in relation to the African Renaissance in a series of interviews with key exponents of the concept in Nuttall and Michael, "African Renaissance."
7 Lizeka Mda, "Max, Mind Your Own Baas Business," *Star,* 12 July 1999.
8 On the new South African constitution, see South Africa, *The Constitution of the Republic of South Africa;* Chaskalson et al., eds., *Constitutional Law of South Africa;* du Plessis and Corder, *Understanding South Africa's Transitional Bill of Rights;* and Roux, *Constitutional Review.* For the definition of "citizen" under apartheid, see Sharp, "Ethnic Group and Nation," and West, "Confusing Categories."
9 For a useful article complicating the concept of "community" during apartheid, see Thornton and Ramphele, "The Quest for Community."
10 Nuttall and Coetzee, eds., *Negotiating the Past.* On liberal and radical traditions within South African historiography, see Brown et al., eds., *History from South Africa;* La Hausse, "Oral History and South African Historians";

Minkley and Rassool, "Orality"; and Hofmeyr, "*We Spend Our Years as a Tale That Is Told.*"

11 Denoon, "The Isolation of Australian History."

12 See, for example, Darian-Smith, Gunner, and Nuttall, eds., *Text, Theory, Space;* Griffiths and Robin, eds., *Ecology and Empire;* Russell, ed., *Colonial Frontiers;* Thomas, *Possessions;* and Beinart and Coates, *Environment and History.*

13 See Simpson, *Making Representations;* Phillips, "Show Times"; Tapsell Te Arawa, "Taonga, marae, whenua"; and Karp, Kreamer, and Levine, eds., *Museums and Communities.*

14 Vikram Dodd: "Irving: Consigned to History as a Racist Liar," *The Guardian,* 12 April 2000, and "How the Web of Lies Was Unravelled," *The Guardian,* 12 April 2000; Stephen Moss, "History's Verdict on the Holocaust Upheld," *The Guardian,* 12 April 2000; David Pallister, "He Is a Holocaust Denier; He Misstated Evidence," *The Guardian,* 12 April 2000; Jonathan Freedland, "Let's Close the Book," *The Guardian,* 12 April 2000; Clare Dyer, "Judging History," *The Guardian,* 17 April 2000; Gerald Posner, "The World According to David Irving," *The Observer,* 19 March 2000; "Irving's Tag as 'Holocaust Denier' Upheld," *The Guardian,* 21 July 2001.

15 See Young, *The Texture of Memory,* for an analysis of how the Holocaust is commemorated differently and has specific meanings depending on the national context. For an analysis of the stakes involved in Holocaust commemoration in Germany after reunification, see Geyer, "The Politics of Memory in Contemporary Germany," Linenthal, *Preserving Memory,* for an account of the debates concerning the creation of a Holocaust Museum as a national institution in the United States. In addition, a substantial literature debates the significance of the proliferation of Holocaust commemorative activities and memorials in the United States. See Cole, *Images of the Holocaust;* Novick, *The Holocaust in American Life;* and Finkelstein, *The Holocaust Industry.*

16 Parry, "Reconciliation and Remembrance"; James and Van de Vijver, eds., *After the TRC.*

17 Posel, "The TRC Report," was published subsequent to my writing this book, and I am indebted to Neville Alexander, who drew my attention to her analysis in a draft chapter of his monograph, since published as Alexander, *An Ordinary Country.* See especially pages 124–33, where he discusses Posel's analysis of the TRC.

18 For a useful set of essays from a range of disciplines that offer different explanations on the ways memory works but that are all premised on an understanding of memory as constructed and partial, see Antze and Lambek, eds., *Tense Past.*

19 See Brison, "Trauma Narratives"; Caruth, ed., *Trauma;* and Antze and Lambek, eds., *Tense Past.*

20 Cuthbertson, "Embodied Memory."

21 Coombes, "The Art of Memory."

22 Levi, *The Truce;* Delbo, *Auschwitz and After.*

23 Delbo, *Auschwitz and After,* 255.

24 Minkley and Rassool, "Orality."

25 The University of the Witwatersrand houses the History Workshop, a group of social historians who modeled themselves on the British History Workshop, founded in a socialist tradition of "history from below" or "people's history" and the history of popular culture at the trade unionist Ruskin College at Oxford University. Formed in 1977 partly in response to the crisis in black education that had resulted in the 1976 Soweto uprising, the South African version aims to popularize history as a discipline but also to make it more representative of all aspects of South African culture and to produce a better understanding of both black and white working-class experience. Many important collaborative projects were developed through the History Workshop, some of which will be referred to below. But see in particular Witz, *Write Your Own History.* For greater detail on the History Workshop, see Bonner, "New Nation, New History." History Workshop has also been crucial in developing research for the new history curriculum; see Kros, *Trusting to the Process,* and Kros and Greybe, *The Rainbow Nation.* Both the University of the Witwatersrand and the University of the Western Cape, jointly with the University of Cape Town, produced critically innovative diplomas and postgraduate degrees in history and heritage soon after the first democratic elections. These have proved important training grounds for a multiethnic student body.

26 For a useful collection dealing with some of the debates concerning public art, see Mitchell, ed., *Art and the Public Sphere.*

27 See Stewart, *On Longing,* xii and 172; Huyssen, "Monumental Seduction," 192. In the film *Disgraced Monuments,* directed by Laura Mulvey and Mark Lewis, the Russian art historian and critic Natalya Davidova says of the situation in contemporary Russia, a country that is veritably littered with monumental sculpture, "We walk past monuments and we often don't notice them."

28 *The Guardian,* 2 and 5 May 2000; *The Times,* 2 May 2000.

29 *Star,* 27 October 1997. For an analysis on the intended publics for *Tribute* magazine, see Murray, "*Tribute* and Attributed Meaning."

30 *Die Beeld,* 29 September 1992.

31 *Star,* 14 June 1999; *Citizen,* 15 June 1999. *Sowetan,* 17 June 1999, had a satirical cartoon by Zapiro.

32 *City Press,* 14 September 1997; *Rapport,* 14 September 1997.

33 *Citizen,* 30 September 1997; *Star,* 3 October 1997; *Cape Argus,* 2 October 1997.

34 Campschreur and Divendal, eds., *Culture in Another South Africa*. For a criti-
    cal assessment of the conference, see Hayman, "Class, Race or Culture."

35 A number of conferences in the late 1980s had debated the future role of
    museums in a "new" South Africa, and one of the important results of the
    1987 Pietermaritzburg conference, "Museums in a Changing and Divided
    South Africa," was a policy statement outlining the South African Museums
    Association's (SAMA) intention to be at the forefront of democratic trans-
    formation in the museum sector and underlining the association's commit-
    ment to redressing the discriminatory museum practices that reinforced
    apartheid legislation. The document, which became known as the "Pieter-
    maritzburg Declaration," stated the following:

> We the members of the Southern African Museums Association, declare our
> earnest desire:
> 1. That South African Museums in their various programmes purposefully
> direct their efforts to promote the dissemination of information to and enjoy-
> ment of museums by all South Africans;
> 2. that South African museums actively assist all our various communities
> better to understand the circumstances of both their separate and common
> history so as to give them a clearer view of their present relationships and
> thereby how they can be more harmoniously involved one with the other in
> the future;
> 3. that South African museums sincerely strive to be seen to belong to all
> South Africans irrespective of colour, creed or gender;
> 4. that all South Africans be encouraged to express openly their views as to
> how the country's museums may better serve the interest of all in South Africa
> (cited in *South African Museums Association Bulletin* [SAMAB] 18, no. 8 [1989]).

By the 1980s SAMA was best understood as a fairly liberal professional
association. One of the issues that bonded the membership was its opposition to the invidious division of museums into "own" and "general" affairs institutions—a division imposed under the tricameral parliament in
the early 1980s. However, despite some liberalizing elements within SAMA,
they seem to have had very little influence on the display policy of most museums, so that even by 1992 Denver Webb (who was later to become coordinator of the Heritage Sector for the ANC Commission for the Reconstruction
and Transformation of the Arts and Culture in South Africa—CREATE) felt
obliged to report that "The fragmented nature of museum administration,
the fact that SAMA is not a statutory body and the fact that, at the end of the
day, there is a limit to the kind of opposition museums can display to the government that funds them, has meant that the government has not paid too
much attention to the representation made on behalf of the profession by
SAMA (Webb, "National Cultural Policy Project Discussion Document: Museums and Monuments," 1992, 8; ANC Museum Commission Files [here-
after ANC MCF]).

36 Odendaal, " 'Give Life to Learning,' " 4.

37 Ibid., 5–6.

38 Ibid., 6.

39 Ibid., 14.

40 André Odendaal, "ANC Commission for the Reconstruction and Transformation of the Arts and Culture in South Africa, Museums Sector Programme of Action"; discussion document, January 1994, 4 (ANC MCF).

41 Ibid., 2.

42 Ibid., 3.

43 Ibid. See also Lalou Meltzer to André Odendaal, 6 January 1994, where Meltzer draws attention to the inequities of the Castle Management Act and the army's attempts to block transfer of power after the changeover of government in 1994:

> Many millions of rands have been spent on restoring the Castle over the last two decades. Indeed, there is still a Public Works Department contract outstanding for 1994. This massive amount of public money spent, with little visible improved advantage to the public of South Africa, has recently led to an outcry, against army mismanagement of the Castle, by journalists and various societies, such as the historical Society of Cape Town, the Vernacular Architecture Society and the Simon van der Stel Foundation. The result was the passing of a bill (Castle Management Bill) into legislation during December 1993—another hasty and thus ill-thought bit of legislation by the last white parliament. . . . It allows for the constitution of a board of management which includes representatives of the City Council, tourism, Public Works and the Provincial Administration, but by virtue of the other members . . . could still allow the army to dominate. Community needs and the needs of education are thus absent (ANC MCF).

44 Odendaal, "ANC Commission" 3 (ANC MCF).

45 In relation to issues concerning staffing, MUSA is accused of failing to recognize either the relevant trade unions or the need for staff development and skills acquisition programs in order to implement an affirmative action strategy. National museums are seen as prioritized over regional museums, which get short shrift in the MUSA document, thus undermining the kinds of contributions that can usefully be made by museums that have a closer relationship with their provincial and regional communities. Community involvement is criticized as too low a priority in MUSA, with no acknowledgment of the need to involve a broader public in the governance of the museum. This is seen as symptomatic of the lack of proper consultation throughout the research process. In May 1992 Denver Webb had already written "National Cultural Policy Project Discussion Document: Museums and Monuments." Odendaal stresses that this document lays out a series of principles and strategies that the authors of MUSA would have done well to consult prior to publishing their own paper.

46 As late as 21 April 1994, Webb, by this time coordinator of the Heritage Sector of CREATE, reported on a meeting with the Department of National Education (DNE) in Pretoria in which various "unilateral restructuring actions" on the part of the DNE were discussed (ANC MCF).

47 Denver Webb, ANC CREATE, draft press release, 22 April 1994, 1 and 3 (ANC MCF). On 30 March 1994, just prior to the elections in April, the CREATE Sub-Committee on Museums and Heritage Resources held a series of meetings in Cape Town with professional bodies representative of a number of key national museum and heritage organizations. These included SAMA, the Association of Directors of National Collections, and the NMC (see CREATE Sub-Committee on Museums and Heritage Resources, minutes of a meeting with the Association of Directors of National Collections, 30 March, 9.30 A.M.: minutes of a meeting with SAMA, 30 March 1994, 11.30 A.M.: minutes of a meeting with the NMC, 30 March 1994, 2.00 P.M.; all in ANC MCF). This was followed by the meeting in Pretoria with the DNE on 21 April 1994 (see meeting between ANC CREATE and the DNE, 21 April 1994, ANC MCF). For each of these the ANC representatives were André Odendaal, Graham Dominy, Andrew Hall, Aron Mazel, Gordon Metz, and Denver Webb. The ANC objections to MUSA were conveyed at each of these meetings. SAMA, while supporting MUSA at the first chance that museum professionals had been given to have an input in national policy, agreed that MUSA should be seen as a "draft technical report" than as agreed policy.

48 See minutes of meeting between ANC CREATE and the DNE, Pretoria, 21 April 1994, para 3.9 (ANC MCF), where Odendaal says, "The ANC's aim is to unite the museum world so that it can stake its claims for resources and state attention early on in the life of the new government."

49 Webb, ANC CREATE, draft press release, 3. See also minutes of meeting between ANC CREATE and DNE, Pretoria, 21 April 1994, 4 (ANC MCF), where Odendaal says, "Monuments are a sensitive issue and the symbolism of this is important to the ANC."

1 TRANSLATING THE PAST: APARTHEID MONUMENTS IN POSTAPARTHEID SOUTH AFRICA

1 For a useful account of Lenin's monuments program, see Lodder, "Lenin's Plan." For an account of later iconoclastic activity concerning monuments in the former Soviet Union, see Michalski, *Public Monuments.*

2 Neville Dubow, "The Field of Fallen Idols," *Weekly Mail and Guardian,* 29 October–4 November 1993; Dubow draws attention to both the Moscow and Budapest sculpture parks in relation to the debate on South African monuments and the past regime.

3 The epigraph reference to "Boerassic Park" by Pieter Dirk Uys, a comedian whose political satire has consistently poked fun at Afrikaner nationalism,

is from his *One Man One Volt*, which in turn is a pun on the slogans "One man, one vote" and "One settler, one bullet" (cited in Amanda Gouws, "Report of the Robben Island Political Feasibility Study as Commissioned by Peace Visions," unpublished report, May 1994, 16).

4   *Business Day Final*, 10 April 1996.

5   See Department of Arts, Culture, Science, and Technology, *Annual Report*, for funding allocations for 1997–1998 and 1998–1999. See also *The Star*, 19 February 1999. The drop in funds for Robben Island might have been in response to criticism that it was receiving the lion's share of funding despite the fact that many curators argued that calling it a "museum" was misleading and that the work done on the island in no way approximated the range of skills expected of most museum personnel. Such criticisms were aired in the national press. See, for example, *Sunday Independent*, 20 September 1998.

6   *Sunday Independent*, 31 March 1996. Cited from a fax sent by de Jager.

7   For further examples of this tendency in totalitarian regimes, see Golomstock, *Totalitarian Art*, and Michalski, *Public Monuments*.

8   Critics included Marilyn Martin (director of the South African National Gallery), Sandra Prosalendis (director of the District Six Museum), and Neville Dubow (head of Michaelis School of Art). See Glynnis Underhill, "Monumental Row over Proposed R 50-Million Statue of Raised Hand," *Saturday Star*, 6 April 1996; *Sunday Independent*, 31 March 1996; Robert Greig, "Kitsch Is the Kroks' Democratic Right—But Only If They Keep It Private," *Sunday Independent*, 7 April 1996; Neville Dubow, "Arms and the Man," *Weekly Mail and Guardian*, 12 April 1996; Roshana Rossouw, "'Mandela's Hand' Gets the Chop," *Weekly Mail and Guardian*, 4 April 1996; *Citizen*, 1 April 1996; "A Fistful of Reconciliation?" *Weekly Mail and Guardian*, 29 March 1996; Piet Muller, "SA kry nou Moeder van alle Monumente!" *Rapport*, 30 April 1995; Stephen Laufer, "Proposed Memorial Must Remember All Apartheid's Victims," *Business Day Final*, 17 April 1996.

9   *Weekly Mail and Guardian*, 4 April 1996. Sandra Prosalendis was particularly angered by this because of the difficulties of getting funding for her museum over this perid.

10 Ben Temkin, "Finger-Pointing Does Not Help: We Were Dancing in Verwoerd's Bizarre Ballet," *Sunday Independent*, 7 April 1996.

11 Robert Greig, "Kitsch Is the Kroks' Democratic Right—But Only If They Keep It Private," *Sunday Independent*, 7 April 1996. Another attempt at a symbolic riposte to the Voortrekker Monument is the Freedom Park initiative, which forms part of the Legacy Project designed to facilitate the erection of monuments and other public institutions that more adequately represent the experience and historical legacy of the black majority and of groups and individuals previously ignored in apartheid histories. This ongoing ten-year project, mooted in 1998, had by 2000 been allocated a site

on the Salvokop, one of the hills opposite the Voortrekker Monument (interview with Alicia Monis from the Department of Arts and Culture, Pretoria, December 2000). At this early stage a number of commemorative features were planned for what was designed to be one of the key sites for the representation of the new nation and its historical legacy: a garden of remembrance made up of indigenous plants, a possible monument, and a wall of remembrance (interview with Luli Callinicos, Johannesburg, December 2000). See also *Star*, 1 June 2000, in which a government representative describes the project: "It will be the focus for a new patriotism, a new common purpose [and] dedicated to the history of our struggle, the victories and successes." So far none of these has yet materialized, and the only official sign of a challenge to the Voortrekker Monument's prime location came when Joe Modise, at that time minister of defense, presided over a ceremony to rename Voortrekker Hill to what he argued was a reversion to its original name of Thaba Tswane (the Hill of Pretoria) (*Citizen*, 20 March 1998).

12 Hyslop, "Why Did Apartheid's Supporters Capitulate?"

13 Benjamin, "The Task of the Translator," in *Illuminations*; Spivak, "The Politics of Translation," in *Outside in the Teaching Machine*.

14 The use and abuse of Afrikaans is a far more complex issue than this statement suggests. In line with other debates in the field of postcolonial literatures about the appropriateness of using the language of the colonizer as a language of resistance, Afrikaner radicals have similarly debated the use and abuse of their own language. The situation is of course further complicated by the fact that Afrikaans is the primary language of most of the constituency designated "colored" by the apartheid regime in the Western Cape. For useful introductions to the debate, see Willemse, "The Black Afrikaans Writer." *Argus* (Cape Town) ran a series of articles debating the status and relevance of Afrikaans in 1997. In one (25 September 1997) Hein Willemse argued that Afrikaans had a privileged position in South Africa, with an infrastructure specially created to foster the language, and consequently its literature had thrived. But all this had also been at the cost of undermining other African languages that were not given the same kind of cultural, economic, and institutional support during apartheid. Willemse's argument is essentially against the way language is always seen in terms of power plays along ethnic lines; those worried about the diminishing use and status of Afrikaans should "seek common ground with speakers and interested groups of other Southern African languages, not along ethnic lines, but in the interest and defence of this new democracy." This article is a response to Hermann Giliomee's defense of Afrikaans as a language made recently vulnerable by an ANC "conspiracy" to instate English as the lingua franca (*Argus*, 23 September 1997).

15 On the cultural significance of the Great Trek for Afrikaner nationalism, see Hofmeyr, "Building a Nation from Words." On the spectacle of the trek

reconstruction, see Hofmeyr, "Popularizing History," and McClintock, *Imperial Leather*, 370–378.

16 Board of Control of the Voortrekker Monument, *The Voortrekker Monument*, 68.

17 On the "invention" of Afrikaner tradition, see Hofmeyr, "Building a Nation from Words"; O'Meara, *Volkskapitalisme*; and Giliomee, "The Beginnings of Afrikaner Ethnic Consciousness." See also Butler, "Afrikaner Women."

18 Cited in *Historiese Rekord*, 29.

19 Ibid., 24.

20 Delmont, "The Voortrekker Monument," is one of the best sources on the early history of the monument, and I have drawn freely from it for my discussion of the early history of the monument.

21 Board of Control of the Voortrekker Monument, *The Voortrekker Monument*, 34.

22 During apartheid the "Day of the Vow" was a public holiday commemorating the moment when the Voortrekkers took a vow before God that they would hold this day forever sacred and commemorate it to His honor if He granted them victory over the Zulu. Postapartheid it is known as the "Day of Reconciliation" (or Goodwill). There is a nice irony here in that the shaft of light no longer hits its intended target due to the idiosyncrasies of planetary activity.

23 Hyslop, "Why Was the White Right Unable?," 148.

24 Grundlingh and Sapire, "From Feverish Festival to Repetitive Ritual?"

25 Ibid., 30–31.

26 Ibid., 32.

27 Ibid., 36.

28 Cited in *Sunday Times Final*, 27 May 1990.

29 Hyslop, "Why Was the White Right Unable?," 151.

30 Ibid., 154.

31 *Citizen*, 8 December 1993.

32 "The Defused Siege," *Cape Times*, 9 December 1993, editorialized that those who besieged the fort had a nerve complaining about the use of black troops to end the siege. It ended with the rejoinder that "They had better get used to the fact that law enforcement is no longer the sole prerogative of whites."

33 *Patriot*, 16 October 1992.

34 As noted in the introduction, in the minutes of the meeting between ANC CREATE and the DNE, Pretoria, 21 April 1994 (ANC MCF), Denver Webb expressed serious concern "at the privatisation of the Voortrekker Monument as an act of unilateral restructuring and the transfer of state funded property to the private sector."

35 National Cultural History Museum Archive, Pretoria; *Die Beeld*, cuttings folder, no date but pre-1993.

36 Ibid.

37 Khan, "Hidden Heritage." See also Krafchik, ed., *The South African Museum*,

where a number of the participants in a workshop of the same name voiced similar concerns about museum publics in South Africa.

38 Frescura, "Monuments."

39 Joe Louw, "A Concrete Symbol of Separate Worlds," *Saturday Star,* 7 November 1992.

40 Ibid.

41 Ibid.

42 Ibid.

43 Cited in Andrew Unsworth, "Tokyo's Groot Trek," *Sunday Times,* 15 December 1996.

44 Ibid.

45 Delmont, "The Voortrekker Monument."

46 Cited in Board of Control of the Voortrekker Monument, *The Voortrekker Monument,* 35.

47 Delmont, "The Voortrekker Monument," 87. For an elaboration of the concept of degeneracy in cultural practice in the late nineteenth century, see Coombes, *Re-Inventing Africa.*

48 Dubow, "Human Origins"; Kuklick, "Contested Monuments."

49 Reported in Kuklick, "Contested Monuments," 152. Kuklick argues, however, that certain aspects of Caton-Thompson's case for an African origin for Great Zimbabwe could also find favor with white settlers since she claims to find traces of foreign influences in the buildings, and they could latch on to such small qualifications in her argument.

50 Ibid., 156.

51 See, for example, *Historical Record* 32, where, on the occasion of the inauguration of the Voortrekker Monument, General Jan Smuts gave an opening address: "The Voortrekker struggle was not against the natives as such, but against barbarous chiefs who, with their Zulu doctrines, made the interior of Natal, the Transvaal and the Free State a wilderness and so unwittingly cleared the country for White settlement."

52 Cited in Robert Brand, "Tutu Pays Visit to 'Symbol of Pain,'" *Star,* 3 July 1996.

53 Ibid.

54 Cited in *Loslyf,* June 1995: 125; translated by Jean Brundrit.

55 Thanks to Isabel Hofmeyr for drawing this to my attention.

56 Board of Control of the Voortrekker Monument, *The Voortrekker Monument,* 31.

57 Ibid., 36.

58 For a useful analysis of Boer women's role in the South African War and their pugilistic skills, see Bradford, "Sisters and Brothers."

59 *Loslyf,* June 1995: 125.

60 Deborah James, South African anthropologist and author now at the London School of Economics, remembers when someone came into a seminar in

which she was participating (at the Institute of African Studies at the University of the Witwatersrand) brandishing a copy of *Loslyf*. According to James, the other participants saw the magazine as hugely influential as a critique of Afrikanerdom. They were less concerned with it as a porn magazine.

61 Louw and Tomaselli, "The Struggle for Legitimacy," 90.
62 Du Preez on SABC English Service, 12 March 1991; cited in Louw and Tomaselli, "Impact," 226.
63 See *Die Beeld,* 7 April and 20 May 1995; *The Star,* 20 May 1995; *Sunday Independent,* 18 February 1996.
64 SABC, *Agenda,* 3 April 1995; transcript and translation by Ronel Verwoerd.
65 Cited in ibid.
66 Cited in ibid.
67 Cited in ibid.
68 Thanks to Ronel Verwoerd for this information.
69 Cited in SABC, *Agenda,* 3 April 1995; transcript and translation by Ronel Verwoerd.
70 Cited in ibid.
71 Cited in ibid.
72 "*Pollie*" is Afrikaans slang for "colored" person, so a number of cultural signifiers are being ironically deployed in this slogan.
73 *Weekly Mail and Guardian,* 1 September 1995.
74 Ibid.
75 "Snuffing Out Censorship," editorial, *Weekly Mail and Guardian,* 15 December 1995. This bill became the Film and Publications Act in 1996 following much debate, as well as ferocious antagonism from the ANC Women's League, who, unlike many other liberal critics, considered the bill to be too lenient. Gaye Davis, "ANC Group Tries to Turn Back Censorship Clock," *Weekly Mail and Guardian,* 16 August 1996. See also "Censorship: Too Little or Too Much?" *Weekly Mail and Guardian,* 4 July 1997; Janet Smith, "Swinging Censors," *Weekly Mail and Guardian,* 27 February 1998.
76 Bafana Khumalo, "Tales from the Heartland," *Weekly Mail and Guardian,* 20 September 1996.
77 Kipnis, "(Male) Desire and (Female) Disgust," 376.
78 Cited in *Weekly Mail and Guardian,* 20 September 1996.
79 *Sunday Times,* 18 January 1998; *Sunday Independent,* 25 January 1998.
80 Cited in *Star,* 21 January 1998.
81 See *Weekly Mail and Guardian,* 23 January 1998, where the art critic Brenda Atkinson delivers a scathing attack on Geers's intended intervention. She suspects him of simple opportunistic self-promotion and also points out that the plane circled over the wrong hill!
82 Ibid.
83 Cited in *Sunday Times,* metro edition, 2 May 1999. *Citizen,* 17 July 1999, lists the names of the organizations that launched the complaint.

84 Rowan Philip, "Fury Grows over Gay Voortrekker Monument Joke," *Sunday Times,* metro edition, 2 May 1999.

85 *Citizen,* 17 July 1999. See also *Sunday Times,* final edition, 18 July 1999.

86 For an essay that advances the argument that the Voortrekker Monument has now become thoroughly incorporated within a global tourist ethos and therefore has diminished in terms of its significance for Afrikaner nationalism, see Grundlingh, "A Cultural Conundrum?"

2 ROBBEN ISLAND: SITE OF MEMORY / SITE OF NATION

1 *Cape Times,* 1930; cited in Hutton, *Robben Island,* 33.

2 Ibid.

3 Ibid.

4 *Argus,* 25 January 1997.

5 Gouws, *Feasibility Study.* The Board of Directors of Peace Visions comprised Ashoek Adhikari, Fikile Bam, Terry Crawford-Browne, Luyanda ka Msumza, Gcina Mhlophe, and Njabulo Ndebele.

6 Gouws, *Feasibility Study,* 2–4, lists the outcomes of these bodies' discussions.

7 "Executive Summary of the Robben Island Political Feasibility Study Report," in Gouws, *Feasibility Study,* n.p. The feasibility study was not just circulated internally but received considerable public attention, with its findings read at a public symposium by the compiler, Amanda Gouws, and *Argus,* 15 May 1994, reporting on this.

8 Gouws, *Feasibility Study,* foreword n.p.

9 Ibid.

10 Ibid., 5.

11 "Executive Summary," in ibid., n.p.

12 Ibid.

13 Ibid.

14 Gouws, *Feasibility Study,* 10.

15 Cited in ibid., 7.

16 Ibid., 6.

17 Deacon, ed. *The Island,* 42–43. Deacon suggests that "Makhanda" is sometimes spelled "Makhana."

18 Deacon, ed., *The Island,* 13.

19 Cited in Gouws, *Feasibility Study,* 5.

20 Ibid.

21 Ibid., 6.

22 Ibid. (emphasis mine), 8.

23 Ibid., 9.

24 Ibid.

25 Ibid.
26 Ibid., 7. Peace Visions was careful to emphasize that the sample of former political prisoners was perhaps too small to glean generalizations but that they seemed to share certain priorities that were worth noting since they were such an important constituency.
27 Ibid.
28 Ibid., 12.
29 Ibid.
30 SAM, press release for "Esiqithini," n.p.; n.d.
31 Davison, "A Place Apart," 3.
32 Ibid.
33 SAM archives, "Esiqithini" Visitors' Comments Book, 6/6/46.
34 Ibid., 8/6/77.
35 Ibid., 9/6/91.
36 Ibid., 15/7/465.
37 Ibid., 17–18/7/500.
38 Ibid., 3–4/7/292.
39 Ibid., 14/6/125.
40 Ibid., 14/6/131.
41 Ibid., 11/6/96.
42 See Worden, "Unwrapping History."
43 Criticisms of the move to the commercial premises engendered enough criticism for Gordon Metz of the Mayibuye Centre to offer a defense in the media, arguing that to see the move simply as a cynical exercise in manipulation and financial gain for Mayibuye was insulting to all those who had worked for the new democracy. See *Cape Times*, 8 August 1995.
44 A celebration banquet to raise funds for the ex–political prisoners' fund and for the RIM for the next five years took place on the island in March 1997. With tickets reportedly costing R 30,000 each and available only to selected invitees, the event was criticized for privileging the international community (with Hilary Clinton and Bill Cosby as two of the guests of honor) and certain business partners who had lent support for the new government's initiatives. See *Cape Times*, 19 March 1997, which reports on an alternative "poor man's banquet" for R 10,000 for a table for ten (with the Cosbys in attendance) that was planned at Sun City to raise funds for the same causes.
45 *Argus*, 13 February 1995.
46 *Argus*, 16 November 1996.
47 Ibid.
48 See *Argus*, 2, 9, 16, and 24 November 1996 and 25 January 1997; *Cape Times*, 30 January 1997; *City Press*, 9 and 14 January 1997.
49 Robben Island received 80 percent of the National Heritage budget in 1998.
50 Cited in *City Press*, 14 January 1997.

51 Kathrada, "Opening Address," 9.
52 *City Press*, 24 December 1995.
53 *Sowetan*, 14 February 1996.
54 *Sunday Times*, final edition, 28 November 1993.
55 *Sunday Times*, 22 December 1996.
56 *Sawubona*, December 2000, 69.
57 *Sunday Independent*, 28 May 2000.
58 Ibid.
59 Ibid.
60 Ibid. See also *Sowetan*, 6 December 1999, which reports that a day after Robben Island was declared a UNESCO World Heritage Site, workers on the island had a day strike. Grievances included differential wages for the same job and the apparent preferential award of tenders for ferry and other services to white as opposed to black operators. *Sunday Independent*, 24 May 1998, similarly reports on a ten-page document from the steering committee of the Robben Island Staffing Association claiming that too few ex–political prisoners had been appointed to the staff. According to André Odendaal, then newly appointed director of the RIM, eight out of eighteen staff members were ex-prisoners. Odendaal saw the complaints as a cynical attempt to affect the imminent appointments of permanent management and staff. Zolile Ndindwa, the Western Cape coordinator of the Ex-Political Prisoners Committee insisted, however, that his office was in daily receipt of complaints about Robben Island and the plight of ex-prisoners.
61 *Sunday Independent*, 28 May 2000.
62 *Sowetan*, 8 May 1997.
63 *Sunday Independent*, 28 May 2000.
64 Bruner, "Tourism in Ghana," 292. My thanks to Ikem Okoye for drawing my attention to this article.
65 I am grateful to Cheryl Finley for this information.
66 Bruner, "Tourism in Ghana," 291.
67 Ibid., 303, n. 13.
68 *Sowetan*, 23 November 2000.
69 I am grateful to Cheryl Finley for this information.
70 Bruner, "Tourism in Ghana," 294.
71 Ibid., 294. Bruner refers to Imahküs Robinson's "Is the Black Man's History Being Whitewashed?" condemning the Ghanaian government's "restoration" of Cape Coast Castle. According to Bruner, it was widely circulated in the American press. He goes on to describe the Ghanaian tourist and development operation, called "One Africa Productions," aimed at providing an "authentic" roots tour for the African American tourists wishing to "reunite" with their African heritage.
72 See Christine Qunta, "This Island of Our Memories," *City Press*, 14 January 1996.

73 Barbara Loftus, "Robben Island, Hallowed Ground of Heroes . . . But It's Just Plain Hell for Tourists. Alcatraz, a Monument to Monsters . . . But a Five-Star Attraction for Visitors," *Saturday Star,* 20 June 1998; Hazel Friedman, "All the Paradoxes of a Nation Fuse on the Island of Shame," *Sunday Independent,* 20 September 1998.

74 For a more interesting comparison with developing tourism on Robben Island, see the article in the *Sunday Independent,* 20 September 1998, where the reporter, Prakash Naidoo, mentions other political prisons that have become tourist "stopovers," bed and breakfasts, or discos—for example, Czech president Vaclav Havel's cell in Prague and the former KGB headquarters in the capital of Kazakhstan, Alma-Ata.

75 Barbara Loftus, "Robben Island, Hallowed Ground of Heroes . . . But It's Just Plain Hell for Tourists. Alcatraz, a Monument to Monsters . . . But a Five-Star Attraction for Visitors," *Saturday Star,* 20 June 1998.

76 Ibid.

77 Ibid.

78 Hazel Friedman, "All the Paradoxes of a Nation Fuse on the Island of Shame," *Sunday Independent,* 20 September 1998.

79 *Sowetan,* 20 December 1996. Rohan airs the grievance that there seems to be no real representation on the island for ex–political prisoners. He says that the image of Robben Island as a symbol of national unity is "highly romanticised."

80 Hazel Friedman, "All the Paradoxes of a Nation Fuse on the Island of Shame," *Sunday Independent,* 20 September 1998. See also Rohan's account of his return to the island, "Feb. 2, 1990, and Victory Is Certain," *Sowetan,* 3 February 2000.

81 Hazel Friedman, "All the Paradoxes of a Nation Fuse on the Island of Shame," *Sunday Independent,* 20 September 1998.

82 See Tim Couzens, "Innocents on the Island," *Sunday Times,* late edition, 5 July 1998, where Couzens describes a tour to the island and visitors' reactions: "Inside names such as Kathrada, Mlambo, Moseneke and Tinto washed over the collective consciousness. Sadly, even Sisulu went largely unrecognised. Walter who?"

83 Cited in the video, *The Story of Robben Island,* shown on the ferry crossing to the island.

84 Owen Mashaba speaking during the tour of the prison.

85 Cooke, *A History of Kilmainham Gaol,* 2.

86 Ibid., 1.

87 Ibid., 11.

88 Kirsty Scott, "Men of Letters, Men of Arms," *Guardian Saturday Review,* 2 December 2000, gets these figures from Richard English, Professor of Politics at Queen's University, Belfast.

89 Loyalist ex-prisoners have felt the need to refute descriptions of their reading

matter as largely body-building magazines, light reading, and pornography in order to stem the consequent embarrassment of the emerging image of the Loyalist as an uneducated thug. However, no Loyalist equivalent to the library found circulating among the Republicans has ever been unearthed. The Scott article cited in note 88 quotes two Loyalist ex-prisoners, Tom Roberts and Martin Snoddon, insisting on the importance of education and reading to their cadre.

90 Cited in Kirsty Scott, "Men of Letters, Men of Arms," *Guardian Saturday Review*, 2 December 2000.

91 See *Ireland and South Africa in Modern Times*, special issue, *Southern African–Irish Studies* 3 (1996).

92 Cited in *Saturday Star*, 10 February 1996.

93 Gordon Metz in *On Campus: The Official Newsletter of the University of the Western Cape* 2, no. 7 (18 March–14 April 1994): 1.

94 Mark Gevisser, "Anne Frank through a Prism of the Present," *Weekly Mail and Guardian*, 19 August 1994.

95 Ibid.

96 Ibid.

97 Ibid.

98 Mark Gevisser, "A Family History That Died in the Holocaust," in *Anne Frank: A Lesson in Humanity*, supplement to the *Weekly Mail and Guardian*, n.d., but available for the opening of the exhibition on 8 March 1994.

99 Chief Rabbi Cyril Harris, "Like Anne, We Need a Belief in Humanity," in *Anne Frank: A Lesson in Humanity*, supplement to the *Weekly Mail and Guardian*, n.d., n.p.

100 Ibid.

101 Cited in Cathy Powers, "Inspiration for Island Prisoners," in *Anne Frank: A Lesson in Humanity*, supplement to the *Weekly Mail and Guardian*, n.d., n.p.

102 According to Rolf Wolfswinkel, a lecturer at the University of Cape Town and a historian of the Holocaust who helped to produce teachers' packs for "Anne Frank in the World," the exhibition had thirty thousand visitors in the first six weeks.

103 "Letters to the Editor," *Argus*, 17 March 1994.

104 Terry Crawford-Browne, *Argus*, weekend edition, 19 March 1994.

105 Ibid.

106 Karel Roskam, "Remember Them for Other Reasons," *Argus*, 10 February 1994.

107 Huyssen, "The Voids of Berlin"; Vidler, *The Architectural Uncanny*.

108 Young, *The Texture of Memory*, 120.

109 Gouws, *Feasibility Study*, 7.

110 See Young, *The Texture of Memory*: "The sum of these dismembered fragments can never approach the whole of what was lost" (133). Young points

out the ritual and symbolic significance of the fragment in Jewish culture (126), and we know that such significance is also evident in the Xhosa and other cultures.

111 See, for example, "The Holocaust Exhibition" at the Imperial War Museum in London.

112 For an interesting analysis of another kind of interior world cut off from other forms of sociality but that created its own social structures and internal polity, see Dening, *Mr. Bligh's Bad Language*, Act 1, "The Ship," where the example is the long exploration voyage ship in the eighteenth century.

113 Cited in Young, *The Texture of Memory*, 135.

114 Ibid., 136–138.

115 Cited in Young, *At Memory's Edge*, 130.

116 Nora, "Between Memory and History."

117 For a detailed account of this project and other work by Jochen Gerz, see Young, *At Memory's Edge*, ch. 5, and Rogoff, "The Aesthetics of Post-History."

118 Kathrada, "Opening Address."

119 See, for example, Meer, *Higher than Hope*; Meredith, *Nelson Mandela*; Sampson, *Mandela*. Mandela's life story has also been produced in illustrated form for children: Case, *What a Gentleman*; Maxim, *Madiba*.

120 See, for example, the following films: *Mandela: Son of Africa*; *Mandela*; and *Nelson Mandela*.

121 Nixon, *Homelands*, 176.

122 Ibid., 178.

123 The speech is reported in *Inside Labour: The New Labour Magazine*, 10. This is illustrated with a photograph of Tony Blair and Mandela embracing, with the caption, "Our newest honorary member—Nelson embraces the Labour Party."

124 *The Guardian*, 29 September 2000; *The Times*, 29 September 2000. It is also true that Mandela has exercised his elder statesman role to criticize the British and U.S. governments on a number of occasions—on one notable occasion when both powers took unilateral action to bomb Iraq and Kosovo without seeking permission from the un Security Council. See Anthony Sampson, "Mandela Condemns 'Policeman' Britain," *The Guardian*, 5 April 2000.

125 Cited in *The Guardian*, 30 April 2001.

126 Ibid.

127 *The Voice*, 8 November 1999, ran a front page item, "Nelson's Column?", on the possibility of Mandela as a statue for the fourth plinth in Trafalgar Square. *The Voice* describes itself as "Britain's *Best* Black Paper."

128 For example, Mac Maharaj, "The Meticulous Genius: Firm on Principle, Flexible in Execution," *Sunday Times*, 19 July 1998; Sharon Chetty, "Paving the Way to Democracy," *Sowetan*, 14 June 2000.

129 For example, special supplement, *The Independent*, 17 July 1998; Ahmed Kathrada, "The Old Man and Me," *The Independent*, weekend review, 18 July 1998.

130 Cited in Nixon, *Homelands*, 183.

131 Ibid., 187. Nixon also points out that in certain senses Mandela draws on an African tradition in recalling a roll of honor praising organizations and groups for their part in the downfall of apartheid. He suggests that its effect as part of the first address in Cape Town was "constructive parochialism, a vital move toward promoting an alternative to the one-nation, one-leader brand of Messianic politics" (184).

132 Ibid., 187.

133 Anthony Sampson, "The Riddle of the Island Which Forged Today's Leaders," *Cape Times*, 23 February 1996.

134 See Sharon Chetty, "Paving the Way to Democracy," *Sowetan*, 14 June 2000, where the author cites Kathrada to this effect.

135 *Cape Times*, 12 June 1996; *Argus*, 19 June 1996.

136 Cited in *City Press*, 12 February 1995. See also Pheko, *Apartheid*.

137 *Sowetan*, 5 January 2000. See also Buntman, "Resistance on Robben Island," 94–97, for a detailed account of the complexities of PAC/ANC politics on the island.

138 Ibid.

139 Ibid.

140 Buntman, "How Best to Resist?"

141 *Sunday Independent*, 20 June 1999.

142 Ahmed Kathrada interview with Mogamad Allie, *Ilifa Labantu* 1 (July 1997), 1. Tensions over heritage issues have erupted elsewhere as well—notably in the case of the statue erected to the memory of Black Consciousness leader Steve Biko in East London in 1997. At the unveiling of the statue AZAPO supporters staged a protest at what they saw as the "highjacking" by the ANC of "their spiritual leader" (*Saturday Star*, 17 September 1997). Mandela used the occasion to appeal to Inkhata, PAC, and AZAPO leaders to work together in the cause of black unity.

143 Cited in *Argus*, 11 February 1995.

144 Cited in Schadeberg, *Voices from the Island*, 25. Mlangeni is a member of the ANC Women's League Committee.

145 Naidoo and Sachs, *Island in Chains*, 114–115.

146 Cited in Robben Island Museum, *Thirty Minutes* (Cape Town: Robben Island Museum, 1997), 20.

147 Interview with Willie Bester, Kuilsrivier, December 2000.

148 Cited in Robben Island Museum, *Thirty Minutes* (Cape Town: Robben Island Museum, 1997), 14.

149 Ibid., 16.

150 *Sowetan*, 13 February 1995.

151 These include Kuzwayo, *Call Me Woman;* Sikakane, *A Window on Soweto;* Makhoere, *No Child's Play;* and Ramphele, *A Life.*

152 Middleton, *Convictions,* 117–118. See also Schalkwyk, "Writing from Prison," and Harlow, *Barred.*

153 Feinberg was director of the Publications and Audio-Visual Department of IDAF while in exile in London from 1975 to 1991. He is also a poet.

154 *Star,* 14 December 1996.

155 Ibid.

156 Department of Arts, Culture, Science and Technology, "The National Legacy Project," describes the initiative as follows: "Shortly after the inauguration of President Mandela on 27 April 1994, DACST and the Office of the President were inundated with requests from diverse sources for official approval for the erection of monuments, museums, statues, commemorations of great leaders and historic events. . . . DACST realized that a coherent policy framework was necessary that would articulate an overall vision and purpose for these requests that would substantially contribute to reconciliation and nation building. . . . Clearly, the variety of requests with their overlaps, different representations and multiple perspectives of our heritage called for a coherent set of principles and criteria to harmonize these many initiatives. These criteria, inter alia, include: affirming cultural diversity, redress of past imbalances in the approval of requests, linking heritage with RDP [Reconstruction and Development Programme] and GEAR [Growth and Employment Policy], ownership through public consultation, organizational and financial aspects of the Legacy Project" (n.d., n.p.).

157 See Lodge, *Black Politics;* Wells, *We Now Demand!;* Joseph, *Tomorrow's Sun,* ch. 3; Baard, *My Spirit Is Not Banned;* and Resha, *Mangoana Tsoara Thipa Ka Bohaleng.* I am grateful to Alicia Monis from the Department of Arts, Culture, Science, and Technology for providing documentation on the 1956 women's march.

158 Becker, "The New Monument."

159 See ibid. I am grateful to Becker and to another judge, Luli Callinicos, for discussion on the monument commission and to Alicia Monis for discussion on the project and for facilitating the visit to the monument.

160 Interview with Luli Callinicos, Johannesburg, December 2000.

161 Ibid.

162 Becker, "The New Monument."

163 Cited in *Citizen,* 18 October 2000.

164 *Findings of the Adjudication Panel for the Competition for the Monument to the Women of South Africa,* n.d., n.p. This was confirmed by Berni Searle, one of the artists involved in running the workshops, who told me in December 2000 that the workshops lacked any follow-up and that the levels of competitors' skills were too varied for the workshops to be effective.

165 Cited in *Sunday Times,* extra, 29 October 2000. See also the case of Dorothey

Molefe, the mother of Hector Petersen, who was reported in the *City Press* as saying that she and the name of her late son had been exploited for twenty-two years by individuals and political organizations to further their own aims. One of her grievances concerned not having been consulted over a project in which her son's portrait was supposed to be incorporated as part of a public mosaic and presented at a special ceremony to Brigitte Mabandla at the Holy Cross Anglican Church in Phefeni Soweto. She was reported as intending to boycott the ceremony, to which she had been invited only at the eleventh hour. She also claimed she had not been informed about another monument erected to Petersen in Soweto the previous year. While all this attention was given to her son, Molefe and her family, who were described as "destitute," had been promised some support but had not received any. Molefe claimed she was not interested in cashing in on her son's death and heroism, but she was fed up with others doing so. *City Press*, 16 August 1998.

166 Cited in *Citizen*, 3 August 2000.

167 See "On the Ground: A Monument by the People for the People," proposal document by Extra Mural Projects, n.p.

168 See "The Presence of the Pass," proposal document, n.p.

169 Interview with Jeremy Wafer, Durban, December 2000.

170 KwaZulu Natal has in fact become the focus of the AIDS pandemic in South Africa since it has the highest proportion of AIDS / HIV infected individuals in the country. Durban has been the most overtly concerned with the secrecy and the stigmatizing of AIDS / HIV sufferers. Dlamini's case has certainly done much to force the issue into the open. It has resulted in some extraordinary public displays (such as the wrapping of a major municipal building with a huge AIDS ribbon by the Durban Art Gallery) and a concerted effort to transform the vilification of AIDS / HIV sufferers into a positive representation. On occasion some unlikely combinations have effectively resituated the status of AIDS / HIV sufferers. In one such instance red AIDS ribbons had been integrated into the promotional campaign for the Miss Durban competition at Durban City Hall in December 2000.

3 DISTRICT SIX: THE ARCHAEOLOGY OF MEMORY

1 These include Neville Alexander, Fakile Bam, and Lionel Davis.

2 Cited in Garth King, "Picking up the Strands of Our Heritage"; District Six Museum Archives, unattributed cutting.

3 Cited in Centre for Intergroup Studies, *Apartheid vs. People*, 11.

4 Ibid.

5 Ibid. For further details on some of the tensions between the City Council and national government with regard to District Six, see Hart, "Political Manipulation," 125.

6 See Department of Arts, Culture, Science and Technology, "Details of Institutions Receiving Financial Assistance under Programme 2" (Pretoria:
   Department of Arts, Culture, Science and Technology, 1999), for details
   of funding allocations to heritage institutions from 1997 to 1999. In an
   interview in Cape Town, December 2000, Sandra Prosalendis reported that
   the District Six Museum received only R 150,000 while Robben Island received R 28 million. The Robben Island figure is confirmed in the DACST
   report.
7 For example, *Weekly Mail and Guardian,* 26 April 1996.
8 Major donors to the museum are the Ford Foundation (United States);
   Joseph Rowntree Charitable Trust (United Kingdom); Pro Helvetia SDC
   (Switzerland); the governments of Norway, Spain, the Netherlands, and
   South Africa; the Swedish International Development Agency (SIDA); and
   USAID.
9 "Iziko, Museums of Cape Town," official brochure (Cape Town, 2000), inside cover.
10 Ibid., front cover.
11 Interview with Sandra Prosalendis, Cape Town, December 2000.
12 Rassool and Prosalendis, eds., *Recalling Community,* 179.
13 Kathrada, "Opening Address," 11.
14 In Rassool and Prosalendis, eds., *Recalling Community,* 82.
15 See Rassool, "Introduction," x, where the author explicitly states that exploring fissures and tensions is one of the aims of the museum.
16 See Nagia, "Land Restitution in District Six," 177. The epigraph at the beginning of this chapter is from this interview.
17 Prosalendis, "District Six," 141.
18 Ibid., 142.
19 See Van Niekerk, *Triomf.* Through the prism of a poor white family living in
   the township of Triomf, Van Niekerk's novel, which won the Noma Award
   for the best book in Africa in any language and was named by the *Weekly
   Mail and Guardian* as the best Afrikaans novel of the decade, is a perceptive analysis of the often disastrous effects of apartheid policy on the very
   constituencies it was intended to benefit.
20 For detailed analyses of the role of the Non-European Unity Movement and
   other organizations in the struggle over District Six, see Soudien, "District
   Six," and Dudley, "Forced Removals."
21 For an analysis of Western Cape politics in relation to "colored" identities,
   see Pickel, *Coloured Ethnicity and Identity.*
22 Steven Robins, "No-Name People Who Kept Cogs of Apartheid Oiled," *Cape
   Times,* 6 August 1997.
23 Ibid.
24 Townsend and Monis, "Report on . . . Charter Workshop." See also Krafchik,
   ed., *The South African Museum,* where Lucien le Grange, one of the trustees

of the District Six Museum, says the following: "If one is talking about negotiating new partnerships, I think we have to be a bit wary of a number of
new phrases such as 'democracy' and 'empowerment.' We need to give substance to these notions if we want to move forward in terms of cultural preservation. Perhaps empowerment does not mean co-option, but must work
through all the levels of administration of museums. The boards should
begin to represent the communities in which museums are situated, and
not only the boards but the various decision-making structures that sit below
them. Communities who are potential users of museums should be actively
involved in deciding and planning projects. All levels of museum work, from
administration to staging public programmes, will require the input of community, cultural and educational institutions, whose knowledge of community needs are vital for museum education in the future" (27).

25   Townsend and Monis, "Report on . . . Charter Workshop," 1.
26   Freud, *Introductory Lectures*, 488.
27   See Tony Morphet, "An Archaeology of Memory," *Weekly Mail and Guard-
     ian,* 30 February 1995. Morphet reviews the opening of the museum's first
     exhibition, "Streets," and suggests that from the balcony, the floor map re-
     sembles "a carefully excavated and labeled archaeological site. The Museum
     creates an archaeology of memory."
28   Delport, "Signposts for Retrieval," 40.
29   Interview with Sandra Prosalendis, Cape Town, December 2000. Soudien,
     "Holding on to the Past," cautions against romanticizing District Six but
     at the same time analyzes the political and social effects of such idealized
     memories as "harmony," "hybridization," and "sharing" in the commemora-
     tion of District Six. See also Rive, "District Six"; after cataloguing the slum
     aspects of the district, Rive goes on to acknowledge, "But what many news-
     papers failed to say, either deliberately or by default, was that District Six
     had a mind and soul of its own. It had a homogeneity that created a sense of
     belonging. It became more than a geographically defined area. It developed
     a separate and unique attitude. It cultivated a sharp, urban inclusivity, the
     type which cockneys have in the East End of London and black Americans
     in Harlem" (112). See also Omar, "The Murder of District Six."
30   Stewart, *On Longing*, 23.
31   Ibid.
32   Battaglia, "On Practical Nostalgia."
33   Ibid., 78.
34   Ibid.
35   Boym, *The Future of Nostalgia*, xvi.
36   Ibid., xviii.
37   For a thorough description and analysis of the project by its curator, see Del-
     port, "Signposts for Retrieval."

38 Prosalendis, "District Six," 137.

39 In the museum's brochure, *The District Six Museum Foundation* (Cape Town: District Six Museum, n.d.), which contains Stan Abrahams's text for a self-guided tour of the district, Abrahams places the date of the plaque as 1971; he says it was laid by the Reverend Peter Storey and that "People were so scared of the Apartheid Government that it was difficult to find someone to make the plaque. Since then the plaque has been defaced twice and pulled off the wall once."

40 Delport, "Signposts for Retrieval," 36. For Delport, what she calls "aesthetic form" is a crucial component of effective memory work and one that she sees as integral to the museum, where "aesthetic form [can be seen] as a vehicle for advancing the perceptive and interpretative capacities of all people, as also their sense of potency in this world" (44).

41 Interview with Sandra Prosalendis, Cape Town, December 2000; interview with Revainer Gwayi, Cape Town, December 2000.

42 Prosalendis, "District Six," 138.

43 Benjamin, "A Berlin Chronicle," in *Reflections*.

44 Ibid., 30.

45 McEachern, "Working with Memory." McEachern, however, presents the museum position as if it were an official hegemonic position, as opposed to the views of the ex-residents. This is a misrepresentation of the governing structure of the museum, the majority of whose board of trustees and foundation members are either former District Six residents or family members, with some academics, museum directors, and others.

46 Abrahams, *The District Six Museum Foundation*.

47 Prosalendis, "District Six," 136.

48 Merseyside Maritime Museum, *Transatlantic Slavery History Trail* (Liverpool: Merseyside Maritime Museum, 1998).

49 Abrahams, *The District Six Museum Foundation*.

50 Ibid.

51 Ibid.

52 Martin Hall, "District Six March"; http//www.districtsix.co.za/archte.htm,6.

53 Meyer, "Introduction" to the catalog of the project, 1.

54 Alexander, "A Homing Pigeon's View," 10.

55 According to Meyer, over seven thousand people attended the opening on Heritage Day ("Introduction," 1).

56 Bedford and Murinik, "Remembering That Place," 22.

57 For a fascinating account of the importance of Carnival for District Six, see Jeppie, "Popular Culture."

58 Bradley, ed., *Rachel Whiteread*.

59 This text is on a plaque at the entrance to *Rod's Room*.

60 Delport, "Digging Deeper in District Six," 154.

61 Ngcelwane, *Sala Kahle, District Six*, 11.

62 Ibid.

63 Ibid., 9.

64 Interview with Sandra Prosalendis, Cape Town, December 2000.

65 Omar, "The Murder of District Six," 194; Dudley, "Forced Removals."

66 Delport, "Digging Deeper in District Six," 159.

67 See Prosalendis, "District Six"; Prosalendis insists that District Six has provided an example for other South African communities that were displaced through the Group Areas Act: "The process of documenting this experience has assisted other affected communities in recalling how they might too fight to win back their dignity and even their land" (141).

68 *Sunday Times*, 27 April 1997.

69 B. Anderson, *Imagined Communities*.

70 *Sunday Times*, 3 December 1995.

71 Ibid.

72 Ibid.

73 Centre for Intergroup Studies, *Apartheid vs. People*, 12.

74 *Cape Times*, metro edition, 25 June 1995.

75 *Cape Times*, metro edition, 3 December 1995.

76 *Financial Mail*, 29 April 1994.

77 Ibid.

78 *Cape Times*, metro edition, 17 July 1994.

79 Ibid.

80 Cited in ibid.

81 See "Land-Locked: A Level-Headed and Realistic Start to the Restitution Process Bodes Well for an Uncertain Journey Ahead," *Finance Week*, 9 March 1995. This was the cover story for the week, and it gave a detailed account of the setting up of the Land Claims Court and the act.

82 Ibid.

83 *Financial Mail*, 4 August 1995.

84 *Weekly Mail and Guardian*, 22 September 1995.

85 Cited in *Weekly Mail and Guardian*, 6 September 1996.

86 Ibid.

87 Ibid.

88 Cited in *Sunday Times*, Cape metro edition, 13 October 1996.

89 Cited in ibid.

90 *Sunday Times*, Cape metro edition, 27 October 1996.

91 Cited in ibid.

92 *Business Day*, 22 July 1997.

93 Ibid.

94 *Argus*, 6 August 1997.

95 "New Tussle Over District Six," *Argus*, 5 August 1997.

96   *Sunday Times,* extra, 1 February 1998; *Argus,* 5 August 1997; *Argus Sunday Insight,* 9 August 1997; *Cape Times,* 6 August 1997.
97   Cited in *Cape Times,* 6 August 1997.
98   Ibid.
99   Cited in ibid.
100   *Business Day,* 23 November 1999.
101   *Star,* 23 November 2000.

4   NEW HISTORIES FOR OLD: MUSEOLOGICAL STRATEGIES

1   Coetzee and Van der Waal, eds., *The Conservation of Culture.*
2   Denver A. Webb, "National Cultural Policy Project Discussion Document: Museums and Monuments," May 1992, 20 (ANC MCF).
3   Schrire, *Adapt or Die.*
4   Coetzee and Van der Waal, eds., *The Conservation of Culture,* 356.
5   Cited in ibid., 92.
6   Tomaselli and Ramgobin, "Culture and Conservation," 106.
7   Ibid., 106–107; their emphasis.
8   Ibid., 114; their emphasis.
9   Ibid., 116.
10   Ibid., 117–119. For the full text of the Freedom Charter, see Mandela, *The Struggle Is My Life,* 50–54.
11   Tomaselli and Ramgobin, "Culture and Conservation," 121.
12   The missionary museum at Genadendal in the Western Cape was cited as a successful instance of community involvement.
13   Webb, "National Monuments in the Ciskei," 326.
14   Ibid., 331.
15   Rassool and Witz, "South Africa," 350.
16   See MacKenzie, *The Empire of Nature;* Beinart and Coates, *Environment and History;* D. Anderson and Grove, eds., *Conservation Policies;* Griffiths and Robin, eds., *Ecology and Empire.*
17   Rassool and Witz, "South Africa," 352.
18   Bunn, "Comparative Barbarism," 38.
19   Carruthers, "Nationhood and National Parks," 128.
20   Ibid., 129.
21   Bunn, "Comparative Barbarism," 39.
22   Carruthers, "Nationhood and National Parks," 126.
23   Ibid., 127.
24   Ranger, " 'Great Spaces Washed with Sun.' " See also Ranger, *Voices from the Rocks.*
25   See also Australian National Parks and Wildlife Service, *Uluru.*
26   Ranger, " 'Great Spaces Washed with Sun,' " 161.

27 Ibid., 162.

28 Ibid., 161.

29 Wilmsen, *Land Filled with Flies;* cited in Ranger, "'Great Spaces Washed with Sun,'" 162.

30 For details of the lease agreement, see Australian National Parks and Wildlife Service, *Uluru,* 6–7. The traditional owners were granted title on 26 October 1985, when Governor General Ninian Stephens presented the title deeds.

31 See Haynes, *Seeking the Centre,* and McGrath, "Travels to a Distant Past."

32 See Rassool and Witz, "South Africa," 338–339, on the dwindling numbers of visitors to South Africa between 1973 and 1986.

33 Ibid., 341. See also Mokaba, *Tourism.*

34 Section 24 of the Bill of Rights in the *Draft Final Constitution of the Republic of South Africa;* cited in Department of Environmental Affairs and Tourism, *An Environmental Policy,* 9.

35 Department of Environmental Affairs and Tourism, *An Environmental Policy,* 14.

36 Ibid., 15.

37 Department of Environmental Affairs and Tourism, *Green Paper on Conservation,* 5.

38 Department of Environmental Affairs and Tourism, *An Environmental Policy,* 16.

39 Department of Environmental Affairs and Tourism, *Green Paper on Conservation,* 5.

40 On the implications of various conventions and agreements on biological diversity for indigenous peoples in Australia, see Fourmile, "Respecting Our Knowledge."

41 Department of Environmental Affairs and Tourism, *Green Paper on Conservation,* 53–54.

42 Ibid., 5.

43 Ibid., 21.

44 African National Congress, *The Reconstruction and Development Programme,* 4; the ANC's summary of the RDP, which was agreed by all parties in parliament in 1994, was: "The RDP is an integrated, coherent socio-economic policy framework. It seeks to mobilise all our people and our country's resources toward the final eradication of apartheid and the building of a democratic, non-racial and non-sexist future" (1). The RDP experienced some delivery problems and was duly criticized for being bureaucratically unwieldy. In 1996 the government shifted its focus to GEAR, designed to encourage economic development and fiscal reform to promote foreign investment, initially with a view to enhancing delivery of the RDP agenda.

45 Küsel et al., "Revitalising the Nation's Heritage," 1.

46 Ibid., 4.

47 Ibid.

48 Ibid., 6.

49 Ibid., 6–7.

50 Ibid., 7.

51 Küsel, "No Building, No Problem," 23.

52 De Jong and Van Coller, "The Development of Tswaing Crater Museum," 2.

53 De Jong, ed., *Museums and the Environment*.

54 De Jong, "The Development of the Pretoria Saltpan," 4.

55 Ibid., 1.

56 De Jong, "The Tswaing Crater Museum," 2.

57 De Jong, "The Development of the Pretoria Saltpan," 6.

58 Ibid., 8.

59 Ibid., 1.

60 De Jong and Van Coller, "The Development of Tswaing Crater Museum," 2.

61 http://www.global.co.za/-nchm/tswmngmt.htm, 2.

62 See Minutes of the Tswaing Forum, 10 September 1994; the eligibility issue for funding the Tswaing Forum itself was discussed (5, 10).

63 African National Congress, *The Reconstruction and Development Programme*, 4–7.

64 Cited in Molobi, "The Star," 17.

65 Horn, "How Many People?," 119.

66 For a useful summary of the growth of Winterveld and the difficulties its legacy presents for cooperation between surrounding communities in the new dispensation, see de Clerq, "Community Participation." Much of my summary of the history of the community is drawn from this article.

67 Ibid.

68 Horn, "How Many People?," 118.

69 De Jong, "The Development of the Pretoria Saltpan," 12.

70 Minutes of the meeting to establish the Tswaing Forum, 9 October 1993, 7.

71 Cited in ibid., 8.

72 Ibid.

73 Ibid., 12.

74 For a detailed history of civic associations, see Swilling, "Civic Associations."

75 Shubane, "Civics."

76 De Jong and Van Coller, "The Development of the Tswaing Crater Museum," 4.

77 De Jong, "The Development of the Pretoria Saltpan," 11.

78 Handwritten document containing suggestions for job creation, community involvement, and human resources development. Some of the suggestions made here are corroborated in the Minutes of the Tswaing Forum Educational Committee, 17 March 1994.

79 Minutes of the Tswaing Executive Committee, 1 March 1994, 4.

80 Ibid.

81 Minutes of the Tswaing Forum, 11 June 1994, 5.

82 Ibid., 6. There is evidence of considerable tension between the official civic associations and the homeless people's associations. Some civic leaders consider the latter an illegitimate form of association that compromises their powers as spokespeople for their communities. See Shubane, "Civics," 37.

83 Minutes of the Tswaing Forum, 15 January 1994, 10.

84 Ibid., 11.

85 Ibid.

86 Ibid.

87 Ibid., 14.

88 Küsel, "People Participate," 65.

89 Ibid.

90 Minutes of the Tswaing Informative [sic] Meeting, 10 February 1994, 1.

91 Ibid.

92 Ibid., 2. At the same meeting another representative suggested that members of the squatters' area should be invited to the planning and educational meeting at Tswaing on 19 February so that they could be properly informed about the project.

93 Interview with Abe Damaneyt, Tswaing, November 1994.

94 *Toyi-toyi* is the term given to the particular form of vocal protest march with raised fists that is practiced in South Africa and that was a feature of any mass political rally.

95 Ibid.

96 Minutes of the Tswaing Forum, 11 June 1994, 11.

97 Ibid., 10 September 1994, 6.

98 Minutes of the Tswaing Planning Committee, 13 July 1994, 2.

99 Van Riet and Van den Berg, *Zoning Proposals*, 14–15.

100 Ibid., 16.

101 Ibid., Plan 11.

102 Küsel, "People Participate," 67.

103 On the early history of the collections, see Nettleton, "Arts and Africana."

104 R. F. Kennedy, "Treasures and Trash: A History of the Africana Museum" (typescript, n. d.); cited in Nettleton, "Arts and Africana," 70.

105 Bruce and Saks, "Frankly Speaking."

106 Nettleton, "Arts and Africana," 67.

107 Van Tonder, "From Mausoleum to Museum," 7.

108 "Networking Brief," no name; Museum Africa, n. d.

109 Ben-Guri, "Shaping the Museum," 1.

110 Ibid., 4.

111 Ibid., 6. Ben-Guri says that 283 individuals completed the survey. See "Networking Brief," no name; Museum Africa, n. d., 3, for the list of history topics.

112 Ben-Guri, "Shaping the Museum," 1.

113 Ibid., 7.

114 Integrated Marketing Research, "Africana Museum," 6 and 9.

115 Ibid., 16.

116 Ibid., 71.

117 Ben-Guri, "Shaping the Museum," 1.

118 Ben-Guri, "Progress Report," 1. The museum team was comprised of Ronit Ben-Guri, Ann Wanless, Maria Burger, and Nadia Cohen.

119 Ibid.

120 "Proposal for a Community Education Project," no name; Africana Museum, March 1994.

121 Unfortunately the poster project was not completed in time for the opening of the museum.

122 Minutes of meeting between museum staff and Luli Callinicos; Museum Africa, 16 April 1991.

123 Bruce and Saks, "Frankly Speaking," 240–241.

124 See Sharp, "Roots and Development."

125 Goodwin, "A New Direction," 5.

126 Thornton, "Culture," 25.

127 Goodwin, "A Hall of Cultural History."

128 Ibid.

129 Ibid.

130 Saks, "Motivations," 1.

131 Ibid., 2. Ben-Guri, Kathy Brookes, Saks, and Goodwin agreed in a meeting (31 October 1991) to the chronological / culture divide on the basis of logistics.

132 Management Committee, Culture and Recreation Committee, Culture and Recreation Directorate, Libraries and Museums Department, "New Africana Museum Project—Newtown: Relocation, Interiors, Display Furniture and Opening Exhibition," unpublished document, Museum Africa, n. d., 4.

133 De Wet, "Thokoza Squatters' Shack," 97.

134 Ibid.

135 "Transformations in Johannesburg, the Home, Section Three, Thokoza," unpublished design brief, Museum Africa, n. d.

136 Cited in *Citizen*, 18 October 1999.

137 "Transformations in Johannesburg, the Home, Section Three, Alexandra," unpublished design brief, Museum Africa, n. d.

138 Cited in ibid.

139 Ibid.

140 Ibid.

141 Ibid.

142 Ibid.

143 Ibid.

144 Ibid.

145 Cited in Louise Marsland, "Saving Shack Life for Posterity," *Star*, 30 July 1994.

146 Ivor Powell, "Something New, Something Old," *Weekly Mail and Guardian*, 12 August 1994.

147 Ibid.

148 Elliot Makhaya, "Africana Museum Goes Ethnic," *Sowetan*, 11 May 1994; Judith Matloff, "Getting a Wider View of History," *Pretoria News*, 19 September 1994.

149 Cited in Louise Marsland, "Saving Shacks Life for Posterity," *Saturday Star*, 30 July 1994.

150 Cited in Mapula Sibanda, "Welcome to Our Humble Home . . . Step Inside — and Take a Trip Back in Time," *City Press*, 30 March 1997.

151 Cited in *Sunday Times*, section 2, 1996 (undated cutting, Times Media library).

152 Ibid. Sandton is a wealthy middle-class suburb of Johannesburg.

153 Interview with Sam Nyambose, Johannesburg, December 2000.

154 Cited in Louise Marsland, "Saving Shack Life for Posterity."

155 See Dhlomo, "Zwelethu Mthethwa," where Mthethwa says, "My objective is to present clear messages to both the initiated and the uninitiated in society. . . . My aim is to be heard, seen and understood by the person I photograph in Paarl, Cape Town, as well as the viewer in Madrid, Spain" (70, 74).

156 Cited in ibid., 75. See also Bester, "Interview with Zwelethu Mthethwa."

157 Published in book form as Younge, ed., *Picture Cape Town*.

158 Taylor, "The Moment Between," 7.

159 Ibid.

160 Deon van Tonder, "The Sounds of the City: Township Jazz and the Sounds of Defiance," unpublished exhibition script, Museum Africa, n. d., 1.

161 The only other museum display that treated labor relations with any degree of complexity and seriousness was the local history museum, KwaMuhle in Durban, which had an important display explaining what became known as the "Durban System."

162 Berning and Dominy, "The Presentation," 6.

163 Kros, "Experiencing a Century," 28.

164 Ibid., 29.

165 Mark Gevisser, "Some Miner Changes to Gold's History," *Weekly Mail and Guardian*, 8–15 April 1993; cited in Kros, "Experiencing a Century," 41.

166 Kros, "Experiencing a Century," 34.

167 Berning and Dominy, "The Presentation," 7.

168 Rassool and Witz, "South Africa," 343.

169 Ibid.

170 Berning and Dominy, "The Presentation," 8.

171 Ibid.

172 Ann Wanless, "Work," unpublished design brief, Museum Africa, 10 December 1993.

173 Interview with Martha Paya, Johannesburg, December 2000.

174 Ibid.

175 Ann Wanless, "Work," unpublished design brief, Museum Africa, 10 December 1993.

176 Cited in *Citizen*, 24 April 1995. See also Callinicos: *Gold and Workers, Working Life*, and *A Place in the City*.

177 Cited in *Citizen*, 24 April 1995.

178 Cited in *Sowetan*, 25 January 1995.

179 Ibid.

180 Ibid.

181 Interview with Luli Callinicos, Johannesburg, December 2000.

182 Cited in Thami Tshabalala, "Workers' Museum That Preserves Vital History of Brutality Faces Cash Crunch," *Sunday Independent*, 29 August 1999.

183 Ward and Worden, "Commemorating, Suppressing."

184 See Cornell, "Whatever Became of Cape Slavery?" which looks at such absences and suggests what could be done to address these in four such museums: Bo Kaap, Groot Constantia, the South African Cultural History Museum, and the Vergelegen wine estate in Somerset West, a suburb of Cape Town.

185 Ward and Worden, "Commemorating, Suppressing," 204.

186 Ibid., 209.

187 See ibid., where the authors cite Mbeki's "I Am an African" speech in 1996; he singles out Malay slaves exclusively, thereby, they argue, excluding all other slave descendants (215).

188 *Slave Route Project Newsletter*, no. 1 (July 1998): 1.

189 *Slave Route Project Newsletter*, no. 3 (September 1998): 1.

190 *Slave Route Project Newsletter*, no. 2 (August 1998): 3.

191 The other project director is Shareen Parker, and research assistants are Najma Mohame and Gwyneth Albertyn.

192 Farieda Khan, "Reclaiming Our Past: The Elim Slave Route Pilot Project," *Slave Route Project Newsletter*, no. 2 (August 1998): 3.

193 Helene Vollgraaff and Sue Newton-King, "The Dutch East India Company's Slave Lodge," *Slave Route Project Newsletter*, no. 3 (September 1998): 1–3.

194 *Slave Route Project Newsletter*, no. 3 (September 1998): 8. The fact that an entrepreneurial venture such as Living History Productions existed at the time is indicative of the optimistic sense that South Africa was on the verge of a "heritage industry."

195 Farieda Khan, "Commemorating the Emancipation Centenary in the Western Cape," *Slave Route Project Newsletter*, no. 4 (November 1998): 2–7; Nigel

Worden, "Controversies over Commemorating Emancipation in Jamaica and Mauritius," ibid., 6 and 8.

196 Interview with Nigel Worden, Cape Town, December 2000.

197 Ibid.

198 Ibid. Worden spoke of Wally Serota's response in 1995 to some of the research proposals made in connection with the UNESCO Slave Route Project. Worden felt that because his proposed project was concerned to particularize and historicize the practice and experience of slavery (in this case with specific reference to its manifestations in the Western Cape), Serote saw it as raising too many historical divisions that might have repercussions for a contemporary politics of national unity.

199 Worden, "The Forgotten Region," 4.

200 Ibid., 5.

5 WHAT'S IN A NAME? THE PLACE OF "ETHNICITY" IN THE "NEW" SOUTH AFRICA

1 The epigraph above is from one of the Khoisan representatives at the opening of the "Miscast" exhibition at the South African National Gallery, 13 April 1996 (discussed below); from the video of the proceedings made by Jon Weinberg, head of exhibitions at the gallery. I am grateful to Pippa Skotnes for supplying me with a copy.

2 For a series of essays dealing with the challenges of creating national museums in Australia, Canada, and New Zealand, see McIntyre and Wehner, eds., *National Museums*.

3 For other useful works that address such questions, see Bennett, ed., *Multicultural States;* Appadurai, "Disjuncture"; and Beckett, "Contested Images."

4 See Beckett, "Contested Images," for a particularly clear exposition of the multiple ways the term has been appropriated in various national contexts. See also Wilmsen and McAllister, eds., *The Politics of Difference*. Thanks to Henrietta Moore for bringing the latter to my attention.

5 For a useful collection dealing with the implications for the Aboriginal peoples of Australia of the Mabo judgment (1992) in Queensland and the subsequent Native Title Act (1993) and National Native Title Tribunal, see Cowlishaw and Kondos, eds., *Mabo and Australia*.

6 For an outline of this policy, see Manne, "The Stolen Generations."

7 A number of journals devoted special issues to debunking the celebrations; see, for example, Janson and Macintyre, eds. *Making the Bicentenary*, and *The Wake of Utopia*, special issue, *Third Text* 21 (1992–1993).

8 For a summary of the debate over the "naming" of different groups of hunter-gatherers in southern Africa, see Wilmsen, *Land Filled with Flies*, esp. 24–32. See also Robins, "Land Struggles."

9   For a thoughtful argument elaborating the ambivalences of such appropria-
    tions for Native Americans, see Durham, "Cowboys and. . . ."
10 See Legassick and Rassool, *Skeletons in the Cupboard;* Fauvelle-Aymer, "Des
    Murs d'Augsbourg"; and Morris, "Trophy Skulls."
11 Morris, "Trophy Skulls," 73.
12 See, for example, Coombes, *Reinventing Africa;* Rydell, *All the World's a Fair;*
    Schneider, *An Empire for the Masses;* and Lindfors, ed., *Africans on Stage.*
13 Dell, "Museums."
14 See Gordon, "'Bains' Bushmen.'"
15 Dubow, *Scientific Racism* 25 n. 13.
16 See Witz, "Commemorations and Conflicts," 268–269.
17 Witz, "Commemorations and Conflicts," 275, citing Central Archive Depot,
    Pretoria, *Memorandum on Native Affairs Exhibit at Jan van Riebeeck Festival
    Fair,* NTS 9787 987/400 (2 November 1951), Part 1.
18 Sharp, "Roots and Development," 19; cited in Witz, "Commemorations and
    Conflicts," 291.
19 Witz, "Commemorations and Conflicts," 296.
20 Ibid. Witz is citing *Die Huisgenoot,* 21 March 1952.
21 Witz, "Commemorations and Conflicts," 298.
22 Ibid. See also Gould, *The Flamingo's Smile,* 293. Gould's ch. 19 is an essay on
    Saartjie Baartman and points to another forgotten moment of retort from a
    subject assumed to be mute: Baartman, interrogated in a court case, demon-
    strates her competence in no less than three languages—her own, French,
    and Dutch.
23 See Dubow, *Scientific Racism,* chs. 2 and 3, for an account of the ways in
    which the origins of Bushmen were debated in academic circles in South
    Africa.
24 Rousseau, "The Great Trek," 89.
25 Ibid., 49.
26 Davison, "Material Culture," 104. See also Coombes, *Reinventing Africa.*
27 South African Museum, *Annual Report to the Trustees* (1856); cited in Davi-
    son, "Material Culture," 104.
28 Guenther, "From 'Brutal Savages.'"
29 Gould, *The Flamingo's Smile,* 294.
30 See Guenther, "From 'Brutal Savages.'"
31 Davison, "Material Culture," 105.
32 Dubow, *Scientific Racism,* 114.
33 Ibid.
34 Davison, "Human Subjects," 168. See also Von Luschan to W. L. Gelater,
    20 December 1906, where he writes of the Bushman cast he has sent to the
    SAM. His letter makes it clear that he considers the extinction of the Bush-
    men to be inevitable. SAM Archives.

35 Cited in Davison, "Human Subjects," 168.

36 Ibid.

37 Ibid.

38 There are numerous instances in the Drury papers where it is clear that casting had to stop because the individual could not bear the process. See, for example, SAM Archives, Physical Anthropology File: Bushman File, Correspondence A-H, Drury Papers (Folder F 1), Description of Bushmen from Kalahari District Mokgalagadi: "Jan Bookpens, Bushman, sentenced at Upington, on 27 October 1903, to detention in the Reformatory, for theft of stock." In the margin in pencil is marked, "Was unfortunately unable to stand the modelling." In the same file, for an individual identified as Klass Zepot: "Bush boy also from Upington [Reformatory] from Kalahari natives of a low type. The boy could not stand the modelling." See also Urry, "'Notes,'" and Coombes, *Reinventing Africa,* ch. 7.

39 Gilman, "Black Bodies, White Bodies"; Gould, *The Flamingo's Smile.*

40 Cited in Davison, "Human Subjects," 173.

41 Ibid., 169.

42 Drury and Drennan; cited in Skotnes, "The Politics of Bushman Representations."

43 Davison, "Human Subjects," 171.

44 Ibid., 174.

45 Cited in ibid., 179.

46 Davison, "Material Culture," 157 n. 27.

47 Ibid., 180.

48 Ibid., 158.

49 Cited in ibid., 159.

50 For a record of some visitors' reactions to the SAM and in particular their responses to the diorama, see ibid., 162.

51 *Cape Times,* 26 January 1960. This cartoon is reproduced in Davison, "Material Culture," where it is used to make the point that although the museum was *technically* not segregated by this date, the general perception of it was as a segregated institution. Davison gives no other commentary on the cartoon and does not locate it in the political context that gives it much of its power.

52 *Cape Times,* 9 December 1993.

53 Ritchie, "Dig the Herders"; cited in Davison, "Material Culture," 160 n. 30. My thanks to Lindsay Hooper, collections manager at SAM, for suggesting the shop where I might find these postcards.

54 Davison, "Material Culture," 163.

55 Cited in ibid.

56 Ibid., 164.

57 Ibid., 184.

58 Ibid., 191.

59 Skotnes, "The Politics of Bushmen Representations," 2 of unpublished manuscript.

60 Ibid.

61 Cited in Krafchik, ed., *The South African Museum*, 21.

62 Cited in Adams, "Postcard from Cape Town."

63 Coombes, "Inventing the 'Post-Colonial.'"

64 Cited in Davison, "Material Culture," 191.

65 Ibid., 193.

66 Ibid.

67 Ibid.

68 Greg Dening, *Mr. Bligh's Bad Language*, 178.

69 See in particular Dowson and Lewis-Williams, "Myths."

70 Weinberg, "Footprints in the Sand." See Bester and Buntman, "Bushman(ia)," for a review of Weinberg's photographs that acknowledges them as an important attempt to debunk the myth of a timeless people but ultimately sees them as failing to deal with the complex and asymmetrical power relations involved in taking photographs under such conditions.

71 Skotnes, "The Politics of Bushman Representation," 14–15 of unpublished manuscript.

72 *Sunday Independent*, 26 May 1996. See also Robins's critique of "Miscast," "Silence in My Father's House."

73 Cited in *Sunday Independent*, 26 May 1996.

74 Cited in Rehana Roussouw, "Setting History Straight—Or Another Chance to Gape?" *Weekly Mail and Guardian*, 19–25 April 1996.

75 Lane, "Breaking the Mould?," 7.

76 Video footage of Khoisan Forum, South African National Gallery, Cape Town, 13 April 1996.

77 Cited in *Weekly Mail and Guardian*, 15 December 1995.

78 Cited in *Weekly Mail and Guardian*, 2 February 1996.

79 Cited in *Weekly Mail and Guardian*, 16 February 1996.

80 Ibid.

81 *Weekly Mail and Guardian*, 3 May 1996 (reported speech nonattributed). In 1998 the case for the return of Baartman's remains received more publicity when the South African filmmaker Zola Maseko's film, *The Life and Times of Sara Baartman*, won a prize at the Ouagadougou film festival and was shown on South African television in October 1998 to much acclaim and attention in the national media. In January 1999 the World Archaeological Congress, held in Cape Town, also publicized the campaign to have Baartman's remains returned. By October 2000 another highly publicized campaign to return the remains of the San warrior known as "El Negro" from Spain had been successful.

82 Cited in *City Press*, 5 May 1996.

83 Cited in *Sowetan*, 3 May 1996.

84 See Robins, "Land Struggles." Robins argues that tourist myths have sometimes served the San well, both economically and in terms of getting publicity for their land claims, and that the San have often knowingly promoted an image of themselves that has on occasion exploited an ethnographic present and an ethnic essentialism to good effect.

85 Sara [Saartjie] Baartman's human remains were finally returned to South Africa in 2002, to be buried in her homeland in the Eastern Cape.

6 NEW SUBJECTIVITIES FOR THE NEW NATION

1 Opening address, HRVC Hearing, East London; as reported on SABC 2 TV, 15 April 1996; my emphasis. See also "The Mandate," in *Truth and Reconciliation Commission of South Africa Report*, 1:48–102.

2 For comparative views on the validity of truth commissions and war tribunals in South Africa and Chile, Argentina, El Salvador, Uruguay, and Eastern and Central Europe, see Boraine, Levy, and Scheffer, eds., *Dealing with the Past*; Boraine and Levy, eds., *The Healing of a Nation?* For more critical accounts of the effects of such commissions, see *Wounded Nations, Broken Lives*.

3 The 1986–1994 Ugandan commission of inquiry into violations of human rights held public victim hearings, but these were considerably fewer in number than in South Africa. See *Index on Censorship* 5 (1996): 148–150 for a list of truth commissions and war tribunals held internationally between 1971 and 1996.

4 See Desmond Tutu, "Foreword," in *Truth and Reconciliation Commission of South Africa Report*; Tutu singles out the South African media for special thanks and explains the reason for welcoming their participation: "We are particularly grateful for the work of SABC (South African Broadcasting Corporation) radio, which communicated in all our official languages to ensure that even the illiterate did not miss out. We want to mention, too, the special television programme that was broadcast on Sunday evenings—giving a summary of the previous week's events at the Commission and a preview of the coming week's events. No wonder these television and radio programmes won prestigious awards—on which we congratulate them. The media helped to ensure that the Commission's process was as inclusive and as non-elitist as possible" (1:19–20).

5 For developments of this criticism, see Parry, "Reconciliation and Remembrance"; Harris: "Confessing the Truth," and "'Unearthing' the 'Essential' Past"; James and Van de Vijver, eds., *After the TRC*.

6 For work that does address the complexities of such hybridity, see Brah and Coombes, eds., *Hybridity and Its Discontents*; Lazarus, *Nationalism*; Thomas,

Entangled Objects; Philips, *Trading Identities;* Parry, "Resistance Theory"; Coombes, "The Distance between Two Points."

7   Three exhibitions dealing with international feminist art practice, held in 1980 at London's Institute of Contemporary Art, were instrumental in bringing such issues onto the agenda in the art establishment. Two dealt specifically with installation and performance as feminist strategy: "About Time, Video, Performance and Installation by 21 Women Artists" and "Issue: Social Strategies by Women Artists." For a more recent analysis of the relationship between feminism and performance, see Phelan, *Unmarked,* and de Zegher, ed., *Inside the Visible.*

8   The case of Steve Biko was, of course, one of the most notorious instances of such denial. See Woods, *Biko,* esp. ch. 5, which contains transcripts of some of the inquest proceedings.

9   The exhibition was part of the Cape Town One City Festival in 1999.

10 Berni Searle, "Proposal Document for *Traces,*" produced for the exhibition "Towards—Transit: New Visual Languages in South Africa" (Zurich: Die Blaue Saal, 1999), 4 n.2.

11 Ibid., 4.

12 Personal correspondence from Berni Searle, 10 May 2001.

13 See Gordon, " 'Bains' Bushmen.' " See also Dubow, *Scientific Racism.*

14 On the complex history of Khoisan displacement and criminalization at the hands of successive colonial and apartheid regimes, see chapter 5 above and Wilmsen, *Land Filled with Flies;* Deacon and Dowson, eds., *Voices from the Past;* and Legassick and Rassool, *Skeletons in the Cupboard.*

15 Cited in Botha, ed., *Bloedlyn,* 10.

16 See Freud, "The Uncanny," where Freud writes: "The 'double' was originally an insurance against destruction to the ego, an 'energetic denial of the power of death,' as Rank says: and probably the 'immortal' soul was the first 'double' of the body. This invention of doubling as a preservation against extinction has its counterpart in the language of dreams, which is fond of representing castration by a doubling or multiplication of the genital symbol . . . and when this stage has been left behind the double takes on a different aspect. From having been an assurance of immortality, it becomes the ghastly harbinger of death." See also Barthes, *Camera Lucida,* 96, where Barthes discusses the way in which the photographic process necessarily produces a double of the body and consequently could be said to signal death and mortality by figuring absence or loss.

17 See Coombes, "Skin Deep."

18 Thanks to Penny Siopis for bringing my attention to this film and to Jacqueline Maingard for discussion and a copy of the film.

19 Meintjes, "Women's Consciousness," 3.

20 See Ardener, "Sexual Insult," and Ifeka-Moller, "Female Militancy."

21 Cited in Bester, interview with Tracey Rose, 92.

22 Richards, "Graft." Richards's definition of "graft" is useful here: "In cutting into and across 'difference,' 'Graft' enjoins the discourse of 'hybridity' without disavowing the violence and the desire which underpins cultural fusion. 'Graft' marks tensions between metaphors of nature and culture, and the way cultural discourse (dis)articulates these tensions. . . . 'Graft' is about disfigurations, cultural error, the sometimes violent aesthetic of the imperfect fit, the parasitic in the symbiotic" (234–235).

23 See Chinzima, "Point of No Return," where Tracey Rose says that *Span II* "is a tribute to women who were put on display like Saartjie Baartman" (89).

24 Interview with Tracey Rose, Johannesburg, August 1999. See also Lundstrom and Pierre, eds., *Democracy's Image*, 93.

25 Atkinson and Breitz, eds., 89.

26 Cited in Bester, "Interview with Tracey Rose," 93.

27 Ibid., 92.

28 Interview with Tracey Rose, Johannesburg, August 1999.

29 Cited in Bester, "Interview with Senzeni Marasela," 119.

30 Ibid., 118.

31 Ibid.

32 Interview with Clive van den Berg, Johannesburg, August 1999.

33 Van den Berg, "Memorials without Facts," 13.

34 Ibid.

35 The new South African constitution was drafted in 1993 but ratified only in 1996. An interim Bill of Rights was adopted in 1994, but Section 20A of the Sexual Offences Act, relating to gay male sex, was eliminated only in 1998. There was no mention of lesbians except with reference to unnatural sexual acts.

36 Interview with Jean Brundrit, Cape Town, August 1999.

37 See Bester, "Interview with Jean Brundrit," 101.

38 Christene vir die Waarheid to Mevrou Swart, 21 July 1997. See also Lundstrom and Pierre, eds., *Democracy's Image*, 100.

39 *Cape Times,* 17 February 1999.

40 *Cape Times,* 18, 22, and 24 February 1999. See also Gevisser and Cameron, eds., *Defiant Desire,* for an important critical and historically informed collection dealing with gay and lesbian experience in South Africa.

41 Published as Coombes, "Gender, 'Race,' Ethnicity." For an insightful account of other work by Siopis, see Law, "Penny Siopis: The Story Teller."

42 Ibid., 115.

43 Ibid., 117.

44 Ibid.

1 See Mace, *Trafalgar Square.*
2 South Africa House Archives, Box 1/101/36, "Murals, Paintings, Pictures," Folder 1/101/36, vol. 4, *Journal of Decorative Art,* 21 June 1934, regarding forthcoming feature in July issue. G. W. Klerck to J. S. Cleland, 21 July 1934, regarding said article, declared that "This will serve to show the interest taken in London in these specimens of South African Art." Cleland was chief architect at the Public Works Department, Pretoria. See also *Fortune* (New York), 21 November 1934, requesting photos of the murals and art for a possible feature and referring to article on South Africa House in the October issue of the British-based art and design journal *Studio.* Despite the fact that not all the commissions were completed by 1934, Te Water was able to write in glowing terms to Mr. Cleland that "the building continues to be a centre of very great interest—hundreds of people passing through every week." South Africa House archive, Box 1/101/8, "Special Decorations," Folder 1/101/8, vol. 2, Te Water to Cleland, 6 February 1934.
3 "South Africa House: A Short Description," mimeographed, n. d., 16.
4 South Africa House Archives, Box 1/101/36, "Murals, Paintings, Pictures," Folder 1/101/36, vol. 4, A. Wheaton and Co., Ltd., Educational Publishers and Contractors to Schools, Exeter, to Mr. McDonald, Publicity Department, South Africa House, 16 August 1934, requesting photographs of the murals in the High Commission building for a forthcoming book on the history of South Africa being prepared by a South African author. See also South Africa House Archives, Box 1/101/36/36, Annex/36A/36/1/37, Folder 1/101/36, vol. 6, Maskew Miller Ltd., Adderley Street, Cape Town, to Klerck, 9 July 1936, requesting colored reproduction of Jan Juta's mural of Van Riebeeck for teaching texts for "English Readers for the Standards."
5 South Africa House Archives, "Special Decorations," Folder 1/101/8, vol. 1, Minutes of Meeting to Discuss Arrangements for Services to the New Building, Held at South Africa House, 27 May 1930. Those present were the high commissioner, C. T. Te Water; secretary to the high commissioner, J. G. Hubball; secretary for public works, O. E. Staten, and J. S. Cleland.
6 Ibid.
7 South Africa House Archives, Permanent HCO, "Special Decorations 1930–1934," Folder 1/101/8, vol. 1, Baker to Mr. Klerck, 26 October 1931 and 9 November 1931; vol. 2, Baker to Te Water, 25 August 1932.
8 South Africa House, "Wall Paintings on the Fourth Floor of South Africa House: A Short Description," pamphlet, n. d., n. p.
9 See Hamilton, *Terrific Majesty.*
10 On the rise in Zulu ethnic nationalism over this period, see Marks, "Patriotism, Patriarchy and Purity." The Zulu cultural organization, Inkatha, was formed in 1922–1923 and revived in 1928.

11 Hamilton, *Terrific Majesty,* 161.

12 See Coombes, *Reinventing Africa,* esp. ch. 5; Lindfors, "Charles Dickens and the Zulus"; Erlmann, " 'Spectatorial Lust.' "

13 Hamilton, *Terrific Majesty,* 161 and 168.

14 South Africa House Archives, Permanent HCO, "Special Decorations 1930–1934," Folder 1/101/8, vol. 1, handwritten memo dated 20 March 1933, suggesting that a letter was written to Baker about this issue.

15 "South Africa House: A Short Description," mimeographed, n. d., 16.

16 Ibid., 24, describes the frieze around the cinema thus: "The escutcheons incorporated in the frieze are representative of the various races that have been concerned with the history of the Union of South Africa—the Navigators' Cross and Wheels to represent the early Portuguese navigators; the ship *Goede Hoop* that carried Van Riebeeck to the Cape; the assegai, shield and native huts of the Native Races; the Royal Lion of Holland and the monogram of the Dutch East India Company; the Lions of England; the Land Quest Symbol and the Fleur de Lys and Bible to represent the Huguenots."

17 See *Die Burger,* 6, 7, 9, and 10 June 1934.

18 See South African House Archives, Box 1/101/36, "Murals, Paintings, Pictures," Folder 1/101/36, vol. 4, J. A. Smith to J. S. Cleland, 11 June 1934. Smith, the art editor of *Die Burger,* took the precaution of sending copies of the relevant articles on the controversy to Cleland, who was Te Water's main correspondent and collaborator at the South African end. His letter pointedly begins by drawing attention to Cleland's linguistic deficiency (as an English speaker) and therefore his assumed political leanings (as someone of English as opposed to Afrikaner origin); he suggests that Cleland would need to employ "somebody to translate [the copies] very carefully for you." Furthermore, Smith sympathizes with the criticisms of Juta's work as being "based on historical and religious-sentimental grounds, which to my mind are quite justified." He continues: "The Dutch and in particular people belonging to the Dutch Reformed Churches and other Protestant churches, I am afraid, will not be satisfied with anything less than the removal of a picture representing Van Riebeek [*sic*], as it seems to do, as a Catholic praying under a cross. Van Riebeek landed just after the bitter religious strife between Catholic and Protestants in Europe and founded a colony to whom he and his Government invited the Hugenots [*sic*] as a refuge. You will thus appreciate the grounds for the strong protests against Juta's wrong interpretation." Cleland was ruffled enough to have cabled Te Water at the onset of the criticisms and followed up with copies of Smith's letter and the articles from *Die Burger.* (See South Africa House Archives, Box 1/101/36, "Murals, Paintings, Pictures," Folder 1/101/36, vol. 4, J. S. Cleland to Te Water, 18 June 1934.) In frustration, Te Water cabled a staccato defense of the artist: "Panels not intended as photographs of events, but artistic interpretation thereof. Original cartoons approved by architect and

myself and much admired by Minister of the Netherlands. We [Te Water] had full knowledge of licence taken. Cannot believe critics do not know licence permissable [sic] mural rendering historic events, used by all masters of this art." (See South Africa House Archives, Box 1/101/36, "Murals, Paintings, Pictures," Folder 1/101/36, vol. 4, Te Water to Cleland, annotated cablegram, 14 June 1934.) This was followed by an even more exasperated letter from Te Water to Cleland ending, "God in Heaven! Cannot we have art for art's sake? Over my dead body, my dear Cleland, and yours, I hope, before bowing to the iconoclasts. I tell Juta that he is in the happy position of being notorious now instead of famous. Really the next best thing for an artist." (See South Africa House Archives, Box 1/101/36, "Murals, Paintings, Pictures," Folder 1/101/36, vol. 4, Te Water to Cleland. It seems that the offending panel was removed. In Box 1/101/36/36, Annex/36A/36/1/37, Folder 1/101/36, vol. 6, Klerck to Miller, 28 August 1936, notes that "Owing to certain criticisms from religious bodies," the panel is now in the South African National Gallery in Cape Town.) One of the other major South African artists of the period who had benefited from large commissions for South Africa House, J. H. Pierneef, was quoted as having maligned Juta's Voortrekker and Van Riebeeck panels as "horrible monstrosities" (cited in *Sunday Times*, n. d.; cutting in South Africa House Archives, Box 1/101/36, "Murals, Paintings, Pictures," Folder 1/101/36, vol. 4). Pierneef reputedly addressed his remarks to a gathering of the Suidafrikaanse Akademie van Taal, Lettere en Juns (South African Academy of Language, Literature, and Art) in Bloemfontein on 20 October and was instrumental in promoting a proposal that "the Academy decides to direct attention to the panels and statues at South Africa House as they are not fair towards the Dutch seeing the part played by them in the founding of the white settlement in South Africa" (cited in *Pretoria News*, n. d.; cutting in South Africa House Archives, Box 1/101/36, "Murals, Paintings, Pictures," Folder 1/101/36, vol. 4). The art historian and specialist on the work of Pierneef, Nico Coetzee, in a personal communication to me (20 November 2000) reported Pierneef's antagonism to Juta as motivated by artistic competition as well as Pierneef's known antagonism to Jews. In a controversy that erupted over another Juta commission, in Pretoria City Hall, slurs were cast on Juta's reputation on the basis of his putative Jewishness.

19 South Africa House Archives, Box 1/101/36 "Murals, Paintings, Pictures," Folder 1/101/36, vol. 4; *Sunday Times* cutting, n. d.

20 South Africa House Archives, Box Permanent HCO, "Special Decorations 1930–1934," 1/101/8, vol. 1, Baker to Te Water, 3 and 11 November 1932.

21 De Smidt, "Rationale," 1.

22 Ibid., 3.

23 Ibid.

24 Senzeni Marasela, "Proposal for South Africa House" (2001), 2.

25 Ibid., 1.

26 Berni Searle, "Proposal for South Africa House" (2001), 1.

27 Ibid.

28 Ibid.

29 Ibid.

30 Sue Williamson, "Proposal for South Africa House" (2002), 1.

31 Ibid.

BIBLIOGRAPHY

ARCHIVAL SOURCES

ANC Museum Commission Files. Mayibuye Centre, University of the Western Cape.

National Cultural History Museum, Pretoria. Documents relating to the development of the Tswaing Crater Museum.

Museum Africa, Johannesburg. Papers relating to the development of Museum Africa.

South Africa House, Trafalgar Square, London. Permanent HCO, Special Decoration 1930–1934.

SAM (South African Museum, Cape Town). Correspondence and Papers relating to James Drury. Papers relating to the "Esiqithini" exhibition.

PERIODICALS

(published in South Africa unless otherwise indicated)

Die Beeld	*The Observer* (London)
Business Day	*Patriot*
Cape Argus	*Pretoria News*
Cape Times	*Rapport*
The Citizen	*Saturday Star*
City Press	*Slave Route Project Newsletter*
Die Burger	*South African Museums*
Evening News	*Association Bulletin*
Finance Week	*Sowetan*
Financial Mail	*Sunday Independent*
Fortune (New York)	*Sunday Times*
The Guardian (London)	*Sunday Times* (London)
In Focus	*Star*
Learn and Teach	*The Times* (London)
Loslyf	*Weekly Mail and Guardian*

PUBLISHED SOURCES

Abrahams, Stan. *The District Six Museum Foundation.* Cape Town: District Six Museum, n.d.

Adams, Gene. "Postcard from Cape Town." *Museums Journal,* April 1994: 22.

African National Congress. *The Reconstruction and Development Programme.* Johannesburg: Umanyano Publications, 1994.

Alexander, Neville. "A Homing Pigeon's View of Forced Removals." In Soudien and Meyer, eds., *The District Six Public Sculpture Project,* 10.

———. *An Ordinary Country: Issues in the Transition from Apartheid to Democracy in South Africa.* Pietermaritzburg: University of Natal Press, 2002.

———. *Robben Island Dossier, 1964–1974.* Cape Town: University of Cape Town Press, 1994.

Alexander, P. F., R. Hutchinson, and D. Schreuder, eds. *Africa Today.* Canberra: Australian National University, 1996.

Anderson, Benedict. *Imagined Communities: Reflections on the Origins and Spread of Nationalism.* London: Verso, 1983.

Anderson, David, and Richard Grove, eds. *Conservation Policies in Africa: Peoples, Policies and Practice.* Cambridge: Cambridge University Press, 1987.

Antze, Paul, and Michael Lambek, eds. *Tense Past: Cultural Essays in Trauma and Memory.* London: Routledge, 1996.

Appadurai, Arjun. "Disjuncture and Difference in the Global Cultural Economy." *Public Culture* 2 (1990): 1–24.

Ardener, Shirley. "Sexual Insult and Female Militancy." In Ardener, ed., *Perceiving Women,* 29–55.

———, ed. *Perceiving Women.* London: Dent and Sons, 1975.

Atkinson, Brenda, and Candice Breitz, eds. *Grey Areas: Representation, Identity and Politics in Contemporary South African Art.* Johannesburg: Chalkham Hill Press, 1999.

Australian National Parks and Wildlife Service, Uluru-Kata Tjuta Board of Management. *Uluru (Ayers Rock-Mount Olga) National Park: Plan of Management.* Canberra: Australian National Parks and Wildlife Service, 1991.

Baard, Frances, as told to Barbara Schreiner. *My Spirit Is Not Banned.* Harare: Zimbabwe Publishing House, 1986.

Bal, Mieke, Jonathan Crewe, and Leo Spitzer, eds. *Acts of Memory: Cultural Recall in the Present.* Hanover, N.H.: University Press of New England, 1999.

Barthes, Roland. *Camera Lucida: Reflections on Photography.* Trans. Richard Howard. New York: Hill and Wang, 1981.

Battaglia, Debbora. "On Practical Nostalgia: Self-Prospecting among Urban Trobrianders." In *Rhetorics of Self-Making.* Ed. Debbora Battaglia, 77–96. Berkeley: University of California Press, 1995.

Becker, Rayda. "The New Monument to the Women of South Africa." *African Arts* 33, no. 4 (winter 2000): 1–6.

Beckett, Jeremy. "Contested Images: Perspectives on the Indigenous Terrain in the Late 20th Century." *Identities* 3 (1996): 1–13.

Bedford, Emma, and Tracey Murinik. "Remembering That Place." In Soudien and Meyer, eds., *The District Six Public Sculpture Project,* 12–22.

Beinart, William, and Peter Coates. *Environment and History: The Taming of Nature in the United States of America and South Africa.* London: Routledge, 1995.

Ben-Guri, Ronit. "Progress Report on Travelling Exhibition." Unpublished. Museum Africa, 18 October 1990.

———. "Shaping the Museum of the Future: A Community Project." Unpublished report. Museum Africa, September 1990.

Benjamin, Walter. *Illuminations.* New York: Schocken Books, 1969.

———. *Reflections.* New York: Schocken Books, 1986.

Bennett, David, ed. *Multicultural States: Rethinking Difference and Identity.* New York: Routledge, 1998.

Berning, Gillian, and Graham Dominy. "The Presentation of the Industrial Past in South African Museums: A Critique." *SAMAB* 19 (1992 for 1990): 1–14.

Bester, Rory. "Interview with Jean Brundrit." In Lundstrom and Pierre, eds., *Democracy's Image,* 82–83.

———. "Interview with Tracey Rose." In Lundstrom and Pierre, eds., *Democracy's Image,* 90–93.

———. "Interview with Zwelethu Mthethwa." In Lundstrom and Pierre, eds., *Democracy's Image,* 82–83.

Bester, Rory, and Barbara Buntman. "Bushman(ia) and Photographic Intervention." *African Arts,* winter 1999: 50–59.

Board of Control of the Voortrekker Monument. *The Voortrekker Monument, Pretoria.* Pretoria: Board of Control of the Voortrekker Monument, 1954.

Bonner, Philip. "New Nation, New History: The History Workshop in South Africa 1977–1994." *Journal of American History* 81, no. 3 (1994): 977–985.

Boonzaier, Emile, and John Sharp, eds. *South African Keywords: The Uses and Abuses of Political Concepts.* Cape Town: David Philip, 1988.

Boraine, Alex, and Janet Levy, eds. *The Healing of a Nation?* Cape Town: Justice in Transition, 1995.

Boraine, Alex, Janet Levy, and Ronel Scheffer, eds. *Dealing with the Past: Truth and Reconciliation in South Africa.* Cape Town: Institute for Democracy in South Africa, 1994.

Botha, Lien, ed. *Bloedlyn.* Vlaeberg: Lien Botha, 1999.

Boym, Svetlana. *The Future of Nostalgia.* New York: Basic Books, 2001.

Bradford, Helen. "Sisters and Brothers: Gendering Africaner Nationalism, 1895–1902." Unpublished seminar paper, Institute of Commonwealth Studies, London, 19 March 1997.

Bradley, Fiona, ed. *Rachel Whiteread: Shedding Life.* London: Tate Gallery, 1996.

Brah, Avtar, and Annie E. Coombes, eds. *Hybridity and Its Discontents: Politics, Science, Culture.* London: Routledge, 2000.

Brison, Susan J. "Trauma Narratives and the Remaking of the Self." In Bal, Crewe, and Spitzer, eds., *Acts of Memory,* 39–55.

Brown, Joshua, Patrick Manning, Karin Shapiro, John Wiener, Belinda Bozzoli, and Peter Delius, eds. *History from South Africa: Alternative Visions and Practices.* Philadelphia, Pa.: Temple University Press, 1991.

Bruce, Hilary, and David Saks. "Frankly Speaking." *Museum* 44, no. 4 (1992): 238–241.

Bruner, Edward M. "Tourism in Ghana: The Representation of Slavery and the Return of the Black Diaspora." *American Anthropologist* 98, no. 2 (1996): 290–304.

Bundy, Colin. *Re-Making the Past: New Perspectives in South African History.* Cape Town: University of Cape Town Press, 1986.

Bunn, David. "Comparative Barbarism: Game Reserves, Sugar Plantations, and the

Modernization of the South African Landscape." In Darian-Smith, Gunner, and Nuttall, eds., *Text, Theory, Space*, 37–53.

Buntman, Fran. "How Best to Resist? Robben Island after 1976." In Deacon, ed., *The Island*, 137–166.

———. "Resistance on Robben Island 1963–1976." In Deacon, ed., *The Island*, 93–136.

Butler, Jeffrey. "Afrikaner Women and the Creation of Ethnicity in a Small South African Town, 1902–1950." In Vail, ed., *The Creation of Tribalism in Southern Africa*, 55–81.

Callinicos, Luli. *Gold and Workers*. Johannesburg: Ravan Press, 1981.

———. *A Place in the City: The Rand on the Eve of Apartheid*. Johannesburg: Ravan Press, 1993.

——— . *Working Life 1886–1940: Factories, Townships and Popular Culture on the Rand*. Johannesburg: Ravan Press, 1987.

Campschreur, Willem, and Joost Divendal, eds. *Culture in Another South Africa*. London: Zed, 1989.

Carruthers, Jane. "Nationhood and National Parks: Comparative Examples from the Post-Imperial Experience." In Griffiths and Robin, eds., *Ecology and Empire*, 125–139.

Caruth, Cathy, ed. *Trauma: Explorations in Memory*. Baltimore: Johns Hopkins University Press, 1995.

Case, Dianne. *What a Gentleman*. Wynberg: Kwagga Publishers, 1997.

Centre for Intergroup Studies. *Apartheid vs. People*. Cape Town: University of Cape Town, 1980.

Chaskalson, M., J. Kentridge, J. Klaaren, G. Marcus, D. Spitz, and S. Woolman, eds. *Constitutional Law of South Africa*. Cape Town: Juta, 1996.

Chinzima, Pitso. "Point of No Return in Contemporary South African Art: Reflections on the Past, the Present and the Future. Interviews with Tracey Rose, Shanti Govender and Ntsoaki Molefe." In Atkinson and Breitz, eds., *Grey Areas*, 85–93.

Coetzee, Ingrid, and Gerhard-Mark van der Waal, eds. *The Conservation of Culture: Changing Contexts and Challenges; Proceedings of the South African Conference on the Conservation of Culture, Cape Town, 6–10 June 1988*. Pretoria: South African Conference on the Conservation of Culture, 1988.

Cole, Tim. *Images of the Holocaust: The Myth of the "Shoah Business."* London: Duckworth, 1999.

Comaroff, Jean and John. *Of Revelation and Revolution*, vols. 1 and 2. Chicago: University of Chicago Press, 1991 and 1997.

Cooke, Pat. *A History of Kilmainham Gaol 1796–1924*. Dublin: Government Stationary Office, 1995.

Coombes, Annie E. "The Art of Memory." *Third Text* 52 (2002): 45–52.

———. "The Distance between Two Points: Global Culture and the Liberal Dilemma." In *Travellers' Tales: Narratives of Home and Displacement*. Ed. George Robertson, Melinda Mash, Lisa Tickner, et al., 177–186. London: Routledge, 1994.

———. "Gender, 'Race,' Ethnicity in Art Practice in Post-Apartheid South Africa: Annie E. Coombes and Penny Siopis in Conversation." *Feminist Review*, no. 55 (spring 1997): 110–129.

———. "Inventing the 'Post-Colonial': Hybridity and Constituency in Contemporary Curating." *New Formations*, no. 18 (winter 1992): 39–52.

———. *Reinventing Africa: Museums, Material Culture and Popular Imagination in Late Victorian and Edwardian England*. New Haven: Yale University Press, 1994.

———. "Skin Deep / Bodies of Evidence: The Work of Berni Searle." In *Authentic / Ex-Centric: Conceptualism in Contemporary African Art*. Ed. Salah M. Hassan and Olu Oguibe, 178–199. Ithaca: Forum for African Arts, 2001.

———, ed. *Revisiting Settler Colonialism: Colonialism, Decolonisation and Resistance in Australia, New Zealand, Canada and South Africa*. Manchester: Manchester University Press, 2003.

Cornell, Carohn. "Whatever Became of Cape Slavery in Western Cape Museums?" *Kronos*, 1998–1999: 259–279.

Cowlishaw, Gillian, and Vivienne Kondos, eds. *Mabo and Australia: On Recognising Native Title after Two Hundred Years. Australian Journal of Anthropology*, special issue, 6, nos. 1 and 2 (1995).

Cuthbertson, Roberta. "Embodied Memory, Transcendence, and Telling: Recounting Trauma, Re-Establishing Self." *New Literary History* 26 (1995): 169–195.

Darian-Smith, Kate, Liz Gunner, and Sarah Nuttall, eds. *Text, Theory, Space: Land, Literature and History in South Africa and Australia*. London: Routledge, 1996.

Davison, Patricia. "Human Subjects as Museum Objects: A Project to Make Life-Casts of 'Bushmen' and 'Hottentots,' 1907–1924." *Annals of the South African Museum* 102 (1993): 165–183.

———. "Material Culture, Context and Meaning." Ph.D. dissertation, University of Cape Town, 1991.

———. "A Place Apart." Press release for "Esiqithini."

Deacon, Harriet, ed. *The Island: A History of Robben Island 1488–1990*. Cape Town: David Philip, 1996.

Deacon, Janette, and Thomas A. Dowson, eds. *Voices from the Past:/Xam Bushmen and the Bleek and Lloyd Collection*. Johannesburg: Witwatersrand University Press, 1996.

de Clerq, Francine. "Putting Community Participation into Development Work: The Difficult Case of Winterveld." *Development Southern Africa* 11, no. 3 (1994): 379–393.

de Jong, Robert. "The Development of the Pretoria Saltpan (Tswaing) as an Enviro-Museum." Unpublished discussion document. Pretoria, July 1994.

———. "The Tswaing Crater Museum." Unpublished discussion document. Pretoria, August 1994.

de Jong, Robert, and Helen van Coller. "The Development of Tswaing Crater Museum: A Museum for the People, by the People." Unpublished discussion document. October 1994.

de Jong, Robert, ed. *Museums and the Environment*. Pretoria: South African Museums Association, 1993.

Delbo, Charlotte. *Auschwitz and After*. New Haven: Yale University Press, 1995.

Dell, Elizabeth A. "Museums and the Representation of 'Savage South Africa.'" Ph.D. dissertation, School of Oriental and African Studies, University of London, 1994.

Delmont, Elizabeth. "The Voortrekker Monument: Monolith to Myth." *South African Historical Journal* 29 (1993): 76–101.

Delport, Peggy. "Signposts for Retrieval: A Visual Framework for Enabling Memory of Place and Time." In Rassool and Prosalendis, eds., *Recalling Community*, 31–46.

Dening, Greg. "Digging Deeper in District Six: Features and Interfaces in a Curatorial Landscape." In Rasool and Prosalendis, eds., *Recalling Community*, 154–64.

———. *Mr. Bligh's Bad Language: Passion, Power and Theatre on the Bounty.* Cambridge: Cambridge University Press, 1992.

Denoon, Donald. "The Isolation of Australian History." *Historical Studies* 22, no. 87 (1986): 252–260.

———. *Settler Capitalism: The Dynamics of Dependent Development in the Southern Hemisphere.* Oxford: Clarendon Press, 1983.

Department of Arts, Culture, Science, and Technology. *Annual Report.* Pretoria: Department of Arts, Culture, Science, and Technology, 1999.

Department of Environmental Affairs and Tourism. *An Environmental Policy for South Africa: Green Paper for Public Discussion.* Pretoria: Department of Environmental Affairs and Tourism, October 1996.

———. *Green Paper on the Conservation and Sustainable Use of South Africa's Biological Diversity.* Pretoria: Department of Environmental Affairs and Tourism, October 1996.

de Smidt, Lorna. "Rationale for the Refurbishment of South Africa House." Unpublished discussion document. 2000.

de Wet, Sandra. "Thokoza Squatters' Shack." *Africana Notes and News* 30, no. 3 (1992): 97–98.

de Zegher, M. Catherine, ed. *Inside the Visible: An Elliptical Traverse of Twentieth Century Art in, of, and from the Feminine.* Kortrijk: Kanaal Art Foundation, 1996.

Dhlomo, Bongi. "Zwelethu Mthethwa Talks about His Photographs." In *Liberated Voices: Contemporary Art from South Africa.* Ed. Frank Herreman, 65–81. New York: Museum for African Art, 1999.

Dowson, Thomas A., and David Lewis-Williams. "Myths, Museums and Southern African Rock Art." In *Contested Images: Diversity in Southern African Rock Art Research,* 385–402. Johannesburg: Witwatersrand University Press, 1994.

Dubow, Saul. "Human Origins, Race Typology and the Other Raymond Dart." In Alexander, Hutchison, and Schreuder, eds., *Africa Today,* 245–279.

———. *Scientific Racism in Modern South Africa.* Cambridge: Cambridge University Press, 1995.

Dudley, Richard. "Forced Removals: The Essential Meanings of District Six." In Jeppie and Soudien, eds., *The Struggle for District Six,* 197–203.

du Plessis, L., and H. Corder. *Understanding South Africa's Transitional Bill of Rights.* Cape Town: Juta, 1994.

Durham, Jimmie. "Cowboys and . . ." *Third Text* 12 (1990): 5–20.

Erlmann, Veit. "'Spectatorial Lust': The African Choir in England, 1891–1893." In Lindfors, ed., *Africans on Stage,* 107–134.

Fauvelle-Aymer, François-Xavier. "Des murs d'Augsbourg aux vitrines du Cap: Cinq siècles d'histoire du regard sur le corps des Khoisan." *Cahiers d'études africaines* 39, nos. 155–156 (1999): 539–561.

Finkelstein, Norman. *The Holocaust Industry.* London: Verso, 2000.

Fourmile, Henrietta. "Respecting Our Knowledge: National Research Institutions and Their Obligations to Indigenous and Local Communities under Article 8 (J) and Related Provisions of the Convention on Biological Diversity." *Humanities Research* 1 (2000): 41–55.

Frescura, F. "Monuments and the Monumentalisation of Myths." Paper presented at "Myths, Monuments, Museums" conference. History Workshop, University of the Witwatersrand, July 1992.

Freud, Sigmund. *Introductory Lectures on Psychoanalysis.* Trans. James Strachey. Harmondsworth: Penguin Books, 1973.

———. "The Uncanny." In *The Complete Psychological Works of Sigmund Freud.* Ed. and trans. James Strachey, 17: 234–235. London: Hogarth Press, 1953–1973.

Fugard, Athol, John Kani, and Winston Ntshona. *The Island.* In *The Township Plays.* Athol Fugard. Oxford: Oxford University Press, 1993.

Gevisser, Mark, and Edwin Cameron, eds. *Defiant Desire: Gay and Lesbian Lives in South Africa.* Johannesburg: Raven Press, 1994.

Geyer, Michael. "The Politics of Memory in Contemporary Germany." In *Radical Evil.* Ed. Joan Copjec, 169–200. London: Verso, 1996.

Giliomee, Hermann. "The Beginnings of Afrikaner Ethnic Consciousness, 1850–1915." In Vail, ed., *The Creation of Tribalism in Southern Africa,* 21–54.

Gilman, Sander L. "Black Bodies, White Bodies: Toward an Iconography of Female Sexuality in Late Nineteenth-Century Art, Medicine, and Literature." In *"Race," Writing and Difference.* Ed. Henry Louis Gates Jr., 223–261. Chicago: University of Chicago Press, 1986.

Golomstock, Igor. *Totalitarian Art in the Soviet Union, the Third Reich, Fascist Italy and the People's Republic of China.* London: Collins-Harvill, 1989.

Goodwin, Eric. "A Hall of Cultural History." Unpublished discussion paper. Museum Africa, 25 October 1991.

———. "A New Direction for Cultural History." Discussion paper. Museum Africa, 14 October 1991.

Gordon, Robert J. " 'Bains' Bushmen': Scenes at the Empire Exhibition, 1936." In Lindfors, ed., *Africans on Stage,* 266–289.

Gould, Stephen J. *The Flamingo's Smile: Reflections on Natural History.* Harmondsworth: Penguin Books, 1986.

Gouws, Amanda. *Report of the Robben Island Political Feasibility Study as Commissioned by Peace Visions.* Cape Town: Peace Visions, 1994.

Griffiths, Tom, and Libby Robin, eds. *Ecology and Empire: Environmental History of Settler Societies.* Melbourne: Melbourne University Press, 1997.

Grundlingh, Albert. "A Cultural Conundrum? Old Monuments and New Regimes: The Voortrekker Monument as Symbol of Afrikaner Power in a Post-Apartheid South Africa." *Radical History Review* 81 (2001): 95–112.

Grundlingh, Albert, and Hilary Sapire. "From Feverish Festival to Repetitive Ritual? The Changing Fortunes of Great Trek Mythology in an Industrializing South Africa, 1938–1988." *South African Historical Journal* 21 (1989): 19–37.

Guenther, Mathias. "From 'Brutal Savages' to 'Harmless People': Notes on the Changing Western Image of the Bushmen." *Paideuma* 26 (1980): 123–140.

Hamilton, Carolyn. *Terrific Majesty: The Powers of Shaka Zulu and the Limits of Historical Invention.* Cambridge, Mass.: Harvard University Press, 1998.

Harlow, Barbara. *Barred: Women, Writing, and Political Detention.* Hanover, N.H.: Wesleyan University Press, 1992.

Harris, Brent. "Confessing the Truth: Shaping Silences through the Amnesty Process." *Kronos* 26 (2000): 76–88.

———. " 'Unearthing' the 'Essential' Past: The Making of a Public 'National' Memory through the Truth and Reconciliation Commission, 1994–1998." M.A. mini-thesis. Cape Town: University of the Western Cape, 1998.

Hart, Deborah M. "Political Manipulation of Urban Space: The Razing of District Six, Cape Town." In Jeppie and Soudien, eds., *The Struggle for District Six*, 117–142.

Hayman, G. P. "Class, Race or Culture: Who Is the Enemy? The Botswana 'Culture and Resistance' Conference." *Critical Arts* 2, no. 3 (1982): 33–38.

Haynes, Roslynn D. *Seeking the Centre: The Australian Desert in Literature, Art and Film.* Cambridge: Cambridge University Press, 1998.

Herreman, Frank, and Mark D'Amato, eds. *Liberated Voices: Contemporary Art from South Africa.* New York: Museum for African Art, 1999.

Historiese Rekord van die Inseening van die Voortrekker Monument, 16de Desember 1949 (Historical record of the consecration of the Voortrekker Monument, 16 December 1949). Johannesburg: Insercor Industrial Services, 1949.

Hofmeyr, Isabel. "Building a Nation from Words: Afrikaans Language, Literature and Ethnic Identity, 1902–1924." In *The Politics of Race, Class and Nationalism in Twentieth Century South Africa.* Ed. S. Marks and S. Trapido. New York: Longman, 1987.

———. "Popularizing History: The Case of Gustav Preller." *Journal of African History* 29 (1998): 521–535.

———. *"We Spend Our Years as a Tale That Is Told": Oral Historical Narrative in a South African Chiefdom.* Johannesburg: Witwatersrand University Press, 1993.

Horn, Andre C. "How Many People Are There in the Winterveld? What a Proper Census Should Show." *Urban Forum* 8, no. 1 (1997): 117–132.

Hutton, Barbara. *Robben Island: Symbol of Resistance.* Johannesburg: SACHED, 1994.

Huyssen, Andreas. "Monumental Seduction." In Bal, Crewe, and Spitzer, eds., *Acts of Memory*, 191–207.

———. *Twilight Memories: Marking Time in a Culture of Amnesia.* New York: Routledge, 1995.

———. "The Voids of Berlin." *Critical Inquiry* 24, no. 1 (1997): 57–81.

Hyslop, J. "Why Did Apartheid's Supporters Capitulate? 'Whiteness,' Class and Consumption in Urban South Africa, 1985–1995." Unpublished paper, 1998.

———. "Why Was the White Right Unable to Stop South Africa's Democratic Transition?" In Alexander, Hutchison, and Schreuder, eds., *Africa Today*, 145–165.

Ifeka-Moller, Caroline. "Female Militancy and Colonial Revolt: The Women's War of 1929, Eastern Nigeria." In Ardener, ed., *Perceiving Women*, 127–159.

Integrated Marketing Research. "Africana Museum Research Report." Unpublished. March 1994.

Ireland and South Africa in Modern Times. Special issue, *Southern African–Irish Studies* 3 (1996).

James, Wilmot, and Linda van de Vijver, eds. *After the TRC: Reflections on Truth and Reconciliation in South Africa.* Claremont: David Philip, 2000.

Janson, Susan, and Stuart Macintyre, eds. *Making the Bicentenary.* Special issue, *Australian Historical Studies* 23, no. 91 (1988).

Jeppie, Shamil. "Popular Culture and Carnival in Cape Town: The 1940s and 1950s." In Jeppie and Soudien, eds., *The Struggle for District Six*, 67–87.

Jeppie, Shamil, and Crain Soudien, eds. *The Struggle for District Six, Past and Present.* Cape Town: Buchu Books, 1990.

Joseph, Helen. *Tomorrow's Sun.* London: Hutchinson, 1966.

Karp, Ivan, Christine Muller Kreamer, and Steven D. Levine, eds. *Museums and Communities: The Politics of Public Culture.* Washington: Smithsonian Institution Press, 1992.

Kathrada, Ahmed M. "Opening Address." Delivered 26 May 1993. In *The Robben Island Exhibition: Esiqithini.* Cape Town: South African Museum and Mayibuye Books, 1996.

Khan, Farieda. "Hidden Heritage: Our Past, Our Future." Paper presented at "Myths, Monuments, Museums" conference. History Workshop, University of the Witwatersrand, July 1992.

Kipnis, Laura. "(Male) Desire and (Female) Disgust: Reading Hustler." In *Cultural Studies.* Ed. Lawrence Grossberg, Cary Nelson, and Paula Treichler, 373–391. New York: Routledge, Chapman, and Hall, 1992.

Krafchik, Bryan, ed. *The South African Museum and Its Public: Negotiating Partnerships.* Cape Town: South African Museum, 1994.

Kros, Cynthia. "Experiencing a Century in a Day? Making More of Gold Reef City." *South African Historical Journal* 29 (1993): 28–43.

———. *Trusting to the Process: Reflections on the Flaws in the Negotiating of the History Curriculum in South Africa.* History Curriculum Research Project of Cambridge University Press and History Workshop, University of the Witwatersrand, vol. 1, 1996.

Kros, Cynthia, and Shelley Greybe. *The Rainbow Nation vs. Healing Old Wounds: An Investigation into Teacher and Pupil Attitudes to Standard Three History.* History Curriculum Research Project of Cambridge University Press and History Workshop, University of the Witwatersrand, vol. 2, 1997.

Kuklick, H. "Contested Monuments: The Politics of Archaeology in Southern Africa." *History of Anthropology* 7 (1991): 135–169.

Küsel, Udo. "No Building, No Problem." *Museums Journal,* April 1994.

———. "People Participate to Create Sustainable Environment." *In Focus,* May–June 1996: 65–67.

Küsel, Udo, Robert de Jong, Helen van Coller, and Kobus Basson. "Revitalising the Nation's Heritage: A Discussion Document on the Involvement of South African Museums in the Reconstruction and Development Programme." Manuscript. Pretoria, November 1994.

Kuzwayo, Ellen. *Call Me Woman.* Johannesburg: Ravan Press, 1985.

La Hausse, Paul. "Oral History and South African Historians." In Brown, et al., eds., *History from South Africa,* 342–50.

Lane, Paul. "Breaking the Mould? Exhibiting Khoisan in Southern African Museums." *Anthropology Today* 12, no. 5 (October 1996): 3–10.

Law, Jennifer A. "Penny Siopis: The Storyteller." In Herreman, ed., *Liberated Voices,* 93–109.

Lazarus, Neil. *Nationalism and Cultural Practice in a Postcolonial World.* Cambridge: Cambridge University Press, 1999.

Legassick, Martin, and Ciraj Rassool. *Skeletons in the Cupboard: South African Mu-*

seums and the Trade in Human Remains 1907–1917. Cape Town: South African Museum and McGregor Museum, 2000.

Levi, Primo. *The Truce*. London: Vintage, 1996.

Lindfors, Bernth. "Charles Dickens and the Zulus." In Lindfors, ed., *Africans on Stage*, 62–80.

———, ed. *Africans on Stage: Studies in Ethnological Show Business*. Bloomington: Indiana University Press, 1999.

Linenthal, Edward T. *Preserving Memory: The Struggle to Create America's Holocaust Museum*. New York: Penguin, 1995.

Lipstadt, Deborah. *Denying the Holocaust: The Growing Assault on Truth and Memory*. New York: Penguin, 1995.

Lodder, Christina. "Lenin's Plan for Monumental Propaganda." In *Art of the Soviets: Painting, Sculpture and Architecture in a One-Party State, 1917–1992*. Ed. Matthew Cullerne Brown and Brandon Taylor, 16–32. Manchester: Manchester University Press, 1993.

Lodge, Tom. *Black Politics in South Africa since 1945*. Johannesburg: Ravan Press, 1985.

Louw, P. Eric, and Keyan Tomaselli. "Impact of the 1990 Reforms on the 'Alternative Media.' " In Tomaselli and Louw, eds., *The Alternative Press in South Africa*, 222–226.

———. "The Struggle for Legitimacy: State Pressures on the Media." In Tomaselli and Louw, eds., *The Alternative Press in South Africa*, 77–92.

Lundstrom, Jan-Erik, and Katarina Pierre, eds. *Democracy's Image: Photography and Visual Art after Apartheid*. Umea: BildMuseet, 1998.

Mace, Rodney. *Trafalgar Square: Emblem of Empire*. London: Lawrence and Wishart, 1976.

MacKenzie, John M. *The Empire of Nature: Hunting, Conservation and British Imperialism*. Manchester: Manchester University Press, 1988.

McClintock, A. *Imperial Leather: Race, Gender and Sexuality in the Colonial Contest*. London: Routledge, 1995.

McEachern, Charmaine. "Working with Memory: The District Six Museum in the New South Africa." *Social Analysis* 42, no. 2 (July 1998): 48–72.

McGrath, Ann. "Travels to a Distant Past: The Mythology of the Outback." *Australian Cultural History* 10 (1991): 113–124.

McIntyre, Darryl, and Kirsten Wehner, eds. *National Museums: Negotiating Histories Conference Proceedings*. Canberra: National Museum of Australia, 2001.

Makhoere, Caesarina Kona. *No Child's Play: In Prison under Apartheid*. London: Women's Press, 1988.

Makoba, Malegapuru William, ed. *African Renaissance*. Sandton: Mafube Publishing, and Cape Town: Tafelberg Publishers, 1999.

Mandela, Nelson. *The Struggle Is My Life*. London: International Defence and Aid Fund for South Africa, 1986.

Manne, Robert. "The Stolen Generations." In *Essays on Australian Reconciliation*. Ed. Michelle Grattan, 129–139. Melbourne: Black, 2000.

Marks, Shula. "Patriotism, Patriarchy and Purity: Natal and the Politics of Zulu Ethnic Consciousness." In Vail, ed., *The Creation of Tribalism in Southern Africa*, 215–40.

Marks, Shula, and Stanley Trapido, eds. *The Politics of Race, Clan, and Nationalism in Twentieth-Century South Africa*. New York: Longman, 1987.

Maxim, Lionel J. *Madiba the Rainbow Man*. Wynberg: Asjen, 1997.

Meer, Fatima. *Higher Than Hope*. London: Hamish Hamilton, 1988.

Meintjes, Sheila. "Women's Consciousness and the Body Politic: Naked Protest, Dobsonville 1990." Paper presented at the fifteenth biennial conference of the South African Historical Society. July 1995.

Meredith, Martin. *Nelson Mandela: A Biography*. Ringwood: Penguin Books Australia, 1997.

Meyer, Renate. "Introduction." In Soudien and Meyer, eds., *The District Six Public Sculpture Project*.

Michalski, Sergiusz. *Public Monuments: Art in Political Bondage 1870–1997*. London: Reaktion Books, 1998.

Middleton, Joan. *Convictions: A Woman Political Prisoner Remembers*. Johannesburg: Ravan Press, 1998.

Minkley, Gary, and Ciraj Rassool. "Orality, Memory, and Social History in South Africa." In Nuttall and Coetzee, eds., *Negotiating the Past*, 89–99.

Mitchell, W. J. T., ed. *Art and the Public Sphere*. Chicago: University of Chicago Press, 1990.

Mokaba, Peter. *Tourism: A Development and Reconstruction Perspective*. Johannesburg: African National Congress, 1994.

Molobi, Saul. "The Star That Fell from the Sky." *Learn and Teach*, March 1994.

Morris, Alan G. "Trophy Skulls, Museums and the San." In Skotnes, ed., *Miscast, the Bushmen*, 67–79.

Murray, Sally-Ann. "*Tribute* and Attributed Meaning: Reading 'the Magazine.'" *Current Writing* 6, no. 2 (1994): 63–76.

Nagia, Anwah (interviewed by Colin Miller). "Land Restitution in District Six: Settling a Traumatic Landscape." In Rassool and Prosalendis, eds., *Recalling Community*.

Naidoo, Indres, and Albie Sachs. *Island in Chains: Ten Years on Robben Island by Prisoner 885/63*. Harmondsworth: Penguin Books, 1982.

Ndebele, Njabulo. "Memory, Metaphor and the Triumph of Narrative." In Nuttall and Coetzee, eds., *Negotiating the Past*, 19–28.

Nettleton, Anitra. "Arts and Africana: Hierarchies of Material Culture." *South African Historical Journal* 29 (1993): 61–75.

Nixon, Rob. *Homelands, Harlem and Hollywood*. New York: Routledge, 1994.

Ngcelwane, Nomvuyo. *Sala Kahle, District Six: An African Woman's Perspective*. Cape Town: Kwela Books, 1998.

Nora, Pierre. "Between Memory and History: Les lieux de mémoir." Trans. Marc Roudebush. *Representations* 26 (1989): 13–25.

Novick, Peter. *The Holocaust in American Life*. New York: Houghton Mifflin, 1999.

Nuttall, Sarah, and Carli Coetzee, eds. *Negotiating the Past: The Making of Memory in South Africa*. Cape Town: Oxford University Press, 1998.

Nuttall, Sarah, and Cheryl-Ann Michael. "African Renaissance." In Nuttall and Michael, eds., *Senses of Culture, African Culture Studies*, 107–126.

———. *Senses of Culture: South African Culture Studies*. Cape Town: Oxford University Press, 2000.

Odendaal, André. "'Giving Life to Learning': The Way Ahead for Museums in a Democratic South Africa." Paper presented on behalf of CREATE at SAMA annual conference, East London, 23 May 1994.

Omar, Dullah. "The Murder of District Six: Some Thoughts and Reminiscences." In Jeppie and Soudien, eds., *The Struggle for District Six*, 192–196.

O'Meara, Dan. *Volkskapitalisme: Class, Capital and Ideology in the Development of Afrikaner Nationalism 1934–1948.* Johannesburg: Ravan Press, and Cambridge: Cambridge University Press, 1983.

Parry, Benita. "Reconciliation and Remembrance." *pretexts* 5, nos. 1–2 (1995): 84–96.

———. "Resistance Theory / Theorising Resistance, or Two Cheers for Nativism." In *Colonial Discourse / Postcolonial Theory*. Ed. Francis Barker, Peter Hulme, and Margaret Iversen, 172–196. Manchester: Manchester University Press, 1994.

Pheko, Motsoko. *Apartheid: The Story of a Dispossessed People.* London: Marram Books, 1984.

Phelan, Peggy. *Unmarked: The Politics of Performance.* New York: Routledge, 1993.

Phillips, Ruth B. "Show Times: De-Celebrating the Canadian Nation, Decolonising the Canadian Museum, 1967–1992." In Coombes, ed., *Revisiting Settler Colonialism*.

———. *Trading Identities.* Seattle: University of Washington Press, 1999.

Pickel, Birgit. *Coloured Ethnicity and Identity: A Case Study in the Former Coloured Areas in the Western Cape / South Africa.* Hamburg: Lit Verlag, 1997.

Posel, Deborah. "The TRC Report: What Kind of History? What Kind of Truth?" In Posel and Simpson, eds., *Commissioning the Past*, 147–172.

Posel, Deborah, and Graeme Simpson. *Commissioning the Past: Understanding South Africa's Truth and Reconciliation Commission.* Johannesburg: Witwatersrand University Press, 2002.

Prosalendis, Sandra. "District Six—Kanaladorp." *Nordisk Museologi* 1 (1999): 135–146.

Ramphele, Mamphela. *A Life.* Claremont: David Philip, 1995.

Ranger, Terence. "'Great Spaces Washed with Sun': The Matapos and Uluru Compared." In Darian-Smith, Gunner, and Nuttall, eds., *Text, Theory, Space*, 157–171.

———. *Voices from the Rocks: Nature, Culture and History in the Matapos Hills of Zimbabwe.* Oxford: James Currey, 1999.

Rassool, Ciraj. "Introduction: Recalling Community in Cape Town." In Rassool and Prosalendis, eds., *Recalling Community*.

Rassool, Ciraj, and Leslie Witz. "South Africa: A World in One Country; Moments in International Tourist Encounters with Wildlife, the Primitive and the Modern." *Cahiers d'études africaines* 143, nos. 36–3 (1996): 335–371.

Rassool, Ciraj, and Sandra Prosalendis, eds. *Recalling Community in Cape Town.* Cape Town: District Six Museum, 2001.

Resha, Maggie. *'Mangoana Tsoara Thipa Ka Bohaleng; My Life in the Struggle.* Johannesburg: Congress of South African Writers, 1991.

Richards, Colin. "Graft." In *Trade Routes: History and Geography, the Second Johannesburg Biennale.* Ed. Matthew DeBord, 234–237. Johannesburg: Greater Johannesburg Metropolitan Council, 1997.

Ritchie, G. "Dig the Herders / Display the Hottentots: The Production and Presentation of Knowledge about the Past." M.A. thesis, University of Cape Town, 1990.

Rive, Richard. "District Six: Fact and Fiction." In Jeppie and Soudien, eds., *The Struggle for District Six.*

Robins, Steven. "Land Struggles and the Politics and Ethics of Representing 'Bushman' History and Identity." *Kronos* 26 (August 2000): 56–75.

———. "Silence in My Father's House: Memory, Nationalism and Narratives of the Body." In Nuttall and Coetzee, eds., *Negotiating the Past*, 120–140.

Rogoff, Irit. "The Aesthetics of Post-History: A German Perspective." In *Vision and Textuality.* Ed. Stephen Melville and Bill Readings, 115–146. Durham: Duke University Press, 1995.

Rousseau, I. J. "The Great Trek and Its Problems." In *Historiese Rekord van die Inseening van die Voortrekker Monument / Historical Record of the Consecration of the Voortrekker Monument.* Johannesburg: Insercor Industrial Services, 16 December 1949, 89–94.

Roux, T. *Constitutional Review of Social Reform Legislation in South Africa: A "Civil Society" Model.* Cape Town: University of Cape Town Press, 1995.

Russell, Lynette, ed. *Colonial Frontiers: Indigenous-European Encounters in Settler Societies.* Manchester: Manchester University Press, 2001.

Rydell, Robert W. *All the World's a Fair: Visions of Empire at American International Expositions, 1876–1916.* Chicago: University of Chicago Press, 1984.

Saks, David. "Motivations behind the Chrono-Cultural Division in the Museum." Position paper. Museum Africa, 24 October 1991.

Sampson, Anthony. *Mandela.* London: HarperCollins, 1999.

Schadeberg, Jürgen, comp. and photog. *Voices from the Island.* Johannesburg: Ravan Press, 1994.

Schalkwyk, David. "Writing from Prison." In Nuttall and Michael, eds., *Senses of Culture*, 178–197.

Schneider, William H. *An Empire for the Masses: The French Popular Image of Africa, 1870–1900.* Westview, Conn.: Greenwood, 1982.

Schrire, R. *Adapt or Die: The End of White Politics in South Africa.* Cape Town: Foreign Policy Association, 1991.

Sharp, John. "Ethnic Group and Nation: The Apartheid Vision in South Africa." In Boonzaier and Sharp, eds., *South African Keywords*, 79–100.

———. "The Roots and Development of Volkekunde in South Africa." *Journal of Southern African Studies* 8, no. 1 (1981): 16–31.

Shubane, Khehla. "Civics as a Building Ground for a Democratic Civil Society." *Die Suid-Afrikaan*, February–March 1993: 35–37.

Sikakane, Joyce. *A Window on Soweto.* London: IDAF, 1977.

Simpson, Moira. *Making Representations: Museums in the Post-Colonial Era.* London: Routledge, 1996.

Skotnes, Pippa. "The Politics of Bushman Representations." In *Images and Empires: Visuality in Colonial and Postcolonial Africa.* Ed. Paul Landau and Deborah Kaspin. Berkeley: University of California Press, 2002.

———, ed. *Miscast: Negotiating the Presence of the Bushmen.* Cape Town: University of Cape Town Press, 1996.

Soudien, Crain. "District Six: From Protest to Protest." In Jeppie and Soudien, eds., *The Struggle for District Six*, 143–182.

————. "Holding on to the Past: Working with the 'Myths' of District Six." In Rassool and Prosalendis, eds., *Recalling Community*, 97–105.

Soudien, Crain, and Renate Meyer, eds. *The District Six Public Sculpture Project*. Cape Town: District Six Museum Foundation, 1997.

South Africa. *The Constitution of the Republic of South Africa*. Pretoria, 1996.

Spivak, Gayatri Chakravorty. *Outside in the Teaching Machine*. New York: Routledge, 1993.

Stewart, Susan. *On Longing: Narratives of the Miniature, the Gigantic, the Souvenir, the Collection*. Durham: Duke University Press, 1993.

Swilling, Mark. "Civic Associations in South Africa." *Urban Forum* 4, no. 2 (1993): 15–36.

Tapsell Te Arawa, Paul. "Taonga, marae, whenua—Negotiating Custodianship." In Coombes, ed., *Revisiting Settler Colonialism*.

Taylor, Jane. "The Moment Between." In Younge, ed., *Picture Cape Town*.

Third Text: The Wake of Utopia. Special issue, *Third Text* 21 (1992–1993).

Thomas, Nicholas. *Entangled Objects: Exchange, Material Culture and Colonialism in the Pacific*. Cambridge, Mass.: Harvard University Press, 1991.

————. *Possessions: Indigenous Art / Colonial Culture*. London: Thames and Hudson, 1999.

Thornton, Robert. "Culture: A Contemporary Definition." In Boonzaier and Sharp, eds., *South African Keywords*, 17–28.

Thornton, Robert, and Mamphela Ramphele. "The Quest for Community." In Boonzaier and Sharp, eds., *South African Keywords*, 29–40.

Tomaselli, Keyan, and Mewa Ramgobin. "Culture and Conservation: Whose Interests?" In Coetzee and van der Waal, eds., *The Conservation of Culture*, 105–127.

Tomaselli, Keyan, and P. Eric Louw, eds. *The Alternative Press in South Africa*. Bellville: Anthropos Publishers, 1991.

Tomaselli, Keyan, Ruth Tomaselli, and Johan Muller, eds. *Narrating the Crisis: Hegemony and the South African Press*. Johannesburg: Richard Lyon, 1987.

Townsend, Lesley Freedman, and Alicia Monis. "Report on the National Monuments Council/International Council on Monuments and Sites (ICOMOS) Heritage Conservation Charter Workshop Which Took Place on 31 January 1997 at the Offices of the National Monuments Council (NMC), 111 Harrington Street, Cape Town." Unpublished draft report. Cape Town, 1997.

Truth and Reconciliation Commission of South Africa Report. 5 vols. Cape Town: Truth and Reconciliation Commission, 1998.

Urry, James. "'Notes and Queries on Anthropology' and the Development of Field Methods in British Anthropology 1870–1920." *Proceedings of the Royal Anthropological Institute*, 1973: 45–57.

Vail, Leroy, ed. *The Creation of Tribalism in Southern Africa*. Berkeley: University of California Press, 1989.

Van den Berg, Clive. "Memorials without Facts." *Performance Research: A Journal of Performance Arts* 3, no. 2 (1998): 10–14.

Van Niekerk, Marlene. *Triomf*. Trans. Leon de Kock. London: Little, Brown, 1999.

Van Riet, Willem, and Erika van den Berg. *Tswaing Crater Museum: Zoning Proposals Report*. Pretoria: National Cultural History Museum, 1994.

Van Tonder, Deon. "From Mausoleum to Museum: Revisiting Public History at the Inauguration of Museum Africa, Newtown." *South African Historical Journal* 31 (1994): 1–19.

Vidler, Anthony. *The Architectural Uncanny: Essays in the Modern Unhomely.* Cambridge: MIT Press, 1996.

Ward, Kerry, and Nigel Worden. "Commemorating, Suppressing, and Invoking Cape Slavery." In Nuttall and Coetzee, eds., *Negotiating the Past,* 201–217.

Webb, Denver A. "National Monuments in the Ciskei—First World Luxuries in a Third World Context?" In Coetzee and Van der Waal, eds., *The Conservation of Culture,* 232–236.

Weinberg, Paul. "Footprints in the Sand." In Skotnes, ed., *Miscast,* 331–341.

Wells, Julia C. *We Now Demand! The History of Women's Resistance to Pass Laws in South Africa.* Johannesburg: Witwatersrand University Press, 1993.

West, Martin. "Confusing Categories: Population Groups, National States and Citizenship." In Boonzaier and Sharp, eds., *South African Keywords,* 100–111.

Willemse, Hein. "The Black Afrikaans Writer: A Continuing Dichotomy." *Triquarterly* 69 (1987): 236–246.

Wilmsen, Edwin N. *Land Filled with Flies: A Political Economy of the Kalahari.* Chicago: University of Chicago Press, 1989.

Wilmsen, Edward, and Patrick McAllister, eds. *The Politics of Difference: Ethnic Premises in a World of Power.* Chicago: University of Chicago Press, 1996.

Witz, Leslie. "Commemorations and Conflicts in the Production of South African National Pasts: The 1952 Jan van Riebeeck Tercentenary Festival." Ph.D. dissertation, University of Cape Town, 1997.

———. *Write Your Own History.* Johannesburg: SACHED Trust, Braamfontein: Ravan Press, 1988.

Woods, Donald. *Biko.* Harmondsworth: Penguin Books, 1978.

Worden, Nigel. "The Forgotten Region: Commemorations of Slavery in Mauritius and South Africa." Manuscript, 2000.

———. "Unwrapping History at the Cape Town Waterfront." Paper presented at "Myths, Monuments, Museums" conference. History workshop, University of the Witwatersrand, July 1992.

Wounded Nations, Broken Lives: Truth Commissions and War Tribunals. Special issue. *Index on Censorship* 5 (1996).

Young, James. *At Memory's Edge: After-Images of the Holocaust in Contemporary Art and Architecture.* New Haven: Yale University Press, 2000.

———. *The Texture of Memory: Holocaust Memorials and Meaning.* New Haven: Yale University Press, 1993.

Younge, Gavin, ed. *Picture Cape Town: Landmarks of a New Generation.* Los Angeles: Getty Conservation Institute, 1996.

FILMS

Disgraced Monuments. 1994. Directors Laura Mulvey and Mark Lewis. Broadcast Channel 4 TV, 6 June 1994.

Mandela. 1996. Director Philip Saville. IMC Video, South Africa.

Mandela: Son of Africa, Father of a Nation. 1995. Directors Jo Menell and Angus Gibson. Island Pictures, South Africa.

Nelson Mandela: The Struggle Is My Life. Director Lionel Ngakane. Film Resource Unit, South Africa.

Uku Hamba 'ze—To Walk Naked. 1995. Directors Sheila Meintjes, Jacqueline Maingard, and Heather Thompson. Independent video production.

INDEX

Illustrations are indicated in the index by use of italics.

Gerz, Jochen, 91; Harburg Monument against Fascism, 92; 2,146 Stones—Monument against Racism, 93, *94*
Gevisser, Mark, 84–86, 196
Godfrain, Jacques, 241
Gold Reef City, 195–201
Goodman, Gwelo, 292–93: *South African Fruit and Vegetables, 293; Groot Constantia, 293*
Goodwin, Eric, 178
Gould, Stephen J., 215
Government Gazette, 16
Granary, The, 248
Gray, Charles, Justice, 7
Great Trek (1838): anniversary celebrations, 31; narrative, 25, 28, 53; reconstruction, 26; representations, 30–32; rewriting, 49. *See also* Voortrekker Monument
Griqua National Conference (GNC), 238
Griquas: recognition as indigenous, 240
Grobler, Lorette, 33–34
Grogan, Tony: cartoon, *223*
Grundlingh, Albert, 30, 31
Guenther, Mathias, 215
Guguletu Seven: monument, 110; evidence at Truth and Reconciliation Commission, 236

Haddon, A. C., 215
Haggard, Rider, 285
Hall, Martin, 133
Hallbeck, Hans Peter, 203
Hamilton, Carolyn, 285
Hands Off District Six Committee (HODSC), 131
Hanekom, Derek, 146, 147
Hart, Frederick, 91
Hartzenberg, Randolph, 134; *Salt Tower* (sculpture), *135*
Hartzenbergh, Ferdie, 31–32
Hattingh, Ryk, 49: *Sing Jy Van Bomme* (Singing about bombs) (play), 43
Hertzog, James, 280–81
"Historic Site Museums of Conscience": District Six Museum as one of, 119
history, 3–14, 56, 86, 207; absences from, 251, 290, 293; alienation from, 116; of complicity and degradation, 132; cultural, 177, 178; of everyday life, 199; funding, 22, 65, 71, 118–20, 181, 200–201; and heritage debates, 5–6, 20, 33–34, 48, 120, 206–7; as "heritage trails," 131; of labor, 153, 197, 293; of mining,

196, 197; national, 56–57, 66, 95, 114, 208; occluded, 205, 206, 278, 131; policy, 14–17, 150; of political alliances, 122; precolonial, 206; private sponsorship, 56, 68; recovery, *127*, 128, 200; representation of, 289; reinterpretation, 12, 194, 230; sanitized version of, 196; of settlers, 157, 174, 206, 215; of slavery, 153, 201–5; "struggle," 120; USAID, 70; writing, 33. *See also* Bushmen; District Six; Khoisan; liberation struggle; Robben Island
History Workshop, University of the Witwatersrand, 175, 177, 246, 299 n.25
Hobhouse, Emily, 39
Holmes, Marcus, 108
Holocaust: and apartheid, 83–95; Auschwitz, 89 (monument, 91); Dachau, 90; death camps, 69, 88; denial, 7–8; Nazism, 86–87; and Robben Island, 83–84, 87–88, 90–91, 93
Holocaust Memorial Museum, Washington, D.C., 88, 231, 238, 240
homelessness, 181, 182, 188, 189. *See also* housing; informal settlements; townships
Homeless People's Association, 170, 171–72
homosexuality, 262, 265, 266, 269, 270
Horniman Museum, 215
"Hottentot," 208, 215. *See also* Bushmen; Khoisan
housing, 147, 155, 179, 194, 254; rehousing, 144. *See also* homelessness; informal settlements; townships
Howard, John, 157
human rights, 84; violations, 7, 123
Human Rights Violations Commission (HRVC), 243
Hustler, 39, 49
Hyslop, Jonathan, 30, 32

imperialism. *See* colonialism
indigeneity, 159, 163, 207, 208, 210, 251, 283, 291; Aboriginals of Australia, 207; aboriginal peoples of South Africa, 213, 215; ancestry and, 202; essentialism and, 156, 157; ethnic absolutism and, 3, 40; "ethnic minority" framework and, 250; ethnic nationalism and, 151–52; "indigenous flower," 40, *41;* Native Americans, 209. *See also* Griquas
informal housing settlements, 166, 170, 172, 181–82, 188–89, 195; Crossroads, 192; images of, 189–95; slum clearance,

monuments (*continued*)
44; funding, 22, 65, 71, 118–20, 181,
200–201; Harburg Monument against
Fascism, 92; Mandela's arm, 22–23, *24;*
Nasionale Vrouemonument, 39; and
"performances," 50–51; to political pris-
oners, 66; and "reconciliation," 39, 47,
69; translation of, 25, 35, 37, 39; 2,146
Stones—Monument against Racism,
93, *94;* vandalism, 152, 170. *See also*
AIDS / HIV; Ciskei; Guguletu Seven;
Holocaust, Auschwitz; Monument to
the Women of South Africa; Strijdom, J.
G.; Taalmonument (Afrikaans Language
Monument); Thokoza; Voortrekker
Monument
Moonsammy, Roshnie, 200
Moore, Henry, 91
Moretele districts, 165
Morkel, Gerald, 144
Morris, S. S., 118
Mpanza, James Sofasonke, 181
Mthethwa, Zwelethu, 189–93
Mtshali, Lionel, 68
Mugabe, Robert, 156
Mulvey, Laura, and Mark Lewis: *Disgraced
Monuments* (documentary), 19–20
Murinik, Tracey, 134
Murphy, Yvonne, 82
Murray, Brett, 134
Musée de l'Homme, 240
Museum Africa, 84, 139, 174–79, 194,
195, 200. *See also* "Birds in a Cornfield"
(exhibition)
museums: absences from history, 153, 205;
and accessibility, 194; collections, 209,
241; debates, 17, 149–54, 177–78; fund-
ing, 22, 65, 71, 118–20, 181, 200–201;
and land claims, 160–63; legislation and
policy, 15–17, 205; and the Khoisan, 209;
and "nation-building," 5, 48, 162; open
air, 160, 161; practice, 160–61, 224–
25, 227; public participation, 4, 175–76;
and Reconstruction and Development
Programme, 160–62, 166; role of, 206–
7. *See also* Africana Museum; Anne
Frank Centre; Bo-Kaap Museum; District Six Museum; Holocaust Memorial
Museum; Horniman Museum; Jewish Museum Annex; KwaMuhle Local
History Museum; Mayibuye Centre;
Musée de l'Homme; Museum Africa;

National Cultural History Museum;
Newtown Workers' Library and Mu-
seum; Robben Island, Museum; South
African Cultural History Museum; South
African Museum; South African Mu-
seum Association; Temporary Museum
of Totalitarian Art; Transvaal Museum;
Tswaing Crater Museum; Voortrekker
Monument, Museum
Museums, Monuments and Heraldry,
Commission on (CMMH). *See* Recon-
struction and Transformation of the Arts
and Culture, Commission for (CREATE)
"Museums and the Reconstruction and
Development Programme (RDP)" (con-
ference), 160–63, 166
"Museums for South Africa Intersectoral
Investigation for National Policy" (MUSA)
(report), 15, 16, 301 n.45
musical culture, 194
"Myths, Monuments, Museums" (confer-
ence), 19, *21,* 33

Nagia, Anwah, 145, 146, 147
Naidoo, Indres: *Island in Chains,* 101
Namibia, 211
Nasionale Vrouemonument, 39
National Association for the Advancement
of Colored People (NAACP), 71
National Commission of Culture,
Ghana, 71
National Cultural History Museum, 160,
163, 164, 166, 168; archives, 204; re-
named Slave Lodge, 203–4
National Cultural Liberation Movement,
Inkatha, 151–52
National Education, Department of, 17
National Gallery, 84, 143, 213, 230, 248,
255, 257
National Monuments Council (NMC),
16–17, 123
National Parks Board of Trustees, 154, 155
National Party (NP), 28, 30–31, 280–81; and
District Six, 122; and Nazi sympathies,
87; and Robben Island, 57
National Tourism Forum, 158
"national unity" government, 3, 10, 55,
204–5
Native Affairs, Department of, 210
Native Trust and Land Act (1936), 165, 167
Nature Conservation and Museums, De-
partment of, 58
Ndebele, 156, 165

ANNIE E. COOMBES teaches in the School of History of Art, Film, and Visual Media at Birkbeck College, University of London, where she is Director of Graduate Studies. Her previous books include *Reinventing Africa: Museums, Material Culture and Popular Imagination in Late Victorian and Edwardian England* (1994) and *Hybridity and Its Discontents: Politics, Science, Culture* (2000), coedited with Avtar Brah.